Understanding Development

D0569518

STOC DYNNWYD YMAITH
LLYFRGELL COLEG MENAI
WITHDRAWN LIBRARY STOCK

LLYFRGELL COLEG MENAI LIBRARY
108441

For Mum, Dad, Shaun, Tracey, Emma and Anna

108441

LLYFRGELL COLEG MENAI V
SAFLE FFRIDDOEDD
BANGOR GWYNEDD LL57 2TP

Understanding Development

Issues and Debates

PAUL HOPPER

polity

Copyright © Paul Hopper 2012

The right of Paul Hopper to be identified as Author of this Work has been asserted in accordance with the UK Copyright, Designs and Patents Act 1988.

First published in 2012 by Polity Press
Reprinted 2012

Polity Press
65 Bridge Street
Cambridge CB2 1UR, UK

Polity Press
350 Main Street
Malden, MA 02148, USA

All rights reserved. Except for the quotation of short passages for the purpose of criticism and review, no part of this publication may be reproduced, stored in a retrieval system, or transmitted, in any form or by any means, electronic, mechanical, photocopying, recording or otherwise, without the prior permission of the publisher.

ISBN-13: 978-0-7456-3894-2
ISBN-13: 978-0-7456-3895-9(pb)

A catalogue record for this book is available from the British Library.

Typeset in 9.5 on 13 pt Swift Light
by Servis Filmsetting Ltd, Stockport, Cheshire
Printed and bound by MPG Books Group, UK

The publisher has used its best endeavours to ensure that the URLs for external websites referred to in this book are correct and active at the time of going to press. However, the publisher has no responsibility for the websites and can make no guarantee that a site will remain live or that the content is or will remain appropriate.

Every effort has been made to trace all copyright holders, but if any have been inadvertently overlooked the publisher will be pleased to include any necessary credits in any subsequent reprint or edition.

For further information on Polity, visit our website: www.politybooks.com

Contents

Acknowledgements

I am extremely grateful to Dr Louise Knight, Emma Hutchinson and David Winters, and their colleagues at Polity Press, for their extremely helpful advice and professional assistance at every stage in the production of this book. I would also like to thank my three anonymous reviewers who provided me with extensive notes on my manuscript and much to think about. This book has been enhanced because of their contribution. Of course, it goes without saying that the errors that remain are my own.

In their different ways, the following colleagues in the Faculty of Arts at the University of Brighton enabled me to write this book: Anne Boddington, Paddy Maguire, Jonathan Woodham, Anne Galliot, Mark Devenney, Vicky Margree, Lucy Noakes and Peter Jackson. Without their support this book may not have seen the light of day. Thanks must also go to Andrea Cornwall and Tobias Denskus at the Institute of Development Studies at the University of Sussex.

My 'Race and Racism' undergraduate students on the BA Humanities and Cultural and Historical Studies degrees at the University of Brighton deserve special mention. both for allowing me to course-test this book and for their enthusiasm. Likewise, my undergraduate students on our BA Globalization: History, Politics, Culture degree enabled me to fine-tune the book. I thoroughly enjoyed teaching and working with you all.

Finally, I would like to thank my brother, Shaun Hopper, for sorting out my never-ending computer and internet access problems. As with my previous books, I dedicate this book to my family.

Acronyms and Abbreviations

AAPPG	Africa All Party Parliamentary Group
ACP	Africa, the Caribbean and the Pacific region
ADB	African Development Bank
ADF	African Development Fund
AERC	African Economic Research Consortium
AFTA	ASEAN Free Trade Area initiative
AIDS	Acquired Immune Deficiency Syndrome
ART	anti-retroviral therapy
ARV	anti-retroviral
ASEAN	South-East Asian Nations
ASI	Adam Smith Institute
ATPC	African Trade Policy Centre
AU	African Union
BNA	Basic Needs Approach
BWIs	Bretton Woods Institutions
CAP	Common Agricultural Policy
CBDR	'common but differentiated responsibilities'
CBOs	community-based organizations
CFCs	chlorofluorocarbons
CGD	Commission on Growth and Development
CHS	Commission on Human Security
CSD	Commission on Sustainable Development
CSOs	civil society organizations
DAC	Development Assistance Committee
DAWN	Development Alternatives for Women in a New Era
DDR	disarmament, demobilization and reintegration
DFID	UK Department for International Development
DPKO	UN Department for Peacekeeping Operations
ECLA	Economic Commission for Latin America
ECLAC	Economic Commission for Latin America and the Caribbean
ECOSOC	United Nations Economic and Social Council
EFA	Education for All
EHIPC	Enhanced Heavily Indebted Poor Countries Initiative
EJM	Environmental Justice Movement
EPAs	Economic Partnership Agreements

ESAF	Enhanced Structural Adjustment Facility
EU	European Union
FAO	Food and Agriculture Organization of the United Nations
FDI	foreign direct investment
FIDES	Fonds d'Investissement pour le Développement Economique et Social
FLO	Fairtrade Labelling Organizations International
FTAs	free trade agreements
G-77	Group of 77 countries
G8	Group of 8 countries (Canada, France, Germany, Italy, Japan, Russia, the UK and the USA)
GAD	Gender and Development
GATS	General Agreement on Trade in Services
GATT	General Agreement on Tariffs and Trade
GDI	Gender-related Development Index
GDP	gross domestic product
GEF	Global Environment Facility
GEG	Global Environmental Governance
GEO	Global Environment Outlook
GHI	Global Hunger Index
GII	Gender Inequality Index
GNI	gross national income
GNP	gross national product
GOARN	Global Outbreak Alert and Response Network (part of the WHO)
GROs	grassroots organizations
HDI	United Nations Human Development Index
HDR	Human Development Report
HIPC	Heavily Indebted Poor Countries Initiative
HPI	Human Poverty Index
HSRP	Human Security Report Project
HSU	UN Human Security Unit
ICANN	Internet Corporation for Assigned Names and Numbers
ICC	International Criminal Court
ICPD	International Conference on Population and Development
ICTs	information and communication technologies
IDA	International Development Association
IDC	International Development Committee (UK)
IDS	Institute of Development Studies (Brighton, UK)
IFIs	international financial institutions
IFPRI	International Food Policy Research Institute
IGO	international intergovernmental organization
ILO	International Labour Organization
IMF	International Monetary Fund

INGOs	international non-governmental organizations
IPA	International Peace Academy
IPCC	Intergovernmental Panel on Climate Change
IPDs	infectious and parasitic diseases
IPFA	Information Project for Africa
IPRs	intellectual property rights
ISI	import substitution industrialization
ITU	International Telecommunication Union
KRIBP	Kribhco Indo-British Farming Project
LA21	Local Agenda 21
LDCs	least developed countries
LEDCs	less economically developed countries
LICUS	low income under stress
MDGs	Millennium Development Goals
MDRI	Multilateral Debt Relief Initiative
MEAs	multilateral environmental agreements
MEDCs	more economically developed countries
MMR	maternal mortality rate
MNCs	multinational corporations
MSF	*Médecins Sans Frontières* (Doctors Without Borders)
MERCOSUR	Southern Cone Common Market
NAFTA	North American Free Trade Agreement
NAM	Non-Aligned Movement
NATO	North Atlantic Treaty Organization
NGOs	non-governmental organizations
NICs	newly industrializing countries
NIEs	newly industrializing economies
NIEO	New International Economic Order
NNGOs	northern non-governmental organizations
NPA	New Policy Agenda
NSDS	national sustainable development strategy
OAU	Organisation of African Unity
ODA	Official Development Assistance
ODI	UK Overseas Development Institute
OECD	Organization for Economic Co-operation and Development
OPEC	Organization of Petroleum Exporting Countries
P5	Permanent Five members of the UN Security Council (China, France,Russia, the UK and the USA)
PAR	Participatory Action Research
PEPFAR	US President's Emergency Plan for AIDS Relief
PPA	Participatory Poverty Assessments
PRA	participatory rural appraisal
PRGF	Poverty Reduction and Growth Facility
PRSs	Poverty Reduction Strategies

PUA	Participatory Urban Appraisal
PWC	Post-Washington Consensus
R2P	responsibility to protect
RIIA	Royal Institute of International Affairs
RRA	Rapid Rural Appraisal
SADC	Southern African Development Community
SAF	Structural Adjustment Facility
SAPs	structural adjustment programmes
SAPRIN	Structural Adjustment Participatory Review International Network
SARS	severe acute respiratory syndrome
SDT	special and differential treatment
SMS	Short Message Service
SNGOs	Southern non-governmental organizations
TB	tuberculosis
TNCs	transnational corporations
TRIPs	Trade-Related Aspects of Intellectual Property Rights
UN	United Nations
UNAIDS	Joint United Nations Programme on HIV/AIDS
UNCED	United Nations Conference on Environment and Development
UNCELA	United Nations Economic Commission for Latin America
UNCTAD	United Nations Conference on Trade and Development
UNDESA	United Nations Department of Economic and Social Affairs
UNDP	United Nations Development Programmes
UNECA	United Nations Economic Commission for Africa
UNEF	United Nations Emergency Force
UNEP	United Nations Environment Programme
UNESCO	United Nations Educational, Scientific and Cultural Organization
UNFPA	United Nations Population Fund
UNGA	United Nations General Assembly
UNHCR	United Nations High Commissioner for Refugees
UNICEF	United Nations International Children's Fund
UNIFEM	United Nations Development Fund for Women
UNODC	United Nations Office on Drugs and Crime
UNPD	United Nations Population Division
UNPROFOR	United Nations Protection Force
UNRISD	United Nations Research Institute for Social Development
UNU	United Nations University
USAID	United States Agency for International Development
WAD	Women and Development
WB	World Bank
WBIEG	World Bank Independent Evaluation Group
WCED	World Commission on Environment and Development

WDI	World Development Indicators
WED	Women, Environment and Development
WEF	World Economic Forum
WEO	World Environment Organization
WFP	World Food Programme
WHO	World Health Organization
WID	Women in Development
WIDER	World Institute for Development Economics Research
WSF	World Social Forum
WSSD	World Summit on Sustainable Development
WTO	World Trade Organization
WWF	World Wide Fund for Nature

Boxes

Introduction: Understanding Development

- A brief history of development
- Development and the United Nations system
- Conceptualizing development
- The UN Millennium Development Goals
- Globalization, poverty and inequality

A number of development issues have recently attracted international attention, notably:

- The Make Poverty History campaign and the decision by the G8 leaders at the Gleneagles Summit of July 2005 to cancel the debts of some of the poorest countries in the world.
- The United Nations Millennium Development goals to reduce global poverty and improve living standards by 2015, most notably halving the number of people living on less than US$1 per day between 1990 and 2015.
- The claim by a number of international health agencies that the number of people infected with HIV will rise to 60 million by 2015.
- The sharp increase in world food prices in 2008, which caused riots in countries like Haiti and Indonesia, and led to fears that developing countries would miss international poverty targets.
- The UN Population Division's estimation that the world's population will rise to 9.1 billion by 2050, with virtually all the growth occurring in the developing world.
- The series of reports produced by the Intergovernmental Panel on Climate Change (IPCC) during 2007, which indicated that global warming was more advanced than had previously been anticipated.
- The rise in the number of people living in fragile and failed states. In its *World Development Report 2011*, the World Bank estimates that more than 1.5 billion people live in countries affected by violent conflict, and the cycles of violence are causing chronic insecurity as well as undermining development (World Bank 2011).

This book investigates these and related development areas that are defining our age. Each chapter deals with the main issues and debates surrounding a particular development topic, including conflict and security, gender, foreign aid and debt, health and education, the environment and globalization.

In investigating these areas, case studies from countries and regions throughout the world will be drawn upon, but also development strategies will be evaluated, ranging from institutionally promoted structural adjustment programmes (SAPs) to participatory approaches carried out at a local level in which non-governmental organizations (NGOs) often play a key role.

In short, this is an issues-driven introduction to development that covers the major aspects of both development theory and practice. It therefore differs from conventional introductory works on development. Thus, while the history of the subject and the major approaches to it are dealt with in the early part of the book, and returned to repeatedly, the main focus is upon the development topics and debates that tend to generate the most interest and passion among practitioners and non-practitioners alike.[1]

There are a number of additional themes and claims that run through this book and, taken together, ensure that this book is distinct from other works in the field. Firstly, it is emphasized that development must be understood within the broader context of globalization and environmental decline, but also that these forces are having tangible development effects (chapters 9 and 10). Put simply, development is taking place within a period of unprecedented international interconnectedness – whether in the form of trade, finance, governance, communication or some other human activity – that informs the nature of development but also has consequences for the environment. In turn, this heightens the need to pursue development that is environmentally sustainable, especially given an escalating global population. It is therefore a work that explores the intricate interrelationships between development, globalization and the environment. Further complicating matters is the fact that development, globalization and the environment are multidimensional, complex and contested phenomena.

Secondly, in investigating the complex and contested nature of development, it will be shown how the different development theories are a product of particular histories, political and philosophical positions, and academic disciplines or discourses. More broadly, it means that development is inextricably bound up with issues of power and political influence. As for complexity, this work will indicate the extent to which aspects of development are interdependent. For example, dealing with an issue like population growth requires exploring the interrelationship between, among other things, gender (and specifically the correlation between women's status and reproductive choices), international health and educational awareness programmes, the cultural norms and values of particular societies, the level of global poverty and inequality, and the nature of welfare systems within individual countries.

Thirdly, understanding the divergent development trajectories of countries and regions requires examining the intersection between development policies, structural/global factors and local contexts or conditions, with the latter informed by influences such as history, cultural values, colonial legacies and the nature of political authority. Fourthly, and following on from the previous point, in focusing upon the ways in which these forces intersect, the plural nature of development soon becomes apparent, with development trajectories and strategies the product of numerous processes and interventions by many agencies (Grillo and Stirrat 1997). In short, there are diverse and multiple forms of development taking place. Hence, this work adheres to the increasingly accepted view that development must be conceived of in pluralistic terms, as *developments*. Finally, it will be shown that encapsulating this complexity necessitates adopting an interdisciplinary approach to development and synthesizing insights from a range of disciplines.

Before analysing the key issues and debates surrounding development, we need to understand the meaning and nature of development. A useful starting point in this regard is to survey the history of development. This will now be undertaken before going on to examine the wider institutional and policy-making (i.e., the UN Millennium Development Goals) framework that is shaping development as well as some of the different ways of conceptualizing development. The Introduction will conclude with a consideration of the global context in which development is taking place, namely globalization and the increasingly complex patterns of global poverty and inequality.

A brief history of development

The origins of development are disputed, but for many writers on this subject its intellectual roots lie with the European Enlightenment of the eighteenth century.[2] The themes that run through this particular episode in human history, notably those of progress, rationalism and modernity, have exerted an enormous influence upon development and for some (for good or ill) they underpin the whole project.[3] Indeed, the notion of becoming modern and modernizing are often viewed as both the goal and the process of development. Further contributing to this mode of thought were the dominant themes of the nineteenth century in the form of science, capitalism, industrialization and imperialism.

1940s and 1950s

Development in its contemporary guise emerged after the Second World War, with the creation of the UN and in particular institutions like the World Bank (WB) and the International Monetary Fund (IMF) that were designed to bring about post-war reconstruction and international economic stability, respectively (see Helleiner 2006).

However, some of the development approaches and policies of the 1940s and 1950s had to an extent been outlined in the 1920s and 1930s, although putting them into practice was disrupted by the Great Depression and then the Second World War. More specifically, the emergence of some aspects of development policy and practice can arguably be traced to colonial development prior to 1940. For example, the contemporary practice of aid provision can be traced to this period. In 1929, the Colonial Development Act (CDA) was passed in the UK, which set up a Colonial Development Fund (CDF) to allocate relatively small amounts of British government money to colonial economic development. There were parallel developments in France, with the creation of the Fonds d'Investissement pour le Développement Economique et Social (FIDES) in 1946. Indeed, such policies led to the 'developmentalist colonialism of the 1940s and 1950s' (Cooper 2002: 197). In the case of Africa, what has been termed a 'second colonial occupation' began, with increased investment by Britain and France in the transport infrastructures, education systems and agricultural production of their African colonies. In this vein, Uma Kothari has sought to reconstruct 'the colonial genealogies of development' (2005: 50) by interviewing former colonial officers who subsequently worked in development. She argues that mainstream development studies neglects its colonial past and is, perhaps unwittingly, seeking to portray development as something distinct and 'good'.

But it is important not to overstate the relationship between colonialism and development, especially as they are driven by different motives. Thus, the 'second colonial occupation of Africa' has also been viewed as an attempt by the colonial powers to develop their colonies as trading partners that contributed to the colonial economy. Others see it as way of Britain and France trying to nullify the growing domestic and international criticism of colonialism. Likewise, the CDA has been viewed as a UK response to the Great Depression and the economic crisis rather than as an example of British philanthropy. In sum, for its critics, colonialism was an exploitative and extractive enterprise whose association with development is therefore questionable.

For many, a defining moment in the history of development was the inaugural address given by President Truman on 20 January 1949. In his speech, Truman announced his plan for a 'fair deal' for the rest of the world, declaring that:

> We must embark on a bold new program for making the benefits of our scientific advances and industrial progress available for the improvement and growth of underdeveloped areas. The old imperialism – exploitation for foreign profit – has no place in our plans. What we envisage is a program of development, based on concepts of democratic fair dealing. (Truman 1967)

Many writers identify 'underdeveloped areas' as the key phrase in this speech, viewing it as the moment when the condition of underdevelopment emerges and the task of development begins (e.g., Dodds 2002; Escobar 1995b; Esteva 1992; Potter et al. 2004).[4] For critics, the real purpose of Truman's speech was to get developing countries to look to the United States as a source of support and as a model to emulate, and in doing so he was preparing the way for American hegemony in the post-war period (Esteva 1992: 6). This claim formed part of a wider critique of the West that it was engaged in establishing a range of neo-colonial relationships through development (Nkrumah 1965). Indeed, for many in the South, development was simply a continuation of the forms of trusteeship pursued by some European powers towards the end of their colonial rule.[5] From their perspective, development was a patronizing project that enabled the West to continue dictating to the non-western world. Furthermore, modernization theory, the dominant development approach in the 1950s, was considered to be a part of this process as it promoted a European conception of development.

Even at this early stage, counter-theories and approaches to the domination of development by the North existed. In this period it took the form of structuralism, which emerged from Latin America. Indeed, structuralists advocated protectionism and forms of disengagement from the international economy, such as import substitution industrialization (ISI), in order to nurture development in the region. Likewise, many anti-colonial and nationalist leaders – like Mohandas (Mahatma) Gandhi in India, Kwame Nkrumah (1965) in Ghana, and Julius Nyerere (1967a, 1967b) in Tanzania – articulated positions on development as part of their drive for autonomy and independence.

1960s

Modernization theory continued to define development as the 1960s – the first United Nations Development Decade – began. As the decade progressed, another significant trend in the history of development emerged in the form of increasingly critical perspectives being articulated by writers from the South (e.g., Samir Amin, Arghiri Emmanuel and Andre Gunder Frank).[6] This criticism was reinforced by the fact that anticipated levels of economic growth had failed to materialize in the South and, in countries where growth had been achieved, the benefits were unevenly distributed. For southern writers, the plight of their countries was due to the nature of the international economic system, which had established the South's dependency upon the North by creating unfair terms of trade, among other measures (see chapter 1).

1970s

In the 1970s, the appeal of dependency theories was strengthened by the persistence and deepening of global inequalities, with some countries showing little sign of breaking free from 'underdevelopment'. International agencies like the International Labour Organization (ILO) and the World Bank responded by turning their attention to 'redistribution with growth' and 'basic needs'. These philosophies continued to stress the necessity of economic growth, but placed greater emphasis upon gearing development towards meeting the needs of the poor. The decade was also marked by certain other changes of focus within development. In particular, there were signs of greater appreciation of the ways in which gender is implicated in development, as well as the different experiences by women and men of underdevelopment. Similarly, growing environmental awareness was encouraged by the 1972 UN Stockholm Conference on the Human Environment. Finally, economic growth and development for all countries was profoundly shaped by disputes over energy, and specifically the oil crises of this decade, which contributed to recession, inflation and debt (see chapter 8).

1980s

A notable feature of the 1980s was the debt crisis faced by developing countries, especially in Africa and Latin America, as they struggled to cope with high interest rates (chapter 8). Debt servicing was made more difficult by the weak international demand for their exports and declining commodity prices, a by-product of the slowing down of the world economy in the late 1970s, which became a global economic recession in the early 1980s. Both Africa and Latin America were also confronted with declining foreign direct investment (FDI), which was a consequence of unfavourable lending conditions during this period (Hewitt 2000). All of this meant that many developing countries sought financial assistance from international financial institutions (IFIs) like the World Bank and the IMF during this period. This context and the widely perceived shortcomings of statist theories of development, a view encouraged by the collapse of the state socialist regimes in Eastern Europe, contributed to neo-liberalism becoming the new orthodoxy within development. The shift to neo-liberalism was confirmed by the World Bank/IMF's structural adjustment programmes (SAPs), which meant that financial assistance for developing countries was conditional upon them reducing state socio-economic activity and participating in global markets.

The 1980s was also the decade when the concept of sustainable development gained increasing acceptance within development circles. Indeed, in 1987 the World Commission on Environment and Development was held, out of which emerged the influential Brundtland Report, *Our Common Future* (chapter 9). Interestingly, at the very time that sustainable development was being articulated in development conferences, countries in East Asia were starting to enjoy rapid export-oriented economic growth.

1990s

During the 1990s, with neo-liberalism continuing to guide official thinking, post-development perspectives began to gain currency with the nature and purpose of development increasingly questioned. Above all, the cultural bias of development was emphasized, with many writers highlighting its European Enlightenment roots and arguing that such Eurocentrism could only be challenged by turning to grassroots approaches and valuing indigenous knowledge. Indeed, culture became an increasingly important theme within development (see Schech and Haggis 2000).

Outside of debates within academia, the unpredictability of development was highlighted by the Asian financial crisis of 1997, with the effects felt far beyond this region. Nevertheless, the economic rise of China and India continued, as did environmental concerns over fossil fuel-driven economic growth. The signing of the Kyoto Accord in 1997 was an attempt by much – though not all – of the international community to address the serious issue of global warming caused by carbon dioxide emissions and other greenhouse gases (chapter 9). Towards the end of the decade, as a result of the widespread criticism of SAPs, the World Bank began to employ the vocabulary of local engagement, participation and poverty reduction. This shift was reflected in the World Bank's promotion of Poverty Reduction Strategies (PRSs), which places the onus upon developing countries themselves formulating their own development approaches based on local consultation. However, critics have questioned the amount of local input that goes into these strategies, and argue that the neo-liberal emphasis upon markets and a minimal state persists within the documents and policies of the IFIs.

The new millennium

Today, as we move further into the twenty-first century, the contested nature of development has never been more apparent as neo-liberalism, participatory approaches, post-development perspectives and sustainable development all compete to define contemporary development theory and practice and do so within the context of globalization, world population growth and environmental decline. Furthermore, issues and debates that came to the forefront in the final years of the twentieth century, like debt, the international terms of trade, the role of aid, conditionality, 'good governance', human security and the environment, look set to continue to be important in this century.

Development and the United Nations system

As will now be shown, the UN system provides the overarching institutional framework within which contemporary development takes place. Some of the key development agencies and institutions within the UN system are also outlined, and in subsequent chapters they are examined in more detail in relation to the issues and debates surrounding development.

In the post-war period, a number of international institutions have been set up to foster development. Indeed, when the UN was created in the aftermath of the Second World War, the need to address development and related issues was acknowledged in its Charter. However, this commitment was broadly defined and expressed and arguably it was not until the early 1960s, with the launch of the UN First Development Decade, that the UN began to engage seriously with development. Reflecting the emerging critical literature of the time, a literature that was to evolve into dependency theory, figures within the UN like Raúl Prebisch and his colleagues at the UN's Economic Commission for Latin America (ECLA) began to urge that the organization take a more sympathetic stance towards the plight of developing nations, and for northern governments to do more to help them (Thomas and Allen 2000: 200).

Concern about the nature of the economic relationships between developing countries and the West led to the setting up of the United Nations Commission for Trade and Development (UNCTAD) in 1964. Its task is to integrate developing nations into the global economy, and it has become a focus for their economic grievances. But in truth UNCTAD has little substantive power and influence – certainly in comparison with the World Bank and the IMF that the western powers dominate and prefer to deal with – and consequently it has an uneven record of achievement. Martin Khor (2003) emphasizes the extent to which the more interventionist UN and its agencies are in competition with the neo-liberal IMF–WB–WTO trinity over the future course of global economic governance, with much of the differences between them centring upon a philosophical dispute over the role of the market in development.

The UN is funded from a combination of voluntary contributions and the assessed contributions of countries. A range of criteria is employed to determine a country's contribution to the UN, but of high importance is their respective GNP and per capita income. This funding system means that the UN is heavily reliant upon national governments fulfilling their financial commitments. However, in 1998, 85 member states owed the UN a total of US$990 million in unpaid contributions. Obviously, funding has a major influence upon how the UN system operates, determining not only the nature and scope of its development activity but also arguably how critical the UN and its agencies, and in particular its representatives, can be of member states.

The Economic and Social Council (ECOSOC)

As its title suggests, this organ of the UN was established to coordinate the economic and social aspects of its work, encompassing the different agencies, organizations and programmes that cover this sphere of activity. Key specialized agencies under its auspices include the World Bank and the IMF, although, in the case of these two organizations, such is their importance that effectively they are operating separately from the rest of the UN. The World Bank and the IMF are known as the Bretton Woods Institutions (BWIs) because they were established on 1 July 1944 during a conference of 44 countries in Bretton Woods, New Hampshire.

The World Bank

The initial task of the World Bank was to drive reconstruction in the post-war period. Subsequently, it has gone on to provide LEDCs with loans and grants worth many billions of dollars. In 2009, it had a membership of 186 countries – with entry into the IMF a prerequisite for membership of the World Bank – and it sees its role as promoting economic development and reducing poverty.

From the late 1970s onwards, the prevailing neo-liberal philosophy within the World Bank was that achieving these ends required reducing the role of the state and 'getting prices right'. It led to charges that the World Bank was relegating the human and environmental dimensions of development, which critics argued was evident in its funding of environmentally harmful projects, like the Sardar Sarovar dam project on the Narmada River in northwest India (Peet 2003). However, the World Bank responded in 1993 by setting up the Inspection Panel in order to monitor the social and environmental record of the projects and countries that it is involved with. Moreover, a combination of criticism of SAPs and their disappointing performance, belated acknowledgement of the role of governance in Asian economic growth, and the influence of academic scholarship (e.g., Evans et al. 1985), has led to a greater appreciation of the state's role in development within World Bank circles.

International Monetary Fund

The IMF has performed its macro-economic role of securing the international monetary system by helping countries overcome balance-of-payments problems and other economic crises through a combination of financial loans and technical advice. Thus, the IMF has negotiated loan packages with Mexico in the 1980s, South-East Asia and Russia in the late 1990s, and Argentina in 2001. In fact, 56 countries took out loans under the Structural Adjustment Facility (SAF) between 1986 and 1999. More recently, richer nations like the USA – concerned that the Chinese yuan and some other Asian currencies are too low, enabling these countries to boost their exports – have been pushing for the IMF to ensure that currencies are correctly valued. The IMF also played a prominent role in setting up the Highly Indebted Poor Countries initiative (HIPC) in 1996 designed to reduce the massive debt burden of many developing countries (chapter 8).

To it critics, the IMF has a history of enforcing a one-size-fits-all model that has been inapplicable in certain countries and regions and has led to real hardships, notably in the form of budget cuts. For example, during the Asian financial crisis of the late 1990s, the IMF insisted that the countries affected must respond by cutting their budget deficits, a move that led to governments cutting back on their social welfare spending. In addition, anti-globalization groups contend that IMF market liberalization has enabled large multinational corporations to encroach further into the economies of developing countries, often at the expense of their domestic industries.

World Bank and IMF responses

Defenders of these institutions maintain that they have helped to ensure the continued smooth running of the international economy, and indeed overseen its expansion. Moreover, their intervention has enabled numerous states to overcome financial crises and they have provided funding that has enabled many more states in the South to continue to develop and modernize. This turnaround has been possible because of the low interest loans that have been provided under the SAF and its successor, the Enhanced Structural Adjustment Facility (ESAF), as well as the technical assistance on economic policies that they provide for recipients and members generally. Where their interventions have not had the desired effect, advocates of the World Bank and the IMF argue, unsurprisingly, that this is because governments have invariably ignored their prescriptions (Madslien 2004).

Officials within both the World Bank and the IMF also maintain that they have been responding constructively to criticism. For example, ESAF has been replaced by the so-called Poverty Reduction and Growth Facility (PRGF), which places greater emphasis upon consulting local opinion, and national governments and aid organizations playing a greater role in the formulation of policy. This policy shift, which is a part of the emerging Post-Washington Consensus (PWC), stems from a joint meeting of the IMF and the World Bank in 1999, and entails individual countries compiling their own poverty reduction strategies as the basis for determining lending and debt relief. However, critics have argued that, by continuing to emphasize financial discipline, the IMF has a more restrictive conception of the PWC when it comes to dealing with poverty and inequality (Öniş and Şenses 2005).

Finally, in thinking about development in relation to the United Nations system, it is important not to overemphasize the power and influence of the leading institutions within it. This is because other agents are also actively involved in development (see p. 12). In particular, developing countries and their respective governments should not be thought of as playing a passive role in this process. Indeed, in multiple and diverse ways they will help to frame, negotiate and contest development.

Conceptualizing development

In addition to its diverse history and institutional complexity, there are other factors that add to the difficulty of conceptualizing development. In particular, there are a range of perspectives on development as will now be shown.

What is intended by development?

At a very basic level, development has been defined simply as change (Brookfield 1975). Robert Chambers (1997) adds a positive spin to this definition by describing development as 'good change'. Of course, others may disagree with this view and consider development to be 'bad change'. For this reason, we need to probe a little deeper when thinking about development and acknowledge, as Cowen and Shenton have noted, that the real issue is 'what is intended by development?' rather than simply a concern with 'what is development?' (1996: viii). But what makes it more difficult to determine the intention of development is that over time it has accrued many different approaches, theories and areas of interests so that it has become a multifaceted phenomenon. Furthermore, development is not simply confined to the developing world; rather it is something that all countries and regions experience, although the focus within development studies has been upon countries in the South which are perceived as being insufficiently economically developed, at least from the perspective of many in the North.

Conceptualizing development is further complicated by the fact that its nature and meaning has changed over time. It has evolved from a concept concerned primarily with economic growth to one which pays more attention to the quality of human life, a shift that has entailed attaching greater weight to the attainment of political freedom and social welfare targets. This pattern reflects the post-war dominance of development by economics, but also how other academic disciplines have come to exert greater influence upon the subject in the recent period (see chapters 1 and 2).

Reflecting these changes, from the late 1980s onwards the United Nations Development Programme (UNDP) began to employ the Human Development Index (HDI) as an alternative measurement of development to GDP. This is encapsulated in the 2000/2001 *Human Development Report* (UNDP 2001), which emphasizes the importance of having a range of opportunities in order to lead productive and creative lives, and to develop our human capabilities. Development from this perspective is about 'expanding the choices people have to lead lives that they value' (UNDP 2001: 9). Hence the HDI acknowledges that the most basic of human capabilities are to lead long and healthy lives, to be knowledgeable through access to education, and to have the necessary resources to achieve a decent standard of living. The focus is therefore upon human well-being. For many people working within development, this goal also entails the ability to participate in the life of the community, human security and empowerment. Of course, economic growth continues to be an important determinant of development, and indeed helps to provide the resources necessary to attain human well-being, a point acknowledged within the HDI which continues to factor in an economic measurement in the form of per capita income.

A key theme within human-centred development is the notion of empowerment. This concept has received particular attention in relation to the position of women (chapter 4) and participation (chapter 7). In the case of the latter, for example, there are some advocates of participatory development who believe empowerment necessitates a reduced role for 'experts' in the development process. This broader conception of development can also be found in Amartya Sen's influential work *Development as Freedom* (2001) in which he makes the case for development being oriented towards enhancing human freedom and the provision of choice and opportunity for people, employing the vocabulary of 'entitlements' and 'capabilities'. It also reflects the increased prominence of human rights, as well as ethical and moral agendas, within development over the last decade or so (Corbridge 1998b; Elliott 2002).

The complexities of development

Beyond debates about the type of development that is being pursued, there are other factors that can shape the course of development within a given country. Such factors can include the influence of culture and history, the degree of political stability and social cohesion in the country, geography and natural resource endowment, as well as the particular development strategy that is being pursued. Furthermore, there is often a problem in determining the extent of development in a society, even if we view it in purely economic terms. This is due to difficulties in gaining access to data in some developing countries, for reasons ranging from the lack of adequate data-gathering mechanisms and institutions to the control of such information by governments.

Further complicating matters is the fact that there is a range of actors and agencies in the development process, including international institutions, states or governments, bilateral donors, NGOs, aid agencies, households, private companies, local communities, individuals, multilateral organizations, and development workers (see Porter, Allen and Thompson 1991).

As Cowen and Shenton have noted, it means that development 'comes to be defined in a multiplicity of ways because there are a multiplicity of "developers" who are entrusted with the task of development' (1996: 4). Moreover, exponents of particular theoretical approaches differ in who they consider to be the main actors or agents of development. For example, dependency theorists focus their attention upon the state, while neo-liberal writers stress the importance of NGOs and the private sector. In addition, the role and significance of particular actors and agents in development can change. For example, the developmental state was the pivotal development institution for much of the post-war period before declining in the late 1970s, while more recently there have been calls for it to be revived (chapter 10).

Alan Thomas (2000) has expressed concern that development is increasingly viewed as the practice of development agencies like multilateral organizations, governments, NGOs and social movements that conceptualize development in terms of alleviating problems and setting targets (ibid.: 774). While recognizing the contribution of these agencies in combating poverty, Thomas believes that accepting this as *the* main meaning of development diminishes its complexity, ambiguity and multidimensionality. In particular, it relegates within development the view of it as a historical process of social change and of striving for the desirable society (ibid.: 773). In short, development becomes simply whatever is done in the name of development (ibid.: 777). Furthermore, the target-based approach to poverty neglects the fact that dealing effectively with such complex issues invariably requires deeper structural changes to societies. As Thomas puts it:

targets are inherently unidimensional and as such represent a very limited vision of social transformation, while the application of techniques designed to achieve such targets tends to simplify theory to the idea that large-scale social change may be achieved straightforwardly by deliberate actions, or even that poverty reduction may be achieved by targeting the poor without the need for broader social change, and thus provides an equally limited view of the historical process of development. (A. Thomas 2000: 778)

The UN Millennium Development Goals

The UN Millennium Development Goals are the type of trend within development that Alan Thomas (2000) has expressed disquiet about. In September 2000, the UN adopted the Millennium Development Goals (MDGs) that synthesized the various declarations and targets from the numerous international summits and conferences held during the 1990s. These consisted of eight goals and were to be achieved by 2015 (see Boxes 0.1 and 0.2). The MDGs followed the United Nations Millennium Declaration, and, taken together, they

---

Box 0.1 The UN Millennium Development Goals

The UN adopted the MDGs in September 2000, which consist of eight goals that were to be achieved by 2015:

- Goal 1: Eradicate extreme poverty and hunger.
- Goal 2: Achieve universal primary education.
- Goal 3: Promote gender equality and empower women.
- Goal 4: Reduce child mortality.
- Goal 5: Improve maternal health.
- Goal 6: Combat HIV/AIDS, malaria and other diseases.
- Goal 7: Ensure environmental sustainability.
- Goal 8: Develop a global partnership for development.

(*Source*: UNMDG 2005)

Box 0.2 The UN Millennium Development Targets

In order to meet the MDGs, specific targets were established for each goal. Notable among them were the following:

- For Goal 1: Reduce by half the proportion of people living on less than a dollar a day and the proportion of people who suffer from hunger.
- For Goal 2: Ensure that all boys and girls complete a full course of primary schooling.
- For Goal 3: Eliminate gender disparity in primary and secondary education preferably by 2005, and at all levels by 2015.
- For Goal 4: Reduce by two-thirds the mortality rate among children under five.
- For Goal 5: Reduce by three-quarters the maternal mortality ratio.
- For Goal 6: Halt and begin to reverse the spread of HIV/AIDS and the incidence of malaria and other major diseases.
- For Goal 7: Reduce by half the proportion of people without sustainable access to safe drinking water.
- For Goal 8: Develop further an open trading and financial system that is rule-based, predictable and non-discriminatory.

(*Source*: UNMDG 2005)

formed a universal framework for pursuing development and eradicating extreme poverty. The wider significance of this project was that it constituted a clear statement of the nature and purpose of development (Willis 2005). From the perspective of the UN, creating a common agenda would encourage joined-up thinking and action within international development.

However, the Millennium Development Goals have attracted criticism. Some critics question the usefulness of the goals, while others believe the time frames are unrealistic to achieve such ambitious goals (see Black and White 2006). Such concerns were being expressed prior to the global recession, which led to the world's poorest countries losing US$1trillion (£600 billion) from their economies in 2009, making it even more difficult to achieve the MDGs (Seager 2009). From a broader perspective, Ashwani Saith (2006) raises the possibility that the MDGs and their respective targets have the potential to distort the development policy agenda by influencing the priorities and direction of academic research and investigation.

Some commentators have questioned the lack of emphasis upon rights within the MDGs. It means, as Salil Shetty, the Secretary-General of Amnesty International has argued, that we are faced with the contradiction of governments continuing to 'violate the human rights of the same people whose lives they have committed to improving under the UN MDGs framework' (Kelly 2011). For Shetty, development and the MDGs need to be less target orientated. Instead, they need to be based upon the principles of accountability and enforceability that comes from human rights frameworks, as well as the recognition that the issues involved frequently entail more complex systemic changes. For example, to tackle effectively maternal mortality requires addressing the issue of women's sexual and reproductive rights, and in many societies this will necessitate change and citizens being able to claim their rights and hold their governments to account (ibid.).

The UN's mid-term report

In 2007, the UN took stock of how close the international community was to achieving the Millennium Development Goals by 2015. *The Millennium Development Goals Report 2007* (UNMDG 2007) states that, while considerable progress had been made in some areas and in certain regions (notably Asia), there was still a considerable way to go to achieve these goals and we may struggle to meet some of them. In sub-Saharan Africa, no country was in line to halve extreme poverty, achieve universal primary education and reverse the HIV/AIDs epidemic by 2015. In the case of the latter, the number of people living with HIV/AIDS worldwide in 2007 had risen sixfold to 40 million since 2001 (ibid.: 18). More generally, alleviating hunger and disease worldwide in 2015 (MDG Goals 1 and 6) seemed unlikely in 2007. As for the second MDG goal of achieving universal primary education, while the number of children attending primary school in Africa had risen by 13 per cent since 2000 to stand at 70 per cent in 2007, on a global scale, one in 10 young children were still not attending school. Similarly, meeting the 2015 target of reducing the child mortality rate by two-thirds (MDG Goal 4) would require a 70 per cent reduction from the level that it was in 2007.

A major reason for this uneven picture was that in general wealthy nations were providing insufficient aid to poorer countries, and in some cases they were not honouring existing aid commitments. This was borne out by the fact that the improvements experienced by countries in Asia, many of whom were achieving a reduction in poverty levels and child hunger, lie mainly with their own rapid economic growth, rather than foreign aid. The UN Secretary-General, Ban Ki-moon, used these findings to urge richer countries to increase substantially their international aid budgets. As we will see in chapter 8, there is a long history of richer countries not fulfilling their aid commitments. In fact, very few countries ever meet the agreed UN target of providing 0.7 per cent of their national income to development aid each year, and there is now much talk of 'aid fatigue' as levels of official development assistance (ODA) begin to decline. However, the report concluded that while the collective record to date was mixed, the MDGs were still achievable if immediate action was taken, something that would also necessitate nationally owned development strategies and budgets being aligned with them. Worryingly, the report also acknowledged that this scenario only applies before the effects of global warming are really felt (ibid.: 3).

Globalization, poverty and inequality

For many people working in development, its primary purpose is to tackle global poverty and inequality. However, there remains a dispute about whether levels of world poverty and income inequality have risen or fallen in the past two or three decades.[7] Indeed, the nature of the interrelationships between poverty, inequality and globalization is the source of much debate (e.g., Held and Kaya 2007; Kaplinsky 2005). But what can be stated with greater certainty is that patterns of global poverty and inequality have become increasingly complex, and this forms the broader context for contemporary international development, as will now be shown.

According to the UNDP (2001), at the start of the new millennium, approximately 1.2 billion lived on less than US$1 a day (70 per cent are female), and 2.8 billion on less than US$2 a day. Of the 1.2 billion, 800 million were located in South Asia and sub-Saharan Africa. Yet the number of people living in absolute poverty declined from 33 per cent in 1981 to 18 per cent in 2001. This reduction is largely down to the rapid economic growth of countries like China and India. Indeed, the fast economic growth of the two most populous nations not only impacts upon the global poverty rate, but is also disguising the divergence between rich and low-income countries (World Bank 2005b: 7).

A more recent World Bank report published in 2008 by Shaohua Chen

LLYFRGELL COLEG MENAI LIBRARY

and Martin Ravallion (2008) confirmed that there has been strong progress towards reducing overall poverty: 1.4 billion people in the developing world were living on less than US$1.25 a day in 2005 compared to 1.9 billion in 1981. However, new cost-of-living data suggest poverty has been more widespread across the developing world over the past 25 years than previously estimated, with up to 400 million more people living in poverty than earlier thought. Moreover, regional differences in poverty reduction trends persist. For example, poverty in East Asia has fallen from nearly 80 per cent of the population living on less than US$1.25 a day in 1981 to less than 20 per cent in 2005, whereas, in sub-Saharan Africa, the US$1.25 a day poverty rate has shown no sustained decline over the whole period since 1981, starting and ending at 50 per cent (ibid.). Current trajectories suggest that about a billion people will still live on less than US$1.25 a day in 2015, and this is without factoring in the impact that rising food and fuel prices since 2005 and the global financial crisis will have upon poor people and poverty reduction.

Numerous studies of poverty and inequality reinforce this complex picture. Based on his research of household surveys for 1988, 1993 and 1998, Branko Milanovic (2005, 2007) detects an uneven pattern: global inequality increased strongly between 1988 and 1993, but then displayed a minor decline in the subsequent five years. As he puts it: 'inequality among people in the world today is extremely high, though its direction of change is unclear' (2007: 32). Likewise, Glenn Firebaugh (2003) contends that income inequality between nations has declined, but it has risen within nations. In particular, there has been the rise in inequality within countries like China, India, Russia, Sweden, the UK and the United States.

The UNU/WIDER study on the links between poverty, inequality and growth confirms the view that within-country income inequality has risen in most countries since the early 1980s (Cornia and Court 2001). Much of Latin America (notably Brazil), the former Soviet bloc and Southern Africa, as well as countries like Pakistan, have levels of inequality that undermine attempts at poverty reduction (ibid.: 24). While China's rapid economic growth has reduced absolute poverty within the country, it has also contributed to a sharp increase in inequality that threatens future poverty reduction, with some of its citizens accumulating considerable wealth in the new economy (ibid.: 8–9). There have also been notable increases in inequality within Malaysia, Thailand and Hong Kong as they too have advanced economically. Likewise, the economic benefits of India's rapid development have been unevenly shared. A wealthy elite has emerged in the country – in 2005, India had 47 billionaires compared with 10 in France – while more than three-quarters of its 1.2 billion people have to get by on less than £1.30 a day, and this is despite a reduction in absolute poverty levels (Wilson 2010).

There has also been a marked rise in regional and rural–urban inequality in the recent period (Cornia and Court 2001). In the case of China, patterns of inequality reflect the divide that exists between coastal provinces like

Guangdong, which are integrated into the international economy, and the underdeveloped regions in the west of the country that are not. However, the absolute number of poor is also increasing in urban areas worldwide, and faster than in rural areas in some countries, with writers now discussing the 'urbanization of poverty' (UN–Habitat 2003: xxvi). Even within relatively wealthy cities, like Mumbai and Rio de Janeiro, areas of extreme poverty are often adjacent to areas of affluence, with the rich able to shelter in gated communities. Indeed, in 2003, the number of people living in slums was almost 1 billion, with the majority of them in developing regions (ibid.: xxv).

Thus, the income and wealth generated by the fast economic growth of countries like China, India and Brazil has generally not been evenly spread within those societies. Indeed, within many of them it has led to the formation of wealthy new elites, many of whom are globally connected, often with their counterparts in the developed world. At the same time, the level of inequality within many northern countries has significantly increased and poverty remains an everyday fact of life for some citizens, especially those living in urban areas. From a global perspective, all of this is leading to a blurring of the developing and developed worlds.

Measuring global poverty and inequality

In determining levels of global poverty and inequality, much depends upon what is being measured and how averages are employed (see Boxes 0.3–0.6). This task is made more difficult by the fact that data are often manipulated or difficult to access. Some governments play down the extent of domestic poverty in case such information is used by their opponents against them. Poverty is typically measured at the household level, but this can generate its own problems as households often contain their own inequalities and in particular they can be highly gendered institutions. Poverty surveys often neglect differences in household composition and the number of women in paid employment. Milanovic (2007) argues that, because we do not always have access to detailed household survey data from many countries, we should avoid making generalizations in relation to these areas.

The incidence of poverty is shaped by how poverty is defined, which can be on the basis of income, consumption or capability. Capability refers to quality of life outcomes, like longevity, education and health. For Sen (1981, 2001), poverty is the deprivation of basic capabilities rather than merely low income. Capability is the substantive 'freedom to achieve various lifestyles' (2001: 75). Development should therefore be about us utilizing and expanding our capabilities, and hence our freedom, as a means of enriching our lives (ibid.: 3).[8]

Likewise, inequality is more than just divergences in income or wealth between or within countries. It also refers, for instance, to differences in consumption expenditure levels and in access to education, health care and other social services. Some commentators emphasize the political dimension to

Box 0.3 Levels of inequality

- National inequality refers to the distribution of income among people within each country. For development specialists and others working in the field, it is more practicable to focus upon tackling inequality at this level. Moreover, reducing disparities within countries can help to reduce the overall level of global inequality.
- International inequality is the economic disparity that exists between countries.
- Global inequality refers to income differences between all individual people in the world, and includes inter-country as well as intra-country inequalities.

(*Sources*: Cornia and Court 2001; Held and Kaya 2007)

Box 0.4 Income inequality

- While there are different types of inequality, income inequality refers to the inequality of the distribution of household income among the population of a country.
- The standard measure of income inequality is the Gini coefficient, which is measured on a scale of 0 (perfect equality) to 1 (perfect inequality). Thus, the higher the Gini coefficient, the more unequal the society. A country with a Gini coefficient above 0.5 is considered to have a highly unequal income distribution.
- The Gini Index, which also measures income inequality, ranges from 0 (perfect equality) to 100 (perfect inequality).
- The level of income inequality depends primarily on the distribution of wages and assets, as well as on government policy.

(*Source*: Cornia and Court 2001)

Box 0.5 Defining poverty

- Most approaches to poverty are economic and oriented towards quantifying it usually by establishing a poverty line, such as people living on less than US$1 per day (the standard measure of poverty), adjusting for differences in purchasing power across different currencies.
- Purchasing Power Parity (PPP) 'is a method of adjusting relative incomes in different countries to take account of the fact that market exchange rates do not accurately reflect purchasing power' (Wade 2003: 43–4). In other words, it takes into account international differences in relative prices.
- From 2005, the international poverty lines of US$1.25 a day (extreme poverty), which is equivalent to the US$1 per day poverty line introduced in 1981 after adjustment for inflation, and US$2 a day (poverty) were established.
- While much attention is devoted to low income, poverty is a multidimensional phenomenon that also encompasses quality of life issues like: health and access to health care; education and employment prospects; security and well-being; and societal participation, although, for some writers on poverty, income underpins many of these other areas (White 2002). Given the multidimensional nature of poverty, it follows that its different aspects affect various population groups in different ways. The poor are therefore heterogeneous.
- Absolute poverty describes a condition where incomes are so low that even a minimum standard of nutrition, shelter and personal necessities cannot be maintained (World Bank 1975: 19).
- Relative poverty refers to people who do not enjoy a sense of well-being and/or are materially disadvantaged compared to others living in the same society. Peter Townsend defines relative poverty as 'the absence or inadequacy of those diets, amenities, standards, services and activities which are common or customary in society' (Townsend 1979).

Box 0.6 The Human Poverty Index

There is growing recognition of the complexity of poverty and that understanding it cannot simply be explained by economics and poverty lines. For example, a poverty line does not reveal information about wider access to public services or the extent of sup-porting family networks. Likewise, a household existing above the poverty line does not describe the experiences of individual members within the household, the size of the family, and the position of women and children within it (Sen 1981).

In an attempt to improve upon the economic focus of conventional methods of determining poverty, the UNDP has devised the Human Poverty Index (HPI) that seeks to measure deprivation. Under this scheme, poverty for developing countries is calculated in terms of the percentage of the population who are illiterate, not expected to live to age 40, and do not enjoy decent standards of living (defined as access to treated water supplies and health care, and the percentage of children under five who are under-weight) (UNDP 2002). Furthermore, there have been some advances in relation to these areas. For example, average life expectancy in low-income countries has risen from 48 to 63 years since the 1960s (DFID 2006: 57), although in countries like Botswana this advance has been reversed by the impact of HIV/AIDS (chapter 3).

However, the HDI has been criticized for continuing to employ a quantitative – as opposed to a qualitative – approach to poverty. In other words, it does not incorporate the actual experiences of poverty of those involved (McIlwaine 2002; Willis 2005: 14). In this regard, it does not include the understandings of poverty based on social exclusion, marginalization and other factors difficult to measure qualitatively.

inequality, regarding it as entailing differences in levels of political participa-tion, such as voting rights (Justino, Litchfield and Whitehead 2003). Inequality is also a plural phenomenon reflected in gender, racial, ethnic, class and age inequalities.

Lastly, determining what is happening internationally with regard to poverty and inequality is made more difficult by the fact that, while they are distinct phenomena, they are also multidimensional and interrelated concepts. For example, writers on inequality argue that achieving substantive poverty reduction requires addressing the unequal economic and social condi-tions that serve to perpetuate poverty. Persistent inequalities lead to poverty traps because it becomes virtually impossible for certain population groups to be economically and socially mobile, which undermines efforts to reduce poverty (Justino, Litchfield and Whitehead 2003).

Explaining global poverty and inequality

The reasons for the emergence of complex patterns of poverty and inequality are numerous and varied, but ultimately will be context specific, shaped by the intersection of global, local, regional and national factors and processes. Nevertheless, general explanations for the high incidence of poverty and inequality include: the level of debt in poor countries; legacies of colonial-ism; the failure of aid programmes; the impact of technological change upon levels and types of employment; the social division created by an abundance of natural resources (the 'resource curse'); internal mismanagement and inappropriate development strategies; and politically unstable and corrupt states. In this vein, Paul Collier (2007) maintains that the poorest countries are caught in one or more of four traps: the conflict trap; the natural resource trap; the trap of being landlocked with bad neighbours; and the trap of bad governance in a small country.

For many writers, it is aspects of globalization, such as trade openness and worldwide production processes, which are determining contemporary patterns of poverty and inequality. Thus, while the poor lack the financial resources to adapt readily to the greater competition which results from opening up economies to global markets, those with resources and the productive capacity can take advantage of the export opportunities that this presents (Glewwe and Hall 1998). For example, the smallholder farmers and landless labourers that make up Brazil's more than 10 million rural poor remain largely outside of its growing agricultural export market, which is dominated by large commercial farms (UNDP 2005: 123).

In contrast, advocates of globalization argue that countries which have integrated into the international economy, like China and India, have experienced significant increases in per capita wealth and poverty reduction (Dollar and Kraay 2002a; Wolf 2004). Dollar and Kraay contend that globalizing developing countries grew at 5.0 per cent per capita in the 1990s, while for rich countries and non-globalizing developing countries, growth was only 2.2 per cent per capita and 1.4 per cent per capita, respectively (2002b: 18). For Dollar and Kraay, growth generally benefits the poor as much as everyone else. Hence, growth-enhancing policies like fiscal discipline and openness to international trade 'should be at the centre of successful poverty reduction strategies' (2001: 32).

However, Grahame Thompson (2007) questions the existence of globalization and a global economic system, maintaining that economic activity is mainly conducted nationally and regionally, and occurs primarily between developed countries. He is therefore sceptical of discussions about the impact of globalization on global inequality, and argues that inequalities should be examined on a national and regional basis. Brune and Garrett (2005) contend that there is no consensus in the relevant literatures on how globalization has affected inequality both among and within countries because there is a basic lack of agreement over how to measure globalization and to draw causal inferences about its effects.

Martin Wolf maintains that we need to look to domestic factors and policies rather than globalization to account for the persistence of global inequality, which is reflected in the disparities in national economic performance within the South (Wade and Wolf 2003). On the theme of domestic factors, the *World Development Report 2006* argues that a major obstacle to equality is that the predetermined circumstances of human beings and the social groups a person is born into (race, gender, place of birth, family origins) continue to determine whether people succeed economically, socially, and politically (World Bank 2005b: 19). The report estimates that between one-third and one-half of the inequalities within countries can be explained by 'between-group', differences with the poor, people in rural areas, women, and those of low caste or status generally having reduced access to education, land and credit. For instance, in 1996, the infant mortality rate in Rio de Janeiro was 3.3 per cent, less than half the 7.4 per cent in the more rural north-east Brazil (ibid.: 55).

For Cornia and Court, the rise of within-country income inequality since the early 1980s is down to the 'excessively liberal economic policy regimes' and the way in which economic reform policies like structural adjustment have been carried out (2001: 1). Thus, the emphasis upon reduced regulation and employment protection, as well as wage flexibility, has been more signifi-cant than traditional causes of inequality, like the nature of land ownership, urban bias, and inequality in education (ibid.: 6). Indeed, the deregulation of labour markets since the 1980s is widely considered to have increased income inequality (see Cornia 2005). The greater emphasis upon flexibility in the workplace has enabled some skilled workers to enjoy higher earnings, but more broadly it has diminished the bargaining power of trade unions, result-ing in greater job insecurity and an erosion of minimum wages. Likewise, the SAPRIN (2004) investigation into the impact of structural adjustment maintains that poverty has been increased through privatization programmes and cuts in public goods and services. The effects were especially felt in Africa because of the high level of public sector employment. In Nigeria, around 60 per cent of jobs were in the public sector, and it is estimated that up to one million workers were made redundant because of SAPs between 1984 and 1989 (Mohan et al. 2000: 64).

Tackling global poverty and inequality

Numerous proposals to alleviate poverty and reduce inequality have been developed (see Collier 2007; Cornia and Court 2001; McKay 1997; Smith 2005), but the most concerted international effort to reduce poverty are the Millennium Development Goals. As we saw in the previous section, the Millennium Development target in relation to poverty is to reduce by half the proportion of people living on less than a dollar a day, which is generally used to denote extreme poverty, and the proportion of people who suffer from hunger (Box 0.2). However, this particular aspect of the Millennium Development project has also attracted criticism. Ashwani Saith (2006) con-tends the MDGs neglect poverty and deprivation within advanced industrial economies, but also fail to address the persistence of high levels of global inequality. More broadly, the multidimensional and subjective nature of pov-erty is marginalized by the emphasis upon quantitative targets, income and economic growth (White 2006).

Unfortunately, the global economic crisis has derailed progress against

Box 0.7 The Kuznets curve

The economist Simon Kuznets (1955) maintained that, as a country experiences economic growth, inequality also rises. This is because some population groups will benefit from these new economic conditions, while others will not. At the higher levels of economic growth and income generation, inequality starts to decline as the wealth spreads to the rest of society. The end of the development process sees a new equilibrium of high incomes and low inequality. For Kuznets, figuratively speaking, this whole process takes the form of an inverted U-shape. However, the Kuznets curve has been criticized. In particular, it is argued that there is no guarantee or in-built mechanism that ensures the increased income will spread to the poorest population groups in society (Killick 2002b).

Kuznets Inverted U-Curve

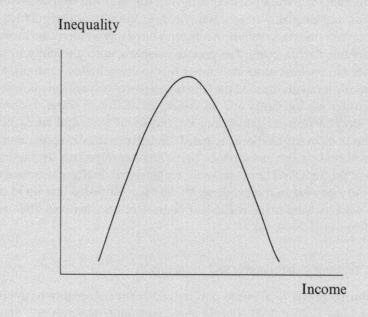

poverty. According to *The Millennium Development Goals Report*, in 2009, an estimated 55 million to 90 million more people were living in extreme poverty than anticipated before the crisis (UNMDG 2009: 4). The report notes that, as well as reducing aid from some donor nations, the crisis meant fewer trade opportunities for developing countries and a lack of economic growth (ibid.: 4).

However, the interrelationships between economic growth, inequality and poverty reduction are complex and contested (Box 0.7). High levels of poverty and inequality can restrict economic growth, which on the face of it can make it more difficult to reduce poverty (Cornia and Court 2001: 1). For instance, persistent high inequalities can limit the size of a country's skilled workforce because disadvantaged groups are more likely to be illiterate and to suffer from poor health (Justino, Litchfield and Whitehead 2003; Kanbur and Lustig 1999; Wilkinson 2005). Highly unequal societies also struggle to generate national demand because poorer population groups lack the financial means to buy domestic goods and services.

Yet until relatively recently policy-makers in the IFIs have neglected the issue of inequality, choosing instead to prioritize economic growth through a neo-liberal or market-led policy approach (chapter 1). But as was indicated above, rapid economic growth can also exacerbate inequalities. Indeed, a major report by the UN Economic and Social Affairs Department found that in 2005, despite considerable economic growth in many regions and improved living standards in some places, inequality between and within countries was greater than it was in 1995 and poverty remained entrenched (United Nations 2005b). The report concludes that: '[f]ocusing exclusively on economic growth and income generation as a development strategy is ineffective, as it leads to the accumulation of wealth by a few and deepens the poverty of many' (ibid.: 1). Thus, '[i]gnoring inequality in the pursuit of development is perilous' (ibid.). The World Bank's World Development Report 2006: Equity and Development similarly concludes that tackling inequality is the key to development, conceding that economic growth will not be enough to end world poverty and that it will require forms of redistribution (World Bank 2005b). These reports reflect a growing awareness that tackling poverty and inequality requires a mixture of policies, including government intervention, institutional reform, redistribution and investment in education, depending on local conditions, and cannot simply be left to pro-growth policies. In other words, economic growth is not the same as development.

As well as helping to build a more broad-base or inclusive economy, there are other reasons for tackling inequality and poverty. In particular, high levels of inequality can undermine social cohesion within a country, as well as encourage crime and social and political unrest. In turn, such conditions erode trust and social capital within a society, and these are regarded as essential prerequisites of commerce and democracy (see chapter 7). These tendencies can therefore hinder the process of economic and social development. For this reason, alongside important considerations of fairness and social justice, addressing the complex patterns of global poverty and inequality is likely to be an integral part of development in the twenty-first century.

Summary

- Development is a contested area of study as is evident in the different disciplinary and theoretical approaches to the subject.
- The dominant conception of development has changed over time, and today there is much greater emphasis upon quality-of-life issues.
- Development is now taking place within the context of globalization and increasing evidence of global environmental decline.

- Since 1980, patterns of global poverty and inequality have become increasingly complex.

RECOMMENDED READING

- Useful introductory works to development are: Robert Potter, Tony Binns, Jennifer Elliott and David Smith's *Geographies of Development* (2004) and Kate Willis, *Theories and Practices of Development* (2005).
- For globalization, poverty and inequality, see David Held and Ayse Kaya (eds), *Global Inequality* (2007) and Raphael Kaplinsky, *Globalization, Poverty and Inequality* (2005).

WEBSITES

- www.undp.org: Provides a comprehensive and up-to-date picture of development.
- www.un.org/millenniumgoals: Website of the *UN Millennium Development Goals* (UNMDG 2005), from where it is possible to access *The Millennium Development Goals Report 2007*.

CHAPTER 1

Theorizing Development

- From three worlds to the North–South divide
- The major economic approaches to development
- The East Asian 'miracle'

To understand development requires knowledge of how this subject has evolved, as well as the major theoretical approaches that have defined it, and addressing these areas is the concern of this first chapter. It begins by looking at how this subject has been conceptualized from a geographical perspective, considering the spatializing of development through an examination of 'the Third World' and 'the North–South divide'. The second section surveys the history of economic theories of development, including modernization theory, structuralism, dependency theory and the rise of the neo-liberal paradigm in the 1980s. The East Asian development experience is a useful testing ground for the leading development theories and consequently is examined in the final section. It also provides evidence of the difficulties of pursuing development within the existing international economic order.

From three worlds to the North–South divide

From its very beginnings, there has been a strong spatial dimension to development, with the world divided at various times into different regions or blocs to indicate different stages and types of economic development, including 'core' and 'periphery', a 'world system' and the idea of semi-peripheries (see p. 36). The most well-known attempt at spatial division in relation to development has been to describe the planet as consisting of three worlds.

The making of 'the Third World'

As was stated in the Introduction, development in its contemporary guise began to emerge in the aftermath of the international economic and political turmoil created by the Second World War. However, it was also shaped by the emergence of the Third World. Indeed, dealing with problems and challenges faced by the Third World gave development much of its impetus and moral purpose. Furthermore, as European colonial rule came to an end in the two of three decades following 1945, development was firmly on the agendas of the leaders of the newly independent countries, both as a means of consolidating independence and of strengthening their own political positions.

Thus, the notion of a 'Third World' began to be articulated in the late 1940s and early 1950s as the decolonization process was getting under way in Africa, Asia and the Caribbean, but also as the future of international affairs appeared to be between two alternatives worlds: either that offered by Washington or that by Moscow (Harris 1986).[1] It was initially a deeply political concept because it highlighted global divisions and inequalities, and as such constituted a critique of the existing international order (see Worsley 1964). Indeed, the Third World rejected the notion of a world divided into two, offering the prospect of a new type of politics that did not take the path of either Soviet socialism or western capitalism (Merriam 1988).

In line with the rejection of the international status quo, as well as desiring to thwart and remain outside of the Cold War, the Non-Aligned Movement (NAM) emerged during the 1950s, coming to prominence with the Bandung Conference in 1955. The forms of cooperation upon which NAM was based, and encouraged, helped to ensure that developing countries remained significant players during the Cold War. Indeed, the NAM contributed to the establishment of UNCTAD (see Introduction) and the Group of 77 (G-77) at the UN that led to the practice of southern states voting together as a bloc on issues like trade. In the 1970s, the NAM contributed to southern calls for a New International Economic Order (NIEO) to replace the US-dominated Bretton Woods system with an international economic system more in tune with the interests of the Third World.

Following this initial radicalism, the term 'the Third World' entered into everyday usage during the Cold War period coming simply to denote a set of countries and geographical regions, which today are commonly referred to as developing countries or the developing world (Harris 1986: 7). These are otherwise known as LEDCs (less economically developed countries), and are generally taken to include countries from Latin America, Asia, Africa and the Caribbean, and are distinguished from MEDCs (more economically developed countries) which can be found in the industrialized West. The following are typical of the criteria that are frequently used to define Third World countries:

- relatively low per capita (for each person) incomes;
- mainly agriculturally based economies with low levels of technology, and reliant upon primary exports;
- ruled by a colonial power in the past;
- sizeable populations and growth rates, but also shorter life expectancies and higher rates of infant mortality;
- a low degree of social mobility;
- societies in which, religion, custom and tradition continue to exert a strong influence;
- lower levels of educational attainment, reflected in higher rates of illiteracy.

(adapted from Hoogvelt 1982; Merriam 1988; Rapley 2007)

However, the problem with the above categorization of the Third World is that it is Eurocentric and largely an economic interpretation. The emphasis upon wealth generation, technology and breaking free from tradition is rooted in the European conception of modernity, and specifically notions of progress, rationalism, science and materialism (see chapter 2). Thus, when it comes to classifying the Third World, much rests upon the criteria that we employ and who has the power to determine such classificatory systems.

Criticisms of the concept of the Third World

Some commentators consider that a global socio-economic classification scheme with only three categories is too broad to reflect the great diversity of economies, cultures, political systems and values that exists throughout the world (Norwine and Gonzalez 1988: 1). Even within the category of the Third World, it includes some of the world's wealthiest and poorest nations in terms of per capita incomes. There is also considerable diversity within the First World. Berger (1994) points to the existence of underclasses within First World societies, who can live in conditions equivalent to and in some cases worse than those found in the Third World.[2] Furthermore, while some of the criteria cited above may have been broadly applicable immediately after 1945, since then newly indus- trializing countries (NICs) like Brazil, Mexico and the Asian 'tiger economies' of Hong Kong, Singapore, South Korea and Taiwan, have enjoyed a rate of eco- nomic growth that has effectively enabled them to leave this condition behind. Moreover, in the case of China and India, such has been the extent of their economic development, it is now widely accepted that they will become world superpowers later this century. More generally, there are also huge differences amongst those countries labelled 'Third World' with regard to their experiences of colonialism, their economic systems (ranging from capitalist/private enter- prise economies to state-run economies) and their political systems (multi-party democracies, theocracies, authoritarian regimes). So great is this internal diver- sity that for some the idea of the Third World is simply a myth (Naipaul 1985).

Many neo-liberals similarly consider the Third World to be an artificial con- struct, emerging as a result of western guilt over Europe's colonial past and its legacies. In the contemporary period, this sentiment has become bound up with the politics of foreign aid, with the inference that there is an element of moral blackmail at work on the part of Third World governments. Indeed, from a neo-liberal perspective, what distinguishes countries of the Third World is that their governments 'with the odd exception, demand and receive' foreign aid (Bauer 1981: 87). This pattern is based upon an underlying assump- tion that responsibility for their condition lies with the West and hence they should receive compensation in the form of official aid from it, which western governments go along with in order to assuage their guilt. Peter Bauer has gone so far as to argue that: 'The Third World is the creation of foreign aid: without foreign aid there is no Third World' (ibid.).

Another school of thought in relation to the Third World is the belief that it is more appropriate to conceptualize four worlds. From an economic perspective, the Third World includes developing nations with significant economic potential and/or natural resources, such as Argentina, Egypt, Nigeria, Mexico, Iran and Saudi Arabia, whereas the Fourth World would designate the worst economic hardship cases, like Bangladesh, Burkino Faso, Chad, Haiti, Laos, Nepal, Ethiopia and Somalia (Merriam 1988: 18). Others have asserted the existence of a Fourth World in terms of culture and politics, rather than economics. For example, George Manuel and Michael Posluns in *The Fourth World: An Indian Reality* (1974) identify a Fourth World consisting of indigenous peoples, like the Indians of the Americas, the Lapps of northern Scandinavia, the Canadian Inuit and the aborigines of Australia that are subsumed by majority cultures in the countries in which they live (see also the special edition of *Antipode*, 1981, 13(1)).

In contrast, some people believe that even three worlds are two worlds too many because ultimately all human beings live on the same planet and share a common humanity, and we should therefore not seek to construct divisions between ourselves that can potentially lead to competition and conflict. While this view has been articulated by Third World leaders like Indira Gandhi and Julius Nyerere, the former prime minister of India and president of Tanzania, respectively, it has been criticized for being idealistic. For example, Allen Merriam (1988) concedes that global unity represents a noble ideal, but it ignores the persistence of tangible cultural, political and economic differences and inequalities in the world. Likewise, Jim Norwine and Alfonso Gonzalez (1988) argue that living in Third World conditions is an everyday reality for millions of people across the globe. Moreover, the number of people transcending their Third World living conditions has been questioned. For example, the combined population of the 'Asian tiger' economies was only 73 million in 1992, and hence only a small proportion of the total population in the Third World. In the case of Brazil and Mexico, they have not been able to spread their economic growth and are still confronted with high income inequality and poverty (Parkins 1996: 54). Indeed, as we have seen, the levels of global poverty and inequality remain high, and may even be increasing. For such reasons, Peter Worsley insists that the Third World 'is not a myth' (1984: 339).

The North–South divide

However, a number of factors have militated against the continued usage of the concept of the Third World. Firstly, and most obviously, the Second World had disappeared by the early 1990s with the collapse of the Soviet bloc, effectively rendering the concept of a Third World illogical (see Bayart 1991). Further complicating matters has been the growing regionalization of world politics since the 1980s, with a number of regional groupings and organizations being set up, such as the European Union, NAFTA (the North American

Free Trade Agreement), ASEAN (the South-East Asian Nations), SADC (the Southern African Development Community) and MERCOSUR (Southern Cone Common Market) in Latin America.

Secondly, a more general problem with the concept of the Third World is that it implies its peoples and countries have been left behind. It also suggests that in order to escape their condition they should become more like the First World (i.e., the West). As a result, many governments in the developing world reject the concept of the Third World, preferring instead that of the South, which has the advantage of implicitly moving away from the idea that their countries have to move up an imaginary international league table.[3]

Thirdly, and following on from the previous point, the notion of a global North–South divide gained credence when the influential UN-sponsored Brandt Commission reported on global inequality and poverty in 1980 and 1983 (Brandt Commission 1980, 1983). Significantly, the Brandt Commission, which was chaired by the former Chancellor of West Germany, Willy Brandt, raised doubts about the appropriateness of conceptualizing a number of different and discrete worlds because it misunderstood the nature of global interdependence.

However, the concept of the North–South divide is not without its critics. In particular, it is pointed out that this dichotomy overlooks the fact that, geographically speaking, parts of Africa and Asia fall within the northern hemisphere while advanced industrial countries like Australia and New Zealand, which are considered to be part of the North, are in the southern hemisphere. And as with the Third World, the South contains countries and cities like Malaysia, Singapore and Mumbai that from an economic perspective outstrip many of their northern counterparts. Interestingly, and perhaps revealingly, the Brandt Report refrains from discussing definitions of the North and South. Nevertheless, this conceptualization of the world is now common within development studies and is the terminology that will generally be employed here. Furthermore, as many commentators have observed, irrespective of the intellectual coherence and validity of concepts like 'the Third World' and the 'South', they do serve a useful role in reminding us of the persistence of profound inequalities on our planet (e.g., Dodds 2002).

Accounting for and addressing the challenges faced by the South has generated numerous theories within development, and the major economic approaches will now be examined.

Major economic approaches to development

As will be come clear, some of these approaches were not originally designed to contribute to development but have subsequently gone on to exert considerable influence upon this field of study. The approaches are dealt with here in broadly chronological order, although, as indicated in the Introduction, their influence has spilled over into different periods and in most cases continues to the present day.

Economic growth theory

Keynesianism is the approach most associated with economic growth theory, and it came to exert an enormous influence upon governments throughout the world after 1945. Named after the British economist John Maynard Keynes (1883–1946), it emerged from the crisis of confidence in the market following the Great Depression of the early 1930s, which itself was preceded by the Wall Street Crash of 1929.

In *The General Theory of Employment, Interest and Money* (1936), Keynes emphasized the positive role that governments could play in stimulating economic growth through investment in new infrastructure projects and the like, even if this meant them having to borrow money to do so. For Keynes, the reason this would lead to economic growth was because of 'the multiplier effect' of such an action. Thus, such investment could help to soak up unemployment within a given country, thereby increasing the purchasing power of its citizens, enabling them to buy more goods and services, which would in turn help to generate economic growth. Of course, if the citizens choose to purchase the goods and services of other countries, then the wealth generated for the country pursuing this approach will be reduced. Moreover, because Keynes was primarily interested in short-term stabilization in already industrialized economies rather than the long-term issue of underdevelopment, he did not directly contribute to development theory (Blomström and Hettne 1984: 12). Nevertheless, Keynes's work is a direct challenge to the faith of classical economists in the market, and subsequently contributed to the notion of the active and interventionist developmental state in the post-war period with his work being utilized by development theorists (Preston 1996).

Modernization theory

Modernization theory has been formed from numerous disciplines, notably economics, sociology, geography, politics and psychology (see Haines 2000; Peet with Hartwick 1999). The common theme running through the various modernization theories is a linear conception of history which sees countries moving from being traditional to modern societies (see Boxes 1.1 and 1.2). Tradition and custom act as a fetter upon development and progress and, once countries start to break free from these vestiges of the past, they can enjoy substantial growth. Modernization theorists have therefore tended to locate the causes for underdevelopment in conditions and structures within countries, rather than in any external forces or factors (Haines 2000). Different modernization theorists have had their own remedies for enabling developing countries to 'take off': it could require increased savings and investment; the West providing its expertise; the formation of westernizing elites or simply the dissemination of liberal capitalist values (Apter 1965; Rapley 2007; Weiner 1966). There is therefore a strong cultural dimension to modernization theory, with

Box 1.1 Walt Rostow's stages of economic growth

In *The Stages of Economic Growth: A Non-Communist Manifesto* (1960), the economic historian Walt Rostow presents the most well-known modernization thesis, viewing it as a five-stage process:

1 *'Traditional society'*. This is the initial phase in which society and economy is relatively static, agrarian, hierarchical, and organized along family and clan lines, with pre-Newtonian science and technology.
2 The *'preconditions'* stage. During this stage, the ingredients for industrial growth, including the building of the necessary physical infrastructure, come together to make industrialization possible. These preconditions include:

   - A transformation in agriculture yielding higher productivity on the land to sustain industrial and urban growth and release surplus labour.
   - Developments in transport, such as ports, docks, canals, roads or railways which extend markets.
   - The development of the ancillary services for industry, especially banking, and saving and investment rates exceeding population growth rates.
   - A basic level of skilled labour and productive and technological capacity.
   - An increased exploitation of raw materials, either domestic or imported.

3 *'Take-off'*. This occurs when the manufacturing sector lifts away from its economic base. The most significant characteristics of 'take-off' are: that it takes only 2 or 3 decades; a doubling in the proportion of national income which is productively invested; the growth of certain major industries to form 'leading sectors' within the economy.
4 *'The drive to maturity'*. Following take-off, the economy then moves into this next stage. This is a lengthy phase – up to six decades or more – but it is also the period when the process of industrial growth becomes sustained or irreversible, and more sophisticated technology and work processes are introduced.
5 The age of *'high mass consumption'*. When economic growth within a country has been sustained for a sufficient length of time, this final stage will be reached. It is characterized by the manufacturing sector focusing upon the production of consumer goods and their respective citizens now earning sufficient income to be able to purchase these products. In addition, there is increased spending on welfare services.

the values and practices of the West, which had already undergone this process, considered more suited to development than those of other societies (see chapter 2). This position reflects the fact that emerging from the late 1940s onwards, modernization theory was caught up in the Cold War politics of the era. In this regard, from the perspective of western governments, modernization constituted an alternative path to development for the Third World from that offered to them by the Soviet bloc and communism. Indeed, this was a time when some academics, particularly in the USA, were declaring that we had reached 'the end of ideology'.

However, modernization theory has attracted considerable criticism. In particular, its linear conception of history is considered to underplay the extent to which societies can take divergent paths and even resist modernizing processes by seeking to hold onto aspects of their past. Moreover, even the most modern societies will still contain elements of their past traditions. Modernity is therefore not a distinct epoch, an all-or-nothing condition. In addition, there is growing acceptance of the concept of multiple modernities, whereby the process of

Box 1.2 A critique of Rostow's thesis

Since the publication of his book, Rostow's model has been criticized on numerous grounds, including the following:

1 Rostow has been accused of homogenizing societies and underplaying the extent to which the particular conditions within them – their resource endowment, population size, the nature of their political systems and cultural characteristics – will shape their development trajectory. For instance, authoritarian societies are less likely to allow entrepreneurship to flourish than more open societies. Political upheavals, like revolutions, can also hold back industrialization.

2 Many economic historians challenge Rostow's 'take-off' thesis, arguing that economic growth tends to be more evolutionary. There are few historical examples of economies doubling their rate of productive investment within 30 years.

3 Rostow's linear model of development has been questioned, with critics stressing that economies can retard after displaying signs of rapid change (Binns 2002).

4 Alexander Gerschenkron contends that most economies start from a condition of deprivation rather than preconditions, and, as other economies progress, the pressure to catch up becomes acute, which invariably leads the state to step in to speed up industrializing processes and substitute itself for other agents of change where they are missing. For example, the state can provide capital and build infrastructure when these prerequisites for development are absent. This role performed by the state explains how latecomers are often able to industrialize in rapid spurts. From Gerschenkron's perspective, therefore, Rostow's model can only account for the first nation to industrialize (i.e., Britain) and cannot explain the development of those countries that follow in its wake.

5 Tony Binns (1994, 2002) has argued that Rostow essentially presents an economic growth model, which is not necessarily the same as development. For example, a country can industrialize and enjoy considerable economic growth without this prosperity being distributed evenly or fairly throughout the population.

6 Finally, critics have argued that economic development simply lacks the precision that Rostow presents. In this regard, the factors that he describes as preconditions may occur at almost any stage of the growth process.

modernization is informed by the particular cultural and historical traditions of individual societies (chapter 2; Eisenstadt 2002, 2003). In this regard, a further criticism of modernization theorists is that they simply assume that the western model of development is universally applicable and can be readily adopted by southern countries (Martinussen 1997). Such a philosophy also underplays the extent to which international conditions may preclude development in the South. As will be shown below, there is a considerable body of work arguing that developing countries are largely powerless to control their destiny because of the nature of the existing international economic order. Indeed, critics argue that a basic flaw of modernization theory is that it is too focused upon endogenous (internal) factors at the expense of exogenous or external factors. It therefore presents only a partial insight into development.

Structuralism

Structuralism gained influence in the 1950s, particularly among Latin American governments, and was so named because its exponents focused upon the structures of the international economy in accounting for patterns of development and underdevelopment (see Clarke 2002). Structuralism was less a school of thought than a broad tradition, but it was strongest in Latin America, due in large part to the attempts of its advocates to explain the relative lack of development in the region. At the forefront of this approach were Raúl Prebisch (1950), the Brazilian economist Celso Furtado (1963, 1964), and the UN Economic Commission for Latin America (ECLA). The scope of ECLA's work was later broadened to include the countries of the Caribbean, and this was reflected in a resolution passed in 1984 that incorporated them into the title so that it became the UN Economic Commission for Latin America and the Caribbean (ECLAC).

ECLA itself was established in 1948 – in fact Prebisch became its Secretary-General – in order to promote the Latin American perspective in the world. This approach differed significantly from modernization theory in the sense that it was based upon the notion that development should not be dictated by European models, but instead should be geared to the realities on the ground within the developing world, which from the ECLA perspective meant Latin America. Indeed, structuralism was often presented by its advocates as an alternative paradigm – devised by social scientists from the South – to the modernization paradigm of the North, although it never challenged either capitalism or the capitalist route to development, and merely sought reform of the capitalist trade system.

Drawing on the work of Keynes, structuralists also viewed governmental intervention as a means of stimulating economic development. More specifically, they argued that developing countries should rely upon state action in a dual sense if they wanted to improve their plight. Firstly, the governments of developing countries should actively encourage industrialization through measures such as planning and providing financial and infrastructural support because they could not rely upon the free market to achieve this end. Structuralism therefore shares with modernization theory a faith in industrialization.

Secondly, governments should adopt protectionist policies, like imposing import tariffs that served to raise the price of foreign goods coming into their countries, in order to protect their own newly emerging industries. Without such measures, indigenous industries within the developing world would struggle to survive under conditions of international free trade because it placed them in direct competition with powerful industries in the North. Prebisch (1950) and other structuralists argued that the existence of established industries in the West meant that the development experience of the non-western world would inevitably be different. In other words, while European industries had matured over time without facing significant international economic competition or constraints, this development trajectory was not possible for industries and countries of the South which had to operate within an established international economic system. For some structuralists, this could even involve countries of the South trading among themselves if it meant they avoided becoming dependent upon the North. But the most notable aspect of structuralism was the type of development it encouraged, namely that of import-substitution industrialization.[4]

Import-substitution industrialization (ISI) During the 1950s and 1960s, many governments in the developing world believed the most effective way of breaking out of unequal trading relationships with the West was by becoming more self-reliant and pursuing a policy of ISI. Consequently, there was an attempt to end reliance upon imports and to concentrate upon developing domestic manufacturing and creating more employment. This approach was intended to facilitate industrialization to the extent that products could be manufactured with export value. In practice, ISI entailed the state driving economic development through a combination of measures such as subsidizing industries, nationalization, the discouragement of foreign direct investment (FDI), and protectionist trade policies. ISI was adopted in many Latin American countries as early as the 1930s – largely in response to the Great Depression – and in some Asian and African countries from the 1950s onwards.

However, the economic track record of ISI was mixed. While manufacturing production increased annually by 6.3 per cent on average in Latin America in the 1960s (Sheahan 1987: 85), many manufacturing industries found it difficult to flourish in countries where their own domestic markets were small due to factors ranging from limited population size to low incomes. In addition, those countries with slender resources found the switch away from cash-crop production tended to rapidly reduce their foreign exchange earnings. This meant that developing countries had less money to purchase imports, including the very production technology upon which ISI depended. There was also resistance within these societies from the land-owning groups that had traditionally benefited from primary product exports. Indeed, the general charge against ISI is that, in the rush to industrialize, the agricultural sector was frequently neglected in developing societies (Rapley 2007: 51). Furthermore, the tariff barriers that were imposed to protect indigenous industry from imported manufactured goods merely led foreign companies to set up local assembly plants as a way of maintaining their export sales. It highlighted the difficulty that countries face in trying to delink themselves from the international economy. In addition, ISI was making industries in the developing world uncompetitive and hence inefficient because they were being artificially protected by tariffs.

Finally, the recurring charge raised against structuralists and all those who advocated statist theories of development was that they had unrealistic expectations of the state, ignoring the bureaucracy, incompetence and corruption that have plagued many states throughout the world. For many of the preceding reasons, most developing countries from the late 1970s onwards became more geared towards export-oriented industrialization (Willis 2005: 69). Latin American countries in particular began to abandon ISI following the debt crisis the region suffered in 1982 (see chapter 8 of this book).

Dependency theory

The origins of this approach can in part be traced to dissatisfaction with many of the claims made by modernization theorists, with critics noting the dearth of evidence that modernization theory was actually working. By the 1960s, the lack of economic development in the South and the persistence of global inequality meant that attention was increasingly directed towards explaining this state of affairs, especially among radical and neo-Marxist critics, some of whose writings came to constitute what became known as dependency theory. Their general position is that international capitalism increases disparities in levels of development because it is based upon a series of imperialistic and exploitative relationships which enable the North to extract wealth from the South.

In Capitalism and Underdevelopment in Latin America (1967), André Gunder Frank – using the examples of Brazil and Chile to make his case – argues that underdevelopment is directly linked to development elsewhere in the world. This is because, dating back to the sixteenth century, capitalism has been based upon a chain of metropolitan–periphery relations that ensures development and domination for the metropolitan countries (First World) and underdevelopment and dependency for those countries on the periphery (Third World). In the post-war period, for dependency theorists, these relations have included the nature of the international division of labour, high interest repayments on loans provided by western banks and governments, royalties, and fees for patents and information services, which along with repatriated profits and capital flight has resulted in money flowing out of the South and into the North, and ensures that the former remains reliant upon the latter. Arghiri Emmanuel, in *Unequal Exchange: A Study of the Imperialism of Trade* (1972), makes a wider point with regard to this relationship, maintaining that free trade always favours the more developed powers because they have the greater productive capacity and are therefore able to produce goods more quickly and cheaply. So, where such conditions prevail, they will inevitably serve to exacerbate existing inequalities between countries and deepen the dependency relationship.

Samir Amin cites the legacy of colonialism in accounting for the lack of development in the South. During the colonial period, production in the colonies was tailored to European markets with the consequence that today many of them remain essentially one-product economies (cocoa, bananas, cane sugar, etc.), which makes them extremely susceptible to fluctuations in price on the international markets. In *Accumulation on a World Scale: Critique of the Theory of Underdevelopment* (1974), Amin maintains that this imposed specialization is now inhibiting the development of countries in the South. Furthermore, because there are so many developing countries that are dependent upon exporting foodstuffs and raw materials, prices remain low.

Other writers (e.g., Emmanuel 1972) point to the structure of the international economy, arguing that unfairness is built into the system, with western countries being able to determine the terms of trade through controlling import and export prices in world markets. From the dependency perspective, there is a basic unequal exchange at work: a low value is attached to primary commodities (raw materials and foodstuffs) from the South whereas manufactured goods produced in the North are highly priced. In short, following decolonization, the ex-colonies entered an international economy that had already been shaped by their former colonial masters and had to do so on their terms. As a result, the levels of debt of countries in the South continued to grow, ensuring that they remain dependent upon western countries for loans and had to accept their terms and conditions. For many in the South, it has meant that the North has been operating a form of neo-colonialism during the post-war period.[5] This means that the former colonies had achieved constitutional or political independence, what is often called 'flag independence', but they remain economically dependent upon the industrialized North and therefore have not achieved true independence.

In sum, radical and neo-Marxist writings, especially during the 1960s and 1970s, were dominated by the idea that international capitalism blocks development by ensuring that countries of the South remain dependent upon the industrialized North.

World-systems theory   While still part of the radical tradition, world-systems theory nevertheless sought to refine the sense within dependency theory that capitalism perpetuated a permanent core–periphery dualism. In this regard, Immanuel Wallerstein (1974, 1979), who first developed world-systems analysis, offers a more fluid conception of international economic and spatial divisions under capitalism, identifying 'core', 'periphery' and 'semi-periphery' categories, with the latter made up of the NICs of East Asia and Latin America. Most importantly, from his perspective, it is possible for countries to move in and out of these categories as they develop or suffer relative economic decline as other countries catch up with or overtake them. This also means the fate of countries is not simply determined by global economic patterns and structures and can in fact be influenced by internal dynamics (Potter et al. 2004: 112). Recognition of this reality makes it easier to account for the economic transformation of countries like China and India, and their changing status in the world. Although some writers have criticized the looseness of Wallerstein's categorization, arguing that it leads to problems when it comes to determining which countries belong to which particular categories (Haines 2000: 43).

Criticisms of dependency theory

A number of criticisms have been raised against dependency theory, some of which will now be outlined.

(i) Dependency is overstated At the heart of this particular criticism is the claim that dependency theorists overplay the extent and nature of dependency, with some critics even challenging whether a dependency relationship exists between the South and the North. This has led, it is claimed, to a distorted picture of conditions in the pre-dependence period, which is invariably idealized and viewed as functioning effectively until the arrival of western countries. Similarly, recent economic developments are considered to challenge dependency theory. A central premise of dependency theory is that capitalism accentuates existing differences in levels of development, which led many dependency theorists to contend that the USA, as the most powerful metropolitan society, would continue to prosper at the expense of the underdevelopment of countries on the periphery (Brewer 1990: 23). In reality, the USA has suffered relative economic decline since the early 1970s as other countries – notably China, India and countries in South-East Asia – have started to catch up and in some areas of manufacturing out-produce it (Wallerstein 2003). Such has been the rapid pace of capitalist development of the NICs that some writers maintain it is no longer feasible to talk about a 'Third World' (Harris 1986).

Cristóbal Kay in *Latin American Theories of Development and Underdevelopment* (1989) provides a useful overview of this whole debate, arguing – as have others – the analyses of dependency theorists are too pessimistic because they ignore the fact that capitalism can lead to development for non-western countries. However, Kay accepts that they will never completely catch up because it is not in the interests of advanced industrialized societies to let them do so, which means that regions like Latin America face a future where they are never able to achieve full development.

(ii) Dependency theory underplays the internal causes of underdevelopment Critics of dependency theory argue that by emphasizing the role of western powers and the nature of the international economic system, they underplay the extent to which domestic factors contribute to underdevelopment in the South. This forms part of a broader charge against dependency theory that it focuses excessively upon the economic, and thereby neglects the influence of political, social, cultural and environmental factors in shaping development. In particular, the role played by local elites is now recognized as a major determining factor upon the nature and extent of development. For example, corrupt and authoritarian elites in a number of African states have been accused of not only siphoning off the wealth of their countries, but also of pursuing inappropriate strategies for achieving economic growth. Indeed, George Ayittey in *Africa Betrayed* (1992) accuses African elites of implementing a form of black neo-colonialism. Dependency theorists respond to this particular criticism by arguing that they do not deny the maintenance of dependency has been aided by local elites. The wealth secured by these elites is their reward for perpetuating the dependency relationship, while their fellow citizens suffer economic

hardship. It means that not only have forms of dependency been established between the centre and the periphery, but this has also resulted in extreme inequalities within so-called peripheral societies.

(iii) What hope does dependency theory offer to the developing world? Critics argue that dependency theory does not offer countries of the South a practicable way forward to attain economic development. By identifying dependency as the root cause of their underdevelopment and poverty, it sees no escape from this condition until their dependency is ended. Dependency theory is therefore premised upon either developing countries disconnecting from the global economy – something that is increasingly difficult under conditions of globalization – or the creation of a new international economic system, and as such it presents all-or-nothing solutions to the problems of the developing world. Consequently, few specific strategies for improving the economic per-formance of developing societies have emerged from this tradition. Indeed, from the dependency perspective, countries of the South will struggle to pursue such strategies because of the very conditions under which they oper-ate. Furthermore, given that international capitalism, at least at this current juncture, would seem to be secure for the foreseeable future, what hope does dependency theory offer to the developing world?

The response of dependency theorists

Unsurprisingly, dependency theorists and their supporters have refuted many of these criticisms. To begin with they note that many of the criticisms of dependency theory emanate from unsympathetic northern writers, especially from those working within the neo-liberal tradition. As we will see in the next section, on ideological and philosophical grounds, neo-liberals are funda-mentally opposed to dependency theory and have been accused of presenting straw man characterizations of it. In this regard, Robert Packenham (1998) stresses the importance of recognizing the varieties of dependency thinking.

Advocates of dependency theory point out that the theorization of depend-ency theorists actually contained many of the points raised by these critiques, especially in the more sociological and political work of writers like Fernando Henrique Cardoso (see Cardoso 1977). In *Dependency and Development in Latin America* (first published in 1969), Cardoso and his co-writer, Enzo Faletto, emphasize the political and social nature of economic development and hence are very much concerned with the particular. Thus, while Cardoso and Faletto identify the following four general stages in Latin America's economic development, they also acknowledge the unique histories of individual coun-tries and focus upon their respective historical backgrounds:

1. The period of outward expansion: this is the early outward expansion of newly independent countries.

2. Development and social change: the emergence of the middle classes and the growing political role played by them.
3. Nationalism and populism: the emergence of social and political forces of development in the formation of domestic markets.
4. The internationalization of the market: the new dependence on international markets.

For Cardoso and Faletto, Latin America's economic dependency stems not merely from the domination of the world market by the international capitalism of multinational corporations but also from the complex interplay of domestic political structures, organizations, classes, social movements, and historically conditioned alliances. An additional way in which Cardoso presents a more nuanced account of dependency theory is his acknowledgement that dependency was not a permanent or even a stable condition, and that development was 'a dynamic and multidimensional process' (Sánchez-Rodríguez 2006: 65). For example, international capitalism was evolving and the emergence of a new international division of labour involving the transfer of manufacturing industry from the North to developing countries provided new opportunities for the latter (ibid.: 62; see also chapter 10 this of book). Moreover, contrary to one of the criticisms of dependency theory, Cardoso was aware of the internal constraints acting upon development in Latin American countries. For instance, he acknowledged and even campaigned against the clientelism and corruption that existed in Brazil, although he maintained that this condition was a product of its dependent status (Font 2001).

Of course, this dispute between dependency theorists and their critics further highlights the contested nature of development. And as will now be shown, from the 1970s onwards, a further challenge to dependency theory came in the guise of neo-liberalism.

Neo-liberalism

Neo-liberalism is an economic and political project with a particular set of policies and approaches to governmentality. It is based on an ideological understanding of the role of states and markets, as well as the relationship between the individual and society. This ideological understanding is that of the so-called 'New Right' that gained considerable influence in national and international policy-making circles in the 1980s due to factors such as the demise of the Bretton Woods system in the early 1970s, increased international economic instability during that decade, and growing criticism of Keynesian economics and statist planning approaches (see Preston 1996). The intellectual origins of neo-liberalism can be traced to the market libertarianism of Friedrich von Hayek (see F. A. Hayek, *The Road to Serfdom*, 1971 [1944]) and the monetarist economics of Milton Friedman and the Chicago School.

Within development circles, neo-liberalism really took off during the 1980s after the intellectual groundwork had been laid by theorists in the previous decade (see Toye 1993). Indeed, aided by being actively promoted by the Reagan administration in the US and the Thatcher government in the UK, neo-liberalism became the new development orthodoxy in the 1980s. Most significantly, the neo-liberal agenda was taken up by the IFIs and informed both their structural adjustment programmes (see chapter 8) and the *World Development Report*, published by the World Bank in 1983.

At the heart of neo-liberalism lies a particular conception of the state, one that performs a minimum of functions but also facilitates entrepreneurial freedom, private ownership, free markets and free trade (Harvey 2005). From a development viewpoint, the purpose of establishing such conditions is that they encourage the free operation of global markets, which in turn is seen as an essential tool for development. Ultimately, from the neo-liberal perspective, even the particular characteristics of societies are relatively unimportant in the development process as what is more relevant is that countries operate under market conditions and allow for individual freedom, both of which entail the role of the state being kept to a minimum (Bauer 1981).

In the 1980s in particular, neo-liberal ideas were actively championed within development by economists like Harry Johnson (1964, 1971), Peter Bauer (1972, 1981), Douglas North, Ian Little (1979, 1982), Bela Balassa (1971, 1981), Deepak Lal (1983) and Michael Beanstock, many of whom were connected to the World Bank and the IMF. Their general position was that countries should rely on the market as their means of achieving economic development, letting it determine economic decisions like prices and wage levels in order that the efficiency of their economy was maximized. For example, it was estimated that LEDCs would only need to achieve 3 per cent growth per annum to alleviate their debt problems, and this income could be achieved by freely trading within an open international economy and selling their primary goods to the North (Little, Scitovsky and Scott 1970).

For neo-liberals, if countries are to pursue export-oriented development strategies, it requires an end to protectionist measures like tariffs, quotas and subsidies that serve to restrict trade. But governments must also refrain from controlling and directing their national economies because their decisions are invariably governed by political rather than economic considerations. Moreover, whenever government tries to sponsor economic progress through heavy state involvement, it tends to undermine development by generating excessive bureaucracy which stifles the economy as well as the initiative and entrepreneurship of other economic actors. Thus, what unites neo-liberal economists is hostility to Keynesianism and all structuralist theories of economic development and planning as these are perceived to be inefficient and lead to poor rates of economic growth. Indeed, the neo-liberal approach to development has been portrayed as a 'counter-revolution', one that sought to displace existing development theories (Toye 1987, 1993).

As well as trade liberalization, other neo-liberal themes like privatization,

deregulation, fiscal austerity, financial liberalization and currency devaluation are seen as a means of achieving economic growth and attracting more
FDI. Neo-liberals argue that such a policy shift would lead to increased
employment and poverty reduction within developing countries (Toye 1987,
1993). Currency devaluation, for example, would mean that the agricultural
products of developing countries were cheaper on export markets, and they
would therefore be likely to sell more produce. Furthermore, trade liberalization ensures that domestic producers are not artificially protected and have
to be internationally competitive in order to survive, which in turn helps to
improve the overall efficiency of the economy (Chang 2003b: 111).

Criticism of neo-liberalism   Critics of the neo-liberal approach to development
reject the above claims on a number of grounds. In particular, the merits of
the free market as a tool for development are disputed, with opponents arguing that it produces comparatively low levels of economic growth, and other
factors are more important in this regard. Indeed, economic development is
invariably the product of a range of factors, which come together in often very
complex ways, and cannot be reduced to a single or primary factor. Moreover,
the consequence of being exposed to global markets is that many domestic
producers in the South struggle to compete with their counterparts in the
North who frequently enjoy greater productive capacity and technological
superiority.

   As for the actual record of neo-liberalism, this will be returned to in more
detail in chapter 8, but for now it should be noted that the FDI emanating
from the North has generally been directed at developing countries considered to have economic potential and/or desirable natural resources, rather
than being universally spread. Moreover, not only has the wealth-generation
promised by neo-liberals been uneven, but there are scant signs that this
wealth has trickled down to the poor within developing countries and, if anything, has actually deepened their internal income inequalities (Haines 2000:
49). Finally, to take a broader perspective, it is claimed that the operation of
free-market global capitalism generates its own social, political and environmental costs, notably diminishing the environmental resources of developing
countries as they seek to compete in the global marketplace, a theme that will
be returned to in chapter 9.

The East Asian 'miracle'

For neo-liberals, the spectacular economic success of the Asian 'tiger economies' of Taiwan, Singapore, South Korea and Hong Kong vindicated their
views (e.g., Balassa 1982). In the 1960s, these former colonial economies
were weak and economically underdeveloped, but since the late 1970s they
have enjoyed remarkable economic growth becoming newly industrializing
countries (NICs). From a neo-liberal perspective, contrary to the views of some

dependency theorists, their rise demonstrated that it is possible to achieve significant development within the existing international capitalist economy. In the region, they joined Japan, which had steadily built its economic success since 1945, and were in turn joined by second-generation NICs in the form of Indonesia, Malaysia and Thailand from the mid-1980s, who similarly began to display rapid economic growth. Together, in the second half of the twentieth century, they enjoyed the fastest economic growth in human history (Chang 2003b). Their experience, also demonstrated, it was argued, the value of pursuing export-driven growth through participation in world markets. Indeed, this was the theme of a World Bank report that was published in 1993, entitled *The East Asian Miracle*, which also stressed that the East Asian experience, particularly in the case of the second-generation NICs, showed the importance of reducing the role of state in the economy and being open to world trade and FDI.

However, the East Asian 'miracle' is deeply contested. In particular, the neo-liberal/World Bank interpretation of the East Asian development experience has attracted criticism. Neo-liberals are accused of employing a selective reading of the economic success enjoyed by East Asian countries, focusing solely upon the aspects that fit their thesis and downplaying the additional factors that contributed to their growth. Critics contend that, with the possible exception of Hong Kong which was always more market-oriented, it was public policy rather than global markets that paved the way for their swift economic growth. For example, the huge state investment in education undertaken by countries like South Korea during the 1960s helped to produce a well-educated and highly skilled workforce. In addition, industrial policy was state-directed with a strong emphasis upon technology and catching up with established industrial powers. Similarly, economic growth was further encouraged by the high savings rates within these countries (Amsden 1992). Questions have also been raised about the nature of East Asian development, with critics noting that the rewards of economic growth have been unevenly distributed confined mainly to people living in urban areas, while poverty and inequality persist and much of the employment that has been generated is casual (Dixon 1999: 219).

The East Asian crisis

The debate between neo-liberals and their critics over East Asia has been further complicated by the financial crisis that hit the region in 1997. The crisis began on 2 July 1997, when the Thai currency, the baht, collapsed under pressure from currency speculators. The origins of the crisis can be traced back to international concerns about the high current account deficits held by a number of countries in the region, including Thailand, as well as the condition of economic governance generally, and with it dawning upon investors how little they knew of the economies in which they had invested (Garnaut

1998: 14). In the case of Thailand, in the months leading up to the collapse there was declining confidence that it would be able to manage its huge current-account deficit, not helped by a reduction in the country's export growth, which was leading investors to begin engaging in capital flight. The financial instability experienced by Thailand soon spread, with investment capital withdrawing from much of the region as the crisis in confidence in the condition of the economies spread, notably in Indonesia, Malaysia, the Philippines and South Korea. For example, in the case of Indonesia, its GDP growth fell from 8.0 per cent in 1996 to –13.2 per cent in 1998. Similarly, Thailand's own downturn went from GDP growth of 5.5 per cent in 1996 to –10.4 per cent in 1998 (Rigg 2002: 27). In order to deal with the severity of the problem, the IMF implemented the costliest refinancing package in history, amounting to US$110 billion (Wade 2004a: xxv).

However, another feature of the crisis was that the countries in the region were affected in varying ways and not all suffered in the way that Thailand did. This particularly applies to Taiwan and Japan. The decade-long economic stagnation experienced by Japan has generated its own debates and further highlights the extent of the diversity that exists in the region and its attendant complexity, while Taiwan emerged from the crisis relatively unscathed (Chang 2003b: 117; Wade 2004a). But this was not just a financial crisis; rather, it was one that has had considerable human and political effects in the region, including contributing to changes of government in Indonesia, South Korea and Thailand (Rigg 2002). Moreover, the economic fallout of the crisis was not confined to the East Asia and by the following year, it had spread throughout the world, including to Russia and Brazil, both of whom experienced financially related difficulties.

The IMF attached strict conditions to the refinancing package it put together for the region and East Asian countries were in no position to object. Critics argue that the World Bank and the IMF, backed and actively encouraged by the US Treasury, exploited this moment to impose a neo-liberal agenda upon the region, which included implementing austere budget cuts, high interest rates and improving financial market regulation, as well as demands that countries in the region should roll back the powers of state and allow greater access to foreign ownership in the financial service and banking sectors (Willis 2005: 60). As a result of some of these measures, many firms were forced into bankruptcy and the region entered a period of deep recession (Stiglitz 2002). Such was the resentment within the region to these conditions that it generated discussion about the need for Asia to develop its own financial institutions in order to reduce reliance upon what were and continue to be perceived as western-dominated IFIs (Rigg 2002: 32). The IFIs justified their approach by arguing the crisis was due to a range of regional deficiencies: the region's governments had proved ineffective at regulating their respective financial sectors; there was a lack of transparency in the management of corporations; some governments had been excessively intervening in financial markets, with accusations of 'crony capitalism'; and East Asian institutions were in general ill-suited to dealing with the mobility of international capital. Of course, this rather undermined their earlier claims that East Asia was a neo-liberal success story that should be emulated by other countries and regions.

There are many writers that dispute the institutional account of the crisis and postulate a range of other contributory factors. Most notably, many argue that international financial and capital markets were liberalized too rapidly and excessively, which merely serves to generate instability (Stiglitz 2002: 89). Related to this point is the claim that foreign investors simply panicked and they have been accused of displaying a herd-like mentality (Rigg 2002: 29). Some point to the failings of the IFIs themselves, ranging from the general – actively promoting liberalization policies, overseeing unstable exchange rates and having inadequate crisis supervisory mechanisms – to the specific, notably that IMF criticism of East Asian countries encouraged capital flight. Other writers point to the close integration of markets and trade that exists in the Pacific Asian region as a factor in the crisis. Thus, while intra-regional trade was key reason for the region's economic growth, this high level of interconnectedness also aided the rapid spread of the financial crisis (Dixon 1999).

As we have seen, the contested nature of the East Asian development experience is reflected in the fact that some writers believe – contrary to the neo-liberal thesis – that economic success was built upon the developmental state in the region, which in turn was undermined by the global financial speculation that neo-liberalism encouraged (see Rapley 2007; Stiglitz 2002; Wade 2000, 2004a). In truth, however, such is the extent of the diversity between the different countries in the region that it makes it difficult to reach a firm conclusion. For instance, the second-generation NICs were more market-oriented and less reliant upon state intervention to facilitate their development than their predecessors. Indeed, it is perhaps unlikely that any development case study will ever adhere to a single development model or explanatory theory. Instead, it is likely that there will be a range of influences and processes at work. This point is borne out by the fact that similar themes and ideas can be found in the different schools of thought. For example, the necessity of investing in people or human capital, especially in the area of education, is a theme that can be detected in the writings of both neo-liberals and developmental state theorists. Likewise, as Joseph Stiglitz (2002) has observed, both neo-liberals and a number of the Asian economies attached considerable importance to establishing macro-stability (e.g., low inflation).[6]

Conclusion

Thus, the East Asian development experience has become an ideational battleground and is a classic example of the contested nature of development. What this case study also highlights is that when evaluating the merits of development approaches, it is essential to take into account the significance of the local, national and regional contexts as well as how they intersect with structural/global factors.

Summary

- The North–South divide has come to replace the notion of three worlds within development studies.
- The major economic theories of development often remain at an abstract level and neglect the significance of what is taking place within specific contexts.
- The major theories of development have struggled to account for the East Asian development experience, largely because it is not a uniform phenomenon.

RECOMMENDED READING

- For an informative work on the Third World, see Nigel Harris's *The End of the Third World* (1986), while both of the reports by the Brandt Commission (1980, 1983) make an effective case for conceptualizing the world in the form of a North–South divide.
- For informative books on the major theoretical approaches to development, see J. Martinussen, *Society, State and Market: A Guide to Competing Theories of Development* (1997) and Richard Peet's (with Elaine Hartwick) *Theories of Development* (1999).
- Raúl Prebisch's *The Economic Development of Latin America and Its Principal Problems* (1950) is a classic work on structuralism.
- For influential works in the dependency tradition, see Samir Amin's *Accumulation on a World Scale: A Critique of the Theory of Underdevelopment* (1974) and Fernando Henrique Cardoso and Enzo Faletto's *Dependency and Development in Latin America* (first published in 1969).
- For the neo-liberal case, see Peter Bauer's *Equality, the Third World and Economic Delusion* (1981) and Deepak Lal's *The Poverty of Development Economics* (1983).
- For contrasting accounts of East Asian development, see the World Bank's report *The East Asian Miracle* (1993) and R. H. McLeod and R. Garnaut (eds), *East Asia in Crisis: From Being a Miracle to Needing One?* (1998).

WEBSITES

- www.ids.ac.uk: Institute for Development Studies (Sussex).
- www.adamsmith.org: Run by the Adam Smith Institute, an organization dedicated to disseminating his work, especially in relation to the market.

CHAPTER 2

Approaching Development

- Culture and development
- Anthropology and development
- Post-developmentalism

Cultural and anthropological approaches to development have contributed significantly to this subject area, and this is despite the fact that, for much of the post-war period, economic theories like dependency theory and neo-liberalism have predominated. More recently, cultural and anthropological accounts have attracted increasing attention as part of a wider questioning and re-evaluation of development.[1] In this regard, as well as examining these disciplinary areas, the chapter will also consider a range of post-development perspectives, outlining their intellectual origins as well as indicating key writers and their respective criticisms of development. It will be suggested that the value of these approaches lies with the fact that they force us to re-evaluate our conceptions of development.

Culture and development

The nature of the relationship between culture and development is complex and contested. In the post-war period, modernization theorists identified culture as a major factor inhibiting the development of 'Third World' societies. It was argued that, once these countries were able to break free from their respective cultural traditions, they would be able to achieve increased economic growth and move to new stages of development. In short, for modernization theorists, developing countries had to be more like western societies. Today, however, it is increasingly recognized that culture is informing development in multiple ways, nationally, regionally, locally and globally, as will now be shown.

Global culture and development

The more intensive and extensive forms of human interconnectedness that constitute contemporary globalization are considered to have significant cultural consequences, and for some commentators these processes are resulting in cultural homogenization that is eroding local cultures and facilitating the emergence of a global culture. If this is occurring, then it would mean that a global culture is not only providing the context in which development takes place but also is likely to be informing the type of development pursued by many countries. However, the nature of this culture is a source of contestation, with opinion ranging from writers who deny its existence to those that delineate it as a form of cultural imperialism.

Americanization   For some writers, global culture is defined by the United States through a combination of its economic, political and military power. It is able to shape global culture at a popular level through its domination of the media and entertainment industries. Most of the leading media entertainment conglomerates, like Time-Warner, CBS and Walt Disney, are American. Moreover, American brands (Levi-Strauss, Burger King, McDonald's, Pepsi, Coca-Cola and Pizza Hut), music, street fashions and other aspects of its popular culture have global appeal. The USA also leads the field in information technology, and enjoys certain advantages over its competitors by being there at the start of the information revolution and shaping information systems and processes (Nye 2002). As the world's most powerful country, the USA is able to exert enormous international cultural and political influence, especially via the UN system (Wade 2007), while its MNCs and TNCs are spreading American business attitudes and practices through their global operations, notably in the form of long working days and weeks. Even economically developed countries like Spain struggle to resist this pressure, with American working practices cited as a contributory factor behind the decline of the Spanish siesta.

However, on a number of grounds, the conception of global culture as Americanization is problematic. To begin with, other countries and non-American organizations are also significant players in the media and entertainment industries, notably Sony, the Australia-based News Corporation, al-Jazeera, and CII (dubbed the 'French CNN'). In addition, there are aspects of American cultural and political life that do not enjoy universal appeal, notably the minimal state and individualism. There also appears to be something of a backlash against American influence in many parts of the world, with some writers detecting a growing anti-Americanism (e.g., Sardar and Wyn Davies 2002). Indeed, Immanuel Wallerstein (2003) detects an erosion of US power that begins with America's relative economic decline from the 1970s onwards. Indeed, America's loss of influence is regarded by some commentators as an indication that we have entered an era of genuine globalization (e.g., Taylor 2001).

McDonaldization   For George Ritzer (1993), global culture takes the form of 'McDonaldization', which he defines as 'the process whereby the principles of the fast-food restaurant are coming to dominate more and more sectors of American society as well as the rest of the world' (ibid.: 19). Ritzer's thesis draws upon the work of the German sociologist Max Weber (1864–1920) who maintained that modern societies are driven by principles of rationality, calculability, predictability and efficiency. For Ritzer, such principles are employed by McDonald's but also by other businesses and modern institutions throughout the world. The cumulative effect of these tendencies is the standardization of contemporary life and, as such, this model is a more complete form of cultural homogenization than Americanization.

However, critics of the McDonaldization thesis point to the continued existence of different modes of organization as well as business cultures and practices (see Smart 1999). Indeed, Japanese management and production methods, like the 'just-in-time' or *kanban* system of work organization, have been adopted by companies in Europe and the USA. Moreover, McDonald's may not be the great cultural homogenizer that it is often presented to be. It has shown itself to be sensitive to local cultural conditions by adapting its outlets and products to reflect the national tastes and preferences in the different countries in which it operates. For example, McDonald's in France serves beer, but this is not the case in the US and the UK. The organization therefore demonstrates a degree of heterogeneity that would seem to challenge the McDonaldization thesis (Watson 1997), although it could be countered that McDonald's is pursuing this more locally oriented approach because it is effective and profitable, and therefore ultimately it is still driven by principles of rationality, calculability, predictability and efficiency.

Furthermore, there is now growing acceptance among writers on cultural globalization that the global and the local are engaged in an ongoing process of interaction (see Hopper 2007). In fact, far from being a top-down process, some writers emphasize the possibility of cultural flows moving from the local to the global, and informing the global in the process (e.g., Cvetkovich and Kellner 1997). For Roland Robertson (1992), the global and local interpenetrate to the extent that 'glocalization' is perhaps a more appropriate concept to describe this condition.

Westernization   The global cultural spread of westernization dates back to European colonialism and the imposition by Europeans of their own institutions and practices upon their colonial subjects, such as their legal and political systems, conceptions of property ownership, languages, the wage-labour system, and the nation-state. For post-development writers (see p. 56), concepts like the state and production have been so pervasively spread by development 'that people everywhere have been caught up in a western perception of reality' (W. Sachs 1992: 5). And arguably forms of western cultural domination persist under contemporary globalization. For example, ICTs and transnational media have helped to spread the English language, which is now spoken by about a quarter of the human race, leading to some linguists forecasting that over 90 per cent of non-English languages could die out during this century (Wurm 1996).

Beyond the issue of language, there is also a sense that global culture is dominated by western values and ideologies. Non-western critics argue that they are being encouraged to consume not only western goods, but also to buy into western lifestyles, especially the emphasis upon individualism. This is reinforced on the part of western governments by their attempt to push their particular conception of human rights upon the non-western world, using their dominant position within international institutions to achieve this end. Indeed, western individualism is said to permeate the UN Declaration of Human Rights and is championed by western governments, irrespective of its appropriateness for non-western societies, some of which are more religious and community based. Similarly, it is claimed that IFIs are promoting essentially a western conception of what constitutes development, namely the establishment of liberal democratic market-based societies.

However, critics of the concept of westernization point to other forces contributing to globalization, like the spread of Islam and Buddhism, but also to the fact that western societies are becoming more culturally diverse, a development that is engendering debates about the nature of western identity and the possible decline of western cultural hegemony (see J. Friedman 1999).

Global culture and capitalism For writers on the Left, capitalism is the real driving force behind globalization, and it is generating a universal consumerist culture. Leslie Sklair (2002) maintains that consumerism contributes to the survival of capitalism because it strives to convince people that such a lifestyle offers them fulfilment. To paraphrase Sklair, the culture ideology of consumerism provides much of the glue that holds the global system together: 'Without consumerism, the rationale for continuous capitalist accumulation dissolves' (2002: 116). Moreover, the function performed by consumerism highlights how the global capitalist system is continuously seeking to sustain itself, something that Sklair believes is evident in the attempt to extend capitalist relations to the Third World.

Inextricably linked to this capitalist-generated global consumerist culture are a set of outlooks and values, like profit maximization, a belief in the market, materialism, individualism and personal fulfilment. In short, this universal culture establishes both the purpose of development and the means of attaining it. However, the problem with this perspective is that it is effectively a denial of human agency, viewing people as essentially passive consumers and neglecting the extent to which we construct our own cultural outlooks and often seek to resist dominant cultures.

Global culture and modernity For many sociologists, the global culture being generated by globalization is that of modernity. More specifically, globalization is spreading the forces associated with modernization, like capitalism, rationalization, democratization, liberalism and industrialization (e.g., Giddens 1990; Spybey 1996). Indeed, for some writers, the forms of cultural homogenization outlined here, like McDonaldization and westernization, are part of this more profound process. As we saw in the previous chapter, for modernization theorists what is driving the project of modernity are the values and benefits associated with it, notably progress, improved living standards, and material well-being.

However, there is growing acceptance of different conceptions of modernity, such as Islamic and Asian modernities, and that the western model is not the only route to modernization and may actually be inappropriate for some cultures and societies (see Eisenstadt 2002, 2003).

Global culture: critical perspectives Beyond debates about the possible form that it may be taking, some critics simply reject the concept of global culture. For them, it is unable to encapsulate the sheer diversity and complexity of contemporary global cultural flows of people, products, sounds, images and information, as well as the reactions they are provoking. Global cultural flows do not only emanate from the USA or the West, rather at any single moment images, symbols, ideas, advertisements, films and other cultural forms will be emanating from multiple sources and travelling in multiple directions across the globe. For example, there are forms of cultural interaction taking place between parts of Africa and Asia as well as within these continents.

Moreover, notions of westernization or Americanization neglect the possibility of cultural counter-flows in the form of cuisines, fashion, religion, music, films (e.g., 'Bollywood') and other influences travelling to the West from other countries. Indeed, for hybridity theorists, contemporary globalization is leading to increased cultural mixing (see Nederveen Pieterse 2004). From their perspective, this means that contemporary globalizing processes introduce even greater heterogeneity into cultural constructs, like 'the West' and 'America', which are already hybrid creations. In turn, this raises the issue of what we mean by westernization and Americanization. Indeed, it is often claimed that we are witnessing a blurring of 'the West' and 'the East' as cultures intermingle and regions become less distinct.

Rather than think of global culture as a common culture, Mike Featherstone maintains that we should conceive of it as a field in which differences and power struggles are played out (1995: 14). This approach allows for the existence of numerous globalizing cultures in the contemporary period, including Islam, environmentalism, westernization and McDonaldization, while acknowledging that some of these cultures may be more influential than others. And it is within this shifting and complex global cultural context that development is taking place.

Culture and development: historical perspectives

Further complicating the nature of the relationship between culture and development is the fact that the influence of the former upon the latter has a long but disputed history.

Protestantism and development   In *The Protestant Ethic and the Spirit of Capitalism* (first published in 1904/05), Max Weber made a direct link between culture and economic development. For Weber, the Protestant faith and the demands it placed upon its adherents – notably encouraging them to work hard and save money to achieve salvation – contributed to the emergence of capitalism in parts of early modern Europe, notably in Germany. Based upon a study of different Protestant traditions – and in particular Calvinism, which took off and spread across Western Europe in the seventeenth century – Weber maintained that this 'ascetic Protestantism' produced a disciplined workforce and ensured capital accumulation which could then be invested and these were constitutive elements of capitalist economic development in the region.

However, the historical accuracy of Weber's thesis has been criticized as, arguably, early capitalism preceded and informed Protestantism, with Calvinism developing in European cities where commerce and early forms of industrial capitalism were already established. Weber has also been criticized for his portrayal of Protestantism and Calvinism in particular, as its founder John Calvin frowned upon attempts to gain an abundance of earthly riches. Hence there must be some doubt that it was a faith that readily facilitated the accumulation of wealth and capital. Nevertheless, Weber's work is important in the sense that he was one of the first writers to recognize that culture can exert a significant influence upon the way that societies and economies develop.

Confucianism and development   More recently, the link between culture and development has been made in relation to the rapid economic growth of the so-called 'Asian tiger' economies, like South Korea, Singapore and Hong Kong. Some commentators attribute this economic success to their Confucian cultures and values, notably the emphasis upon ritual, order, service and respect for authority, and the achievement of these virtues. Value is also placed upon education and hard work, and the community rather than the individual, all of which has served to foster national cohesion and harmony, rather than conflict. Stewart Clegg et al. (1990) maintain that Confucian principles of collectivism and merit must serve as part of the explanation for successful industrial relations and management in East Asia.

A Confucian upbringing involves a central concern for the correct and courteous execution of the individual's duties, and this has arguably contributed to high levels of productivity and manufacturing output. Indeed, the former prime minister of Malaysia, Dr Mahathir Mohamad, contends the West should now learn from the East and adopt Asian values and cultural practices. This is because the 'Asian tigers' have shown that it is possible to enjoy rapid economic growth but also maintain social cohesion.

Culture and underdevelopment   In *Underdevelopment is a State of Mind* (2000), Lawrence E. Harrison argues that culture is the principal explanatory factor accounting for differences in levels of development between the US, Canada and Australia, on the one hand, and Latin America, on the other.[2] While he acknowledges that culture is not an independent entity and is informed by historical and political developments, which also ensures that cultures evolve, he nevertheless considers traditional Hispanic culture to have been a major obstacle to development in Latin America. For example, he observes that both Argentina and Australia are resource rich, remote and underpopulated countries, but while Australia has thrived under a long tradition of democratic capitalism, despite its unpromising origins as a prisoners' colony, Argentina has been plagued by political instability and a failure to maintain durable and progressive institutions, which have greatly hindered its economic growth. Indeed, Harrison is even more specific in the distinctions that he makes, examining a number of different Latin American societies and undertaking comparisons between them. He notes that Costa Rica has been more successful economically than Nicaragua, in spite of possessing fewer natural resources. Again, for Harrison, the answer lies with culture: while the former was settled by pioneer farmers, the latter was settled by conquistadors, a difference that was to have a profound impact upon their future historical development and one that continues to exert an influence today.

Culture and development: a critique

The claim that culture is the primary determinant of development has been challenged. Culture is a notoriously elusive and contested concept, and pinning down what it *is* in order to determine the extent to which it is informing development is a difficult task. Moreover, because cultures are not discrete and bounded entities but overlap and draw from other traditions and influences, they are rarely stable or static. In seeking to make connections with patterns of development, there is therefore a danger of essentializing cultures, reducing them to a core essence and ignoring the diversity that exists within them. This is a charge that can be raised against Harrison's thesis. Moreover, his position can encourage feelings of cultural superiority and even chauvinism on the part of those whose cultures are identified as conducive to development and a sense of inferiority on the part of those whose cultures are considered not to function in this way.

Doubts have also been raised about the contribution of Confucianism to the rapid economic development of the 'Asian tigers'. Given the numerous cultures and religions that exist within these countries, can their economic growth simply be attributed to Confucianism? There is also no single Confucian model but a variety of Confucianisms in the region, reflecting the particular societal conditions in which they are operating. In turn, these Confucianisms are likely to be exerting varying degrees of influence, and this adds to the difficulty of making general pronouncements about the impact of Confucianism upon development. And given that Confucianism has been rooted in the Asia

Pacific region for thousands of years, why has it only recently facilitated the growth of capitalist development? It would strongly suggest that other factors have played a significant role in the economic growth of the region.

The preceding point forms part of a wider critique of the association between culture and development, namely that it underplays other causal factors behind relative underdevelopment, like resource allocation, structural constraints and exploitative relations with other economic powers. In the case of the East Asian societies, their industrial growth may have more to do with the substantial state investment in education and training that was undertaken by their respective governments during the 1960s and 1970s than any cultural explanations (chapter 1). Interestingly, for much of the twentieth century, Confucianism was viewed as a factor holding back East Asian development, with the emphasis upon order, respect for authority, collectivism and hierarchy considered antithetical to creativity and entrepreneurship (Krugman 1994). Likewise, as with Protestantism, there is perhaps some distaste for commercial activity within Confucian philosophy, deemed behaviour unsuitable for educated and courteous gentlemen (Chang 2003b: 119). Finally, as we saw in the discussion of Protestantism above, some of the values identified as 'Confucian' can in fact be found in other cultures, a point that reinforces the notion that cultures are not discrete entities.

Anthropology and development

The often uneasy relationship between anthropology and development is now over a century old (Ferguson 2005; Grillo 2002). This uneasiness stemmed from anthropology's social evolutionist ranking of societies in the late nineteenth century, which was based upon the notion that different human societies have attained different levels of development (Ferguson 2005: 141–2). Postcolonial critics maintain that anthropology was engaged in constructing 'other' cultures, which were invariably conceptualized as 'static', 'traditional' and 'primitive' (Fabian 1983; McGrane 1989), and for many Third World writers this was part of the process of subjugating the colonized. Indeed, the reports of anthropologists were frequently critical of non-western cultures, presenting negative portrayals of many aspects of the lives of indigenous peoples, ranging from their institutions to their cultural practices (Grillo 2002: 55). It was an outlook that betrayed anthropology's own roots in western rationalism and its associated conception of progress (Marcus and Fischer 1986), as well as reflecting the imperial age during which it emerged. In fact, many anthropologists were employed by colonial regimes, and their reports often justified particularly intrusive forms of intervention. For example, the work of anthropologists is said to have informed British colonial policy in Africa (Ferguson 2005: 140). And so tarnished was anthropology's reputation that for many years development experts sought to distance themselves from it.

But today the relationship between anthropology and development has changed in at least two important respects. Firstly, some of the most sub-stantive criticisms of 'development' have emerged from different anthropo-logical voices. Above all, they have been especially critical of conventional mainstream approaches to development, which they consider to be western-dominated and consistently excluding 'the other' in the form of the views and wishes of indigenous peoples. Indeed, the common theme uniting the contributors to the book edited by Mark Hobart entitled *An Anthropological Critique of Development* (1993) is the sense that in relying upon western scientific knowledge and disregarding indigenous perspectives and insights, develop-ment experts are contributing to the growth of ignorance rather than the growth of knowledge.

Secondly, and following on from the previous point, by the last decades of the twentieth century, mainstream approaches to development appeared to be having at best uneven success, and what was even more unacceptable from an anthropological perspective was that such theories had little refer-ence to or engagement with the people that they were supposed to be help-ing. Consequently, from roughly the early 1980s onwards, the relationship between anthropology and development underwent something of a revival. This was aided by the fact that anthropology is able to offer insights into the effects of development policies through empirical research. Indeed, from the perspective of practitioners, anthropology can contribute to development in ways that other disciplines struggle to replicate, most notably by providing situated or grounded analyses of local experiences. Furthermore, the shift to participatory strategies within development (e.g., Nelson and Wright 1995), and putting local people first (e.g., Chambers 1983, 1997), means that anthro-pology is well placed to exert considerable influence upon the future course of this subject area.

There are a number of potential benefits that can accrue from incorporating local knowledge and insights into development. Above all, it arguably leads to the formulation of development strategies and policies more suited to local conditions and the needs and interests of the communities involved. Of course, for this to happen, it requires local knowledge to be properly integrated into development processes, and in this regard development institutions and prac-titioners are frequently charged with simply employing the rhetoric of partici-pation (e.g., Nyamwaya 1997). Secondly, enabling indigenous peoples to have an active input into development decision-making processes enhances local autonomy and, because value is being attached to indigenous know-how, this can in turn contribute to their self-esteem and sense of self-respect (Desai and Potter 2002: 2; see also chapter 7 of this book). Thirdly, the focus of anthropol-ogy upon the local can have environmental benefits because the knowledge and experiences of indigenous peoples of their particular environments – and after all they are more likely to be in tune with their surroundings than development institutions operating on a global level – can be brought into the development process (Croll and Parkin 1992).

However, objections have been raised against anthropology playing a prominent role within development, and much of them centre upon the danger of privileging and even romanticizing 'the local' (Richards 1993), in turn neglecting the crucial role played by international institutions in the development process, although some anthropologists are now addressing this area (see Fox 2005; Harper 2005). For instance, critics note that local conditions can sometimes serve to inhibit or preclude development. This may include existing social structures, the nature of local traditions, customs and cultural practices, and forms of indigenous political authority, all of which can potentially act as a fetter upon development. Moreover, in some instances local knowledge and insights may be partial or simply mistaken (Agrawal 1995). In addition, there is the problem of determining what local opinion *is* and who speaks for 'the local', which entails being aware that it is not dominated by particular interests, and ensuring that minorities and women, for example, are not marginalized from the development process (Grillo 2002: 57). Lastly, given the controversy that has often surrounded development 'experts', some anthropologists are wary of assuming that role themselves (Gardner and Lewis 2005; Gatter 1993).

Anthropology, development and complexity

The relationship between anthropology and development is more complicated than has thus far been suggested. This is because a distinction is often made between the 'anthropology of development' and 'development anthropology'. The latter is considered to be anthropology in practice and consequently is associated with the work of practitioners and experts, while the former is geared towards investigating development as a process that is informed by numerous influences, cultural, political, economic, and the like, and has generated substantive criticisms of development (see Edelman and Haugerud 2005; Grillo and Stirrat 1997). However, this division is increasingly contested as more and more anthropologists draw upon the insights offered by both traditions (e.g., Crewe and Harrison 1998), and anthropology becomes more interdisciplinary, at least within countries outside the United States (Edelman and Haugerud 2005: 40–2).

Globalization further complicates the relationship between anthropology and development. Not only are the processes that constitute globalization likely to be ensuring that cultures are more unstable, but it is also appropriate to enquire whether local cultures actually exist in any meaningful sense under such conditions. Given the intensity and extensity of contemporary cultural and other flows, are there any places in the world that have not yet to some extent been permeated by global influences? If this is the case, then it raises questions about the nature of local knowledge and the issue of distinctiveness. In short, what exactly is it that anthropologists are seeking to incorporate into the development process? Ulf Hannerz (1990, 2003) believes that local cultures are increasingly interconnected so that they form a global discourse of locality. Of course, for anthropologists, such developments challenge their traditional 'fieldwork approach', and it has led them to pay greater attention to how cultures 'travel' (Clifford 1992) and the extent to which cultures and places are constituted by a wider set of social and cultural phenomena (Eriksen 2003).

But we can go too far with this theme. While most places or locations will to some degree be informed by global processes, we should keep in mind that in general people's everyday experiences and behaviour are conditioned by their immediate environment and personal life histories. At the same time, the nature of global flows entails that they must interact with different countries and regions, and their form will frequently be altered within these contexts. In this vein, Jonathan Xavier Inda and Renato Rosaldo (2002) maintain that culture is not simply 'free-floating'. By this they mean that 'cultural flows do not just flow etherally across the globe but are always reinscribed (however partially or fleetingly) in specific cultural environments' (ibid.: 11). This point reinforces a theme of this work, namely the importance of examining the contexts in which global cultural flows are experienced if we are to gain an insight into the ways in which they are being reinscribed. In short, it is only by focusing upon how cultural flows intersect with particular societies and regions, as well as with specific groups and cultures within these locations, that it becomes possible to determine what is actually taking place. In this regard, contemporary anthropologists are increasingly recognizing the necessity of investigating the impact of global and other external influences upon cultures and places (Arce and Long 2000; Eriksen 2003; Gupta and Ferguson 1997; Hannerz 2003).

The dissatisfaction felt by many anthropologists towards development, which has included concerns over how anthropology has been incorporated into this enterprise, has led many of them to contribute to the case for moving beyond development, as will now be shown.

Post-developmentalism

This chapter will end by surveying a range of critical and often overlapping positions on development, including post-structuralist, postcolonial and postmodern perspectives, as well as post-development (sometimes termed 'anti-development' and 'beyond development') writers, who maintain that we should simply give up on the enterprise. As will become clear, a common theme of these critiques is the claim that development is rooted in European intellectual traditions and plays a role in extending western power, serving to dominate, dismiss and transform the local in the process. Indeed, underpinning what will be termed here for the sake of analytical convenience 'post-developmentalism' is an ongoing concern with who, or what, has the power to determine what development is and means (see Crush 1995).

Development is Eurocentric

For many development scholars, and not just those operating within the post-development tradition, development has always been dominated by economics, a discipline that itself has been profoundly shaped by 'the West' and western writers. In *On Ethics and Economics* (1987), Amartya Sen argues that economists portray their discipline as an objective science of universal relevance, when in reality it is rooted in European rationalist thought and hence far from value free. This leads economists to dismiss alternative perspectives and disciplinary approaches, and even to deny their own intellectual heritage (ibid.: 69). For example, there is scant acknowledgement within economics of the work of Ibn' Khaldun (1332–1406), an important Muslim scholar who had already formulated in the fourteenth century many of the ideas that Adam Smith was to postulate in the eighteenth century (Mehmet 1995). There is also an implicit western presumption of superiority at work within development economics in the sense that the non-western world is portrayed as trying to 'catch up', something that of course it can achieve only by following the guidelines laid down by development economics. In recent decades, adhering to western economic orthodoxy has entailed developing countries reducing the role of their respective states and opening up their economies to global markets. In sum, it is claimed that development economics has sought to transplant western norms and solutions into non-western environments, consistently ignoring their respective historical and cultural conditions in the process. Indeed, even its model of an economic actor – that of the rational, competitive, acquisitive individual – will be inapplicable to many non-western societies (ibid.: 136–7).

For some writers, development and development economics have simply been about perpetuating capitalism. In short, there is a view that conventional economic theories have not only distorted the development of non-western societies, but have mainly been about incorporating these societies into the international capitalist economy. In this regard, Ozay Mehmet in *Westernizing the Third World* (1995) argues that mainstream economic theories of development, like modernization theory and neo-liberalism, have functioned as tools of western capitalism, even when this has been unintended by the theorists themselves. For example, their emphasis upon open markets has merely enabled the West to export its goods and products to the developing world, safe in the knowledge that they face little reciprocal competition.

Post-structuralism, postcolonialism, postmodernism and development

Post-structuralists essentially view development as a discourse constituted by a specific set of ideas, concepts, practices and rhetoric or language, and in particular regard it as a modernist regime of knowledge and power. An example of the power–knowledge games at work within development can be seen in the construction of the Third World, which comes to form the lower tier in the hierarchical relationship with the First World (see chapter 1). As the Colombian anthropologist Arturo Escobar has noted in his book *Encountering Development: The Making and Unmaking of the Third World* (1995a), the creation of forms of knowledge about the Third World form an integral part of the process of legitimizing intervention in this world. Indeed, Escobar goes further, arguing that the development agenda identifies abnormalities in the form of poverty, landlessness and backwardness, and associates them with the Third World as a pretext for such intervention, a claim that echoes Edward Said's (1995) view of the way in which colonizing discourses like Orientalism operate. This process also entails the homogenization of the Third World or the South, whereby the diversity that exists within it is simply ignored.

Moreover, from a post-structuralist perspective, discourse analysis can be applied to dependency theory. Thus, while advocates of dependency theory present it as both a radical critique of and an alternative to mainstream development economics, for post-structuralists it remains firmly within this tradition. This is because dependency theory does not question the legitimacy or appropriateness of development, merely the means of attaining it. It has led Arturo Escobar, in an essay entitled 'Imagining a Post-Development Era', to argue that dependency theorists still function 'within the same discursive space of development' as those that they criticize, and they are therefore implicated with one another (1995b: 215). Indeed, dependency theory ensures that development has its own in-built explanatory mechanisms for its shortcomings.

Postcolonial writers are especially anxious to liberate countries of the South from such patterns of thinking, and from western knowledge in general, viewing them, along with the mentalities and socio-economic structures that Europeans left behind, as legacies of colonialism that serves to inhibit their independence and deny the value of their own local knowledge and experiences (Sardar, Nandy, and Davies 1993; Spivak 1987). Postcolonial analyses therefore seek to investigate these divergent experiences, especially with regard to how the former colonial subjects negotiate these legacies (see Radcliffe 2005). Crucially, they also seek to ensure that these experiences are articulated and represented within development.

Postmodernists similarly detect a tendency within development to deny heterogeneity. But in addition, they challenge the European Enlightenment conception of progress that underpins development. In particular, the emphasis upon linearity and teleology within the modernist project, which sees history heading in one direction, namely towards greater progress and development, is rejected by postmodernists who instead identify contingency, complexity and unevenness. Lastly, the emphasis upon pluralism within postmodernism is one reason why it is hard to pin down the postmodern approach to development, although the postmodern epoch is often associated with post-industrial modes of production and consumption (Harvey 1989; Potter et al. 2004: 120).

Thus, a common theme of these perspectives is a criticism of development for being metropolitan-centred and marginalizing local perspectives and initiatives, with postcolonial and postmodern approaches especially insisting upon space for alternative voices and plurality rather than the standard modernist route to development. From their perspective, there are multiple conceptions of, and paths to, development. Therefore, we should move beyond notions of 'traditional' and 'modern' that lie at the heart of mainstream development thinking. In this regard, the Third World state, and more specifically many of its governments, is criticized for facilitating the spread of a modernist paradigm.

Beyond development

Arising from this dissatisfaction with development, a number of post-development perspectives have emerged, notably anti-development and beyond-development approaches. In particular, the notion that development theory had reached an 'impasse' began to be articulated during the 1980s (see Booth 1985; Schuurman 1993). Indeed, some within the developing world began questioning development per se, increasingly viewing it as the 'new religion' that the West was exporting (Nederveen Pieterse 2000b: 175). At the same time, numerous post-development thinkers questioned whether development had ever been a serious project. From their perspective, it was an enterprise that was first and foremost geared to maintaining harmonious relationships in post-war international affairs as this would enable the perpetuation of northern dominance. Some emphasized how development had been destructive of local traditions and indigenous cultures and how some development projects have simply been inappropriate and misconceived. Others stressed how the imposition of development affected the self-esteem of the peoples of the South. Gustavo Esteva was even more scathing in his assessment, declaring simply that 'development stinks' (1987: 135). All of this led to growing calls for an 'end to development' (e.g., Rahnema with Bawtree 1997), a view that Wolfgang Sachs expresses in the following way: 'The idea of development stands like a ruin in the intellectual landscape. Delusion and disappointment, failures and crimes have been the steady companions of development and they tell a common story: it did not work . . . It is time to dismantle this mental structure' (1992: 1).

As we will see in chapter 7, in response to the perceived shortcomings of development, greater onus is being placed upon grassroots participation, and harnessing local knowledge and expertise, including that of social movements, like ecological movements, peasants, women, ethnic minorities, indigenous peoples and squatter movements. Many post-development writers have also taken up this theme, emphasizing the right of people in the South to lead their own lives in their own local communities, free from the imposition of global ideologies like development (Esteva and Prakash 1998; Rist 2002).

Escobar (1995a, 1995b), in particular, has set great store by the emancipatory potential of social movements, regarding them as vehicles for promoting a new kind of democratic and participatory politics, as well as greater egalitarianism. In short, post-development advocates of such movements stress their ethical dimension and consider them to offer an alternative to development, one that is less oriented towards materialism. However, post-development has attracted considerable criticism.

Post-development: critical perspectives

Inaccurate representations of development   In a variety of ways, post-development writers have been accused of overstating their case and misrepresenting many features of development (Drinkwater 1992). Some have been criticized for presenting a one-dimensional account of development, science and technology, one which overlooks the practical benefits they have brought to many countries, like improvements in water provision, better sanitation and easier access to education (Corbridge 1995, 1998a). More broadly, post-development accounts of non-western countries are often oversimplified, playing down the extent of the inequalities and tensions that existed within those societies before the arrival of 'development', but also ignoring the extent of the diversity that exists in the contemporary South (Corbridge 1998a; Simon 1998). Furthermore, even under the global conditions established by the discourse of development, to use post-development terminology, many non-western countries like India, China and the 'Asian tiger' economies have been able to develop at a remarkable rate in the post-war period which has contributed to poverty reduction and in turn helped to increase life expectancy in the region.

Post-development writers are also accused of portraying the relationship between the West and the Third World as simply one of domination and subordination, and thereby underplaying the complex nature of this interaction, and the extent of resistance on the part of developing countries to the imposition of alien ideas. Such an outlook overlooks the genuine attempts on the part of some governments of the North to improve the position of the poor in the South. Indeed, a case could be made that some post-development writers are stereotyping in the way that western policy-makers have been accused of in relation to the Third World (Willis 2005: 207). In this regard, many anthropologists pursue an actor-oriented approach to analysing development, examining those intersections or points at which different bodies of knowledge meet, including those of experts, development practitioners, institutions, national governments, NGOs, indigenous movements and locals, looking at how the actors involved negotiate their way through these varied and often competing conceptions of development (see Apthorpe 1985, 1986; Apthorpe and Gasper 1996; Arce and Long 2000; Hobart 1993; Long and Long 1992). Anthropologists, therefore, seek to look beyond the imposition of western epistemologies and practices upon indigenous peoples that is the theme of many discourse accounts (Arce and Long 2000: 24).

To return to a claim made in the Introduction, development is not a unitary phenomenon but emerges from the interaction of numerous processes and agencies within a range of different contexts, and for this reason it is more appropriate to conceptualize it in the plural, as developments. In this regard, R. D. Grillo maintains that the post-development conception of development as an essentially monolithic regime underpins what he terms the 'myth of development' (1997: 20). This also means, he argues, that we should recognize that the notion of a single discourse of development 'is far too limiting' and begin instead to conceptualize discourses of development (ibid.: 21). In this vein, post-development has been accused of conceptualizing development as simply emerging from modernity, ignoring the fact that the latter concept is contested and arguably exists in the plural (Nederveen Pieterse 2001).

In sum, the post-development notion of a discourse of development dominated by the West risks neglecting the sheer diversity of development agencies, experiences and practices (Corbridge 1995; Rigg 1997). As James Sidaway has noted, development entails and embraces so many things that inevitably there is an element of reductionism which takes place whenever post-development writers seek to pin it down in order to critique it (2002: 18). Such an approach also risks underplaying the extent to which development, or at least the dominant approaches to it, can and do change, a theme that was addressed in the Introduction and will be returned to throughout the book (Brown 1996).[3] Finally, and perhaps the most telling riposte to the claim that development is a western project, is that a number of key themes and theories actually emerged from the South, most notably structuralism and dependency theory (Edelman 1999; Rapley 2007).

Excessive intellectualism   Some post-development writers have been accused of over-intellectualizing development by placing too much emphasis upon discourse and power–knowledge relations. In reality, critics argue, much development involves practical activity that takes place 'on the ground' and hence is shaped by specific material conditions and relations. For this reason, many of the problems associated with development cannot simply be traced to the dominant intellectual traditions that have emanated from Europe. Indeed, post-development writers often present an undifferentiated critique of science, rationality and the Enlightenment, which their defenders maintain are inherently reflexive and therefore do not readily lend themselves to domination. Moreover, in response to Escobar, critics note that poverty is not something that is produced by a development discourse but is an everyday material reality for many people living in the developing world and for this reason development remains the deeply held goal of many located there.[4] In addition, critics note that, despite claiming to articulate the concerns of many in the South, especially the marginalized, the work of a number of post-development writers is firmly located within contemporary academic debates often engaging with key (and often difficult) thinkers, like the French intellectual Michel Foucault, as well as Edward Said. Arguably, post-developmentalists are similarly engaged in their own form of power–knowledge relations.

Critique rather than solutions   One of the frequently heard criticisms of post-modernist and post-structuralist writers is that they are primarily oriented towards presenting a critique of existing practices, content simply to reveal the power games that are operating within this discourse, and have little to offer in the form of coherent and viable alternatives (Grillo and Stirrat 1997; Nederveen Pieterse 2000a). For example, some critics of postmodernism have dismissed it as little more than a celebration of consumerist lifestyles in our late capitalist era (Jameson 1984), while the social movements that Escobar promotes as an alternative to development are effectively being called upon to reshape societies, and there must be some doubt as to whether they will be capable of performing this role, especially as many will be tempted to pursue their particular agendas. As for the emphasis upon the local, and 'remaking the soil of cultures' (Esteva and Prakash 1998), globalization arguably makes it difficult to live as 'a local' because, as Roland Robertson (1992) has suggested, we are now living with constant reference to the global. For example, it is difficult not to make comparisons with lifestyles and living standards of societies in other parts of the world, and this will undoubtedly inform how we act at the local level. Furthermore, the emphasis upon grassroots participation does not deal with the structural dimensions of development, namely the difficulty that many developing countries face in operating within an international economy when the terms of trade are weighted against them.

Finally, and in many ways this is the ultimate criticism of post-development, doubts have been raised about the extent to which it offers something genuinely new or whether it simply remains within the tradition of earlier neo-Marxist and feminist critiques (Corbridge 1998a; Kiely 1999; Sidaway 2002). Indeed, perhaps post-development remains within mainstream development, with for example its emphasis upon grassroots participation merely mirroring the current popularity of participatory approaches within development. Is it the case therefore that post-development has reached its own impasse? Conversely, this criticism of post-development needs to be weighed against the fact hat development's continuing evolution and expansion makes it difficult to formulate ideas and coherent strategies outside of its sphere of interest. For its critics, therefore, development operates to deny the possibility of alternatives.

Conclusion

This chapter has highlighted how development is continuing to evolve, with cultural and anthropological approaches becoming more prominent as part of a broader challenge to the subject. This is despite the fact that the relationship between culture and development is difficult to pin down, reflected in the problematization of global culture and associated notions of cultural homogenization and cultural imperialism. In this regard, 'the West' and 'America' are not just hybrid constructions but also umbrella concepts encompassing and often subsuming considerable diversity within them. Ultimately, however, the ways in which culture intersects with development will be dependent upon particular contexts. In other words, the type of development that is being pursued within societies will be informed by their own local, national and regional cultures, and this will in turn shape the nature of the interaction with global cultural influences. All of this, of course, makes the task of the anthropologist extremely difficult. Nevertheless, anthropology's general insistence that there are multiple development processes in operation, played out within different contexts and involving a range of actors, agencies and external influences, is a productive approach to the study of development. It is, in short, an approach that recognizes the complexity of development.

Summary

- The ways in which culture informs development are complex and contested.
- Anthropology has gained academic credence in the recent period because, in valuing indigenous knowledge and perspectives, it is in accord with the contemporary emphasis upon participation within development.
- A common theme of post-development approaches is to emphasize the constructed nature of development, and how it is inextricably bound up with knowledge and power.

RECOMMENDED READING

- For an introduction to the key debates surrounding culture and development, see Susanne Schech and Jane Haggis, *Culture and Development: A Critical Introduction* (2000).
- For an examination of the nature of the relationship between anthropology and development, see R. D. Grillo and R. L. Stirrat (eds), *Discourses of Development: Anthropological Perspectives* (1997) and Jean-Pierre Olivier de Sardan, *Anthropology and Development* (2005).
- Important post-development texts are Arturo Escobar's *Encountering Development: The Making and Unmaking of the Third World* (1995a) and Wolfgang Sachs (ed.), *The Development Dictionary: A Guide to Knowledge as Power* (1992).
- For a critique of the post-development school of thought, see Trevor Parfitt's *The End of Development* (2002).

CHAPTER 3

Health, Education and Population

- Population and development
- Health and development
- Education and development

This chapter considers quality of life issues in relation to development focusing upon health, education and demography. As will be shown, for many commentators these matters go to the heart of development and they are interdependent. Indeed, a feature of this interdependency is that poverty and a lack of economic development are frequently the underlying factors behind rapid population growth, the spread of disease, and inchoate healthcare and education systems. In the case of population growth, for example, the poor tend to have large families because parents fear that they may well lose some of their children through poverty, but in turn this contributes to sizeable populations that can dissipate a society's resources and thereby contribute to poverty.

There is therefore a need for joined-up thinking and strategies in dealing with these challenges. In this regard, existing international policy approaches will be outlined, including the Millennium Development health and education goals. However, evaluating the effectiveness of these approaches is often made more difficult by the lack of available data. This deficit stems from the under-resourced information-gathering systems that exist in some developing countries, particularly those experiencing conflicts. Patterns of human migration, such as emigration and the internal movement of people from rural to urban areas, can also add to the difficulty of garnering accurate data from some countries, although international surveys, such as the World Fertility Survey and demographic and health surveys, are an additional source of information.

Population and development

Global patterns and trends

At the start of the new millennium, the world's population was nearing 6.1 billion people and growing at an unprecedented rate of approximately 83 million people per year. Despite these figures, fertility rates have actually declined worldwide in recent decades. According to the UN Population Division, total fertility fell from an average of 4.7 children per woman in 1970–5 to 2.6 children per woman in 2005–10 (UNPD 2009a). However, this global figure disguises considerable regional variations, with the decline less marked among the LDCs – notably in sub-Saharan Africa – where fertility remains high: it declined from 6.3 children per woman in 1970–5 to 4.4 in 2005–10 (ibid.).

Moreover, global population growth has been aided by falling mortality rates, especially in the developing world. Based on its research into world mortality, the UNPD contends that life expectancy at birth for the world population rose from 47 years in 1950–5 to 68 years in 2005–10 (UNPD 2009b). Developing countries in particular have benefited from medical and health-care advances, notably in the form of a reduction in infant and child mortality. For example, the wider use of antibiotics has helped to control the spread of diseases. Public health in many developing societies has also been aided by improvements to sanitation and water supply. But there are also wide disparities in levels of mortality across countries and regions due, among other factors, to differential access to safe drinking water, food, sanitation, medical care and other basic human needs (ibid.).

According to the UN Population Division, world population growth is projected to rise to 9.1.billion by 2050 – with India overtaking China as the world's most populous nation by this point – and to 11 billion by 2200 (UNPD 2011). Even allowing for the extraordinary number of people dying from AIDS, the population of LEDCs is projected to increase from 5.6 billion in 2009 to 8.1 billion in 2050. In contrast, the population of MEDCs is projected to grow only from 1.2 billion to 1.3 billion in this timescale (Bremner et al. 2009: 2).

Given that future population growth will occur mainly in the developing world – with the fastest growth in the poorest countries and regions – this will have numerous implications for development, including the potential to undermine existing development projects and strategies. In particular, rapid population growth can place strains upon the educational and healthcare systems of developing countries. Sustaining large populations can also lead to the diminution of a country's natural resources, including the overuse of land for agricultural production, which can lead to soil erosion.

Thus, while in the past some writers have considered a burgeoning population to be evidence of a country's economic growth, increasingly it is regarded as a challenge to development. Consequently, there are regular calls for donors to give more funds to reproductive health programmes for developing countries, and in particular to honour the pledges that they have made at events like the 1994 International Conference on Population and Development (ICPD) in Cairo. According to the United Nations Population Fund (UNFPA), providing contraception for the 200 million women who want it would avert some 52 million pregnancies each year (UNFPA 2011).

Another feature of an escalating population is rapid urbanization. In 2008, more than half of humans – 3.3 billion people – were living in urban areas for the first time in history. This figure will rise to almost 5 billion by 2030, with this urban increase located mainly in the developing world, especially in Africa and Asia (UNFPA 2007). Indeed, the urban population in Africa and Asia is expected to double between 2000 and 2030. Moreover, the number of globally connected megacities – defined as having 10 million or more residents – is growing and they are in many ways operating as the hubs or nodal points of globalization.

However, UNFPA is concerned about how this substantial growth in the world's urban population can be managed, particularly as many of these new urbanites will be poor (ibid.: 1). Substantial flows of people moving to towns and cities in search of work and housing can generate considerable social and economic problems within these urban areas (see Linden 1996). For environmentalists, whenever unbridled population growth takes place in cities with poor urban management, inevitably natural resources are depleted.

Of course, different countries and regions face different demographic challenges. In the case of Europe, an ageing population – that stems from declining birth rates and Europeans living longer – is placing strains upon welfare provision in some countries. The percentage of Europeans over 65 years of age is expected to rise from 15 per cent in 2000 to almost 30 per cent in 2050 (UNDESA 2002: 12). Brazil and China are also starting to develop ageing populations as a result of recent declines in fertility.[1]

Many states in sub-Saharan Africa are confronted with the daily difficulty of sustaining their burgeoning populations. Likewise, the population of Afghanistan, Chad and East Timor will increase threefold by 2050, and it is anticipated that these countries will struggle to meet the basic needs of their respective citizens (UNPD 2011). Within developing societies, large families are often a response to poverty, with the family unit performing a social welfare role for members in the absence of adequate welfare systems. However, in some developing countries, high fertility rates are linked to religion. For example, the Catholic Church's opposition to abortion and the use of contraception has had considerable influence upon personal behaviour in many parts of the developing world. Islamist movements are similarly opposed to the use of contraceptives by women.

The Middle East and North Africa is a developing region that is facing considerable population pressures. A combination of slowly declining fertility rates and rapidly declining death rates led to the region's population size quadrupling in the last half of the twentieth century (Roudi-Fahimi and Kent 2007). Despite recent fertility declines – the population growth rate is slowing in the region from 2.5 to 2.0 per cent per annum – the region's population was approximately 430 million in 2007 and it is projected to surpass 700 million by 2050 (UNPD 2011). Indeed, the Middle East and North Africa is suffering from a demographic bulge that some commentators believe is storing up problems for regimes in the region, especially because there are insufficient jobs for their burgeoning populations. In particular, the region is confronted with a rapidly growing youth population, with one in every three people being between the ages of 10 and 24 while two-thirds of the population in some Gulf States is under the age of 30.

According to a 2003 World Bank Report, the countries of the Middle East and North Africa must create more than 100 million new jobs over the next 20 years or face growing social unrest (BBC 2003a). Avoiding such problems is one important reason why many of these regimes encourage their citizens to seek work abroad. However, in some Persian Gulf countries, foreign workers constitute a large proportion of the domestic labour force, which merely adds to the difficulty of their own citizens finding employment (Roudi-Fahimi and Kent 2007).

States have responded to accelerating population growth in a variety of ways. In the mid-1970s, Indira Gandhi's government introduced a compulsory sterilization programme for Indian government workers with more than two children. More orthodox and effective ways of ensuring population reduction involve the implementation of family planning programmes, including ready access to contraception, reinforced by educational and media campaigns about birth control (Bongaarts 1997; Robey, Rutstein and Morris 1993). It is this approach that most governments now pursue. Indeed, with the notable exception of China (see below), governments now avoid policies aimed at population control as they are increasingly regarded as an unacceptable encroachment on human affairs (Ashford 2001: 40).

China's one-child programme

In 2010, China's population was over just 1.3 billion people, making it the world's most populous country. Moreover, China's population is expected to increase by about roughly 10 million a year, reaching around 1.6 billion in 2050. The Chinese authorities consider this level of population growth is unsustainable in a country that is prone to floods and famine and has relatively low energy, food and water resources. As a result, China introduced a one-child policy in 1979, a measure that was incorporated into the country's 1982 constitution. It stipulates that each couple living in the cities should only have one child, unless one or both of the couple are from an ethnic minority or they are both only children. In contrast, in most rural areas, a couple may have a second child after a break of several years.

It is in the countryside that the efforts at flouting this law have been most successful and where large families can still be found. The government has found it easier to enforce this policy in the cities, and arguably its best means of enforcing it in countryside has been the rise in the price of school fees which acts as a strong deterrent to couples having more children (Rosenthal 2000). As well as penalties and sanctions, the party-state has offered a system of rewards such as a 5–10 per cent salary bonus for those parents limiting their families to one child.

The Chinese government claims that its one-child policy has helped to keep the country's population growth in check, reducing the number of births by around 400 million. A team of independent researchers confirmed in 2007 that China had indeed curtailed its population growth but questioned the extent to which this was due to this specific policy. They attach greater weight to a decline in the fertility rate during the 1970s, resulting from China's modernization and associated changing social and cultural attitudes towards larger families and early marriages, especially in urban areas. Family planning also played an important role in fertility reduction in the 1970s before the advent of the one-child policy, although the researchers acknowledge that the one-child policy has helped to perpetuate this trend, both with regard to attitudes and in turn to fertility rates (Bristow 2007).

However, China's strict family planning policy has been heavily criticized. Human rights groups view it as an infringement upon individual freedom, and point to cases of the authorities putting pressure on women to have abortions in order to attain targets. There is also evidence that state policy has exacerbated the abuse and neglect of girls, with more of them being abandoned or concealed, both of which invariably entails them being deprived of proper childcare and schooling (Hull 1990; Human Rights Watch/Asia 1996). Feminists consider China's one-child population policy to be denying the rights of women to control their own bodies, and there are claims that it has led to forced sterilizations. It is also unpopular amongst many Chinese people because it goes against the value that is traditionally attached to the family and family life in China. Indeed, there is evidence of some couples taking fertility drugs in order to achieve a multiple pregnancy (see Reynolds 2007).

The one-child policy has heightened the prestige attached to the birth of a baby son in China, which stems largely from boys being better able to support their parents in later life whereas girls are considered to become part of another family when they marry. As a result, there has been a rise in the number of female foetuses being aborted – with ultrasound scans increasing this practice – as well as young girls being abandoned and even killed. Such a policy distorts the male/female ratio in China, with government figures indicating that 119 boys are born for every 100 girls, a figure that is 130/100 respectively in some provinces (BBC 2010; see also Box 3.1 for evidence of a gender imbalance in other developing societies). Indeed, men are now believed to outnumber women by more than 60 million and it is predicted that there will be as many as 40 million single men in the country by 2020, with many of them unable to find wives (Lim 2004). It is contributing to the growth in the trafficking of girls and women, with their commercial value rising because of their limited numbers.

The one-child policy is also generating other social and economic problems for China. In particular, with people living 30–40 years longer than they did a century ago, the policy is contributing to an ageing population. This will make it more difficult for China to sustain its rapid economic growth in the future,

Box 3.1 The gender imbalance in some developing societies

In some developing societies, the ratio of men to women is distorted in favour of the former because of the abortion of female foetuses, female infanticide and through the fatal neglect of female children. These practices stem from a preference for sons, due to factors like cultural tradition and poverty. For example, in poor societies lacking welfare systems, boys are regarded as more able to provide assistance to couples in their old age as they generally have better employment prospects. Furthermore, in some Asian societies, daughters tend to move away from the family home at marriage, while sons (with their new spouses) often remain with their parents and continue to provide financial support. Moreover, in parts of India, parents have to pay a substantial dowry for their daughters to the prospective husband's family.

In an influential article entitled 'More than 100 Million Women are Missing' (2008), Amartya Sen identifies numerous societies that have significant numbers of females missing from their populations, notably in South Asia, but also in China. In 1990, there was an estimated 50 million women 'missing' in China while, in India today, the male to female ratio is 1,070/1,000, respectively. For Sen, we need to undertake contextual analyses if we are to understand this phenomenon and how the complex interplay of economic, social, and cultural factors influence regional differences. Alleviating this problem will require tackling differential female education, and employment and economic (including property) rights. More broadly, reducing the levels of female infanticide necessitates enhancing women's status in developing societies.

due to a diminishing labour force (see England 2005). By the middle of this century, the size of China's labour force will have decreased dramatically with a third of Chinese over 60, and there will be only 1.6 working age adults per pensioner, compared with seven before 1979 (Righter 2009). Fewer workers means fewer taxpayers and this is likely to lead to a decrease in social welfare provision, including a potential reduction in care for the elderly.

Influenced by some of the ideas emerging from the 1994 ICPD held in Cairo, from 1995, the Chinese government placed greater emphasis upon improving the quality of family planning services and providing more comprehensive care (Ashford 2001: 37). Similarly, in an effort to deal with some of the problems generated by the one-child policy, some rules have been relaxed. For example, as a way of curbing the abortion of female foetuses and infanticide of baby girls, in rural areas couples may have a second child if their first is a girl (Righter 2009).

At this juncture, the future of China's one-child policy remains unclear. While the state insists that it remains necessary in order to control population growth, it continues to attract considerable opposition. In May 2007, in Guangxi province, in southern China, thousands of villagers attacked family planning officials for imposing heavy fines on families who had too many children (Watts 2007). Many wealthier couples also appear willing to flout the law and have more than one child, knowing that they can afford to pay the fines. This practice is likely to continue as a result of the wealth generated by China's burgeoning economy, although a 2008 survey undertaken by the Pew Research Center found that roughly three in four (76 per cent) of the Chinese population supported the one-child policy (Pew Research Center 2008). In February 2010, the deputy director of China's National Population and Family Planning Commission announced that the one-child policy would remain unaltered during the twelfth five-year plan, which was scheduled to run until 2015 (Phani Kumar 2010). However, in March 2011, according to an online report in the state-run *People's Daily*, the Chinese authorities were considering lifting family-planning restrictions to allow couples to have a second child (Phani Kumar 2011).

Perspectives on population growth and development

The nature of the relationship between population growth and development has generated much controversy and numerous competing views. For the sake of explication, they will be categorized into the following broad perspectives.

Neo-Malthusian perspectives   Modern-day followers of Thomas Malthus (1766– 1834), the eighteenth-century essayist (see his *An Essay on the Principle of Population*, first published in 1798), believe that contemporary population growth is placing unsustainable demands upon the planet's finite resources (e.g., Ehrlich and Ehrlich 1990). Malthus maintained that we must address the prospect of population growth outstripping the means of sustaining it, most notably in the form of food supply. He therefore advocated limiting future population growth through encouraging 'moral restraint' and other measures. Malthus also warned that efforts to raise the poor beyond subsistence level would increase their numbers, and thereby aggravate the problem that he had identified. He envisaged that the economic hardships caused by population growth would force people to have smaller families. Ultimately, Malthus believed the equilibrium between population and resources would be maintained by natural disasters like famine as well as warfare.

Today, Malthusian concerns have become caught up with the issue of global environmental decline (see P. Harrison 1993). Forms of environmental degradation, ranging from pollution to global warming, foreground the problem of resource scarcity, especially as contemporary population increases surpass the rises of earlier epochs. In this regard, prior to 1800, there had only been moderate or gradual rises in world population growth; it is in the modern period that it really takes off, increasing more than sixfold between 1800 and 2000 (Sachs 2005a: 27). For neo-Malthusians, the damage that is being caused to the earth's ecosystems by contemporary population growth necessitates swift and draconian action to rein in our numbers and prevent an ecological catastrophe (Hardin 1993).[2] Kevin Cleaver and Gotz Schreiber (1994) consider such action is especially necessary in sub-Saharan Africa which they consider to be on the verge of environmental catastrophe. Their research emphasizes the extent to which rapid population growth, increasing environmental degradation and poor agricultural performance are interlinked. But for Cleaver and

Schreiber, rapid population growth is the principal factor that is generating this downward spiral and therefore needs to be curbed (see also Timberlake 1985). However, as will now be shown, for others within the development community, neo-Malthusian concerns about population growth are overstated.

Southern perspective For some southern writers, population growth is simply a false issue, stirred up by the developed world in order to keep the LDCs in their underdeveloped condition and to perpetuate their own dominant position (IPFA 1995).[3] They argue that northern countries are concerned that southern population growth will help to shift the global balance of power in favour of the South and also lead to greater competition for resources between the two worlds. In this vein, Frank Furedi (1997) is concerned that the recent shift of the population agenda towards the problems of the environment, gender equality and reproductive health has provided the West with a further opportunity to shape development in the South. Likewise, Furedi continues, the rhetoric of rights and empowerment that is increasingly employed 'is part of the patronizing outlook that can ignore what it does not like on the grounds that it knows best' (ibid.: 169). Lastly, southern writers note that northern countries also experienced rapid population growth as part of their development phase and that to attempt to restrict this process in the South is hypocritical.

There are obviously a range of southern perspectives on the issue of population growth, but an often-stated view is that, for the reasons state above, it is a product of poverty. It follows therefore that alleviating poverty in southern societies is the best way of dealing with this problem. This position was also advocated by the Brandt Commission, which pointed to the need for much greater international assistance to break 'the vicious circle between poverty and high birth rates' (1980: 116).

Development perspectives Since the 1940s, rapid population growth has frequently been portrayed as a problem for development. From this perspective, in order to sustain their burgeoning populations, southern countries have to divert valuable resources away from economic development and poverty reduction. A prerequisite of development is therefore the control of population growth.

However, another view within development is that the processes of modernization and economic development enable developing societies to achieve population reduction (Coale and Hoover 1958). For example, research undertaken on 125 countries for the period 1950–2000 indicates a weak but negative relationship between population growth and per capita GDP. In other words, as income increases, population expands at a slower rate (see Faria, León-Ledesma and Sachsida. 2006). This tendency occurs because there is less need for larger families in developed societies as citizens are protected by their respective welfare states, and specifically their healthcare systems. Within modern societies, there is also likely to be ready access to contraception and family planning services. In addition, women are more likely to prioritize their own education and careers within such societies and delay having children, and have fewer of them than their counterparts in the developing world. Furthermore, better educated women are more likely to be informed about birth control. Indeed, it is in less economically developed regions, notably sub-Saharan Africa, that the fertility rate (the average number of children born per woman) remains high.

Urbanization is another feature of development that can impact upon family size. For instance, some of the basic chores that children will be expected to perform in rural areas are provided by municipal authorities in cities. Moreover, conditions are cramped within the cities of many developing countries, making it impracticable for couples to have large families. Cities also afford women more opportunities than the traditional roles assigned to them in rural areas of being mothers and working in agriculture. Thus, the differences between urban and rural life mean that it is simply not as necessary or practicable for parents in cities to have large families.

In sum, this position is encapsulated in the often-used phrase 'development is the best contraceptive'. However, the assumption that development will lead to a reduction in population growth is problematic. It simply assumes that the development experience of the South will replicate that of the North but, as we have seen, the processes and trajectories of development within the former realm are extremely uneven. It is also the case that factors like culture and gender influence fertility and have to be weighed against this type of general development tendency. Furthermore, environmentalists are concerned that the planet will undergo forms of ecological breakdown before developing countries reach the stage of development that leads to reductions in their populations.

Gender perspectives   For many writers on development, and not just feminist writers, if we are to tackle population growth effectively, we need to address the issue of women's empowerment. From their perspective, when development strategies are established that serve to enhance the position of women, such as improving their access to education, health care and employment, it invariably leads to a reduction in fertility rates (see Sen, Germain and Chen 1994). Such policies make it easier for women to pursue work and careers outside of the family, and entail that it is uneconomic for them simply to stay at home to bring up children. As wage earners, their status is likely to be enhanced within the family, enabling them to exert greater influence upon decision-making, especially when it comes to the issue of reproduction. Of course, this general tendency needs to be weighed against the fact some women still live in cultures where a high value is placed upon large families (see Jeffery and Basu 1997).

The theme of women's empowerment has exerted a considerable influence upon development policy. For example, UNFPA seeks to synthesize three policy areas – reproductive health, women's empowerment, and population and development strategies – recognizing that they are inextricably linked. In particular, the ability of women to make free and informed childbearing decisions lies at their intersection.

The UNFPA strategy is based on the Programme of Action developed at the ICPD held in Cairo in 1994. This document goes beyond the traditional family planning approach to population by arguing for improvements in individual health and well-being, as well as the advancement of women through greater access to education and economic and political power.[4] Reflecting this broader philosophy, the Cairo conference also located the issue of population growth within the context of sustainable development and environmental decline. UNFPA has built on this approach, developing population strategies in relation to key challenges of our time, like climate change (e.g., see UNFPA 2008). However, the ICPD has attracted criticism, with some demographers arguing that it downplayed the problem of population growth because of pressure from women's rights advocates (Ashford 2001: 38; Finkle 1995).

Technological and market perspectives　For technologists, Malthusian concerns about unsustainable population growth underestimate the impact that new technologies can have in alleviating such rises, especially in the area of renewable energy supplies and agricultural production. For example, a significant proportion of all crops are lost to disease and pest before they are harvested and this can be addressed in part through genetic modification to enable the development of more effective pest-resistant and disease-resistant plants, as well as to improve their drought and saline tolerance. Crop yields will also be increased through more efficient use of existing water supplies, better harvesting procedures, improved fertilizers and greater storage facilities (McGourty 2009). Ester Boserup (1993) was an early exponent of this approach. She linked population change with agricultural growth, arguing that as long as population growth is not too rapid, it can serve to stimulate innovation in agricultural production, leading to increased yields.

More broadly, market advocates contend that technologies will emerge in response to market demand. In this way, they argue, the market can help to facilitate a balance between resources and population growth. From their perspective, statist interventions designed to achieve population control are therefore unnecessary. Ultimately, this approach places faith in human ingenuity in dealing with demographic challenges (Simon 1981).

However, critics maintain that there is a leap of faith underpinning this approach. Relying upon market mechanisms overlooks the fact that sometimes markets fail. Critics also caution about placing too much faith in technology. There are widely expressed concerns about the long-term environmental consequences of genetic engineering and the development of new plant strains. Furthermore, while food output has tripled since the 1960s, according to the FAO's 2008 report on *The State of Food Insecurity in the World*, world hunger is increasing, with the number of hungry people estimated at 923 million in 2007, a rise of more than 80 million since the early 1990s (FAO 2008: 2). While much of the blame for this increase may lie with the rise in food prices during this period, it also suggests that there are limits to the productive capacities of agricultural technologies. If so, then it would be wise to continue to work to reduce birth and fertility rates.

In sum, the relationship between population growth and development is a complex one. Indeed, Frank Furedi stresses how the effects of population growth are determined by context and the interaction with the prevailing socio-economic structures and cultural practices (1997: 8). For Furedi, this goes to the heart of the problem with neo-Malthusian approaches, namely that population is considered in isolation from both history and social development as if it adheres to its own autonomous laws (ibid.: 41). It perhaps also goes some way to explaining why many neo-Malthusian concerns and predictions have to date not been realized.

Future scenarios

It is widely anticipated that the world's growing population will exacerbate the problem of hunger and water shortages in some contexts, issues that are likely to be aggravated by global warming as the century progresses. Population growth is also contributing to debates about the 'carrying capacity' of the earth in relation to humans (see Cohen 1995; Seitz 2008). In other words, how many people can the planet support? Furthermore, growing population pressures in some developing nations will lead to increased migration, and in some instances this will generate tensions within host countries. However, this point needs to be weighed against the fact that migration benefits those societies with ageing populations by providing them with a ready source of labour.

Professor John Beddington, the UK Chief Scientific Adviser, contends that the world's growing population, along with success in alleviating poverty in developing countries, will culminate in a 'perfect storm' of food, energy and water shortages by 2030. With the population reaching 8.3 billion by this date, the demand for fresh water will increase by 30 per cent and for food and energy by 50 per cent. He predicts this will lead to cross-border conflicts, public unrest and mass migration as people flee from the worst-affected regions (Sample 2009).

However, there are signs that the world population is growing at a lower rate in the past 20 to 50 years, due to measures like family planning. In this regard, it is also predicted that fertility will decline from 2.6 children per woman in 2005 to slightly over 2 children per woman in 2050 (BBC 2005b). Moreover, according to the Washington-based Population Reference Bureau

(PRB), the populations of some countries will decrease by nearly 40 per cent by 2050, notably in Eastern Europe (BBC 2004b). Similarly, Rosemary Righter (2009) notes that birth rates have fallen below replacement level in more than 70 countries, and she considers that this will help world population to level out at a more manageable 9 billion within 40 years. Indeed, Lutz, Sanderson and Scherbov (2004) envisage world population growth coming to an end during the twenty-first century and it becoming a century of population ageing (see also Pearce 2010).

Health and development

The focus will now turn to examining the health status of populations, as well as some of the key issues in relation to health and development. Health is obviously a quality of life issue for individuals, but it also has implications for economic development, as healthy citizens are likely to be more economically productive.

Measuring health

For the World Health Organization (WHO), health is not merely the absence of disease or infirmity, but also the state of complete physical, mental and social well-being (WHO 1948). However, a range of criteria can be employed in determining the health status of nations. Beyond the quality of health care and the proportion of national income spent upon health, there are other factors that will be influential in this regard, including water supply, sanitation, food security and nutrition, the impact of global warming, the strain that refugees can place upon societies, the legacies of colonialism, and rural–urban differences in access to health provision. Moreover, as we will see in the next section, the nature and quality of education within countries can also profoundly impact upon the health of nations. In addition, an individual's health status will be shaped by factors like housing, family life, educational background and the level of political stability or conflict in their country. All of the above will have an impact upon the life expectancy and the health of peoples within any given society.

As was mentioned at the beginning of this chapter, health and the spread of infectious diseases are inextricably linked to poverty. In the most obvious sense, aspects of poverty such as malnutrition and inadequate shelter and sanitation can increase vulnerability to disease. Likewise, as we have seen, another feature of poverty and underdevelopment is high birth rates and rapid urbanization, and cramped cities provide conditions that are conducive to the spread of diseases like cholera.

However, poor health is not simply due to malnutrition and differential access to resources. This point is vividly illustrated in the case of obesity. Scientists, dieticians and other health practitioners now regularly voice concern about a global epidemic of obesity. It is not only in the developed North where this is a problem, as even in the poorest countries, particularly within urban communities, many people are growing heavier and taller and becoming at risk from what are described as the 'diseases of affluence', such as heart conditions, diabetes and cancer (Radford 2002). In this regard, income is not the key factor; rather it is a matter of lifestyle and environment, most notably the fact that, compared to even the recent past, globally we are eating foods with higher densities of calories and fat – what is sometimes termed the 'McDonaldization of diet' – and less of us are leading physically active lives.

Health is therefore a complex issue, one which cuts across a range of development areas. But despite a proliferation in the number of global health initiatives and agencies, and an increase in global health funding in recent years, many developing countries still do not enjoy adequate healthcare provision (McCoy, Chand and Sridhar 2009). It is estimated that more than half of the population in the world's poorest countries in Africa and Asia lack access to essential medicines (Siddique 2007). Indeed, the extent and persistence of global health inequalities raise enormous challenges for the international community. For example, in 2007, health spending in the UK was on average £1,400 per person, whereas in some sub-Saharan African countries it was as low as £5. Furthermore, there was only one health worker per 1,000 people in some of the latter countries, compared to a European average of one per 100 (Siddique 2007).

Global health check

It is widely anticipated that the future health of the global community is likely to be shaped by the following issues and challenges.

Globalization   Many of the processes of globalization are diminishing the division between domestic and international health. In particular, the greater movement of people around the world due to increased trade, commerce, tourism and migration facilitates the spread of diseases, turning epidemics into pandemics. Since late 2002, there have been a number of epidemics and pandemics, including severe acute respiratory syndrome (SARS), cholera and Ebola haemorrhagic fever in Africa, yellow fever in Africa and Latin America, avian influenza and swine flu.

For developing countries, the rapid spread of communicable diseases is not simply a human tragedy. It can also place a strain on inchoate health systems, as well as cause economic harm when it results in a reduction in foreign trade and tourism. In contrast, northern governments often express concern about the adequacy of southern surveillance systems for monitoring communicable diseases. From a different perspective, Murray Last (1999) emphasizes how the operation of the world economy – another important feature of globalization

– is exacerbating global inequality and poverty which in turn has a very direct impact upon the health of people in some countries and regions.

However, there are aspects of globalization that arguably help to improve the health of the international community. For instance, the WHO has become a worldwide directing and coordinating authority for health. Indeed, within the WHO is the Global Outbreak Alert and Response Network (GOARN), an international response system for epidemics and other public health emergencies. It forms an integral part of global communicable disease surveillance that monitors diseases, evaluates national and international control measures and provides public information and health advice.[5]

Similarly, global communication and media globalization are generating greater public awareness of diseases, as well as being used by governments and health authorities to spread best practice in relation to health care. Global ICTs like the internet also facilitate the formation of global networks of health professionals, NGOs and concerned citizens, allowing them to communicate, share knowledge and information, and monitor official or national responses to disease outbreaks. Indeed, another manifestation of globalization is the growth of international health-oriented NGOs, like *Médecins Sans Frontières* (MSF) (or Doctors Without Borders), which undertake both humanitarian and campaigning activity.

Global shortage of health workers In the *World Health Report 2006 – Working Together for Health*, the WHO warned that a global shortage of health workers was undermining the fight against diseases such as Aids, malaria and tuberculosis, and affecting childhood vaccination campaigns and basic care for pregnant women (WHO 2006). The shortage of health workers reached 4.3 million in 2006. Among the 57 countries facing an acute shortage of doctors and nurses, 36 were in sub-Saharan Africa (ibid.). Indeed, sub-Saharan Africa has 24 per cent of the world's disease, but only 3 per cent of the world's health workers and less than 1 per cent of the total global health budget (Foulkes 2006). Furthermore, the global health worker shortage is jeopardizing the chances of achieving the UNMDGs on health. In addition, many developing countries face a shortage of skilled health workers in poorer rural areas with professionals preferring to work in more affluent urban areas where there is greater access to amenities and entertainment.

The reasons for health worker shortages will obviously be context specific; nevertheless, it is possible to detect a number of common themes:

- Poor remuneration and conditions of service for healthcare workers in developing societies can deter potential entrants into the profession, as well as encourage those who are qualified to emigrate to developed nations (see p. 78).
- In fragile states, civil unrest and personal security concerns can also influence health professionals to migrate.

- Underfunded health systems, which means that some countries do not have sufficient tutors to train health professionals. Moreover, two-thirds of countries in sub-Saharan Africa have only one medical school, and some have none at all (Naicker et al. 2009: 62). Critics of the IFIs maintain that the public sector expenditure limits they imposed upon many developing countries in the 1980s and 1990s led to under-investment in their health infrastructure.
- Weak human resource planning and management. The health systems of some countries are hindered by factors such as excessive bureaucracy and inadequate information-gathering processes, while the lack of career opportunities for health workers makes the recruitment and retention of staff more difficult.
- The size of the health workforce in some developing countries has been reduced by HIV/AIDS. South Africa and Malawi have suffered particularly in this regard, with the latter losing nearly 3 per cent of its health workforce each year to the disease (WHO 2006). In high-prevalence countries, health workers are not only potentially exposed to significant risks in their personal lives, but also at work whenever protective practices and equipment are deficient. More broadly, in countries where AIDS has reached epidemic proportions, it is placing enormous stress upon health systems and staff.

An additional problem confronting many developing nations is that their own health workers are being enticed to go and work in northern countries because of the prospect of higher salaries, improved working conditions, and opportunities for further training and career advancement. In 2002–3, for example, over 3,000 nurses migrated from African states and registered in the UK (Buchan and Dovlo 2004). Moreover, some northern governments are actively recruiting these workers in order to address staff shortages within their own health systems and to deal with the wider problem of their ageing populations. This 'brain drain' of qualified health professionals is enormously harmful to poorer countries, marking a substantial loss in investment and vital skills. It has led the WHO to push for a global code of practice for the international recruitment of health personnel.

In response to the health worker shortage, the *World Health Report 2006* calls for governments to devise national strategies to create an effective health workforce, backed by international donor assistance that especially allows poorer countries to train more staff (WHO 2006).

Climate change   According to the WHO's *World Health Report 2002*, climate change was responsible for 2.4 per cent of diarrhoeal disease worldwide in 2002. However, majority scientific opinion maintains that, as the century progresses, global warming will have an even more profound impact upon global health. It is anticipated that climate change will facilitate the spread and persistence of infectious and parasitic disease (IPDs). In particular, it is predicted that the range of disease-carrying mosquitoes will expand, exposing more people to diseases like dengue fever and malaria (Kent and Yin 2006: 4). And with environmental decline expected to unduly affect southern countries and result in an increase in ecological migrants, this will raise concerns in northern countries about the strains this places on their own health and welfare systems.

HIV/AIDS   Peter Piot, the head of the Joint United Nations Programme on HIV/ AIDS (UNAIDS), has described HIV/AIDS as 'the single greatest threat to continual global development' (Poku 2002: 111). In particular, HIV/AIDS is seen as potentially undermining the development advances that have been made in areas like life expectancy and infant mortality rates. Indeed, '95 per cent of the global distribution of HIV infections and AIDS cases are located in the developing world' (Poku 2005: 7).

The HIV/AIDS epidemic spread from the early 1980s onwards and by 2007 had killed some 25 million people worldwide. During 2008, the number of people living with HIV worldwide rose to an estimated 33.4 million, which meant that the total number of people living with the virus in 2008 was roughly threefold higher than the number in 1990 (UNAIDS 2009b: 7).

HIV/AIDS has an especially detrimental impact upon developing nations because it places an additional strain upon their already limited financial resources. In some countries, HIV/AIDS is overwhelming healthcare services and means that health provision is weighted in favour of curative health care, thereby lessening the amount that can be spent upon other areas (World Bank 2005a). HIV/AIDS also distorts population structures, robbing countries of a large proportion of their most physically active labour force and an important source of income generation.

As well as being a personal tragedy, the deaths caused by AIDS have significant social consequences, decimating families and resulting in a high number of orphans. In *The State of the World's Children* (2005), UNICEF emphasizes the emotional, mental and health challenges that the loss of a parent can create for a child. Furthermore, with 80 per cent of the 15 million children orphaned by AIDS living in Africa, it is placing pressure upon the extended African family, especially in Botswana, Lesotho, Swaziland and Zimbabwe (Carroll and Boseley 2004).

Sub-Saharan Africa has been hardest hit by the HIV/AIDS epidemic, with a high incidence of HIV. Indeed, Botswana, Lesotho and Swaziland have the highest percentage of people who are HIV positive. One explanatory factor behind the spread of the disease is the high level of migrant labour that traverses the continent. Linked to this phenomenon, some commentators believe the prevalence of HIV/AIDS is part of a broader challenge to the African family and family life, where men in particular have fewer scruples about being unfaithful to their partners. However, such patterns of infidelity are not exclusive to Africa and can be found elsewhere in the world where the levels of HIV/AIDS are not as high.

While two-thirds of HIV positive people live in sub-Saharan Africa, there has been a rise in the numbers affected in Asia and Eastern Europe, especially in India, Ukraine and the Russian Federation. Indeed, India now has more people with HIV than South Africa. But beyond these general trends, there exists considerable variation even within countries, with some areas having a higher incidence of HIV than others. As the World Bank has noted in its *Global HIV/AIDS Program of Action*, the extent of this diversity necessitates good surveillance 'to understand the specific transmission dynamics in each context or country in order to design effective interventions' (World Bank 2005a: 13).

Poverty is widely considered to be an underlying factor behind the spread of HIV in developing regions. In some African states, underfunded and inchoate health systems mean that not all of their populations receive adequate health provision, ensuring that some must live with untreated diseases which can aid the rapid transmission of HIV (Sachs 2005b: 323). Likewise, pregnant women with AIDS require treatment to prevent them transmitting the virus to their unborn children. More broadly, research suggests that AIDS prevention strategies must address 'the greater biological susceptibility of poor people to infectious disease' due to factors like poor nutrition (Stillwaggon 2002: 17). Underfunded health systems can also mean that there are insufficient resources for effective family planning services – including limiting the availability of contraception – and HIV/AIDS educational awareness campaigns. Indeed, for UNAIDS, education can 'modify the behaviours that create, increase or perpetuate the risk of HIV infection' (UNAIDS 2009c: 5).

Beyond poverty, the spread of HIV/AIDS can also be facilitated by internal factors within countries. For instance, the HIV prevention programmes of national governments may be inappropriate, a charge that was raised against the South African government of Thabo Mbeki (see Box 3.2). The World Bank contends that efforts against AIDS are often not coordinated well at the national level due to factors ranging from a lack of strategic planning to missing data (World Bank 2005a: 15–16). Some governments, for cultural and social reasons, may not promote effective sex education and shy away from promoting condom use for homosexual men and sex workers. Indeed, condom use is also shaped by wider cultural attitudes, and some countries may require societal change if they are to tackle HIV/AIDS effectively, such as the empowerment of women and changing the attitudes of some men about the desirability of having multiple sexual partners. In this regard, UNAIDS established the *Action Framework* in 2009 to address the persistent gender inequality and human rights violations that place girls and women at greater risk and vulnerability to HIV (UNAIDS 2009a).

UN Millennium Development Goals: Health

As we saw in the Introduction, the UN Millennium Development Goals (MDGs) are an attempt to establish a common international agenda to address the key

Box 3.2 South Africa and HIV/AIDS

In 2008, around 5.5 million people were infected with HIV in South Africa – roughly 1 in 10 of the population – and over 2 million people had already died of AIDS. Numerous reasons have been postulated to explain the high incidence of HIV/AIDS in South Africa, but two in particular stand out.

Firstly, the patterns of trade and human migration that criss-cross South Africa and connect it with the rest of the continent are considered to be a primary factor contributing to the spread of HIV. South Africa is a leading economic power on the continent and major provider of employment and this has led to the formation of an extensive labour migrant system, as well as encouraged a high level of drive-through traffic.

Secondly, the AIDS policies of the former South African president Thabo Mbeki's government have been blamed for exacerbating the problem, and leading to the avoidable deaths of more than a third of a million people in the country (Boseley 2008). During his time in office, Mbeki questioned the link between HIV and AIDS. He argued that poverty was the real cause of the disease because it led to poor nourishment and general ill health, noting that HIV spread much more rapidly in Africa than in developed countries. Indeed, for many years he refused to endorse the wearing of condoms to prevent infection. He also argued that AIDS encourages the perception of Africans as 'germ carriers' (McGreal 2006a).

Mbeki's government was lukewarm about AIDS testing programmes and the provision of anti-retroviral (ARV) drugs, claiming in the case of the latter that they are toxic, dangerous and too expensive. In particular, he questioned the usefulness of ARV drugs in containing the spread of HIV and progression to AIDS, noting that pharmaceutical companies enjoyed increased sales because of such claims (Sachs 2000). As a result, about 700,000 people with HIV were not receiving anti-retroviral drugs in 2006 (Boseley 2006). In 2007, according to UNAIDS, the figure had risen to an estimated 800,000, with less than 20 per cent receiving ARV drugs (McGreal 2006b).

In August 2006, at an international AIDS conference in Toronto, the South African health minister, Manto Tshabalala-Msimang, advocated eating vegetables, including garlic, lemon, beetroot and African potatoes, as a way of managing the disease. It is widely believed that she was appointed to this position because she shared Mbeki's views and was prepared to take on the medical community.

Mbeki was ousted from the leadership of the African National Congress in September 2008 and, since then, the South African state has been attempting to distribute ARV drugs to as many people as possible. However, South Africa is still faced with a thousand HIV-related deaths every day.

challenges within development. In relation to health, as with the other goals, the MDGs are part of a chain of responses that are being pursued in tackling these important areas. There are three UN MDGs that focus specifically on health.

(i) Goal 4: Reduce child mortality   According to *The Millennium Development Goals Report 2009*, the under-five mortality rate has declined steadily worldwide: '[i]n 2007, the global under-five mortality rate was 67 deaths per 1,000 live births, down from 93 in 1990' (UNMDG 2009: 24). Nevertheless, there remains much work to be done in order to achieve the UNMDG target of reducing by two-thirds, between 1990 and 2015, the under-five mortality rate. Many countries in sub-Saharan Africa and Southern Asia have made little or no progress at all.

In particular, sub-Saharan Africa now accounts for half of all deaths among children under five (ibid.: 25).

However, a notable decline in under-five mortality is anticipated in sub-Saharan Africa because of the progress of several key child-survival interventions. These interventions include vitamin A supplementation, the use of insecticide-treated bed nets to prevent malaria, immunization against measles, and anti-retroviral treatment for pregnant mothers who are HIV-positive to prevent transmission of the virus to their babies.

(ii) Goal 5: Improve maternal health   The target for this particular UNMDG is to reduce by three-quarters, between 1990 and 2015, the maternal mortality ratio. There is a stark contrast in the maternal mortality rate between the developed and developing worlds: almost 99 per cent of maternal deaths occur in the latter region. Thus, while one in every seven women in Niger dies of pregnancy-related causes, in Sweden the lifetime risk is one in 17,400 (Seal and Manson 2008).

According to *The Millennium Development Goals Report 2009*, it is UNMDG 5 that has made the least progress, largely due to a lack of funding, especially for family planning programmes. For the developing world as a whole, there were 450 maternal deaths per 100,000 births in 2005 compared to 480 maternal deaths in 1990. Moreover, this small decline during this period reflects progress only in some regions: Eastern Asia, Northern Africa and South-East Asia experienced declines of 30 per cent; for Southern Asia, the figure was a decline of more than 20 per cent; while there was little progress in sub-Saharan Africa (UNMDG 2009: 27). Worryingly, the maternal death rate in sub-Saharan Africa has remained almost unchanged since 2000.

The proportion of births attended by skilled health personnel, which is considered essential to reducing maternal deaths, increased in developing regions from 53 per cent in 1990 to 61 per cent in 2007. However, again it is an uneven picture. Thus, while the number of deliveries attended by skilled health workers (doctors, nurses or midwives) has increased in North Africa and East Asia since 1995, progress remains slow in countries in sub-Saharan Africa and Southern Asia, with more than half of all births still taking place without the assistance of trained personnel.

The Millennium Development Goals Report 2009 also found that fewer than half of pregnant women in developing countries had the benefit of adequate prenatal care, which UNICEF and the WHO consider to be a minimum of four antenatal visits. Such visits aid the detection, treatment and prevention of health problems among pregnant women. However, the proportion of women who received four or more antenatal visits was 'still less than 50 per cent in sub-Saharan Africa and Southern Asia, where the majority of maternal deaths occur' (ibid.).

(iii) Goal 6: Combat HIV/AIDS, malaria and other diseases   With regards to HIV/AIDS, malaria and other major diseases, such as tuberculosis, the aim is to

halt their spread and to start reversing it by 2015. By 2005, US$290 million had been provided by the Global Fund to Fight HIV/AIDS, Tuberculosis and Malaria in 80 countries.

In the case of malaria, significant advances have already been made since the turn of the millennium, with death rates falling in some countries, aided by the UN's distribution of free insecticide-treated mosquito nets and more widely available preventative medicines. According to the *Millennium Development Goals Report 2009*, governments have been adopting more effective anti-malaria strategies 'that would have been out of reach had funding not been available' (UNMDG 2009: 36).

The global incidence of tuberculosis (TB), which is the number of new cases per 100,000 people, is levelling off. However, the number of new cases continues to rise because 'progress has not been fast enough to keep pace with population growth' (ibid.: 38). Consequently, there were an estimated 9.3 million new cases of tuberculosis in 2007, compared to 8.3 million cases in 2000. Tuberculosis prevalence – i.e., the number of TB cases per 100,000 people – and mortality rates are also not falling fast enough to meet global targets (ibid.).

According to the *Millennium Development Goals Report 2009*, new HIV infections and AIDS deaths have peaked. However, 33 million people were still living with HIV in 2007, a number that is growing largely because people infected with the virus are surviving longer (ibid.: 32). Worryingly, the report also found that, on average, 'only about 31 per cent of young men and 19 per cent of young women (aged 15–24) in developing countries have a thorough and accurate understanding of HIV' (ibid.: 33).

More encouragingly, the *Millennium Development Goals Report 2009* argues that access to treatment for HIV/AIDS has widened and contributed to the first decline in AIDS deaths since the epidemic began in the early 1980s. For instance, three million people in the developing regions had access to anti-retroviral drugs in December 2007, a 47 per cent increase on the year before (ibid.: 35). However, the report noted that there was still some way to go to achieve the UNMDG target of universal access to treatment for all those who need it by 2010. Indeed, in 2007, 69 per cent of people who needed anti-retroviral treatment did not have access to the required drugs (ibid.: WHO 2009: 11).

There are also fears that the global financial crisis will erode the advances that have already been made in relation to HIV/AIDS. A report published by MSF in May 2010, indicated that spending by the large international donor agencies (e.g., PEPFAR, UNITAID and the World Bank) on HIV/AIDS treatment had declined in the previous eighteen months, and countries like the USA and the Netherlands were seeking to reduce their payments to the Global Fund (MSF 2010). As a result, eight countries in sub-Saharan Africa had reduced the numbers of people starting on ARV drugs and requested emergency supplies for those already on treatment.

In sum, there has been uneven progress made in relation to the UNMDG health goals, with advances varying considerably between and even within countries and regions. Achieving these goals is dependent upon progress being made in other areas, such as widening access to education and gender equality, and how the anticipated health threats posed by climate change are tackled (WHO, 2009: 10). Future progress will also be linked to the building of effective national health systems and continuing increases in both the amount and the predictability of aid flows. Total global aid for health rose from US$6.8 billion in 2000 to US$16.7 billion in 2006, but experts believe this upward trajectory has to be maintained if the UNMDG health goals are to be attained in 2015 (WHO 2008: 7).

Indeed, in July 2007, Ban Ki-Moon, the United Nations Secretary-General, declared that the Millennium Development goals, including those in relation to health care, would not be met unless richer countries increased significantly their international aid budgets. With regards to the issue of health, he identified particular problems in Africa, arguing that without this additional financial support there is little chance of stemming the HIV/AIDS epidemic on the continent. And at a global level, while child mortality has been declining, it will have to drop dramatically – by as much as 70 per cent – if the 2015 targets are to be met (Bamford 2007).

Education and development

The benefits of education

Education is an integral component of development. Indeed, the type and quality of educational provision that exists within a given country can have a profound impact upon the course and nature of its economic development. As we saw in chapter 1, the high levels of investment in education undertaken by countries like South Korea and Singapore in the 1960s arguably paved the way for their subsequent rapid economic growth. In the case of India, critics have claimed that it has overly focused upon higher education at the expense of school education, and this has contributed to its uneven economic and social development, with the poor largely marginalized from these processes (Sen 2001: 42).

An effective educational system can bring a range of benefits for developing societies. For example, education is linked to a growth in productivity. Research suggests that the output of small farmers increases when they receive a basic education. Indeed, a study of 13 low-income countries indicated that four years of schooling led to an 8 per cent increase in farm production (Lockheed, Jamison and Lau 1980). Similarly, research into risk-taking and innovation among farmers in rural Ethiopia found that education of the household head decreases risk aversion and encourages farmers to adopt innovations (Knight, Weir, and Woldehanna 2003). The authors note that there are also externality benefits to education, with the educated farmers providing an example 'which may be copied by those without education (such as in the adoption and diffusion of innovations)' (ibid.: 19–20). They contend that their 'findings provide an incentive to the Ethiopian government and donor organisations to expand rural schooling from its extremely low level and encourage parents to send their children to school' (ibid.: 20).

Education can have a positive impact upon other aspects of development. For example, UNICEF makes the link between schooling and a reduction in fertility rates, noting how, in Brazil, 'illiterate women have an average of 6.5 children, whereas those with secondary education have 2.5 children' (UNICEF 1999: 7). An integral part of education is also health awareness, which in turn can help to reduce the incidence of preventable illness and death, as we saw above in the case of HIV/AIDS (ibid.: 8).

For many commentators, education should be at the centre of the international development agenda because it is an essential prerequisite for other development goals, such as sustainable development, empowering women, building socially cohesive societies, combating poverty and safeguarding human rights. Education can also help to spread progressive attitudes and practices like tolerance, cultural awareness, respect for others and gender equality that can help to combat racism, xenophobia and sexism within societies. In this vein, education can also contribute to international peace and cooperation by facilitating greater knowledge of other countries that may lead to shared understanding.

Education is beneficial for individuals as well as societies. It provides access to employment and thereby better equips us to look after ourselves and our families. Education can also help to inculcate values like self-discipline, self-motivation and the importance of hard work. Above all, it can potentially allow people to lead more rewarding lives by opening up new career opportunities and introducing them to new ideas. In this vein, Amartya Sen views education as essential in enhancing 'human capability'. Through education, learning and skill formation, we are able to become more productive, thereby contributing to the process of economic expansion, as well as our own self-development (2001: 292–3). Education therefore offers a form of empowerment. For example, literacy is integral to one's sense of well-being because it enables us to participate actively in our societies and economies, as well as allowing us the pleasure of reading and greater access to the arts and culture.

Education in developing societies

The problem confronting developing nations is that the provision of education and, specifically, the setting up and maintenance of state education systems is expensive. Indeed, education in many developing countries has suffered under structural adjustment, with governments compelled to cut educational budgets in order to reduce their debt. For children in some developing countries, these financial constraints can mean not having a local school to attend. And where such schools exist, they will often be underfunded resulting in overcrowding and a lack of adequate educational resources and qualified teachers. For example, in parts of Equatorial Guinea there can be as many as 90 pupils per teacher (UNICEF 1999: 9). In turn, such conditions contribute to the high drop-out rate from schools in some developing countries, as well as the large numbers of pupils having to repeat school years.

There is also the issue of what is the most appropriate form of educational provision for poorer countries. In other words, in relation to facilitating development and enhancing the quality of life of their respective citizens, what level of education (primary, secondary, tertiary or higher education level) should scarce resources be geared towards?

For example, a World Bank report entitled *Higher Education in Developing Societies: Peril and Promise* emphasizes the importance of higher education for LEDCs in terms of allowing them to compete in an increasingly globalized knowledge economy (World Bank 2000b). Alternatively, is it more productive to focus upon the provision of practical and vocational forms of education? In this vein, perhaps education budgets should be concentrated upon the teaching of science and technology as this would arguably better serve a developing country's future prospects.

There is greater consensus over the importance of people attaining literacy within education. Consequently, there is considerable emphasis upon the provision of primary education because this is seen as the best means for people to achieve this skill and thereby to establish a literate citizenry. Indeed, primary education is regarded as a fundamental human right by the UN. Nevertheless, the UN estimated that globally around 115 million primary school-age children remained outside formal education systems in 2000. As a result, adult literacy continues to be a major obstacle to development, with an estimated 880 million adults functionally illiterate in the world. In other words, nearly a billion people entered the twenty-first century 'unable to read a book or sign their names' (UNICEF 1999: 7). Dealing with these issues will also require tackling child labour in the developing world. At the start of the millennium, it was estimated that 250 million children were trapped in child labour, with many of them receiving no schooling whatsoever (ibid.: 9). However, child labour and not sending children to school is often due to poverty, where parents' first priority is to meet everyday subsistence needs.

The quality of education that children receive is obviously dependent upon context. Key factors in this regard range from the nature of governance to the level of conflict that exists within a country. For example, around one-third of the world's 72 million out-of-school children live in only 20 conflict-affected countries (UNESCO forthcoming). In particular, the state is widely considered to play a pivotal role, especially with regard to the level of political commitment to education and the proportion of the national budget that is allocated to it. For example, Pakistan has a literacy rate of only 38 per cent compared to Vietnam's 94 per cent, and this is despite the former country having a higher per capita income than the latter (UNICEF 1999: 80).

Corruption within education is another problem confronting some developing countries (see Hallak and Poisson 2005). This activity can range from bribes and pay-offs in teacher recruitment and promotion to illegal payments for school entrance. It is reflected in the 'leakage' of funds from ministries of education to schools (ibid.: 1). The reasons for corruption are numerous and varied and dependent upon context. However, an underlying problem is the issue of poverty and the low salaries earned by public officials and civil servants, such as teachers (ibid.: 2). Obviously, where corruption exists, it can greatly undermine the quality of the education that young people receive and in turn this will have a detrimental impact upon the long-term development of that country. It can also lead to donors questioning the worth of aid programmes. As a result, many development agencies are calling for the dissemination of strategies designed to improve transparency and accountability in education, including reinforcing regulatory systems and establishing ethical codes of conduct for teachers.

Education for All

During the 1980s, the education budgets and programmes of many developing countries were curtailed by a combination of debt and structural adjustment. In this context, the UN held the World Conference on Education for All in Jomtien (Thailand) in March 1990 that culminated in the World Declaration on Education for All (EFA), which established the world's commitment to educate all of its citizens. It is a rights-based approach to education, underpinned by the Universal Declaration of Human Rights and the Convention on the Rights of the Child. In essence, it decrees that all citizens have the right to benefit from an education that will meet their basic learning needs and which allows them to improve their lives and transform their societies. Thus the Jomtien Conference not only helped to establish that education is a fundamental human right, but also placed education at the heart of the international development agenda (UNICEF 1999: 15).

Towards the end of the 1990s, in a much discussed report entitled *The State of the World's Children* (1999), UNICEF monitored the progress of the international community in ensuring that all children had access to a high-quality education. The report emphasized how EFA is based upon achieving certain targets, namely that: 'schooling should provide the foundation for learning for life; it needs to be accessible, of high quality and flexible; it must be gender sensitive and emphasize girls' education; the state needs to be a key partner; and it should begin with care for the young child' (ibid.: 2). However, crucially the UNICEF report concluded that, despite some progress in relation to these areas, the goal of EFA 'is in danger of being cut short by an apparent dearth of resources and growing indebtedness in the developing world' (ibid.).

In response to this uneven progress, delegates from 164 countries gathered in Dakar, Senegal, for the World Education Forum in April 2000. The

Box 3.3 The Six Education for All Goals

Goal 1: Expanding and improving comprehensive early childhood care and education, especially for the most vulnerable and disadvantaged children.

Goal 2: Ensuring that by 2015 all children, particularly girls, children in difficult circumstances and those belonging to ethnic minorities, have access to, and complete, free and compulsory primary education of good quality.

Goal 3: Ensuring that the learning needs of all young people and adults are met through equitable access to appropriate learning and life skills programmes.

Goal 4: Achieving a 50 per cent improvement in levels of adult literacy by 2015, especially for women, and equitable access to basic and continuing education for all adults.

Goal 5: Eliminating gender disparities in primary and secondary education by 2005, and achieving gender equality in education by 2015, with a focus on ensuring girls' full and equal access to and achievement in basic education of good quality.

Goal 6: Improving all aspects of the quality of education, and ensuring excellence of all, so that recognized and measurable learning outcomes are achieved by all, especially in literacy, numeracy and essential life skills.

(*Source*: World Education Forum 2000)

Dakar Framework for Action – Education for All: Meeting our Collective Commitments was adopted at this event which effectively marked a reaffirmation on the part of the international community to achieve EFA by 2015. In this regard, the participants identified six key educational goals which aim to meet the learning needs of all children, youth and adults by 2015 (see Box 3.3).

The Dakar Framework for Action was based on a detailed analysis of the state of basic education around the world. Known as the EFA 2000 Assessment, it found at the start of a new millennium that:

(i)   Of the more than 800 million children under 6 years of age, fewer than a third benefit from any form of early childhood education.

(ii) Some 113 million children, 60 per cent of whom are girls, have no access to primary schooling.

(iii) At least 880 million adults are illiterate, of whom the majority are women. (World Education Forum 2000: 12)

On the basis of the EFA 2000 Assessment, the Dakar Framework for Action maintained that achieving EFA necessitated 'additional financial support by countries and increased development assistance and debt relief for education by bilateral and multilateral donors, estimated to cost in the order of US$8 billion a year' (ibid.: 10).

Overcoming inequality in education

From a global perspective, there is considerable inequality within education. This is reflected in the differences in the enrolment ratios that exist between developed and developing countries. This discrepancy is especially marked at secondary and tertiary levels, with Africa significantly falling behind other regions. For example, in the case of the tertiary sector, around 40 per cent of the population will go on to this level of education in OECD countries, but the figure is as low as 2 per cent in sub-Saharan Africa (Potter et al. 2004: 218). And just as important as the levels of enrolment is the quality of education that children receive. Funding can again be important in this regard, as some developing societies simply lack the resources to ensure that nationwide there are well equipped schools staffed by professionally trained teachers (Bowden 2002).

Access to education is also highly unequal within some developing societies. In particular, there is often a substantial difference in the number of boys attending schools compared with the number of girls. In some countries, girls will be expected – and in some instances forced – to undertake domestic or subsistence chores rather than attend school. Moreover, even when girls are able to attend schools, they can be confronted with further forms of discrimination. This can range from being encouraged to pursue courses that are considered to be appropriate to their gender through to not being allowed to participate fully and freely in all aspects of school life, such as classroom discussions. For this reason, organizations like UNICEF emphasize the importance of the nature and quality of the education that young people receive (see UNICEF 1999).

The issue of female attendance in schools is important not only on the grounds of fairness but also because studies have revealed strong links between education and health, notably a strong correlation between high levels of infant and child mortality and low levels of maternal education, particularly basic literacy. In other words, education enhances the ability of women to create healthy households within developing societies. More specifically, education ensures they are more likely to benefit from health information and make good use of health services. Education also improves their prospects of earning an independent income that can be channelled into the household, and most importantly it helps them to lead healthier lives. For these reasons, within the area of health and development, considerable emphasis is placed upon the role of female education in promoting good health.

Access to education is also considered to be integral to women's empowerment, providing them with more opportunities and greater control over their lives. Furthermore, studies have shown that education not only improves women's employment prospects, it can also significantly lower levels of fertility. This is because, as women become a more active part of the labour force, they tend to marry later and want fewer children. For example, in the case of Iran, there was a major rise in female literacy and school attendance following the Islamist revolution of 1979 and, as female participation in education grew, the country's fertility rate declined. The average number of births per woman fell from 6.6 in the period 1980–5 to 2.5 for the period 1995–2000 (Sachs 2005b: 317). Again, this highlights the extent to which education, health and population are closely interlinked.

In 2009, the *EFA Global Monitoring Report* argued that the progress towards the EFA goals was being hampered by the failure of governments to tackle persistent inequalities in education (UNESCO 2009). These inequalities were primarily based on gender, income, location, ethnicity, language and disability, and it meant that too many children were 'receiving an education of such poor quality that they leave school without basic literacy and numeracy skills' (ibid.: 3). Hence, if governments believe in Education for All, they will have 'to strengthen their commitment to equity and inclusive education' so that 'children have access to well-funded schools that are responsive to local needs, and employ trained and motivated teachers' (ibid.: 38: 24). In turn, this will require governance reforms that are designed to widen access and participation, improve quality and accountability, and break down inequalities in education. Currently, however, existing approaches to governance reform are failing to attach sufficient weight to equity (ibid.: 4). In short, there is still a long way to go to overcome inequality in education.

UN Millennium Development Goals: Education

The UN Millennium Development Goal 2 is to achieve universal primary education so that all children will be able to complete a full course of primary schooling by 2015. A number of the world's regions are now close to achieving this goal; however, there is still much work that needs to be done in sub-Saharan Africa, Southern Asia and Oceania. In particular, in 2004/5 the UN identified a problem with sub-Saharan Africa, with only 70 per cent of children attending school (BBC 2007b). The UN also expressed concern about the reliability of available data, noting that there were likely to be differences between children enrolling in primary education and actually attending schools on a regular basis, a point that applied not only in Africa but also elsewhere in the developing world. Furthermore, for obvious reasons, data were simply unavailable in some conflict zones.

According to *The Millennium Development Goals Report 2009*, progress is being made towards universal primary education. In the developing world, enrolment coverage in primary education reached 88 per cent in 2007. Encouragingly, 'major breakthroughs have been achieved in sub-Saharan Africa, where enrolment increased by 15 percentage points from 2000 to 2007, and Southern Asia, which gained 11 percentage points over the same period' (UNMDG 2009: 14–15). However, the report also noted that more than 10 per cent of children of primary school age remained out of school. It also warned of the potential detrimental effects of the global economic crisis in terms of leading to a reduction in national spending on education. More broadly, it declared that 'global numbers of out-of-school children are dropping too slowly and too unevenly for the target of universal primary education to be reached by 2015' (ibid.: 15). Moreover, not achieving this target will in turn have a negative impact upon many of the other MDGs and development in general.

Finally, the *2010 Education for All Global Monitoring Report: Reaching the marginalized* warned that the global economic crisis is resulting in a decline in government revenue for the world's poorest countries which means that they have less to spend on education. More specifically, sub-Saharan Africa was 'facing a potential loss of around US$4.6 billion annually in financing for education in 2009 and 2010, equivalent to a 10 per cent reduction in spending per primary school pupil' (UNESCO 2010: 4). The report estimated that in 2010 at least 72 million children were missing out on their right to education (ibid.: 3). While progress has been made, many of the world's poorest countries are a long way from achieving the goals set at Dakar. If we are to meet the Education for All goals by 2015, the report argues, there must be a renewed financing commitment by aid donors and recipient governments alike, as well as greater political determination shown by the international community (ibid.: 38).

Conclusion

Education, health and population growth are both integral aspects of development and closely interrelated, and hence need to be addressed in an integrated fashion. For example, as well as benefiting people, effective educational and healthcare systems increase productivity, a necessary prerequisite of economic development. In turn, research reveals that, as countries develop, life expectancy increases and fertility rates decline, ensuring that population growth is moderated. As Jeffrey Sachs has noted, with just a few exceptions in the Middle East, fertility rates are highest in the poorest and least economically developed countries in the world, with large families serving as a poverty coping strategy (2005b: 323). Of course, the wealth generated by economic development can be invested in health and education. As Roger-Mark De Souza and his co-writers note: 'The most rapid fertility declines have occurred in developing countries that have improved child survival rates and educational levels and have implemented family planning programs' (De Souza, Williams and Meyerson 2003: 37). Furthermore, a more educated citizenry is likely to have greater awareness of health matters and the dangers of unfettered population growth.

However, the funding of the health and educational systems of developing countries continues to be profoundly shaped by the enormous debt that many of them continue to labour under. In addition, resourcing these areas has been made even more difficult by the global economic and financial crisis. For the world's poorest countries, growing financial instability inhibits economic growth and exacerbates the fragile nature of their own economies. It is also likely to lead to a reduction in the amount of foreign aid that developing countries receive from donor agencies as they themselves struggle to cope with the economic downturn.

Summary

- The relationship between population growth and development is complex and ultimately determined by context.
- Achieving the UNMDG health goals is dependent upon progress being made in other areas, such as widening access to education and gender equality.
- Education is not only integral to economic development but also facilitates human capability and flourishing.
- The issues of health, education and population growth are interdependent and profoundly shaped by the levels of poverty and economic development that exist in any given society.

RECOMMENDED READING

- For an insight into the complex relationship between population growth and development, see Frank Furedi, *Population and Development* (1997).
- For an overview of a range of health and development issues, see T. H. MacDonald, *The Global Human Right to Health* (2007).
- For a case study of the impact of HIV/AIDS, see Nana K. Poku, *AIDS in Africa: How the Poor are Dying* (2005).
- UNESCO's *2010 Education for All Global Monitoring Report: Reaching the Marginalized* provides a useful assessment of how close the international community is to attaining the Education for All goals by 2015.

WEBSITES

- www.unfpa.org: Website of the United Nations Population Fund (UNFPA). A useful resource for information on population and reproductive health issues.
- www.prb.org: Website for the Population Reference Bureau that publishes *Population Bulletins*, which are up-to-date and informative articles on many aspects of population and health.
- www.who.int: Website for the WHO, the directing and coordinating authority for health within the United Nations system.
- www.unaids.org: Website for UNAIDS.
- www.unesco.org/en/education: Website for UNESCO (Education).
- www.unicef.org: Website for UNICEF.
- www.worldbank.org/education World Bank Education seeks, among other things, to coordinate education and economic strategies within developing countries.

CHAPTER 4

Gender and Development

- A brief history of gender and development
- Women and development
- Gender and development: critical debates
- Gender and development: future trajectories

Gender refers to socially constructed categories of femininity and masculinity, as opposed to the biological differences between women and men. Gender relations are therefore the socially constructed relations between women and men. The concern of many working within development is with the impact of development strategies and policies upon gender relations, especially with regard to affecting the balance of power between women and men in different societies. Given that women face forms of discrimination and exclusion in most countries, tackling gender inequality can empower women and contribute to their sense of well-being. As we have seen, for many writers attaining this goal for both women and men is the purpose of development. It is part of the trend towards a more people-centred approach to development and away from the preoccupation with economic growth. In this regard, Amartya Sen maintains that the political, economic and social participation of women within development is 'a crucial aspect of development as freedom' (2001: 203).

Thus, this chapter will provide some indication of women's experiences of development as part of a critical examination of the relationship between gender and development. In investigating this area, feminist criticism of development theory and practice, specifically claims about its masculine nature and orientation, will be outlined, as well as the major approaches to gender and development. The chapter will also consider the extent to which these approaches and feminist critiques have challenged mainstream conceptions of development. The final section will explore future trajectories in relation to this subject area, including the growing calls for men to be more fully integrated into gender and development.

A brief history of gender and development

Until the late 1960s, development was assumed to be affecting men and women in the same way, with the economic benefits of growth and modernization

Box 4.1 Gender and development policy approaches: 1950 onwards

Since 1950, a number of gender and development policy approaches have been adopted by development organizations and governments:

- *Welfare (1950s–early 1970s)*: targeted women in their domestic role as wives and mothers. The projects addressed women's practical needs, such as food aid, health and nutrition advice, but also initiated programmes on birth control and childcare. Women were viewed as essentially passive within the development process.
- *Equity (1970s)*: linked with the UN Decade for Women of 1976–85, this approach aimed to eradicate obstacles to women's advancement in the public sphere. It sought to secure gender equality legislation to end the gender discrimination that was preventing women from fully participating in development.
- *Anti-poverty (1970s)*: women's low status and omission from development was due to their income poverty. Consequently, the focus of projects was upon enabling women to enter the workforce and providing them with income-generating opportunities. There was little consideration of patriarchal structures of oppression, especially women's exclusion from the economic and political spheres.
- *The efficiency approach (1980s onwards)*: promoted in the context of structural adjustment, it argued that harnessing the abilities of women was a more effective way of achieving economic development. In turn, this would lead to increased equity between women and men.
- *Empowerment (early 1990s onwards)*: linked to participatory approaches to development, the original focus was on projects devised and run by Southern women. Multiple conceptions of empowerment have emerged, but exponents are united by a desire to seek a significant shift in gender relations.
- *Gender mainstreaming (since 1995)*: this has recently emerged as a strategy to promote gender equality (see p. 112).

(*Source*: Adapted from Momsen 2004; Moser 1993; Richey 2000; Willis 2005)

trickling down to poor families (Momsen 2004: 11). This view changed as part of the broader challenge to modernization theory, but also due to the emergence of 'second wave' feminism and the growing evidence that women were being left behind by the processes of development. Since then, a number of gender and development approaches have emerged, notably Women in Development (WID), Gender and Development (GAD), the empowerment approach, and more recently gender mainstreaming, which is designed to promote gender equality (see Box 4.1 and the third section of this chapter).

The growing interest in gender and development was reflected in the setting up of four UN World Conferences on Women. The first conference was held in Mexico City in 1975 (proclaimed as International Women's Year), addressing the themes of equality, development and peace. It led to the UN declaring 1976–85 the 'Women's Decade', although during this decade the position of women actually deteriorated in terms of access to education, health services and nutrition, as well as increasing workloads (Peet with Hartwick 1999: 164). Following the Mexico City conference, the UN created the United Nations Development Fund for Women (UNIFEM) to target financial aid at the world's poorest women. By 1985, 127 countries had established Ministries for Women or some other form of national machinery to facilitate women's advancement and participation in development (United Nations 1999: 6). These bodies pursued the WID approach (see p. 105), setting up women-centred projects geared to increasing women's incomes that remained apart from mainstream development.

The three other World Conferences on Women were in Copenhagen (1980), Nairobi (1985) and Beijing (1995). The Nairobi conference was notable for the increased presence of southern women and their growing challenge to what was perceived as a northern feminist agenda (ibid.: 165). At Beijing, the Platform for Action (United Nations 1995) was adopted by member governments that established a series of measures designed to achieve women's equality and empowerment, although many states have not subsequently implemented it. Another landmark moment in the relationship between gender and development was the passing in 1973 of the Percy Amendment by the US Congress, which established that a goal of US foreign aid was to improve the status of women in the South by integrating them into development.

However, we are still a long way from achieving gender-equitable development, notably because the state institutions, political systems and legislatures of most countries remain patriarchal or male-dominated. It has led to the exclusion of women from political power, denied them access to important economic resources, and made it difficult to bring about policy change on issues ranging from gender-based violence to wage inequalities. It also helps to explain why, for example, women form approximately 70 per cent of the world's poor and continue to do the lion's share of non-remunerated work. These matters are considered in the next section, although we should also keep in mind the feminist concern about constantly portraying women as victims because it suggests a lack of agency and is the antithesis of self-empowerment.[1]

Women and development

Because it would be impossible to encapsulate the sheer diversity of women's experiences of development, this section simply seeks to identify some of the key issues and debates in relation to this area.[2]

Male bias in the development process?

Numerous writers in the gender and development field point to the marginalization of women from development in areas ranging from the collection of data to the lexicon and concepts associated with development (Evans 1992; Elson 1995a; Kabeer 1994). Diane Elson notes that supposedly neutral terms like 'farmer' and 'worker' are in fact imbued with male bias because 'we soon read of "farmers and their wives" and "workers and their wives", but never of "farmers and their husbands" and "workers and their husbands"' (1995: 9). Likewise the household, which forms the most basic unit of development planning and analysis, is implicitly considered to be headed by a man (see p. 97). In addition, Naila Kabeer (1994) points to the inadequacies of the poverty line as a measuring tool because it provides little insight into the nature of poverty, especially the gender-specific disadvantages that women face.

Feminists maintain that mainstream development economics and economic theory are blind to the gendered nature of societies (Elson 1995a; Folbre 1986; Sen and Grown 1987). For example, because of its claim to be value free or neutral, economic theory and analysis does not take into account the sexual division of labour. It therefore misses the fact that a large proportion of women's work in many parts of the South is unpaid labour, notably in the form of bringing up children and running households. In short, the contribution that women are making to economies is rendered invisible (Elson 1991). As Diane Elson (1995a) notes, this blindness also means that the economic policies do not contain measures to counteract gender inequalities, and as a consequence they serve to perpetuate male bias.

There are also claims that male bias persists within development at an institutional level. The contributors to *Feminisms in Development* (Cornwall, Harrison and Whitehead 2007) identify the various ways in which the arguments of feminist researchers are often depoliticized within development institutions, like bureaucracies, academic institutions, social movements and NGOs as a result of the unequal power relations that exist within them. Similarly, another publication, *Missions and Mandarins: Feminist Engagement with Development Institutions* (Miller and Razavi 1998), examines the various strategies of engagement employed by women working to transform the bureaucratic structures of multilateral institutions, NGOs and state organizations to make them more gender-equitable. This type of research helps to explain why at the Beijing UN Conference on Women in 1995, the 'Woman's Eyes on the Bank' campaign was set up to monitor the impact of the World Bank's policies on women, as well as its attempt to institutionalize gender equity. Women's movements have struggled to influence World Bank policy formulation, due to its organizational and voting mechanisms, the dominance of neo-liberalism and because first and foremost it is an economic institution that has always prioritized its relationship with borrowing countries. Indeed, it was not until 1994 that the World Bank issued a policy paper on gender equity, entitled *Enhancing Women's Involvement in Economic Development* (O'Brien et al. 2000: 42).

Jane Parpart (2007) extends this discussion to consider the 'good governance agenda' promoted by the World Bank and other development agencies, which seeks to improve governance in the South. As Parpart herself notes, in response to the rise in the number of fragile states and high levels of corruption, '[g]overnance has become one of the watchwords of current development discourse' (ibid.: 207). However, she is critical of the governance agenda for neglecting gender and power, and especially for ignoring the relationship between empowerment and national and global structures and discourses. Empowerment, she argues, 'is an empty term if it ignores these factors' (ibid.: 213). Thus, for Parpart, strategies 'to empower women that do not take into account the way women (and men) are situated in an increasingly global economy are bound to fail' (ibid.: 216).

Structural adjustment

For critics, the gender blindness of mainstream development is especially evident with structural adjustment. The programmes, it is argued, have been implemented solely for macro-level economic reasons with insufficient thought given to their impact on the ground. For example, with SAPs insisting upon cuts in the spending of southern governments, the social welfare role has fallen back upon the family, and this has entailed women extending their domestic responsibilities to compensate for the retreating state, particularly in relation to health care (Elson 1991). Pamela Sparr (1994b) points to research indicating that, in countries undergoing structural adjustment, a common pattern emerges whereby: women are more likely than men to become unemployed; working conditions for women deteriorate; and wage differentials between men and women grow.

Structural adjustment aims to encourage export production, but in countries in sub-Saharan Africa, where women dominate agricultural production, it has led to greater workloads for them (O'Brien et al. 2000: 37–8). In many of these societies, women have faced pressure to increase cash-crop production but at the same time are expected to maintain the level of food crops production for their families. During the height of structural adjustment, more women were also looking for waged labour to maintain household incomes and compensate for the reduction in the support provided by the state (Zack-Williams 1995). There is evidence that cumulatively this has had a negative impact upon women's health (Dalla Costa 1995; O'Brien et al. 2000). It has also led to girls' withdrawing from schools to support their mothers, a move that is obviously detrimental to their own careers (Sparr 1994b).

In sum, women have borne the brunt of structural adjustment, and this is despite the fact that at an official level SAPs have been presented as 'gender neutral' by the IFIs (Elson 1995b; Wallace 1991).

Households and families

Feminists maintain that the household is a key arena in which gender relations are shaped and played out. Indeed, Naila Kabeer (1994) contends the household is a primary site for the construction of power relations. For this reason, she is critical of economic models of households within mainstream development theory for ignoring this reality, and in particular for neglecting the nature of gender inequalities within the family unit.

Likewise, for John Friedmann (1992), the double disempowerment of women in both the public and private spheres begins in the household. He argues that 'the overall structure of household relations throughout the world openly discriminates against women and keeps them in a state of permanent subordination vis-à-vis males, both inside the household and in the wider public domain' (ibid.: 109). If this form of social, political and psychological disempowerment is to be tackled, we must seek to build households that can be a source of empowerment for both women and men. In practical terms, for women in disempowered households, this will entail addressing four broad categories: time savings in the completion of household chores; improved health care; acquisition of knowledge, skills and information; expanded income opportunities (ibid.: 116–18). For Friedmann, it is because households are integrated into the wider social relations of production and politics that makes them so important strategically, and it means that the democratization of the household will have wider effects (ibid.: 118–19).

However, as Ann Varley (2002) has noted, households are cultural constructs. This means that the nature of their organization and the functions they perform will reflect the conditions of their respective cultures and societies. We should therefore be wary of making universal statements about the impact of households upon gender relations. Moreover, households are not isolated units but overlap with other households and social groupings like extended families, neighbours and friends. There are also households that simply do not adhere to the nuclear family model, namely those made up of friends and homosexual partners, as well as single-parent family households. Indeed, one-third of the world's households are always female-headed, due to factors like separation, death, conflict and economic migration (Østergaard 1992).

Because it is a sensitive area, governments do not readily seek to intervene in family life. The family is considered to belong to the private realm and, so while government does legislate in this area, there are arguably limits to which the state can redefine gender relations. Indeed, the public–private distinction has had an impact on gender relations in other areas. For example, as Kathleen Staudt (1998) notes, because of the public–private division – with women historically confined to the private sphere – it is only relatively recently that women's rights have become associated with human rights within international law (see also Reilly 2008).

Reproductive choices and population growth

As we saw in the previous chapter, reducing burgeoning population rates within many developing societies is linked to women having greater autonomy in decision-making, something that requires their status being enhanced through greater access to education and being able to pursue careers. If women become significant income generators in their own right, and have access to economic resources, then it is likely to change their role within the family and their respective societies. Of course, the validity of this claim is ultimately dependent upon context. In this regard, McIlwaine (1997) rightly cautions that an enhanced role in the workplace does not necessarily translate into a transformation in gender relations within households. Much depends upon the nature of pre-existing power relations between men and women within households and societies.

Naila Kabeer (1994) notes that, because of their association with mother-hood, women receive a disproportionate amount of attention in population control programmes, and this contrasts with their negligible presence in other areas of development. Development therefore underplays the multiple roles that women perform. Nevertheless, Kabeer recognizes the significance of motherhood in most women's lives. In this regard, she argues that it is impera-tive that population policy is predicated on a respect for women's reproductive health, rights and choices, and this 'cannot be done on the cheap' (ibid.: 221). Indeed, there is continuing concern about the high maternal death rate in developing countries. In 1994, at the International Conference on Population and Development in Cairo, it was estimated that there were some 514,000 maternal deaths a year. A particular problem in this regard is the shortage of skilled health personnel, especially midwives, in poorer countries. In response, the Beijing Declaration that emerged from the UN-sponsored Fourth World Conference on Women stated that: 'The explicit recognition and reaffirmation of the right of all women to control all aspects of their health, in particular their own fertility, is basic to their empowerment' (United Nations 1995: 3).

Access to education and training

As a result of factors like girls in Africa and Asia being more likely to leave school at an earlier age than boys, prior to the implementation of the UNMDGs, 565 million women were illiterate in 1995. Two-thirds of all illiter-ate people are therefore female (UNESCO 1995: 11). In some societies, girls are discouraged from continuing their education or simply withdrawn from schools by their parents in order that they contribute to the household either by performing domestic tasks or by earning an income. For these reasons, UNMDG Goal 3 seeks to eliminate gender disparity at all levels of education by no later than 2015 (Box 4.2).

Nonetheless, we should not overlook the progress that has been made in relation to education. For instance, the adult literacy and school enrolment disparities between men and women were halved between 1970 and 1990 (Hodder 2000: 54). Although as Kathleen Staudt (1998) has observed, even when girls have equal access to education, their educational experiences are often different from those of boys, both in terms of the course content they receive and how they are expected to perform in the classroom.

Employment

Worldwide, the number of women in paid employment rose from 54 per cent in the mid-1950s to just under 70 per cent in 2000 (Rai 2002: 7). Nevertheless,

> ### Box 4.2 MDGs Goal 3: Promote gender equality and empower women
>
> *Target*: Eliminate gender disparity in primary and secondary education, preferably by 2005, and in all levels of education no later than 2015.
>
> This goal aims to reduce the gap between men and women in education and employment. In a number of developing countries women receive little formal education, and this diminishes their economic potential. Invariably, they can only secure temporary, poorly paid or informal work, and this in turn erodes their social status. Indeed, poor, uneducated women are often disenfranchised at every level – from the household to government. Female participation in national assemblies has slowly increased since 1990, but in 2004 women still only occupied 16 per cent of seats worldwide.
>
> (*Source*: UNMDG 2005)

according to the International Labour Organization, women on average earn approximately two-thirds of men's earnings (ILO 2003). Within many developing countries, in addition to the labour that they undertake within the household, women play a key role within agricultural production, particularly in relation to the provision of domestic food supplies. It has been estimated that women provide 60–80 per cent of agricultural labour in Africa and Asia, while in Latin America the figure is approximately 40 per cent (Hodder 2000: 76). Indeed, approximately 70 per cent of the food of tropical Africa is produced by women (Potter et al. 2004: 199).

However, it is in manufacturing that the most profound changes have taken place for women in the recent period, especially within the developing world. This development is part of a wider change to the international division of labour that has been underway since the 1960s, whereby manufacturing is increasingly located in developing societies (chapter 10). MNCs have been at the forefront of this process, relocating and shifting investment from the North to the South, and to South-East Asia and Latin America in particular where labour costs are cheaper. It has led to a significant expansion of employment in the South in this area, and these jobs have been taken up in large numbers by women. Indeed, recent global labour market changes have been described as the 'feminization of labour' (Standing 1989). This term describes the growth in the number of women in paid employment but also reflects the nature and type of work that is being generated, with a strong emphasis upon 'flexibility'. In other words, the work is often temporary, part-time and in the service sector, which women have tended to undertake more than men, combining these jobs with rearing children and their household labour.

There is a view that these developments have led to women earning higher incomes and this is helping to enhance their social status (Lim 1990a). For instance, Linda Lim (1983, 1990a) has observed that wage levels and working conditions in MNCs operating in the South often compare favourably to those offered by local employers, and this has been ignored by gender analyses informed by Marxism and socialism because it does not comply with their ideological approach. In contrast, Ruth Pearson (1998) notes that the increased employment of women has been in export-oriented manufacturing (especially electronics and clothing) – work that is generally undertaken by younger women who are poorly paid. Likewise, the expansion of the low-pay end of the service sector has been a major source of the increase in female employment, as has the informal sector (United Nations 1999). In addition, MNCs are accused of pursuing exploitative practices, with some paying considerably less in wages to southern women workers than to their northern counterparts (Visvanathan et al. 1997). Most importantly, there is little evidence that the greater number of hours women are spending in paid employment is leading to a concomitant reduction in their share of domestic labour. However, Lim (1990b) also emphasizes the social and political opportunities that industrial sector employment provides women in Asia, especially in comparison with their rural counterparts, highlighting examples of labour organization among women workers in multinational export factories.

Of course, what is actually taking place with regard to the nature of women's involvement in industrializing processes will vary from country to country and will be dependent upon their particular backgrounds and status, which dictates the need for contextual analyses. For instance, while globally the growth of the female labour force has been higher than that of men since the 1980s, this does not apply to Africa.

Participatory development

Participatory approaches are often promoted as a better way of incorporating women's perspectives into development. The locally oriented and non-hierarchical way in which NGOs generally operate is considered by their advocates to make them more responsive to women's needs and less susceptible to male bias in comparison with other more centralized and bureaucratic development agencies (Miller and Razavi 1998: 16).

However, Irene Guijt and Meera Kaul Shah (1998b) identify what they term 'gender naivety' within participatory development. They point to the absence of links between participatory development and gender studies, and the lack of gender sensitivity on the part of exponents of the former. For example, the presence of women at community gatherings has often been taken as evidence of inclusivity, a perspective that ignores the dynamics of gender relations within particular societies (ibid.: 3). Furthermore, there are occasional instances of participatory development organizations incorporating gender issues simply in order to secure resources (ibid.: 5–6).

In the case of NGOs, given the sheer size and diversity of the NGO sector, there are inevitably examples of good and bad practice with regard to this area. Indeed, some NGOs have been accused of believing their own rhetoric in relation to gender, and as a result 'their own practices – both within their organizations and their development work – fall far short of achieving real changes in the status and condition of women' (Lewis and Wallace 2000: xii). Indeed, the persistence of particularly masculine cultures or environments has been detected within some NGOs (Mayoux 1998). Of course, the validity of such claims is dependent upon context and the particular NGO concerned. Moreover, some commentators emphasize the positive role that NGOs are performing in relation to gender and development, such as monitoring the implementation of gender-equitable policies (Staudt 2008). There are also a large number of women's NGOs that address matters like the provision of health care, access to credit and community support for women.

Women, conflict and security

As we will see in the next chapter, conflict and security has become increasingly prominent within development. Feminists tend to have a broader conception of security than that emphasized in conventional accounts which tend to place great stress on national security, especially in relation to the international state system. According to J. Ann Tickner (2001, 2008), security from a feminist perspective stems from a reduction in violence, whether physical, ecological, economic, or some other form. Security therefore matters from the bottom-up, rather than the top-down (2008: 270). Undoubtedly, this viewpoint is motivated by the fact that women's experience of war and conflict is often different from that of men. In particular, in nearly all conflicts there are instances of women facing systematic rape, notably during the Bosnian war and Rwandan genocide in the first half of the 1990s. Likewise, when men go off to fight in conflicts, women will assume the role of head of households.

However, academics working in the field of international relations have been criticized for not properly factoring into their analyses the different experiences of conflict for men and women (e.g., Reimann 2002). Some writers also emphasize the extent of gender blindness in humanitarian work, ranging from male bias in the provision of humanitarian aid (Clifton and Gell 2001) to denying women the opportunity to exercise their potential as peace builders (Sweetman 2001). They argue that humanitarian work will be more effective if a gender-sensitive approach is employed.

Women and globalization

The issue of how globalization is impacting upon women's lives tends to polarize opinion. The optimistic view is that women are playing central roles in the formation of a global economy reflected in the worldwide rise in female labour-force participation. It is argued that the greater economic competition introduced by globalization means that employers cannot afford to discriminate and will offer jobs to those best able to perform them, irrespective of their sex (United Nations 1999: 91). However, pessimists point to the growing differentiation and inequality among women which stems from the fact that some countries and regions are actively participating in the globalization of production – defined by the increased flows of commodities, capital and information – while others are not. Thus, East Asian women have generally enjoyed higher incomes as a result of the economic prosperity enjoyed by their globally oriented countries, while the employment prospects and incomes of many women in Africa have arguably suffered because certain regions of the continent are on the margins of globalization.

There are other aspects of globalization that are potentially more positive for women. Worldwide, growing numbers of women are taking advantage of ICTs and forming global and transnational networks in order to exchange ideas and information, provide mutual support and promote their particular agendas and causes (e.g., see WOMANKIND Worldwide listed on p. 115). Similarly, increased female migration is bringing more and more women into contact with different cultures and ideas, and in time this may lead some to question the nature of gender relations within their own societies. Furthermore, those women that are able to send back remittances to family members are likely to earn their appreciation and increased respect, and this may have implications for their future status (Kanji, Tan and Toulmin 2007: xiv). Of course, the gender implications of these developments are dependent upon context. Indeed, to better understand women's experiences of globalization, and to avoid making generalizations about it, we need to undertake contextual analyses, exploring how women armed with their own local discourses engage with and contribute to globalizing processes (Davids and van Driel 2001; Hopper 2006, 2007).

Gender awareness within development

There is recent evidence of growing gender awareness within development, especially in relation to enhancing the position of women. For example, microcredit schemes have given women greater access to loans and finance (see Conclusion to this book). In addition, participatory development approaches are increasingly gender-sensitive and conduct 'gender needs assessments'. Thus, aware of the cultural and familial obstacles that many southern women face in attending meetings, exponents of a Participatory Rural Appraisal (PRA) seek to offset this disadvantage so that they remain fully part of the process (see Chambers 2005: 117; Guijt and Shah 1998a). Nevertheless, as Janet Hunt (2004) has noted, it is not always easy to arrange separate opportunities for women to participate, especially in those societies where women are always accompanied by male relatives.

The measurement of development has also become gender-sensitive. In 1995, the UNDP introduced the Gender Development Index (GDI) and the Gender Empowerment Measure (GEM) (UNDP 1995). The GDI is able to calculate male and female HDIs in terms of the number of years of schooling, employment levels, wage rates, adult literacy and life expectancy (UNDP

Box 4.3 MDGs Goal 5: Improve maternal health

Targets: (1) Reduce by three quarters, between 1990 and 2015, the maternal mortality rate; (2) Achieve, by 2015, universal access to reproductive health.

- Childbirth and pregnancy remain leading causes of disability and death for women in developing countries, while children whose mothers die during childbirth are more likely to suffer poverty and exploitation.
- One of the indicators to measure progress in achieving the first target is an increase in the proportion of births attended by skilled staff.
- For target 2, the intention is to provide reproductive health care to the estimated 200 million women worldwide who have no access to safe contraception.

(*Source*: UNMDG 2005)

Box 4.4 The Millennium Development Goals Report 2008

In this report, the UN reviewed the progress that had been made towards achieving the MDGs. On a positive note, it found the gender parity index in primary education was 95 per cent or higher in six out of ten regions, including the most populous ones. However, the report also identified a number of problem areas in relation to gender:

- Of the 113 countries that failed to achieve gender parity in both primary and secondary school enrolment by the target date of 2005, only 18 are likely to achieve the goal by 2015.
- Almost two-thirds of employed women in the developing world are in vulnerable jobs as own-account or unpaid family workers.
- In one third of developing countries, women account for less than 10 per cent of parliamentarians.
- More than 500,000 prospective mothers in developing countries were still dying annually in childbirth or of complications from pregnancy. The maternal mortality rate (MMR) was especially high in sub-Saharan Africa and Southern Asia. While some countries have recorded an improvement, the UN warned that future reductions in maternal death rates is dependent on the provision of increased resources and trained medical staff in developing countries.

(*Source*: UNMDG 2008)

1998). More recently, the UNDP's latest innovation in measuring inequality – the Gender Inequality Index (GII) – has revealed that women in both developed and developing countries still fall behind men on nearly all measures except life expectancy (UNDP 2010).

Furthermore, the greater the gender disparity in human development, the lower will be a country's GDI relative to its HDI. On this basis, the GDI ranking of Muslim countries like Saudi Arabia and Iran falls short of their HDI ranking by some 20 points (Hodder 2000: 54). As for the GEM, it measures women's achievements in the economic and political spheres in terms of their political participation and decision-making, their economic participation and decision-making, and their power over economic resources (UNDP 1995).

At an institutional level, gender equity and the empowerment of women is Goal 3 of the MDGs (Box 4.2), and improving maternal health is Millennium Development Goal 5 (Box 4.3). However, to date, the international community has only made halting progress towards achieving these goals (see Box 4.4).

Moreover, Pearson (2005) notes that gender goals have often been employed instrumentally within development as a means of attaining other objectives – such as limiting population growth through enhancing women's autonomy and status – rather than as desirable ends in their own right.

Gender and development: critical debates

This section will explore in more detail the different gender and development approaches, focusing upon the critical debates surrounding them. However, it should be borne in mind that – depending upon the particular issue under discussion – the boundaries between the different approaches are often more blurred than presented here.

Women in Development (WID)

WID emerged in the 1970s motivated by a strong sense that women were being excluded from many aspects of development (Tinker 1990). WID writers complained that development planners continued to see women's primary role as housewives rather than as earners, and implicitly assumed that their lives would be improved by more money going into households (Young 2002). In order for women to be integrated into development, WID focused upon strengthening women's position within the labour force and the market economy. In practical terms, this required women having equal access to educational opportunities and credit services, for example.

To achieve their goals, WID advocates sought to increase women's representation within development institutions, a move that was also designed to facilitate greater access to funding and participation in development programmes. Much activity was also spent on projects designed to increase women's earnings, although with mixed success as southern women had little available time to undertake them (Momsen 2004: 13). Reflecting the times, WID campaigners initially found it more productive to couch their cause in the language of alleviating poverty, especially within the household, rather than achieving gender equality (Young 2002: 322).

Within WID, concern was also expressed about the processes of modernization. In her influential book, *Woman's Role in Economic Development* (1970), Danish economist Ester Boserup (1910–1999) argued that modernization affected men and women differently, with the latter increasingly marginalized as countries industrialized and urbanized. For Boserup, women's association with domestic labour and childcare led to new technologies, and associated training and education, becoming the preserve of men. In contrast, within agricultural societies, it was easier for women to combine housework and working on the land (Willis 2005: 128). She envisaged women losing their jobs with the decline of agricultural production and also as larger industries drove domestic industries out of business.

> ### Box 4.5 Criticisms of WID
>
> The broad charge raised against WID is that it could never offer women true empower-ment (Jahan 1995). More specific criticisms of WID include the following:
>
> - The WID acceptance of the market economy neglects the fact that it exacerbates gender inequalities by enabling men to gain job advancement and increased resources.
> - Southern writers criticize WID for underestimating the value of indigenous knowledge and expertise of local women (Marchand and Parpart 1995).
> - The WID focus upon women-only projects, many of which were unable to generate significant income or funding, arguably continued the marginalization of women from mainstream development.
> - WID underestimated the significance of reproduction for women as a result of prioritizing women's participation in the market economy.
> - WID failed to address the nature of relations within households, especially in terms of altering the burden of household tasks
>
> (Peet and Hartwick 1999).

For Boserup and other WID writers, women were capable of playing a much greater role within industry and development generally, and this would in turn increase economic growth within countries. It was therefore more efficient to involve women in development and to harness their capabili-ties, and from the 1980s the WID approach increasingly made its appeal to development planners on these grounds (Moser 1993). In short, women were portrayed as an 'untapped resource' (Moser 1993: 2).

WID emerged out of the liberal feminist tradition, with the term being first articulated by liberal feminists in the USA. It was argued that securing the rights of women would provide them with greater autonomy to participate more fully in the market economy as wage earners. WID therefore did not campaign for the overthrow of existing social structures; rather it sought the more complete integration of women into the existing economic and politi-cal system, and in some cases this took the form of legislative campaigns. For this reason, WID found support from both governments and international development organizations and is still prevalent among women politicians and bureaucrats who are involved with development and aid issues (Schech and Haggis 2000: 90). However, WID has attracted criticism from a variety of sources (see Box 4.5).

Women and Development (WAD)

The WAD position that emerged in the late 1970s was led by southern, Marxist and dependency feminists who maintained that the WID approach ignored both the real source of women's oppression – global capitalism – and the need to change existing power structures. Women were being used in a variety of ways to perpetuate this system, including raising children to become the next generation of workers and providing unpaid labour within households to ensure that their male partners were ready for work each day. Capitalism was

Box 4.6 Development Alternatives with Women for a New Era (DAWN)

The DAWN network emerged from the WAD tradition, although its research has contributed to GAD especially in relation to championing the empowerment of women.

Founded in Bangladore, India, in 1984, DAWN was geared to publicizing the views of developing countries, and in particular 'Third World' women's perspectives. As Gita Sen and Caren Grown, two leading figures within DAWN, put it: '[w]hile gender subordination has universal elements, feminism cannot be based on a rigid concept of universality that negates the wide variation in women's experience' (1987: 18). This led them to call for 'a diversity of feminisms, responsive to the different needs and concerns of different women, and *defined by them for themselves*' (ibid.: 18–19). More broadly, the DAWN network committed itself to 'developing alternative frameworks and methods to attain the goals of economic and social justice, peace, and development free of all forms of oppression by gender, class, race, and nation' (ibid.: 9).

DAWN maintained that meeting everyday survival needs in the form of sufficient income and food was a more pressing matter for Southern women than the gender equality agenda pushed by the western feminist movement (ibid.: 24–5).

However, the extent to which DAWN represents an alternative to conventional development theory and practice has been questioned. Indeed, Sen and Grown have themselves been accused of pursuing a Northern feminist agenda and not listening to Southern women's voices because of their undifferentiated category of women and claims about the universal way that the sexual division of labour operates (e.g., Hirshman 1995).

also dependent upon the exploitation of women who functioned as a cheap source of labour, frequently working in worse conditions and for lower pay than men (Mies 1986). The justification for this disparity was that women's work and earnings were seen as merely supplementary to that of the male breadwinner.

Because of its emphasis upon addressing these structural constraints, there was a strong international dimension to WAD and it is often associated with dependency theory. From this perspective, there was no need – in the manner of WID – to seek the integration of women into the development process as they have always been part of it, as had men; rather, it was the process that was the problem (Pearson 2000: 390). Both sexes were drawn into roles and forms of behaviour that help to sustain existing patterns of global inequality, and therefore the models of development must be transformed (Sen and Grown 1987).

Another recurring theme within WAD is the diverse nature of women's experiences. For WAD writers and activists, mainstream development failed to recognize the extent of this diversity and in particular marginalized the perspective of women from developing societies (Box 4.6). Interestingly, within this approach different perspectives emerged between northern and southern women on development, most notably at the 1975 UN Woman's World Conference in Mexico City. For example, broadly speaking, northern women placed greater emphasis upon achieving gender equality than their southern counterparts. From the perspective of many women living in the Global South, this issue had to be weighed against everyday demands of material survival, a reality that necessitated prioritizing practical matters like access to clean drinking water and having adequate shelter (Sen and Grown 1987; Young 2002).

Critics of WAD argued that it ignored the particular challenges facing women and the nature of gender inequality. WAD was overly focused upon economic production, and consequently neglected the importance of biological reproduction to women's lives (Kabeer 1994). It offered women little practicable support because, rather than pursuing practicable reforms, some accounts insisted that their plight would only be improved by overthrowing international capitalism. But even if this goal were to be achieved, it would not necessarily lead to the transformation of men (Rathgeber 1990). In short, critics argue, WAD underplays the significance of gender relations.

Gender and Development (GAD)

Feminist criticism of WID also paved the way for the emergence of GAD in the 1980s, with the latter increasingly supplanting the former in the policies and programmes of national and international agencies (Østergaard 1992). GAD seeks to address all aspects of women's lives, including in the areas of health and reproduction, education, sexuality, production or labour and the household. At the same time, its focus upon gender constitutes an acknowledgement that the position of women cannot be considered in isolation from that of men (Moser 1993: 2).

GAD originated in the mid-1970s and specifically in work undertaken at the Institute of Development Studies (IDS) in the UK. Initially the intellectual roots of GAD lie in socialist and radical feminism, and this was reflected in the desire to challenge the market economy as well as the economic growth model of development and the institutions that sustained it. Rather than relying upon the market economy, GAD writers believe that women should organize and seek support from their own self-help organizations and local communities.

GAD embodies a diverse range of opinion, but a unifying theme is a belief that WID ignored the damaging impact that inequitable gender relations were having upon women's lives. Thus, WID was accused of neglecting issues like unequal property rights and inheritance laws, domestic violence, family planning and men's abandonment of their children (Edelman and Haugerud 2005: 28). Furthermore, because male superiority was a global phenomenon, discrimination was not confined to southern women, but also experienced by women in the West, notably in the form of unequal labour markets and promotion prospects, as well as the absence of women from positions of authority (see Young, Wokowitz, and McCullagh 1984). For these reasons, advocates of GAD sought to change the power relations between men and women, especially the sexual division of labour, and expected the state to perform a key role in bringing this about.

Rather than simply focusing upon meeting women's practical needs, GAD exponents have pursued a broader analysis of gender within development. This theme has been pushed by Caroline Moser (1993) who distinguishes between women's practical and strategic needs. The former were geared to enhancing women's lives within their existing roles – such as the provision of adequate health facilities to support their role in reproductive activities – while the latter seek to empower women by enhancing their ability to take on new roles through measures such as legal reform to remove gender discrimination (Hunt 2004).[3]

The GAD agenda is a broad one that tackles issues such as patriarchy, racism and capitalism. For example, Kate Young (1993) highlights the need to view gender as part of a wider international system, which includes other forms of social inequality and hierarchies, and it therefore requires taking a holistic approach. She states: '[i]t is therefore necessary to analyze how these other forces (political, religious, racial and economic), intersect with and dynamize gender relations' (ibid.: 187). Hence GAD focuses on the interrelationship between the family, household and the economic and political spheres (Young 1997: 52). For GAD advocates, their approach addresses the complex range of challenges facing women, and southern women in particular, and therefore provides them with a more productive route to achieving emancipation.

Finally, some GAD writers have also criticized the WID approach for encouraging the homogenization of women. In other words, WID underplays the extent of the differences that exist among women, due to factors like religion, age, class or social status, race or ethnicity (Young 2002). Likewise, GAD also challenges the homogenization of households within development, emphasizing both their internal complexity and the unequal nature of gender relations within them (Kabeer 1994). To reflect the diversity of people's circumstances, GAD emphasizes the pluralistic nature of gender relations, including acknowledging that women and men often have the same agendas for achieving basic improvements in their lives.

Women, Environment and Development (WED)

In the 1970s, a number of environmentally aware women writers challenged the dominant model of development, and in particular what they saw as the gendered (masculine) knowledge that underpins it. Broadly speaking, the WED approach equates men's domination of women with their control over nature. From this perspective, industrialization and science have been shaped by masculine values since the Enlightenment and have been guilty of excluding spiritual and holistic thinking. It has led to the pursuit of economic development that has effectively constituted a war against the earth's ecosystems, which are usually portrayed as female by eco-feminists.

LLYFRGELL COLEG MENAI LIBRARY

In *Staying Alive: Women, Ecology and Development* (1989), Vandana Shiva seeks to connect women and the environment by focusing upon their characteristics or traits, their nurturing and caring capacities, and their ability to manage limited food supplies. Writers like Shiva therefore discount gender formation, and identify an organic link between women and nature. Indeed, eco-feminists make the case for local knowledge systems to play a more prominent role within development, and this must include local women's voices being heard. It also follows, they argue, that, if such a linkage exists, it makes sense for environmental programmes to be geared towards women. As Ruth Pearson (2000) notes, in policy terms there are similarities between eco-feminists and WED, with both calling for the prioritization of women within development projects that are related to environmental conservation.

However, critics have questioned the link between women and the environment, viewing it as an essentialist reading of women's biological make-up and their relationship with nature (Agarwal 1997b). Socialist feminists are particularly uneasy about biological claims made in relation to women because potentially this can be used to limit their roles and influence within society (Rocheleau, Thomas-Slayter and Wangari 1996). Others consider the WED emphasis upon women's rural connectedness presents an outdated almost romanticized conception of their lives especially as they increasingly live in urban areas. The WED approach is also charged with ignoring and excluding environmentally sensitive men who may have much to bring to this debate.

Postcolonial perspectives on development

As with the other approaches examined here, there are a variety of postcolonial perspectives on development. However, Chandra Talpade Mohanty has written an influential article entitled 'Under Western Eyes: Feminist Scholarship and Colonial Discourses' (1991) in which she contends that feminist development writings have served to stereotype women of the Global South as tradition-bound and constrained by patriarchal cultures. In particular, 'Third World women' are portrayed as being in a condition from which they must 'escape' and this entails becoming more like liberated women of the West. Such a perspective, Mohanty argues, simply serves to deny the value and legitimacy of women's roles and experiences within the developing world (Schech and Haggis 2002: xviii).[4]

Mohanty's thesis reflects a tension that occasionally surfaces between women of the Global South and Global North. Indeed, southern women have accused northern feminists working in development of pursuing a western liberal rights-based agenda that ignores their respective cultural, racial and class differences (see also Peake and Alissa Trotz 2002). Similarly, Haleh Afshar (1996) is critical of western feminisms for negating 'Third World women's choices of paths of political activism which used the local prevalent ideologies and were often located within religious or maternal discourses' (1996: 1).

Indeed, some southern critics are suspicious of the universalization of gender within development, viewing it as yet another way in which the North is imposing its agenda upon the South (Pearson 2000: 385).

However, many women writers are exploring ways of overcoming these divisions. For example, Ann Ferguson (1998) has stressed the need to build, as she puts it, 'bridge identities'. Ruth Pearson notes that within feminist theory there has been increasing recognition of the complex and multiple identities and interests of women, due to factors like, ethnicity, class, sexuality, religion and culture. The emphasis is now upon *feminisms*, which challenges the 1970s' feminist notion of a universal sisterhood but also means that gender cannot be employed as a universal reference point for analysis (2000: 383). In addition, there is greater awareness that different countries and regions have their own understandings of gender difference and gender roles (ibid.: 385). In turn, this postmodern recognition of diversity and complexity has come to inform gender and development, challenging the notion that women are a homogenous group and allowing space for southern women's voices (see also Lazreg 1988). However, Uma Kothari observes that feminist and postcolonial scholarship does not yet properly inform development, and this may in part be due to the fact that those working in the field see themselves primarily as a practitioners rather than theorists (2002: 51).

Likewise, Jane Parpart stresses the importance of getting planners to investigate and properly incorporate the perspectives of local women into the development process. She advocates a postmodern feminism that 'recognizes the connection between knowledge, language and power, and seeks to understand local knowledge(s), both as sites of resistance and power' (1995: 264). At the same time, Parpart acknowledges the emphasis on difference must be accompanied by the formation of national, regional and global solidarities among women over issues of mutual concern in order to avoid 'dissolving into relativity and political paralysis' (ibid.: 265). For Uma Narayan, an insistence upon cultural difference can lead to 'culture-specific essentialist generalisations that depend on totalising categories', resulting in portrayals of 'western women' and 'Third World women' as separate groups with effectively antithetical cultures (Narayan 1998: 87–8). Furthermore, if cultural hybridity theorists are correct, and cultures are not discrete and stable but are made up of numerous influences and evolve over time, then this offers the basis for dialogue (Nederveen Pieterse 2004).

The empowerment approach

Towards the end of the 1980s, the concept of empowerment gained increasing acceptance within gender and development circles. Linked to the rise of participatory approaches to development, empowerment was taken up by development agencies ranging from NGOs to the World Bank (Young 2002). However, there are multiple understandings of empowerment. It ranges from writers who see it as a form of self-actualization whereby the individual undergoes a transformation from within to the view held by some development institutions that empowerment is simply more productive for societies (Parpart 2002). It is therefore difficult to determine and monitor empowerment. Furthermore, empowerment takes place within the context of evolving and complex gender-differentiated societies 'where women's life experiences may differ widely' (Rowlands 1997: 141).

Jo Rowlands (1997) believes the various ways in which empowerment is defined diminish 'the value of the concept as a tool for analysis or as part of a strategy for change' (ibid.: 8). Moreover, based upon the research evidence provided by two development projects in Honduras, she questions whether genuine empowerment is possible for women without major changes in social attitudes. For Rowlands, empowerment must be seen as a process whereby women and men gain self-confidence so that they are able to participate in all aspects of development, including decision-making (Momsen 2004: 14). The notion that empowerment is both a process and an outcome is also recognized by Parpart, Rai and Staudt (2002), who argue for a feminist interpretation of empowerment, one which recognizes that local empowerment is always embedded in regional, national, as well as global contexts.

Mainstreaming gender equality

In 1995, gender mainstreaming was officially adopted as a worldwide strategy by the UN at its Fourth World Conference on Women in Beijing, and it has subsequently been adopted by intergovernmental organizations like the EU, as well as some national governments and private development institutions. Rather than focusing upon specialized projects for women, gender mainstreaming entails transforming existing policy agendas by integrating a gender perspective into all policies and programmes (Karam 2000; Pearson 2000). To achieve gender equality, the perspectives and experiences of women and men are incorporated into policy design, and participating organizations evaluate the gendered effects of their policies in order to ensure equitable outcomes as well as monitor their own organizational practices and procedures (Tickner 2008).

However, Ruth Pearson (2005) detects a recent tendency for development agencies to withdraw resources and staff from gender equality programmes because it is widely believed that gender has been successfully mainstreamed. More broadly, Elizabeth Prügl and Audrey Lustgarten (2006) question the impact of gender mainstreaming, especially with regard to the extent to which it has diminished gender inequalities within development. They maintain that, while international organizations have incorporated gender mainstreaming, it has been on their terms. As a result, gender mainstreaming has become a public relations and technocratic management process or exercise, one that is not geared to attaining social transformation. Indeed, feminists are concerned that gender mainstreaming has simply become a way of preserving existing development institutions, with some remaining deeply gendered and only paying lip-service to the importance of gender issues (Pearson 2000: 384).

Gender and development: future trajectories

This chapter will conclude by taking stock of where we are now in relation to gender and development (see also Momsen 2004: ch. 9). It will also indicate some of the issues and debates that are likely to become increasingly prominent in the future.

Where are we today?

Even though the field of gender issues in development has expanded, and there have been significant advances in relation to these areas, there remains much work to be done. For example, gender analysis is now built into the programmes of international development institutions and agencies, yet men continue to dominate the positions of power within these bodies (Goetz 1997; Staudt 1998). Likewise, more and more women are participating in the global economy, but in manufacturing (especially in the electronics, textile and garment industries) many are doing so as poorly paid, in some cases home-based, workers, with little or no employment protection (Athreya 2002). Furthermore, gender inequality is especially persistent within households (see Agarwal 1997a). Women's dual role as earners and as unpaid mothers, and the enormous burden this places upon them, has yet to be addressed in any meaningful sense. Having gained wider acceptance of their role as participators in the market economy, this cannot disguise the fact that for many women it has increased their workload.

For the preceding reasons, there continues to be debate over the nature of feminist engagement with development, especially with regard to the amount of influence that feminists have been able to exert upon development theory and practice (see Cornwall, Harrison and Whitehead 2007). For instance, to what extent has feminist criticism redefined the modernist paradigm of development with its preoccupation with economic growth? Have feminist writers provided us with an alternative to development? In truth, the different approaches within gender and development are not questioning the validity of development per se – and this is despite the eco-feminist stance about its harmful environmental impact – merely the means of achieving it and the form it should take. Such issues form part of a broader concern that gender has been drawn into development merely to legitimate it, and in the process feminist objectives have been diluted or lost. As mentioned above, some feminists feel that gender and development has become a technical enterprise rather than a project designed to change power relations and achieve gender transformation (Cornwall, Harrison and Whitehead 2007: 9). In addition, because it is now widely assumed that gender is fully incorporated into development policy, some writers detect 'gender fatigue' within development (Jaquette and Summerfield 2006; Molyneux 2007).

Within gender and development, many of the areas and issues that will require greater attention in the future are linked to globalization. Jane S. Jaquette and Gale Summerfield (2006) stress the importance of implementing policies that ensure women are able to compete in market economies in an increasingly interconnected world. However, as we will see in chapter 10, the processes of globalization are arguably diminishing the capacity of states to protect and provide for their respective citizens. Indeed, both states and international institutions are struggling to deal with the darker side of globalization, notably the various forms of trafficking in women, the regionalization of conflict, increasing insecurity and more complex patterns of poverty and inequality.

Mainstreaming men into gender and development

The changes taking place in gender relations in different parts of the world has raised the issue of whether men should be more fully incorporated into gender and development (see Chant and Gutmann 2000, 2005). A rising female workforce, coupled with unskilled and semi-skilled men facing declining employment prospects, is unsettling gender roles and identities. Similarly, there is growing evidence of boys and young men falling behind their female counterparts in rates of educational attainment (2000: 1). It has stimulated debates about 'troubled masculinities', with some men said to be suffering from low self-esteem as they lose their traditional roles and status within households and the workplace (Safa 1995; Silberschmidt 2001).

However, Chant and Gutmann (2005) note that irrespective of these changes, GAD programmes remain within the WID tradition whereby programmes are essentially designed by and for women. Furthermore, 'without men, gender interventions can only go so far' (ibid.: 241). In other words, moving beyond patriarchal structures and practices will require the efforts of both women and men. Indeed, to exclude men from GAD projects may lead some to oppose measures designed to enhance women's economic and social status, especially among those men that feel they are falling behind. In addition, the diminution of their role and status may lead some men to assume even less responsibilities within households, thereby adding to the workloads of women (Chant 2000). And there are other areas that will be more effectively addressed through the involvement of both men and women, notably domestic violence and the spread of HIV/AIDS.

However, the incorporation of men into gender and development has not been universally welcomed. This is because women have yet to achieve equality with men within the processes of development (Cornwall and White 2000). There are also fears that women's concerns will be marginalized within gender and development as men become more heavily involved. Nonetheless, within gender and development studies there is now a growing body of research on men, masculinity and development (e.g., Greig, Kimmel and Lang 2000). And Andrea Cornwall's contention that we need to acknowledge the complexity of gender and development and of our everyday experiences as women and men, perhaps offers us a way forward:

> It is time to move beyond the old fixed ideas about gender roles and about universal male domination. Time to find ways of thinking about and analysing gender that makes sense of the complexities of people's lived realities . . . Taking complexity seriously does not mean that we need to abandon completely fundamental feminist concerns with women's rights. (Cornwall 1997: 12)

Summary

- Gender only really began to be addressed seriously within development from the late 1960s onwards. From the outset, the focus was upon tackling the forms of exclusion and discrimination suffered by women.
- Gender issues and analysis are now an established part of development thinking and practice.
- Broadly speaking, certain differences persist between women of the North and the South over what constitutes the advancement of women within development.
- There are growing calls for men to be more fully incorporated into gender and development.

RECOMMENDED READING

- Janet Hensall Momsen's *Gender and Development* (2004) is an accessible text that covers the key issues and debates surrounding gender and development.
- On mainstreaming women into all aspects of development, see Rounaq Jahan, *The Elusive Agenda: Mainstreaming Women in Development* (1995).
- For analysis of the role of men within Gender and Development, see Sylvia Chant and Matthew Gutmann, *Mainstreaming Men into Gender and Development* (2000).

WEBSITES

- www.ids.ac.uk/bridge: For access to the BRIDGE *Gender and Participation: Cutting Edge Pack* (2001), a very useful source on participation and gender.
- www.un.org/womenwatch: Monitors women's advancement and empowerment.
- www.womankind.org.uk: Website of WOMANKIND Worldwide, a UK-based women's development charity that focuses on women's legal and human rights. It provides access to research and policy analyses on a range of gender issues.

CHAPTER 5

Conflict, Security and Development

- The merging of development and security
- Fragile and failing states
- Human security
- Peacekeeping
- Post-conflict development
- The reform of the United Nations system

There has been increasing acceptance within development circles that security and development are inextricably linked, and this is reflected in the emergence of the concept of human security (e.g., McGrew and Poku 2007; Picciotto and Weaving 2006; Shaw 2002; C. Thomas 2000). As will be shown, underlying this shift of emphasis is the fact that the majority of conflicts since the early 1990s have been in the South. In turn, this has contributed to an increase in the number of fragile states in the region, a phenomenon that has served to undermine development in a variety of ways. Consideration will also be given to the effectiveness of existing international mechanisms for conflict resolution and management, notably the role of the UN, as well as wider debates about the nature of humanitarian intervention.

The merging of development and security

As will now be shown, for a number of reasons development and security have become more interconnected in the recent period. First, however, the wider geopolitical context in which this transformation has taken place needs to be noted. For Beall, Goodfellow and Putzel (2006), while the incorporation of security concerns into development is not new and was evident in the Cold War era, it has been given additional momentum with the US-led 'War on Terror', particularly at a discursive level in the North. In short, development has come to be viewed as a means of tackling perceived threats from the South. Indeed, Beall and her co-writers contend that this move has not only contributed to a shift of approach towards development on the part of Washington, but its influence can also be seen in the operations of some multilateral development organizations and bilateral donors (see *Reality of Aid 2006 Report* discussed on p. 120 and in chapter 8 in this book).

An increase in the number of fragile states

According to the World Bank, the number of fragile states rose from 17 in 2003 to 26 in 2006, and this is part of a trend that can be traced back to at least the early 1990s (BBC 2006a). Explanations for this phenomenon are examined below, but such has been the extent of the turmoil within some states that concern has been expressed about their ability to contain post-Cold War conflicts and protect their citizens from human rights violations (Horsman and Marshall 1995). Fragile states include such countries as Afghanistan, the Central African Republic, Haiti and Angola, and it is estimated that roughly 500 million people live in these states, with up to half of them living in extreme poverty (BBC 2006a). Indeed, according to the UN, a third of the people living in poverty in the world reside in conflict-affected states (Reality of Aid 2006). Failing states also provide safe havens for terrorist networks, transnational crime, and drug and people traffickers, as is evident in the case of Afghanistan.

Conflict can undermine development

The conflict that helps to produce fragile states can be detrimental to development in numerous ways, including eroding communication, transport and civil (i.e., hospitals, schools) infrastructures. Civil society is also invariably damaged as it becomes difficult for individuals and communities to organize and function under such conditions. Moreover, conflict can lead to a significant reduction in the levels of domestic consumption and FDI. Many parts of Africa are considered to be politically unstable and consequently the continent attracts 'less than 1 per cent of annual global financial flows' (McKay 2004: 155). On average, the economic growth rate of countries affected by civil war declines by 2.2 per cent per year (Collier and Hoeffler 2004a: 5). Conflict can also undermine existing development projects, as well as reverse any development advances that have been made within particular countries. In contrast, as the *World Development Report 2011* has noted, countries that have successfully emerged from violent conflict – like Ethiopia, Mozambique and Rwanda – are making good progress towards reducing poverty (World Bank 2011).

   The central theme of the *World Development Report 2011* (subtitled *Conflict, Security and Development*) is that many states now face cycles of repeated violence, weak governance and instability. The number of civil wars and battle deaths from civil wars has declined over the last 25 years – although civil and interstate wars are still threats in some regions – but few countries can be defined as 'post-conflict' (ibid.: 3). Indeed, conflicts are increasingly ongoing and repeated in the contemporary period. For example, 90 per cent of the civil wars in the 1990s occurred in countries that had already had a civil war in the previous 30 years (ibid.: 2). Furthermore, conflict-afflicted states that achieve a peace settlement frequently remain plagued by high levels of violence and crime, as the citizens of South Africa, El Salvador and Guatemala would testify (ibid.: 5). What makes it more difficult to achieve conflict resolution is that the different forms of violence are often linked to each other. For instance, the Taliban sustains its activities through the illicit Afghan heroin trade (UNODC 2008). The authors of the *World Development Report 2011* note that 'no low-income fragile or conflict-affected country has yet achieved a single MDG' (World Bank 2011: 5). They conclude that 'strengthening legitimate institutions and governance to provide citizen security, justice, and jobs is crucial to break cycles of violence' (ibid.: 2).

It is for the preceding reasons that international development assistance is increasingly oriented towards dealing with conflict within states (discussed on p. 120). Indeed, OECD member states spent approximately US$6 billion on peace work in 2006, through official development assistance and the funding of UN peacekeeping missions (DAC 2008: 1). Occasionally, however, conflict can stimulate certain exports and imports, with some economic actors profiting from the turmoil, including in some cases through various forms of illegal trade (UNCTAD 2004b).

The human cost of conflict

The human cost of conflict is a major reason for the merging of security and development. It is estimated that worldwide around 700,000 people die in armed conflicts or are killed by violence each year (DAC 2008: 1). Civilians have increasingly been targeted in recent conflicts, resulting in the number of displaced people rising from 16 million in 1980 to more than 40 million in 1992 (HSRP 2005: 5). Armed conflicts can also disrupt agricultural production, leading to food shortages and hunger. A report published by the International Food Policy Research Institute (IFPRI) in 2006 revealed that the countries with the highest levels of hunger and malnutrition are plagued by civil wars and violent conflicts (see Wiesmann 2006). Based upon a 119-nation study, the IFPRI report indicated that combatants often use hunger as a weapon by cutting off food supplies, hijacking food aid and destroying crops (ibid.: 5). IFPRI formulated a Global Hunger Index (GHI) and found that nine of the twelve countries with the worst GHI rankings – Angola, Burundi, Cambodia, Eritrea, Ethiopia, Liberia, Sierra Leone, Tajikistan and the Democratic Republic of Congo – were affected by major wars between 1989 and 2003. More specifically, the GHI was 22 per cent higher for war-torn countries than for peaceful countries with comparable levels of economic development (ibid.).

Finally, the human cost of conflict is succinctly encapsulated in this extract from the *World Development Report 2011*: 'People in fragile and conflict-affected states are more than twice as likely to be undernourished as those in other developing countries, more than three times as likely to be unable to send their children to school, twice as likely to see their children die before age five, and more than twice as likely to lack clean water' (World Bank 2011: 5).

Declining aid

The rise in the number of fragile states also has considerable implications for a major tool of development, namely aid provision. In countries with ineffective governance and high levels of corruption and crime, there is an increased likelihood of aid being squandered and embezzled. Indeed, in some instances, aid may even contribute to the problems that states are facing by creating an additional resource to be competed over (Brown et al. 2007). Moreover, the cost of an average civil war in a low-income country – which was US$54 billion (£29bn) in 2004 – can almost wipe out the total worldwide aid budget, which amounted to US$78.6 billion (£42bn) in that year (BBC 2006b). The major consequence of aid being wasted is that donor governments and their respective citizens are inevitably less willing to continue providing this type of assistance, and this may partly explain why, prior to the G8 Gleneagles Summit in 2005, international funding for humanitarian aid was in decline. For these reasons, figures like the former head of the World Bank, Paul Wolfowitz, argue that establishing effective governance and tackling corruption should be a precondition for receiving aid. He sought to attach such conditions to the loans, grants and technical assistance that his institution provided, but critics respond that this can significantly delay the provision of aid to countries.

Growing insecurity

Security has also become a more prominent issue within development because, within the context of globalization, many of the pressing challenges of our time are interconnected, and their effects uneven and contingent. In other words, insecurity arises from global financial crises, world food shortages, resource conflict, transnational terrorism and crime, unpredictable job markets, health scares, growing inequality and poverty, and global environmental hazards, but also because of their interpenetration. Reflecting the growing sense of insecurity, the global private security sector was estimated to be worth US$95 billion in 2005 (RIIA 2005: 6). Furthermore, the prospect of continuing global environmental decline is likely to ensure that the interrelationship between development and security will strengthen as this century progresses. Indeed, it is now widely predicted that conflict in the twenty-first century will increasingly be over natural resources as humanity adjusts to the realities of environmental degradation, resource scarcity and global warming. By embracing security, the development industry is therefore demonstrating its continuing relevance both now and in the future.

Redefining development

The turn to security within development marks a further shift from its economic growth orientation towards a greater emphasis upon quality-of-life issues. As the UNDP has declared: 'If human development is about expanding choice and advancing rights, then violent conflict is the most brutal suppression of human development' (UNDP 2005: 151). Conversely, achieving peace and security creates the appropriate conditions for development, especially poverty reduction. And living free from the threat of intimidation and violence is a necessary prerequisite for human flourishing.

Development and security: critical perspectives

The merging of development and security has generated numerous criticisms. For some critics, northern governmental concern over fragile states is primarily because they harm markets, restrict access to mineral resources, and lead to refugees ending up on their own borders (Bøås and Jennings 2007) while, according to the Reality of Aid *2006 Report*, post-9/11 aid is increasingly being used to fulfil the security objectives of donor governments, with more than a third of aid resources allocated to the wars in Afghanistan and Iraq (IBON Foundation 2007). The US and Australian governments have even changed the mandate of their aid programmes in line with this end. The *Reality of Aid* network has called for aid spending to be focused once again upon poverty eradication.

The contemporary emphasis upon security is seen by some as a form of western imperialism because effective governance is invariably conceptualized as the introduction of democracy, party systems, an independent judiciary and market societies. For Mark Duffield (2001), the merging of security and development facilitates the spread of liberal governance and keeps errant states in line by providing a pretext for external intervention in these countries. Duffield considers the reshaping of developing societies to be problematic on two grounds. Firstly, there is the issue of whether it is legitimate for northern governments to be seeking to transform the social and political systems of developing societies. Secondly, he questions their ability to implement such change – and the difficulties that the US and its coalition partners have faced in establishing stable democratic governance in Iraq since the war of 2004 would seem to bear out this point. As an alternative, Duffield argues for a true cosmopolitan politics based upon common values, rather than relying on the imposition of external norms and values that he maintains is a feature of existing liberal governance. However, for Duffield, the fault does not lie solely with northern governments as they are only one part of the emerging system of global governance that also includes NGOs, private companies, security forces and UN agencies.

Duffield extends these themes in *Development, Security and Unending War* (2007). In this work, he challenges conventional wisdom that increased global interconnectedness means that instability in different parts of the world has security implications for the West and must be dealt with through development and poverty reduction strategies. For him, the securitization of development has little to do with enhancing the lives of people in the developing world and is instead geared to maintaining international stability and ways of life for the dominant powers. Stewart Patrick (2006) has also questioned the view that weak states generate international instability by allowing the spread of terrorism, organized crime, pandemics, environmental degradation and similar forms of cross-border phenomena. This assertion is based upon very little empirical evidence, and any research that has been done into this area invariably presents a much more complex picture. For a variety of reasons, therefore, we need to scrutinize the assumptions that underpin the development–security nexus.

Fragile and failing states

Numerous interpretations have been postulated by academics and development practitioners to account for the high number of fragile states in the contemporary period, many of which are interrelated. Here, the latter explanations are established – almost classic – accounts of conflict within developing societies, but the first two subsections seek to historicize and globally contextualize this phenomenon.

The end of the Cold War and the rise of the 'new wars'

One explanation of the failing state phenomenon is that its origins lie with the end of the Cold War in the late 1980s. This important historical event allowed ethno-cultural tensions to resurface within many societies after having been subsumed for decades by the global ideological conflict between the Soviet bloc and the West during the Cold War. It has led in the post-Cold War period to the emergence of 'new wars' that are intra-state rather than interstate conflicts, and are themselves a reflection of the diminishing authority of some states (Munkler 2005). Mary Kaldor (2001), in particular, has emphasized the ways in which these new civil wars defy the conventional interstate system.

Moreover, in the final years of the Cold War, approximately US$176 billion worth of weaponry was exported to Third World countries between 1987 and 1991 (Ramsbotham, Woodhouse and Miall 2005: 98). The passing of the Cold War, and with it the end of superpower domination, has also made it easier for private arms' dealers to operate. It has meant that the global flow of weapons and other military hardware has continued, particularly into developing countries as many lack the capacity to monitor and control this activity. This amount of weaponry is viewed as a destabilizing factor that is contributing to the conflict within some states. Indeed, some commentators describe the emergence of a 'Kalashnikov culture' in some African countries, reflected in a rise in 'warlordism' and ethnic conflict and in the number of criminal gangs (see Furley 1995).

Adding to the internal instability of some states has been the growing regionalization of world politics and conflict. Since the early 1990s there has been an increasing tendency for conflict to spread from one country to another in certain regions, notably the Balkans, the Caucasus and Central Asia, West Africa, and the Great Lakes area of Africa (see Ramsbotham, Woodhouse and Miall 2005). There may be common factors or sources of conflict in a region, like contested borders, disputes over access to natural resources and minerals, and ethno-cultural differences. But conflict is invariably exacerbated whenever civil wars spill over into neighbouring states through refugees fleeing for protection, the smuggling of weapons, trans-border criminal activity, and the ripple effect of economic upheaval in a war-torn state.

Globalization

Another view is that weak states must be considered within the context of globalization (Clapham 2002). Globalizing processes, like the heightened role of MNCs, global financial flows and institutions, the increased flows of people, trade and capital across borders, and the global drugs and arms trades, are seen as undermining the authority of the nation-state and its ability to protect its citizens. For example, IFIs fuel grievances whenever they insist that struggling countries devalue their economies and cut back on state services in return for financial aid (Keen 2008: 47). Indeed, some writers make explicit connections between aspects of globalization and the growth in anti-state behaviour, like ethno-cultural conflict and civil unrest (Barber 1996; Swain, Amer and Oiendal 2007). In particular, the nation-state is viewed as increasingly powerless in its dealings with non-state actors and privatized networks that operate largely oblivious to territorial boundaries. It also means that developing countries are facing conflicts that increasingly possess both state and non-state dimensions, and many struggle to deal with this complexity.[1] In this regard, a globalizing media has arguably exacerbated conflicts by encouraging some groups to avenge the atrocities committed against their kith and kin that they witness on their television screens (Ahmed 1995). At the same time, the internet and e-mail have enabled cultural fundamentalists and ethno-nationalists to organize their challenge to nation-states.

In sum, there is a view that aspects of globalization have ensured that the nation-state has lost some of its vitality and is contributing to the 'fragile state' phenomenon. However, as we will see in chapter 10, globalization is a contested phenomenon, with some writers sceptical of the notion that it is undermining the nation-state. But while the ways in which the different aspects of globalization are operating remain subject to debate, there is less dispute that mature industrial democracies are better able to resist such pressures than developing countries with inchoate democracies.

Poverty and underdevelopment

Poverty and underdevelopment are considered by some commentators to be the root cause of insecurity, conflict and fragile states (Brainard and Chollet

2007; Stewart and Fitzgerald 2001). The *Human Development Report* of 1994 (UNDP 1994) noted that, of the 79 countries affected by political violence and conflict in that year, 65 were in the developing world. Similarly, according to UNCTAD (2004b), between 1990 and 2001, more LDCs were affected by conflict than were unaffected by it. Indeed, most of the world's armed conflicts occur in sub-Saharan Africa, one of its poorest regions (HSRP 2005: 4). Moreover, conflict can be self-perpetuating because it exacerbates the very conditions – like poverty and economic stagnation – that gave rise to it in the first place, thereby creating a 'conflict trap' from which countries struggle to escape (ibid.; Collier et al. 2003). Furthermore, low-income countries are especially likely to relapse into conflict once a civil war is over (Collier 2007: 27). While economic development presents countries with a way of escaping this condition, it has to be organized on an equitable basis to avoid exacerbating inequalities and creating further tensions (Picciotto and Weaving 2006). Indeed, development can be profoundly disruptive for societies leading to rapid urbanization and industrialization, with some commentators identifying links between modernization and ethnic conflict (Newman 1991).

The 'resource curse' thesis

Some countries suffer from political violence precisely because they are rich in natural resources and minerals as this can encourage corruption, warlordism and foreign exploitation. In such cases, the wealth generated by oil and other mineral resources is frequently confined to elites. This situation can lead to social tensions, with governments relying upon repressive measures to retain law and order (see Hutchful and Aning 2004). Indeed, a notable characteristic of many resource-rich countries is their lack of responsiveness to public opinion (Brown et al. 2007). Moreover, reliance upon natural resource exploitation means that there is less incentive to build diverse and productive economies.

However, the 'resource curse' thesis has been challenged. For example, Jonathan Di John (2007) contends that there is little compelling evidence to prove that oil abundance leads to conflict. While acknowledging that once a conflict has begun some types of natural resources may help to prolong the violence, he maintains that 'factor endowments do not determine politics' (ibid.: 980). As he puts it: '[t]he indeterminacy of oil wealth and violence suggests that the nature of conflicts in mineral-dominant economies does not exist prior to politics' (ibid.). In this vein, Michael Ross notes that '[f]or every resource-rich country that has suffered from violent conflict, two or three have avoided it' (2003: 19). And there are some resource-rich countries, like Botswana, that have remained relatively free from violence and have been able to enjoy significant economic growth.

Greed versus grievance

In their research for the World Bank, Paul Collier and his colleagues point to economic factors as the main drivers of civil wars. They stress that statistical evidence indicates that '[g]reed seems more important than grievance' (2000: 110), with grievance taken to entail factors like political repression, ethno-cultural exclusion and socio-economic inequality, while economic incentives for conflict occur when countries suffer a decline in economic growth or are dependent on primary commodity exports, like timber and rare minerals. The latter incentive means that there is an international trading dimension to contemporary conflicts, with combatants able to secure revenues from poorly regulated global markets, thereby enabling them to continue their campaigns (see Brown et al. 2007). Indeed, this state of affairs has led to the UNDP (2005) to call for 'conflict resource' markets to be restricted. For Collier, the likelihood of conflict is further increased when states have a high proportion of poorly educated young men between the ages of 15 and 24, as they are overwhelmingly the people who join rebellions, and provide rebel movements with the opportunity to acquire lootable assets through the use of violence (Collier 2000: 110). Furthermore, once civil wars have started, interests emerge that only know how to prosper during war and this helps explain their longevity (Collier 2007: 27).

However, Collier et al. are criticized for understating the role of politics, identity and ideology in intra-state wars (Ballentine and Nitzschke 2006). Case studies commissioned by the International Peace Academy (IPA) indicate that economic calculations were not the primary cause of recent armed conflicts. Most importantly, they became relevant only when they were intertwined with factors like government mismanagement, exclusionary and repressive political systems, weak states, security dilemmas and inter-ethnic disputes (Ballentine and Sherman 2003). The studies also suggest that, in certain circumstances, combatant access to economic resources creates opportunities for sustaining conflicts by impacting upon their intensity and character (ibid.: 260).

But the major shortcoming of the 'greed versus grievance' debate concerns the lack of clarity over the meaning of these terms (ibid.: 14). While they commonly designate economic and political motivations, respectively, factors like inequality could potentially fall within both camps (ibid.). In this regard, David Keen (2008) contends that, rather than viewing greed and grievance as separate entities, we will only gain an informed insight into the nature of conflict by examining how they interact. He also maintains that Collier's emphasis upon 'rebel greed' neglects the role that states and other actors beyond the region can play in fuelling war economies. For example, through its trading connections, China has helped to prop up the abusive regimes in Sudan and Zimbabwe (ibid.: 43). Interestingly, in recent writings, Collier and his co-writers have presented a more nuanced interpretation of greed (e.g.,

Collier and Hoeffler 2004a). And in the conclusion to *Understanding Civil War* (2005), which is edited by Paul Collier and Nicholas Sambanis and written by the latter, it is conceded that we should move beyond the 'greed versus griev-ance' debate in favour of a more complex model that considers greed and grievance as inextricably fused motives for civil conflict.

The nature of political authority

For Edward Azar (1990), political institutions in developing societies are fre-quently bureaucratic and authoritarian, and afford limited opportunity for popular participation. It means that the states within these societies are gen-erally unresponsive to the needs of their respective citizens, and this helps to explain the protracted nature of the social conflict that afflicts many of them. As recent events in the Middle East and North Arica vividly illustrate, where political and economic development lags behind expectations, it can lead to escalating demands for change as well as the potential for conflict (World Bank 2011: 5).

The responsibility for this democratic deficit is much debated and much will depend upon particular contexts. In Africa, for example, there is a view that authoritarian states are a colonial legacy. The departing colonialists hast-ily erected democratic structures and did not allow them sufficient time to become embedded within African societies (Throup 1995). Indeed, for some the nation-state itself was a colonial imposition and this goes a long way to explain its fragility in Africa (Davidson 1992). Others contend that authori-tarian rule and unstable states are down to a generation of postcolonial African leaders that have effectively run their countries for their own ends and inflicted enormous harm upon them in the process (Ayittey 1992). On the other hand, dependency writers consider the responsibility for much of the instability in the South lies with the structural conditions of the international economy and the institutions of global governance, rather than with the limitations of their respective governments.

Of course, the preceding interpretations present essentially general explan-atory accounts of the high incidence of conflict-affected states in the South. To understand this phenomenon properly requires undertaking a differentiat-ing and contextualist approach to this subject and examining the particular circumstances within individual societies.

Human security

Development and security have effectively coalesced around the concept of human security. Yet there remains some dispute over its meaning. For example, paragraph 143 of the 2005 UN reform document simply states that, in relation to this issue, 'we commit ourselves to discuss and define the notion of human security in the General Assembly' (United Nations 2005a:

28). Human security is therefore an evolving concept. For example, some writers maintain that establishing democracy is the best way of generating security within societies and achieving human dignity (Large and Sisk 2006). Whereas some commentators see human security approaches as contributing to improved health (e.g., *The Lancet* 2008), other academics stress the extent to which human security is inextricably linked to the environment. More specifically, forms of environmental decline, like erratic rainfall patterns and land degradation, have the potential to create food and water shortages, resource competition and population displacement. For Jon Barnett and Neil Adger (2005), climate change has the potential to undermine human security and may, in conjunction with other socio-political factors like poverty, increase the risk of violent conflict.

There have been a number of significant moments in the evolution of human security, beginning in 1994 with the UNDP's *Human Development Report*. This report articulated a multidimensional conception of human security, one that incorporated areas ranging from personal to environmental security. Moreover, the atrocities committed in Rwanda and Bosnia-Herzegovina in the 1990s emphasized the need for a conception of security that focused more upon individuals and communities. And, reflecting the growing prominence of human security, at its landmark Millennium Summit in September 2000 the UN called upon the international community to work together to achieve not only 'freedom from want', but also 'freedom from fear'. This pronouncement was followed by the setting up of the Commission on Human Security (CHS) in January 2001. It defines human security as seeking 'to protect the vital core of all human lives in ways that enhances human freedoms and human fulfillment' (CHS 2003: 4). In 2005, human security was endorsed by Kofi Annan, the former UN Secretary-General, who placed it at the heart of his *In Larger Freedom* (2005) report and it underpinned his proposals for UN reform, many of which were accepted at the UN Summit in September of that year (discussed on p. 135).

In its 2003 report, *Human Security Now*, the CHS declares that achieving human security entails 'both shielding people from acute threats and empowering people to take charge of their own lives' (ibid.: iv). For the CHS, empowerment and protection are mutually reinforcing. Human security therefore requires integrated and human-centred policies geared to enhancing people's lives and protecting their dignity, and it follows that this means not having to live in abject poverty and suffer from educational deprivations and ill health. Most importantly, the CHS insists that 'human security broadens the focus from the security of borders to the lives of people and communities inside and across those borders' (ibid.: 6). In practical terms, this entails recognizing that the threat to human security comes not only from armed conflict, but also from disease, hunger, economic inequality, environmental pollution and natural disasters that actually kill far more people.

In focusing upon the individual, human security not only constitutes a shift away from traditional state-centred conceptions of security but also reflects the fact that security challenges increasingly come from within states, as opposed to wars between states, in the form of civil conflicts (Jolly and Basu Ray 2006). The CHS emphasizes that human security and national security are mutually reinforcing but notes that states can be the main source of insecurity for individuals and communities, especially in the case of weak states or authoritarian regimes.[2] There is also a sense within the human security literature that, because of contemporary developments like increasingly unpredictable financial markets, global terrorism, transnational crime, global environmental decline and pandemics, states are less able to provide security for their citizens (e.g., Shani, Sato and Pasha 2007). Richard Jolly and Deepayan Basu Ray (2006) stress that the interconnected nature of these factors requires multidimensional, gender sensitive and nationally contextualized analyses. Indeed, for its advocates, human security is more in tune with the interrelated nature of contemporary threats than state-centred conceptions of security (ibid.: 8).

However, the concept of human security has its detractors, with some writers questioning its definitional and intellectual coherence (see Foong-Khong 2001; MacFarlane and Foong-Khong 2006; Paris 2001). In particular, by embracing such a wide range of concerns, there is a danger of the concept becoming almost meaningless. In turn, this makes it extremely difficult to establish priorities and formulate policy in order to achieve human security (Paris 2001). Also, the lack of a commonly accepted definition means that there is always a danger of powerful states interpreting human security to further their own foreign policy objectives. Others challenge the novelty of the concept, arguing that human security concerns are already an established part of the discourse of international relations, albeit using different terminology, and are dealt with by numerous international institutions and agencies (MacFarlane and Foong-Khong 2006). Arguably, the shift from the state to the individual as the focus of security also reflects the greater individualism of our age. In contrast, Lawrence Freedman maintains that, despite its shortcomings, the state remains the best agency for ensuring our security, and we should therefore focus upon building up states in the South so that they are better able to perform this role (Picciotto, Olonisakin and Clarke 2007: xiv).[3]

The Human Security Report

In 2005, the *Human Security Report 2005: War and Peace in the 21st Century*, published by the University of British Colombia's Human Security Report Project (HSRP), challenged the conventional wisdom on contemporary conflict and security. Based on their research, the authors detect a substantial decline in the number of armed conflicts, military coups, genocides and human rights abuse during the previous decade, and all of this is reflected in a reduction in the average number of people killed in conflicts each year. More specifically, 'the number of armed conflicts around the world has declined by more than 40 per cent since the early 1990s' (HSRP 2005: 1), while 'five out of six regions in the developing world saw a net decrease in core human rights abuses between 1994 and 2003' (ibid.: 2). They contend these developments are due to changes that have taken place in the post-Cold War period, notably an unprecedented upsurge in international activism geared to conflict prevention, peacemaking and reconciliation. Free from the paralysis of Cold War politics, the UN Security Council has also been able to play a more active role in maintaining international security, reflected in a fourfold increase in the number of UN peacekeeping operations between 1987 and 1999 (ibid.: 8–9).

The report also notes a decline in the number of international wars due to: the end of colonialism and the Cold War; fear of the consequences of nuclear warfare; and the principle of securing UN Security Council mandates to sanction the use of force becoming more widely accepted. The authors of the report acknowledge that these trends are reversible and we must not be complacent, but they see no reason for pessimism (ibid.: 10).[4] In a subsequent report, the *Human Security Brief 2007*, the HSRP confirmed that the positive security trends had continued. In particular, the dramatic increase in the number of terrorist incidents since 9/11 appeared to have peaked, with fatalities from terrorism declining by some 40 per cent worldwide (see HSRP 2007). And the security situation in sub-Saharan Africa was improving, with the number of conflicts being waged in the region more than halved between 1999 and 2006. For the HSRP, the lack of popular awareness of these positive developments is due to sensationalist media coverage of global security and the overstated claims made by NGOs and international organizations in relation to this area.

Nevertheless, some sixty wars were still being fought in 2005, with the most well-known conflicts – namely those in Afghanistan, Darfur, Iraq and the tribal areas in the north of Pakistan – showing few signs of being resolved. Moreover, from the perspective of the CHS, which advocates a broader conception of human security, the reduction in forms of armed conflict does not mean the human security agenda has been addressed because this still leaves the threats that stem from poverty, hunger, disease and other humanitarian emergencies. In other words, by conceptualizing human security as the protection of individuals from violence, the HSRP has a narrow view of what it means to lead secure and fulfilling lives.

Peacekeeping

It is through peacekeeping and peace-building that the international community responds in a practical way to dealing with conflict, the growth in the number of fragile states and the need to foster human security. Peacekeeping encompasses many different types of tasks, including monitoring and enforcing ceasefires, restoring essential services, clearing landmines, supporting the return of refugees, confidence-building measures, strengthening the rule of law and disarming combatants. Underpinning this activity is the desire to bring security to people living within conflict zones by creating conditions for sustainable peace. Peacekeeping therefore paves the way for peace-building and conflict prevention that are associated with long-term post-conflict development.[5]

The UN Security Council is the key international body responsible for authorizing peacekeeping operations. And it is the UN itself – led by the Department of Peacekeeping Operations (DPKO) – that is at the forefront of these operations and is the main multilateral contributor to international post-conflict stabilization. Furthermore, its activities have increased sevenfold since 1999, with almost 110,000 personnel serving on 20 peace operations in 2008 (UNDPKO 2008: 1). The Security Council also authorizes both joint operations with the other multilateral organizations like the EU, NATO and the African Union, and operations in which it is does not play a direct part, including in the past 'coalitions of willing countries'. Most importantly, the post-Cold War period has seen the UN Security Council extend its peacekeeping remit to include humanitarian intervention.

However, humanitarian intervention raises difficult legal and ethical dilemmas (see Barnett and Weiss 2008; Chatterjee and Scheid 2003; Holzgrefe and Keohane 2003), and in addition entails encroaching upon the principle of state sovereignty (Welsh 2004). It also necessitates building the necessary international consensus and political will, especially as humanitarian intervention often requires the use of military force, although since the early 1990s the UN has generally been cautious about pursuing this particular approach, preferring instead to focus upon conflict prevention (discussed on p. 132). These attendant complexities have meant that the international community has pursued a variety of responses towards humanitarian intervention in the post-Cold War period (see Weiss 2007). For Roland Dannreuther (2007), the humanitarianism underpinning humanitarian intervention is often at odds with the messy nature of the politics surrounding the actual interventions, which invariably entails that the latter are partial and selective. Furthermore, southern governments and even some development practitioners (e.g., Vaux 2007) have questioned the commitment of some northern governments to humanitarianism, especially when their interventions coincide with their own national security objectives.

Ian Smillie and Larry Minear in *The Charity of Nations* (2004) emphasize the extent to which contemporary humanitarianism has a strong commercial dimension for some countries and call for it to be founded upon multilateralism. It would mean, for example, an end to the use of private security firms by the US military and US private-sector companies would not receive reconstruction contracts as was the case during the recent war in Iraq (ibid.: 17; see also Singer 2008). Episodes like the 'humanitarian bombing' of Belgrade by NATO planes during the 1999 Kosovo conflict and the humanitarian claims made by the US to justify the war in Iraq in 2003 are widely considered to have harmed the principle of humanitarian intervention (see Weiss 2004).

Box 5.1 The peacekeeping record of the UN

- *1948:* UN military observers monitored the Armistice Agreement between Israel and its Arab neighbours.
- *1956:* The UN Emergency Force (UNEF) was deployed in the Sinai Peninsula to cover the withdrawal of British, French and Israeli forces from Egypt, following their failed invasion during the Suez crisis. The UNEF helped to maintain peace in the region for a decade.
- *1967:* President Nasser of Egypt ordered the UN troops to withdraw, and war soon broke out again when Israel attacked on 5 June. Fourteen remaining UN soldiers were killed.
- *1993:* Hundreds died when US marines became embroiled in a series of gun battles with Somalia militia. The US troops were there to support the UN force but, soon after, Washington withdrew its contingent and this was followed by the UN doing the same in 1995.
- *1994:* The UN failed to prevent the genocide in Rwanda. In fact, when the slaughter began, many countries withdrew their contingents from the UN peacekeeping force that was stationed in the country.
- *1995:* Thousands of Bosnian Muslims were killed in Srebrenica, a UN Safe Area. The United Nations Protection Force, UNPROFOR, was hampered by a limited mandate and inadequate military resources.
- *2000:* Around 500 peacekeepers were kidnapped and a considerable amount of military hardware stolen by rebels in Sierra Leone in what is widely viewed as a poorly organized operation. Civil war also returned to Angola despite years of UN involvement in the region.
- *2003:* The conflict in Darfur, Sudan, began, and the UN has been unable to halt the ethnic cleansing and other human rights abuses committed in the region. Indeed, it provides a vivid illustration of the difficulties of peacekeeping in the contemporary period (see Box 5.3).

Further undermining contemporary peacekeeping is the UN's mixed track record in relation to this area (see Box 5.1). For instance, the UN/US intervention in Somalia in December 1992 is now widely regarded as a kind of tragic farce (see Rutherford 2008). Likewise, during the Bosnian war, 325 UN personnel were taken hostage by Serb forces in May 1995 and some were used as human shields in order to forestall further UN/NATO military action. In 2000, UN peacekeepers were similarly taken hostage during the conflict in Sierra Leone. It is also the case that in many recent conflicts, the UN has been criticized for intervening too late in the day while, in the case of Rwanda, when the genocide began in April 1994, there was already a small UN peacekeeping force stationed in the country but it was constrained by a limited mandate. It is for these reasons that the UN has undertaken a fundamental review of its approach to peacekeeping (see Box 5.2, The Brahimi Report).

However, the UN faces considerable difficulties in performing its peacekeeping role. It does not have its own military force, and relies upon financial and human resource contributions from member states to carry out peacekeeping. Indeed, 119 countries contributed military and police personnel to UN peacekeeping in January 2008, along with 2,300 UN volunteers from over 160 nations (UNDPKO 2008: 1). Inevitably, there are differing levels of commitment to this activity, dependent upon the particular histories, cultures and capacities of individual countries. Peacekeeping is also made more difficult by the structural and organizational shortcomings that exist within the UN system itself, notably the nature of the membership and decision-making

> **Box 5.2 The Brahimi Report of 2000**
>
> The Report of the Panel on United Nations Peace Operations (A/55/305) was pub-
> lished on 21August 2000 (see Brahimi 2000). The panel was convened by the former
> Secretary-General, Kofi Annan, to undertake a comprehensive review of all aspects
> of UN peacekeeping operations. Chaired by the former foreign minister of Algeria,
> Lakhdar Brahimi, effectively its task was to ensure that the UN's peacekeeping track
> record improved.
>
> The report made 57 recommendations, including proposals designed to ensure
> that the UN peacekeeping forces do not arrive late and ill-equipped to conflicts, and
> that they have the authority to intervene to prevent atrocities. There were also recom-
> mendations concerning UN headquarters for planning and supporting peacekeeping
> operations, particularly with regard to strengthening the Department for Peacekeeping
> Operations (DPKO). And there were proposals for creating a 'rapid reaction force' by
> enhancing the UN's rapid deployment capacities, a measure condemned by critics as
> an attempt to create a UN army. While some of the report's recommendations have
> been implemented, the ability of the UN to pursue 'robust peacekeeping', as urged by
> the Brahimi Report, continues to be hampered by a lack of support from some states.

processes of the Security Council. Indeed, the veto-holding Permanent Five
(P5) members of the Security Council – namely China, France, Russia, the UK
and the USA – had a profound influence upon the conduct of UN peacekeeping
operations in Bosnia and Rwanda.

Interestingly, during 2008 the outgoing head of UN peacekeeping operations, Jean-Marie Gueheno, warned that UN peacekeepers were being over-
stretched, especially in regions like Darfur. He argued that peacekeeping
should support and complement a political agreement, rather than being
used as a substitute for it. In other words, there has to be a peace to keep for
peacekeeping to work (BBC 2008).

Post-conflict development

The end of the Cold War has removed much of the international political
tensions that prevented any meaningful focus upon post-conflict development. It has meant that the 'global security industry', in the form of the
UN, donor governments, regional organizations and CSOs, has been able to
devote more attention and resources to pursuing long-term peace-building
and conflict prevention strategies in many of the world's troubled spots.
Post-conflict development can assume numerous forms, dependent upon the
particular country or context. It can include demobilization, disarmament
and reintegration (DDR) programmes, creating a professional military and
police, the pursuit of conflict resolution and reconciliation measures, ranging
from mediation to human rights investigations, but also social and economic
reconstruction. The latter can include rebuilding a country's infrastructure,
such as its transport networks, energy supplies, and education and health
services (see Junne and Verkoren 2005). Indeed, inclusive social and economic

Box 5.3 Peacekeeping in Darfur

The conflict in Darfur began in 2003 when rebels took up arms to resist alleged government discrimination against the region. The Sudanese government responded by mobilizing Arab Janjaweed militias – accused of widespread atrocities against black Africans – although Khartoum denies this charge. But it was not until July 2007 that an international peacekeeping force (UNAMID) was created from UN and African Union (AU) forces, with China being blamed for some of the delay by backing its Sudanese ally, a country in which it has considerable economic interests. Replacing the AU contingent that had struggled to contain the violence, UNAMID was given a stronger mandate to protect civilians and ensure that humanitarian agencies could operate safely in Darfur. Nevertheless, UN resolution 1769 did not allow UNAMID to intervene to stop the conflict. Moreover, not only was UNAMID a long time coming, it had also been hindered by a lack of resources. Indeed, the operation faced enormous logistical difficulties as a result of the rough terrain, the size of the region and a lack of transport, including a promised 24 helicopters. It also lacked military equipment and even personnel, with only 10,000 of the agreed 26,000 troops and police having arrived in Sudan by September 2008.

As well as a lack of practical support from the international community, UNAMID was hampered by an obstructive Sudanese government that had resented the deployment of non-African forces within its borders (Borger 2008). In fact, UNAMID had been subject to violent attacks, most notably when seven peacekeepers were killed in an ambush in July 2008 carried out by suspected Janjaweed fighters, amid charges that it was part of an attempt to drive the peacekeepers out of the country.

The consequence of this catalogue of problems was that in September 2008 the Darfur crisis showed no signs of coming to an end and African aid agencies were claiming that the UN was failing civilians in the region. Indeed, during that month, the UN's World Food Programme (WFP) threatened to halt food aid distribution in parts of Darfur unless the security situation improved. The UN also estimated that, since the conflict began, around 300,000 people had been killed in the conflict and up to 2.5 million were displaced.

development is widely seen as an essential prerequisite of conflict prevention. There must be a peace dividend not only for ending conflict but also for preventing its recurrence, particularly as states with a recent history of internal violence are nearly 50 per cent more likely to see it return within five years (Collier and Hoeffler 2004a).

The formation of effective governance within troubled societies is similarly considered vital in this regard, especially for countries that are plagued by civil wars and competing factions. In practical terms, this translates as government that is equitable and transparent, with inclusive and democratic institutions, an independent judiciary, a free press and a vibrant civil society. Post-conflict development therefore frequently entails working to change countries in order to alleviate sources of conflict and create more stable and inclusive societies. However, as the recent war in Iraq demonstrated, it is possible to introduce too much change into countries during post-conflict reconstruction. Even the US authorities have now acknowledged that the dismantling of much of Iraq's civil and military infrastructure was a strategic mistake.

The UN has been at the forefront of post-conflict development. In particular, the Human Security Unit (HSU), which is part of the Office for the Coordination of Humanitarian Affairs at the United Nations, dedicates much of its activity to this area (see HSU 2008). For the HSU, establishing a lasting peace is dependent upon building an integrated human security framework that is forged in conjunction with the relevant local and national authorities (HSU 2008: 1). However, conflict evaluation and prevention networks within the OECD's Development Assistance Committee (DAC) consider peace-building and conflict prevention should focus upon four broad areas: equitable socio-economic development; good governance; the reform of security and justice institutions; and truth and reconciliation processes (DAC 2008).

However, there is an ongoing debate over the most effective strategies to achieve conflict prevention and peace-building (see Ramsbotham, Woodhouse, and Miall 2005). This is because to date a number of international conflict management operations have been expensive to implement and achieved only limited success. In the case of Bosnia and Kosovo, for example, the underlying causes of the disputes have yet to be resolved (Dannreuther 2007: 158). Furthermore, when post-conflict development is not properly planned and implemented, it can lead to aid dependency and states effectively being propped up by external security forces for years. Planning and implementation, along with the issue of resources, are widely considered by specialists in the field to be the key determinants of the success or failure of conflict management and resolution programmes. In the case of aid, Paul Collier and Anke Hoeffler (2004b) contend that its effectiveness in conflict prevention is dependent upon the institutional and political context in which it is being employed and how it is targeted. Lastly, there is increasing recognition that post-conflict recovery must also contain a global dimension. In other words, countries will be better able to avoid future conflict if the global economy is based upon equitable trading relations as this would facilitate their economic development (Addison 2004).

The complexities of intervention

While there may be sound reasons for intervening in states and pursuing different forms of post-conflict development, certain factors influence the ability of the international community to perform this role. To begin with, the nature and duration of interventions, and indeed the decision over whether or not to intervene, are profoundly shaped by the conditions within particular countries as well as by the wider global context, such as the 'War on Terror'. Often, there will be multiple causes behind particular conflicts, making it difficult to formulate appropriate responses and strategies (Shaw 2002). At the same time, no government will ever readily seek to become involved in the civil conflicts of other countries because to do so risks becoming embroiled in often highly complex disputes that can last for years and for which there is often a lack of adequate international institutional support mechanisms (Luck 2006; Munslow 2002). Propping up fragile states is made more difficult by the fact that there is often a regional dimension to their instability (Etzioni 2004; Fukuyama 2004). Again, this is illustrated by the experience of the US and its allies in post-conflict Afghanistan and Iraq, and it has led to considerable strains being placed upon the coalitions.

Governments also have to justify the merits of intervention to their own populations, highlighting the national security implications of non-intervention, and generally make the case for diverting domestic resources to other countries. It is especially difficult to justify intervention in countries that have been inflicted with civil wars for generations as there would seem to be limits to what can be achieved. And ultimately UN peacekeeping and peace-building operations have to take into account the views of national governments who will always insist upon having the final say over their own contingents.

Some governments may have particular reasons for not wishing to become involved in post-conflict development in certain countries or regions. For example, some western governments may be reluctant to intervene in their former colonies in order to avoid being accused of imperialism, a charge that has even been raised against the UN in some contexts. At the same time, some former colonial states may blame their former colonial power for their current predicament and hence will be reluctant to have them operating within their borders. Indeed, many writers on the Left emphasize the extent to which western powers are often the main instigators behind conflicts (Chomsky 2000). They are also sustaining an international economy that is increasing inequality and contributing to poverty and resource competition within many developing societies, which is why the majority of the world's conflicts are in the South. In short, we must employ an international political economy critique to understand contemporary conflict. However, this position implies that conflict resolution and management are always likely to be undermined by the international economic order, a contention that many within the peace-building community would reject. Moreover, given that this approach is ultimately dependent upon the overthrow of international capitalism, it offers little practicable help to those caught up in conflict zones.

There is a growing call to shift to the 'peacekeeping from below' approach, whereby the onus should be upon local people devising local solutions to conflict (see Lederach 1997; Ramsbotham, Woodhouse and Miall 2005). It entails NGOs playing a greater role in conflict management and resolution, as many of them have gained considerable knowledge and expertise from operating in the field. Likewise, because grassroots and community-based organizations represent local interests, they are seen by some practitioners as an essential element in the building of a sustainable peace process (Lederach 1997; Reality of Aid 2006). Advocates of this approach maintain that it also enhances the prospects of formulating culturally sensitive peace-building strategies. Moreover, it is hoped that the ways in which NGOs operate – namely through negotiation, mediation and campaigning activity – can help to spread these practices and in turn contribute to civil society and democracy in conflict-afflicted states.

However, NGOs have on occasion been accused of serving western interests and this charge can serve to reduce their credibility and influence in some contexts, whereas grassroots and community-based organizations often lack the necessary political clout to make much of a difference. In the case of the latter, there is also the matter of how representative they are of local opinion (see chapter 8). And as touched upon earlier, one of the effects of conflict is frequently the erosion of civil society. Moreover, a plethora of NGOs operating in a conflict zone can make it difficult to devise and implement coordinated peace-building strategies, especially as some will be pursuing their own approaches to conflict resolution (Ramsbotham, Woodhouse and Miall 2005: 224). Nevertheless, on a broader scale, Mary Kaldor (2003, 2007) considers NGOs and international NGOs (INGOs) to be an important part of the formation of a global civil society that she views as an antidote to the atrocities committed in many contemporary conflicts. For Kaldor, global civil society is underpinned by human rights law, and this includes adhering to stipulations concerning the rules and conduct of war.

The reform of the United Nations system

At this juncture, the UN remains the primary force within the development–security dynamic, and this is despite the criticisms that it has generated. Indeed, in response to these criticisms, the UN has undergone a major review of its processes. It culminated in the signing of a reform document in September 2005 by world leaders at a summit coinciding with the UN's sixtieth anniversary. Here the focus will be solely upon the conflict and security aspects of this document, the central tenets of which are the following:

- It established a 'responsibility to protect' (R2P) principle of intervention in cases of genocide, ethnic cleansing and war crimes, thereby breaking with the convention of non-intervention in a sovereign state unless it represents a security threat to its neighbours. R2P breaks with the principle of non-intervention established in Article 2 [4] of the UN Charter.
- It agreed to the setting up of a new Peace-building Commission geared to helping failed states and countries make the transition from war to peace.
- The reform document condemned terrorism 'in all its forms and manifestations, committed by whomever, wherever and for whatever purposes'. However, no consensus emerged upon the definition of terrorism.
- Finally, the summit also decided upon the establishment of a new Human Rights Council to monitor human rights abuses.

At the time, the reform document was heavily criticized by a number of government leaders, including those of Venezuela, Indonesia, Cuba and Canada. Much of this criticism centred upon what the reform document omitted, notably the lack of agreement on a strategy to prevent the spread of nuclear weapons. The Human Rights Council is also considered by its critics to lack the appropriate powers and is therefore not up to the task. In particular, a number of western governments were concerned to prevent countries with a record of human rights abuses from being allowed to join it. Concern has also been expressed that the Peace-building Commission will be like many other UN agencies – namely New York-based and geared primarily to dealing with governments – when what is required is greater engagement with CSOs on the ground (IDC 2006: 52).

Lastly, there was widespread disappointment that attempts to broaden the membership of the UN Security Council to include more developing nations made no progress (see chapter 7). And some decisions and policy areas were simply deferred to other meetings. Moreover, the human rights abuses that have been committed in Darfur and Zimbabwe since the signing of the reform document have raised further doubts about the effectiveness of the measures that were agreed upon. As has been shown, the interrelationship between development and security is both evolving and complex.

Summary

- Conflict and the concept of human security have become an integral part of development.
- Critics maintain that security has been politically expedient for many northern governments.
- There are numerous factors that account for the rise in conflict within the South, but, to gain a more informed understanding of this phenomenon, we need to examine the particular conditions within individual developing societies.

RECOMMENDED READING

- On security and development, see Anthony McGrew and Nana K. Poku (eds), *Globalization, Development and Human Security* (2007) and Robert Picciotto and Rachel Weaving (eds), *Security and Development* (2006).
- For humanitarian intervention, see Thomas G. Weiss, *Humanitarian Intervention* (2007), and for peacekeeping, see Alex Bellamy, Paul Williams and Stuart Griffin, *Understanding Peacekeeping* (2004).
- On post-conflict development, see Gerd Junne and Willemijn Verkoren (eds), *Postconflict Development: Meeting New Challenges* (2005).

WEBSITES

- www.humansecurity-chs.org/finalreport: Website of the Commission on Human Security from where it is possible to access its 2003 report entitled *Human Security Now*.

- www.humansecurityreport.info: For access to the *Human Security Reports* published by the Human Security Report Project.
- www.humansecuritynetwork.org: Website of the Human Security Network that is made up of UN member states, academics and civil society groups.
- www.un.org/peace/reports: For access to the *Report of the Panel on United Nations Peace Operations* (A/55/305), otherwise known as the Brahimi Report.

CHAPTER 6

Trade and Development

- The free trade debate
- Fair trade and development
- The WTO and the world trading system
- Trade and development: a complex relationship

Trade is widely considered to provide countries with a more effective and long-term developmental route out of poverty than international aid. It is claimed that if Africa could increase its share of world exports by 1 per cent, it would generate US$70 billion, which is around five times more than it receives in international aid (Byers 2003: 55). It is also estimated that if Africa, East Asia, South Asia and Latin America all increased their exports by this figure, the income generated could lift 128 million people out of poverty (Oxfam 2002: 5).

However, the relationship between trade and development provokes much debate, especially with regard to the linkage between trade openness or liberalization and economic growth, as will be shown in the first section of this chapter. The WTO-dominated world trading system, and the trade negotiations that sustain it, are arguably the most disputed issues within development. Here, the complexity of the trade–development relationship will be stressed. More specifically, it will be emphasized that the economic growth achieved by a developing country is dependent upon the particular conditions within it, the nature of its exports and the type of international trading regime that has been established, especially in relation to market access to developed countries. There is therefore a need for a contextualized and differentiated understanding of the trade–development dynamic. It also means that a multilateral trading regime should allow developing countries the space to design trade–development strategies that suit their particular circumstances, rather than insisting that they adhere to universal prescriptions.

The free trade debate

The impact of free trade or trade liberalization upon development is an issue that tends to polarize opinion, even provoking violent protests at the WTO trade talks in Seattle in 1999.[1]

The case for trade liberalization

Advocates of trade liberalization argue for trade barriers to be lowered on the following grounds:

Facilitating development in the South Free traders consider increasing participation in the global economy through trade to be the primary means of achieving development. From their perspective, trade liberalization facilitates economic growth and development in the South by making it easier for the region's producers to sell their products to the widest possible market. In contrast, whenever governments implement tariffs, it raises the prices of imports, making it harder for producers from developing nations to sell their products in these countries. It also means that consumers have to pay unnecessarily high prices for goods and services, and it often results in less choice.

Some governments protect their domestic producers by providing them with financial subsidies in order to reduce their production costs, thereby helping them to increase their levels of production. For free traders, this measure leads to overproduction, lowering the global market prices for particular goods, and again reduces the amount that producers in other countries can earn. In this vein, whenever a government implements quotas, foreign producers are unable to export any more goods to that country beyond a restricted level, even if their particular product is cheaper and of better quality. Moreover, trade liberalizers maintain that it is unwise even for developing countries to pursue the protectionist route because this artificially protects their producers, making them uncompetitive. From their perspective, free trade encourages competition, and this in turn acts as a stimulant to innovation, improved productivity and development.

Arguably, under free trade conditions, developing countries have an economic advantage over developed countries because their wage levels tend to be lower and working hours longer, and hence production costs are cheaper.[2] Indeed, northern governments often accuse their southern counterparts of engaging in unfair competition by not clamping down on child labour, allowing sweatshop conditions and having lax environmental standards. Conversely, many southern governments regard northern concerns about labour and environmental standards and human rights in their countries as simply an opportune way of banning their products. In this regard, free traders argue that the issue of labour exploitation in the developing world is pushed so heavily by northern trade unionists because it is seen as a way of curbing the competition that this source presents and protecting northern jobs (Legrain 2002: 64). It also means that western ethical consumerism can operate as a form of unintended protectionism. Indeed, Martin Wolf (2004) argues that consumer boycotts and export sanctions upon companies and countries in the developing world where labour exploitation is being practised invariably leads to the exploited losing their jobs and incomes, as well as blocking the best way out of poverty for these countries.

Improved resource allocation   Participating in world trade enables developing countries to obtain the materials, goods, services and investment which they lack, and that may well be holding up their development. They are able to purchase these resources from the revenue gained from their own exports. From the perspective of free traders, trade liberalization makes this process much easier because it makes international trade flow and function more smoothly, and in doing so enables developing countries to speed up the development of their productive capacities. Moreover, by entering global markets, developing countries will also gain access to new ideas, information and above all the latest technologies. As we will see in chapter 10, some commentators stress that ICTs can potentially enable developing nations to skip stages of development, with some moving to a post-industrial knowledge-based mode of production. Indeed, it could be argued that the 'network society' is the ultimate free trade model.

Universal benefits   According to the classical economist David Ricardo (1772–1823), due to factors ranging from the quality of its land to its technological capacity, every country has a 'comparative advantage' in producing some good or product (Ricardo 1817). It therefore makes sense to utilize this specialization through open markets. Indeed, maximizing the efficiency of the production process can help to reduce costs. In short, if countries concentrate upon producing what they are best at, and import those goods in which they have a comparative disadvantage, it will be to the benefit of all. In contrast, when governments implement protectionist measures, they often do so for their own political objectives and/or to protect producer interests. As for developing countries, Douglas Irwin maintains that even if a country 'lacks an absolute advantage in any field, it will always have a comparative advantage in the production of some goods', and the income earned from exporting them can be used for development purposes (2005: 32).

Mike Moore (2003), the former head of the WTO, similarly maintains that free trade has the potential to bring universal benefits. Put simply, for writers like Moore, the expansion of world trade can help to raise living standards throughout the world. In this regard, research carried out by Australian academics indicates that halving current average tariff rates would lead to an increase in the world's output of US$450 billion per annum, which translates as each person earning on average an extra US$75 (Morris 2003). World Bank (2001a) research estimates that a liberalized trade regime would increase global economic growth by US$287 billion per annum by 2015 lifting 320 million people out of poverty (Schifferes 2005b).

The Asian development experience   Dating back to the British development experience, which saw Britain reliant upon its maritime power and the export of cotton textiles, free traders have maintained that foreign trade can operate as an engine of growth. In essence, outward-oriented trade leads to growth which in turn provides the productive capacity and incentive to encourage more trade. Continuing this theme in our own time, trade liberalizers point to the strong economic growth that Asia has enjoyed in the recent period, which they claim has come from countries in the region participating in global markets and placing trade at the heart of their development policies (although, as we saw in chapter 1, this view is contested). The growth achieved by their export-oriented approach has led to the number of people in the region who live on less than US$1 per day falling by 0.25 billion between 1990 and 2001.

In contrast, Africa's share of global exports has fallen from nearly 5 per cent in 1980 to under 2 per cent in 2004, and there is growing acceptance among African governments that this is because trade has not been prioritized within their respective development strategies as well as there being excessive controls on international trade (Amoako 2004). Furthermore, it has been estimated that the lack of openness to the international economy has cost Africa on average about 1.2 per cent growth per year (Sachs and Warner 1995b). Addressing this matter was one of the key concerns at the Conference of African Ministers of Finance, Planning and Economic Development held in Kampala, Uganda, in May 2004 (UNECAa 2004). At this conference, it was agreed that there was a need to mainstream trade policies into national development strategies in order to achieve economic growth and poverty reduction (ibid.: 3). Trade liberalizers also note that when the Doha Round of trade talks stalled, which was designed among other things to expand trade liberalization, the governments of many LEDCs argued that the delay was hurting them most of all. In short, it is claimed, that developing nations increasingly recognize the benefits of free trade for their own economies and future development.

Environmental and political benefits   Arguably, there is an environmental theme running through the work of the classical economists David Ricardo and Adam Smith, who made the case for free trade on the grounds that it would encourage national specialization and facilitate efficient use of the earth's scarce resources. By obstructing comparative advantage, protectionism therefore works against the environment. In addition, contemporary economists emphasize that MEDCs are in a better position to tackle environmental degradation than LEDCs because they no longer have to prioritize everyday subsistence needs. Of course, for free traders, the economic growth needed to acquire MEDC status is best achieved through trade liberalization. Moreover, this growth will mean that developing countries are better able to afford the latest green technologies. Free trade also ensures that MNCs, which generally utilize green technologies more than local businesses, are able to set up plants and outlets in different parts of the world, thereby facilitating their dissemination.

Free traders also view trade liberalization as contributing to international peace. In contrast to protectionism, which is a form of economic nationalism that can generate tensions between countries, trade is a human activity that facilitates cultural interaction and in doing so it can help us to gain a more informed understanding of other societies. In this vein, it is argued that trade openness can help to spread democracy through the exchange of ideas that it facilitates. Free traders observe that countries like Chile, South Korea and Taiwan have become more democratic as they have developed trading relationships with the rest of the international community (Wolf 2004: 82). This claim is also a variant of modernization theory which sees a linkage between economic freedom and political freedom. If people are freely operating within market economies and taking responsibility for earning a living and running businesses, it follows that they will soon wish to take greater political control over their lives. However, it is countered that, since the 1970s, a number of the developing countries most actively participating in global markets and enjoying the fastest economic growth have been one-party governments, including China, Indonesia and Singapore.

The case against free trade

Critics of free trade argue that it hinders rather than helps the development of poorer countries, with some insisting that the liberalized world trading system is a contributory factor to the poverty that exists in the developing world (Dunkley 2004; Stiglitz 2002).

The free trade case is overstated   The claim that trade liberalization invariably leads to economic growth for developing countries is disputed, particularly as many of them will be dependent upon a limited range of primary commodities (Yanikkaya 2003). Indeed, the Prebisch–Singer thesis that emerged in the 1950s contends that primary commodity producers do less well under free market systems. This is because under such conditions, whenever incomes rise, the demand for manufactured goods tends to grow more rapidly than demand for primary products like food (see Prebisch 1950).

The benefits of trade liberalization for the least developed countries (LDCs) – defined by their very low per capita incomes, high economic vulnerability to shocks and weak human resources – have also been challenged. In this regard, there are two notable aspects to an UNCTAD report entitled *The Least Developed Countries Report 2004: Linking International Trade with Poverty Reduction* (2004b). Firstly, it notes that most LDCs implemented forms of trade liberalization in the 1990s, albeit often compelled to do so through their involvement in SAPs. Secondly, under these conditions, and despite diversifying their exports and receiving preferential market access from developed and developing countries, LDCs continue to import more than they export and are therefore faced with a worsening trade balance and deepening debt. Even in LDCs that have enjoyed significant export growth, average private consumption per capita has not taken off in the same way. In other words, contrary to the prevailing philosophy within the IFIs and the WTO, in the case of LDCs, a trade-driven approach to development is not necessarily leading to economic growth and sustained poverty reduction.

The UNCTAD report acknowledges that there is a range of factors behind this disappointing picture, including – dependent upon the particular LDC – civil conflict, decreased aid inflows, high population growth and slow export growth. It also accepts that international trade has the potential to play a key role in poverty reduction, but in order for this to happen the appropriate conditions have to be established, notably a fairer multilateral trading system. In this vein, it argues that the extent to which trade liberalization leads to a reduction in poverty is conditioned by the 'level of development of a country and the structure of its economy' (UNCTAD 2004b: 77). Indeed, the central theme of the subsequent UNCTAD (2006b) report is the need for LDCs to develop their productive capacities if they are to achieve sustained economic growth and poverty reduction. Finally, the authors of the 2004 UNCTAD report maintain that poverty reduction in LDCs is dependent upon trade working hand-in-hand with continued aid and debt relief.

The need to nurture developing economies For critics of trade liberalization, the UNCTAD report reinforces their contention that countries in the early stages of development need to protect and develop their economies before exposing them to competitive global markets. Chang points to a long history of countries adopting this approach, with Britain doing so up until the mid-nineteenth century, for example (2002a: 22). Under free trade, LEDCs are unable to nurture nascent industries and hence will always struggle to achieve the degree of diversification necessary for development. Indeed, there is a danger that they become simply specialists in particular areas, notably keeping their traditional role as provider of agricultural and primary commodities for the markets of northern countries (Ocampo and Taylor 1998; Storm 2005).[3] Chang makes the broader point that, under protectionist ISI, 'developing countries used to grow, on average, at double the rate that they are doing today under free trade' (2007: 69). However, Martin Wolf (2004) questions the effectiveness of infant-industry protection measures, including bans on competing imports, arguing that producers inevitably become domestically oriented and uncompetitive.

Some writers argue that, rather than relying upon international trade, a more productive approach to development is to focus upon internal economic priorities like security, good governance, stable trading conditions and investment in education and technology (e.g., Rodrik 1999). This view will be returned to in more detail in the final section. But one benefit of this approach is that it would seem to make developing countries less susceptible to fluctuations in international trading conditions. It also starts to address the concerns of some in the South that, with the rise of Asia and international trading conditions becoming more competitive, northern countries are showing signs of moving away from free trade (Bello 1995).

Free trade benefits the economically powerful It is argued that conditions of free trade will invariably benefit richer developed countries as they have greater productive capacity and the advantage of economies of scale, with which developing countries simply cannot compete. Indeed, Chang (2002a) maintains that knowing that they have this advantage is a primary reason why established economic powers push for free trade. In short, countries lower tariffs as they grow richer, while, among the economically powerful, MNCs particularly benefit from any reduction in trade barriers because it gives them greater access to new markets and the chance to invest and set up branches and outlets in more countries. In fact, MNCs account for 70 per cent of world trade, with approaching a third of it being intra-firm trade conducted between branches of multinationals (UNCTAD 2001). Indeed, Richard Peet (2003) believes the main consequence of the neo-liberal policies pursued by IFIs is to facilitate the profit-maximizing activities of MNCs and TNCs, often at the expense of smaller companies in the developing world.

Another consequence of creating conditions that suit multinationals is that they arguably have been too successful to the point where some exercise virtual monopolies within certain markets and are therefore running counter to the principle of free trade. The global commodity trade, in particular, is concentrated in the hands of a small number of MNCs, with Nestlé and Phillip Morris dominating the coffee industry, for example (Wolf 2004: 206). Likewise, Eric Holt-Giménez and Raj Patel (2009) contend that free trade agreements (FTAs), like the North American Free Trade Agreement (NAFTA), have facilitated the corporate takeover of the world's food systems. It means that countries have lost control of their food systems and are dependent on a volatile global market, one that is dominated by agri-food monopolies. Indeed, the search for profits by agri-businesses has been cited as a contributory factor behind the sharp increase in world food prices in 2008.[4]

As a result of their growing economic power, many MNCs enjoy considerable influence in their dealings with national governments and are able to push for ever greater access to their domestic markets, as well as to largely dictate the conditions under which they operate – a state of affairs that can often be to the detriment of workers. Many anti-globalization groups argue that free trade has simply enabled multinationals to operate sweatshops, with low wage levels and poor labour standards. For their part, national governments will always be reluctant to turn away the investment and jobs that multinationals bring with them (for a critique of these claims, see Wolf 2004, ch. 11).

In *Free Trade and Uneven Development* (2002), Gary Gereffi and his co-writers explore the effects of globalization, trade liberalization and the NAFTA on inter-firm linkages in the textiles and apparel industry. This book is part of a growing number of works on global commodity chains. For Gereffi (2004), the latter are part of a power shift within the global economy from the manufacturing sector to the retail sector. Global retailers like Wal-Mart have enhanced their own economic power through utilizing information technologies and logistics and distribution centre management to gain control of global commodity supply chains. They have developed global sourcing networks that for a low cost make what they need according to their exact specifications. In essence, their decisions increasingly determine where products are made around the world. This model has been criticized for ensuring a global race to the bottom in terms of costs. It means that suppliers struggle to make profits and are wary of complaining for fear that the retailers will go elsewhere for their outsourcing. In turn, it invariably entails that the wages of their workers remain low (ibid.). And because of the higher wages in MEDCs, offshore outsourcing also means a reduction in the amount of jobs available for citizens in the developed world (Gereffi 2007).

Gereffi, Humphrey and Sturgeon (2005) refer to these new network forms as 'global value chains'. They contend that research into these value chains reveals 'that access to developed country markets has become increasingly dependent on participating in global production networks led by firms based in developed countries' (ibid.: 99). For Gereffi, this pattern is evident in the case of Wal-Mart. In essence, Wal-Mart gains its economic power because its sheer size (i.e., its number of US customers) ensures that it provides a gateway into the American economy for overseas suppliers. In this regard, while 6 per cent of Wal-Mart's total merchandise was imported in 1995, this figure had increased tenfold to 60 per cent in 2004 (ibid.).

The social and environmental costs of trade liberalization By benefiting the economically powerful, critics argue, trade liberalization exacerbates existing inequalities both between and within societies, leading to potentially harmful consequences for social and political order. Furthermore, tariffs are an important source of revenue for poor countries. Analysts from Nottingham University estimate that this source provides between 15 and 50 per cent of the public finance for poorer countries (Thurston 2003: 53). Free trade can therefore lead to a reduction in government budgets and in turn to the amount spent on social welfare provision.

For environmentalists, the expansion of world trade encouraged by outward orientation creates environmental costs, notably as a result of the increased transportation, resource depletion and energy usage that it entails. It is also claimed that MNCs take advantage of free trade conditions to relocate to the LDCs because they lack the resources to enforce rigorous environmental regulation regimes. Poorer countries therefore become 'pollution havens' for the world's major polluters (Gallagher 2004), although this concept is disputed (see Letchumanan 2000). Free trade also heightens international economic competition, creating concern among businesses and governments that their counterparts in other countries are not pursuing the same environmental

standards in order to make themselves more competitive. Countries therefore feel pressure to reduce their environmental standards to those with
the poorest record, which results in a 'race to the bottom' (Porter 1999).
Environmentalists therefore seek stronger rules on environmental protection
to be incorporated into all trade deals. Some go further and argue for the establishment of a World Environment Organization (WEO) to counterbalance the
power of the WTO and trade interests (chapter 9).

Free trade in practice   Critics also argue that free trade is always likely to be
undermined by countries and producers pursuing their own interests. Within
the EU, the Common Agricultural Policy (CAP) provides export subsidies
to European farmers and protects them from competition through import
tariffs, while US cotton farmers receive considerable subsidies from their
government. For example, according to a report published by the Fairtrade
Foundation in 2010, during the previous decade the US and EU provided
cotton farms subsidies of US$32 billion (£20 billion), with US cotton farmers
receiving US$24.4 billion of this total. It is estimated that these subsidies cost
West African cotton farmers £155 million a year (Fairtrade Foundation 2010).

Most importantly, northern countries are protecting the very areas that
are key southern exports. At the same time, African governments argue that
they have responded to northern calls for trade liberalization by reducing
their support for agriculture and opening up their economies to foreign
trade under the terms of the SAPs. An Oxfam report contends that southern
countries are opening up their respective economies more rapidly than their
northern counterparts, noting that 'average import tariffs have been halved
in sub-Saharan Africa and South Asia, and cut by two-thirds in Latin America
and East Asia' (2002: 12). Northern governments have therefore been accused
of double standards in relation to this issue (e.g., Oxfam 2002).

Northern governments are also accused of being overly protective of their
intellectual property rights (patents, copyrights and trademarks), which has
resulted in the setting up of TRIPS (Agreement on Trade-Related Aspects of
Intellectual Property Rights) that even covers areas such as educational material and medical equipment and drugs (chapter 10). In crude financial terms,
this translates as northern firms currently earning US$71 billion a year as they
account for 96 per cent of royalties from patents (UNDP 2005: 135). The TRIPS
agreement in effect functions as a form of rent collection for northern countries, while hindering the technological development of southern countries
(Khor 2001b: 46).

Unsurprisingly, the EU and the US reject all of these charges. They maintain
that on average southern countries continue to enjoy higher protection (see
also Bhagwati and Panagariya 2001), and on the grounds of fairness need to
continue opening up their markets. But, as will now be shown, the fair trade
movement has a different conception of fairness in relation to international
trade.

Fair trade and development

The fair trade movement emerged in the second half of the twentieth century because of what its proponents believed was the unfairness of the existing deregulated global trading regime, and with the intention of providing an alternative to this system. However, given that the movement contains a range of opinion, and different organizations have their own initiatives and ways of operating within it, the intention here will simply be to delineate key themes.

In essence, producers in the developing world enter a fair trade partnership in order to receive a fairer price for their goods, and this is measured in terms of giving them a living wage and ensuring that their production costs are met. Moreover, because the price is guaranteed and the fair trade partnership is designed to be a long-term relationship, it provides producers with a degree of financial certainty and continuity that enables them to pursue sustainable development. In addition, certified fair trade initiatives pay a social premium to fund local community infrastructural projects, such as crèches, better roads, and improved health care and sanitation. Fair trade also offers market advice and information to producers, as well as access to credit. Support is also given to democratic groups that represent small-scale producers (cooperatives) and workers (unions). It is also insisted upon that there are no abuses of labour during the production process (Nicholls and Opal 2005).

Fair trade advocates emphasize that their project is based upon 'trade, not aid' (Sachs and Santarius 2007). In other words, it is through their own efforts that the poor will lift themselves out of poverty. For this to happen, however, there must be improved access to northern markets for southern producers, as well as an end to the subsidized competition that they face from northern producers. Beyond this general demand, fair trade campaigners believe there are specific policy issues and areas that need to be revisited, notably that of intellectual property rights and trade rules applied to service sectors like accountancy, banking and insurance. Some fair traders focus on achieving closer regulation of those MNCs operating within developing countries, especially with regard to the rights of workers.

For consumers, the Fairtrade label or kitemark is an indication that, along with producers receiving a fair price, the product meets certain minimal standards in relation to employment conditions and pay, health and safety, and the environment. In turn, fair trade has contributed to an increase in the number of ethical consumers, especially in the West. According to Fairtrade Labelling Organizations International (FLO), an umbrella organization constituted by numerous national initiatives, consumers spent over 2.3 billion euros for Fairtrade certified goods in 2007, a 47 per cent increase on the previous year (FLO 2007: 11). In 2006, there were over one million small-scale producers involved in fair trade (Cooper 2006: 40). And the number of Fairtrade certified producer organizations has risen from 224 in 2001 to 632 in 2007 (FLO 2007: 5).

Fair trade: critical perspectives

Many economists believe that fair trade will never have mass appeal as most people are primarily concerned with purchasing goods as cheaply as possible (Sidwell 2008). In this regard, there are fears that rising food prices will be especially damaging to the fair trade project as people will be even less willing to pay for generally higher-priced fair trade goods. For some, therefore, fair trade is unlikely to achieve a significant reduction in poverty in the South, and targeted developmental aid remains a more effective solution. However, the sales of fair trade goods have risen substantially in the past decade, especially in Europe where they are entering the mainstream and are no longer a niche market (Krier 2005). Moreover, an increasing number of companies are looking to participate in the fair trade system.

Interestingly, some within the fair trade movement itself are critical of the direction it is taking (see Raynolds, Murray and Wilkinson 2007). Some FLO affiliates have been criticized for relegating southern development concerns in their attempt to expand the volume of fair trade sales (ibid.: 225). In particular, there is concern that companies like Nestlé, the world's largest food corporation, are associating themselves with fair trade when many fair traders consider they have been part of the problem. Others, however, regard the latter development as evidence of the broadening appeal of the fair trade message. From their perspective, MNCs have to be engaged with and properly incorporated into the fair trade movement, and this will help to ensure that they are not hijacking the image for their own commercial purposes.

The most serious charge raised against fair trade is that in numerous ways it hinders rather than aids economic development. Firstly, producers in the developing world wishing to participate in the fair trade network must adhere to the regulations laid down by the relevant organizations, and this creates an additional layer of bureaucracy that can only serve to stifle economic growth. Secondly, with some trade justice campaigners calling for poorer countries to raise their trade barriers and to reverse years of liberalization, free traders emphasize the harmful protectionist aspects of fair trade, arguing that developing economies would benefit more from concentrating upon improving the market performance of their key exports (Lindsey 2003). Thirdly, the problem with the price guarantees provided by fair trade is that it not only keeps inefficient producers in business but also encourages overproduction, resulting in a global reduction in the price of commodities and lower returns for non-fair trade producers. Fourthly, because producers are artificially protected, it discourages mechanization and diversification (Lindsey 2003; Sidwell 2008). As a result, many developing societies continue to rely upon a few primary commodities for their export earnings. In short, fair trade is charged with distorting markets and the economies of developing countries.

Marc Sidwell, in a report published by the Adam Smith Institute (ASI) entitled *Unfair Trade* (2008), contends the fair trade movement is essentially a marketing ploy that provides a minority of farmers with a higher price for their goods but at the expense of all the others who do not qualify for Fairtrade certification. He also argues that no more than 10 per cent of the premium that consumers pay for fair trade actually goes to producers, with most of it going to retailers. Moreover, many of these farmers are in Mexico, a relatively developed economy, while poorer countries are often neglected. Unsurprisingly, the ASI report concludes that a more productive way of helping southern producers would be to abolish barriers to trade in the developed world.

Thus, the contribution of fair trade to development in the South is a source of contestation. Furthermore, from an environmental perspective, fair trade does not address the problem of current levels of global consumption and transportation (Johnston 2002). However, the fair trade movement has raised awareness of the difficulties that southern producers can face in participating in global markets and, in purchasing fair trade products, consumers are also commenting upon conventional international trade. In turn, this creates pressure upon the WTO to oversee the formation of an equitable multilateral trading system. And it is to this matter that this chapter will now turn.

The WTO and the world trading system

Between 1948 and 2000, international trade increased by an average of 6.1 per cent every year, and this included an expansion of merchandise trade (goods) as well as trade in services like accountancy, banking and information. However, this growth has been uneven, with 23 countries accounting for 75 per cent of this trade (Gareis and Varwick 2005: 52). For this reason, the world trading system and the lengthy trade negotiations that shape it continue to be controversial issues. Currently, the ninth round of trade talks is in progress, having been reconvened at Doha, the Qatari capital, in November 2001 after being halted following the protests in Seattle in 1999. The trade rounds tend to last many years, due to a combination of: the importance and complexity of the issues being decided upon; governments pursuing their national self-interest; and the fact that the deals are put together as a single all-or-nothing package with members have the right to veto any final deal.

The General Agreement on Tariffs and Trade (GATT)

In the post-war period, a number of international institutions have played a key role in shaping the nature of world trade, beginning with the establishment of GATT in 1947. GATT's first task was to help revive international trade following the upheavals of the Second World War. Throughout its history, GATT pushed a free trade agenda, seeking the reduction of tariffs and the ending of forms of trade discrimination. The demise of GATT can be traced to the Uruguay round of trade negotiations (September 1986–April 1994) becoming bogged down in debates between the USA and Europe over agricultural subsidies. It was replaced by the WTO in 1995, a more influential organization in the sense that it has greater powers but also a wider remit encompassing trade in services like banking and telecommunications and not just merchandise goods, as was the case with GATT.

World Trade Organization

The WTO similarly seeks to promote trade liberalization. It does this by policing free trade agreements, encouraging countries to abolish import tariffs and other trade restrictions, hosting multilateral trade negotiations, and operating as a mediator in trade disputes. The WTO has certain shared arrangements and cooperative practices with the UN, but it is not formally part of the UN system and has its own legal status. Based in Geneva, it is a major international player in its own right with a membership of 152 countries in 2008. Indeed, China spent many years seeking admission before formally joining the WTO in December 2001. Every member is expected to abide by its rulings, and WTO members have the right to endorse its decisions by imposing trade sanctions against countries that breach its rules.

Because of its promotion of free trade, the WTO is associated with economic globalization. Consequently, it has attracted the wrath of anti-globalizers who would like to see it scrapped as part of a broader redesigning of the international trading system along more equitable and environmentally friendly lines. Many within the anti-globalization movement maintain that the WTO is indifferent to the impact of free trade on workers' rights, the environment, health and child labour. Other critics consider the WTO to be too powerful, reflected in its ability to encroach upon the sovereignty of nation-states through its mandatory multilateral agreements.

The WTO is also accused of a lack of openness and accessibility, reflected in the restrictions on media and public access and the behind-the-scenes way that it arrives at decisions, which allows powerful countries to build the necessary 'consensus' to get their policies pushed through. Critics especially want the influence exerted by MNCs upon the WTO's decision-making to be made public, and at the same time for there to be greater input in these processes for CSOs (UNDP 2003b). It is also claimed that northern countries have ensured that they have benefited from any exceptions to the WTO's trade liberalization rules, notably concerning subsidies being given for basic research and development and reducing regional disparities (Chang 2007: 76–7).

From a development perspective, the WTO is charged with paying insufficient attention to the issues affecting developing nations, notably their desire for better access to the markets of western countries, but also for there to be changes in the international terms of trade and, specifically, a rise in the prices of primary commodities. Moreover, in signing up to the WTO, developing countries have to agree to its multilateral trade rules and general stipulations concerning services and intellectual property rights as part of a single undertaking, when often they face particular development challenges requiring the formulation of individual strategies (Storm 2005; UNDP 2003b). In other words, the WTO reduces the ability of LEDCs to pursue national trade policies. And, as we will see, some writers believe this has been the basis of the rapid growth of many Asian economies. Indeed, a UNDP report has argued that the WTO should take greater account of the differing capacities of developing countries by allowing for more flexibility in compliance with its rules and greater policy autonomy (UNDP 2003b: 69). In short, there needs to be a more differentiating and contextualist approach to trade policy.

The general response of the WTO to these criticisms is that three-quarters of its members are from the developing world and development is now firmly a part of its agenda, most notably underpinning the ninth round of trade talks. Furthermore, LEDCs receive 'special and differential treatment' (SDT), such as being able to use export subsidies and raise customs duties whenever increased competition from imports threatens their local industries.[5] Moreover, tariffs have been reduced, not abolished, under the WTO, infant industry protection is still permissible for up to eight years, and ultimately the WTO only covers trade-related policies (Chang 2003d). It is therefore claimed that developing countries can still to a significant extent pursue their own course to economic development.

In response to the charge of lack of democratic accountability, the WTO stresses that its rules were written by its own member states, and it is they that choose its leadership. It is therefore an intergovernmental rather than a supragovernmental organization (*The Economist* 2001: 54). Moreover, unlike the IMF and WB, voting is based upon national sovereignty and not financial contribution. In addition, the WTO's defenders argue that it provides the international community with a number of benefits. Above all, it has helped to prevent the world being plagued by selfish protectionism by putting pressure upon national governments to adhere to collectively negotiated and agreed trade rules. In doing so, it helps to create a stable trading environment for companies and countries. The WTO has also had to deal with more than 200 disputes since 1995, and its supporters maintain that it is more successful at resolving disputes than equivalent organizations, such as the UN. From this perspective, the WTO is a forum for ensuring multilateralism as opposed to unilateralism and bilateralism.

Defenders of the WTO also maintain that its voting procedures and dispute mechanisms enable developing countries to take on the most powerful nations, and such equitableness contrasts sharply with the UN Security Council, for example. For instance, in April 2008, the WTO backed a case brought by Latin American banana growing countries that the EU import duties on bananas flouted world trade rules. The so-called 'banana wars' date back to the 1990s and centre upon Latin American claims that the EU gives preferential treatment to its members' ex-colonies in Africa, the Caribbean and the Pacific region (ACP). Similarly, in June 2008, a WTO panel upheld an earlier ruling, which declared that the subsidies that the US government paid to its cotton growers were illegal and helped them to undercut foreign competitors. This decision meant that Brazil, which brought the case before the WTO in 2002, had the potential to impose retaliatory trade sanctions against the US amounting to billions of dollars.

However, Amin Alavi (2007) notes that in over ten years no sub-Saharan African country had used the WTO's Dispute Settlement Mechanism. He believes that this illustrates the marginal role and position of African countries in the WTO in general and is a reflection of their insignificant share of world trade. Others maintain that the WTO's Dispute Settlement Understanding is simply too costly for the LDCs to use (Storm 2005; UNDP 2003b). The UNDP has called for LDCs to receive support in order to reinforce their legal capacity and representation at the WTO (UNDP 2003b), while Thurston (2003) has argued that their technical capacity to evaluate how they will be affected by liberalization proposals needs to be bolstered. With 33 LDCs having no permanent representative in 2004, their ability to shape agreements and the organization as a whole is limited (UNDP 2005: 146).

The Doha Round

It was originally intended that a final agreement would be reached for the Doha Round of trade talks at a WTO meeting held in Hong Kong in December 2005. At this meeting, it was agreed that rich countries should end export subsidies to farmers by 2013. However, no agreement was reached on reducing import tariffs on agricultural produce. As for cotton, richer countries confirmed that they would phase out export subsidies, but no agreement on the date was set for reducing domestic subsidies for US farmers. This was a matter of great concern to African governments who maintained that it was forcing their own farmers out of the market. And many LEDCs expressed disappointment at the development package that was attached to the rest of the deal. While developing countries secured the right to sell 97 per cent of their goods to developed countries without paying tariffs or being limited by quotas, nevertheless the final arrangement was too full of exemptions to make any real difference to their situation. Japan, for instance, sought to exempt fish, sugar, maize and rice from the agreement.

The end of Doha?

In July 2006, the Doha negotiations were suspended because the EU and the US could not agree on the extent to which they should cut agricultural subsidies to their farmers, nor on when the tariff barriers that protected their producers should be removed. The other major stumbling block was that developing countries had to open up their economies to allow manufactured goods and services from the rest of the world, and some were reluctant to do so.

The next major attempt to complete the Doha Round was at a meeting held in Geneva at the end of July 2008. However, this broke down over a failure to agree on trade rules. India, China and their supporters insisted on the right to impose barriers to protect their farmers when farm imports rose above a certain level, while Washington insisted that this level had been set too low. But perhaps the clearest evidence that the Doha development round had lost its way was that African countries were not even represented in the final negotiations at the Geneva meeting. In April 2011, there was still little sign of the Doha Round of trade talks being completed.

Many NGOs maintain that for the LDCs no trade deal would be better than a bad deal. However, if the Doha Round is not completed, it would raise serious questions about the role and purpose of the WTO, as well as undermine the multilateral trading system. In this regard, there are signs of a weakening commitment to free trade on the part of some northern countries as many of their own industries become increasingly uncompetitive in comparison to some of the dynamic economies in Asia. If northern countries do adopt protectionist measures, it will restrict the access of developing countries to their markets and thereby hinder their economic development.

Moreover, if the Doha negotiations are unsuccessful, then it is likely to lead to a rise in trade disputes between nations. Indeed, following the suspension of the Doha trade round in 2006, China and Vietnam were at loggerheads with the EU over the issue of cheap Asian shoe imports into Europe. In the long term, global trade will be hampered if countries become more litigious and habitually take their individual trade disputes to the WTO's Dispute Settlement Panels, rather than adhering to collectively agreed trade frameworks. There is also the prospect of countries resorting to measures like dumping, whereby a government subsidizes some of its own manufacturing companies to such an extent that it enables them to sell their products abroad for less than the cost of making them, thereby ensuring they enjoy a significant advantage over their competitors.

Another consequence of the delays surrounding the Doha agreement is a growing tendency for governments to seek bilateral and regional arrangements as an alternative to a global trade deal. The US government either negotiated or was negotiating free trade agreements with over twenty countries, although, in the case of countries such as Bahrain and UAE, some of these were as much for strategic as economic objectives. The EU has been seeking to build economic ties with the 69 ACP nations who were former colonies in the form of EU–ACP Economic Partnership Agreements (EPAs). Similarly, there has been a proliferation in the number of bilateral FTAs in the Asia-Pacific region since the turn of the century, along with the consolidation of the ASEAN Free Trade Area (AFTA) initiative. In short, the number of trade agreements has increased rapidly since the Doha Round began, especially free trade agreements (WDI 2008: 339).

Trade liberalizers worry that regionalism will lead to the formation of rival trading blocs and inhibit world trade, although to date there is little evidence of this pattern. As for bilateralism, many LEDCs lack the political influence and productive capacity to enter negotiations with MEDCs on an equal basis, and this may lead to asymmetric bilateral trade agreements being concluded. As was suggested above, the multilateralism upon which the WTO is based ensures that developing nations are afforded at least some negotiating influence and that powerful countries like the US cannot readily ignore the collective pressure brought upon them by the other member states. Bilateral agreements can also make it more difficult for ordinary consumers to gain access to the cheapest goods and foodstuffs. Lastly, bilateral arrangements can restrict the international flow of goods and services and thereby serve to hold back the expansion of world trade that many consider to be essential to poverty reduction (E. Davis 2006).

Trade and development: a complex relationship

Having set out the major debates surrounding trade and development, the intention is now to suggest an appropriate way of conceptualizing this relationship. But in order to understand the impact of trade upon development, we need to take into account the nature of contemporary patterns of international trade.

Contemporary international trade patterns

Reflecting the expansion and greater integration of the global economy, the value of world exports rose to US$9 trillion in 2003, almost doubling during the previous decade (UNDP 2005: 114), while since the mid-1990s developing countries have enjoyed an average increase in export growth of almost 10 per cent a year, compared to the 5 per cent that developed countries have achieved (Moore 2003: 169).[6] It has meant that developing countries' share of world trade has risen from 16 per cent in 1990 to 30 per cent in 2006, although much of this has been driven by countries that are now economic powers in their own right, notably China, Brazil and India (WDI 2008: 318). Interestingly, the share of developing country exports in manufactured goods is growing, while that of food and commodities (excluding fuels) is much smaller and declining (ibid.). Furthermore, there is evidence that developing countries are now trading more with each other and, if this pattern persists, it may in time help to reduce their reliance upon trade with the developed world (Held 2004: 9).

Overall, however, the share of world trade within the developing world is unevenly spread. While Asia's share of world trade has grown consistently in the recent period, reaching 27.8 per cent in 2006, Africa's share has declined since the mid-1950s and constituted only 2.3 per cent of world trade in 2006 (ECIPE 2007; OECD 2007). Asian countries have specialized in manufactured exports, like computers and clothing – although India is increasingly focusing on services – which have risen in value relative to the commodities like coffee and copper that Africa exports. In fact, apart from the recent rise in prices, the price of primary commodities has been falling for two or three decades due to a general problem of structural over-supply (Oxfam 2002: 159), and this has revived southern demands for there to be changes in the international terms of trade. In relation to trade, therefore, Africa is falling behind not just the North but also other developing regions, with the World Bank estimating that the continent's decline in trade represents a loss equivalent to US\$70 billion annually (World Bank 2000a).[7]

Given this disappointing performance, African governments in particular continue to call for improved access to northern markets. But, at the UNECA-sponsored conference for African finance ministers in Kampala, it was recognized that they cannot simply wait for the access issue to be resolved and must instead explore other ways of enhancing their trading position, including diversifying and ending their reliance on commodity exports that are vulnerable to international price falls and the weather (UNECAa 2004). There was also acknowledgement of the need:

- to develop communication and transport infrastructures;
- to make companies more competitive;
- to improve access to trade financing and ICTs;
- to reduce delays at custom points;
- to lessen dependence upon trade taxes through more efficient domestic tax gathering and public spending;
- and to build the manufacturing sector.

In short, there was recognition that urgent action needed to be taken on the domestic front (ibid.: 2–3). In addition, speeding up regional integration by removing trade barriers and creating free trade areas within the continent was considered to be a priority. Thus, rather than simply relying on external or multilateral trade, greater emphasis needed to be placed upon intra-African trade which currently accounts for around only 10 per cent of Africa's total trade (ibid.: 3). Furthermore, it is accepted that Africa was opening up to external markets from the late 1980s onwards at a time when political instability and civil conflict was disrupting many African states, and this inevitably held back growth and reduced the impact of the reforms undertaken (UNECA 2004b).

At the same time, many of the poorest countries in Africa and beyond continue to be wary of free trade, believing that they lack the productive capacity to take advantage of the opportunity it affords and that many of their own farmers would struggle to compete with those of MEDCs. It is for this reason that poorer countries favour the gradual opening up of their economies while maintaining some built-in protections for their farmers and workers. There are some grounds for their concern as recent World Bank research indicates that the major beneficiaries from establishing a fully liberalized trading system would be industrialized countries and the larger developing countries

like Argentina, Brazil and South Africa who are major agricultural exporters (Schifferes 2005b). In contrast, those LEDCs who are food importers, like
Bangladesh, Cameroon and Mozambique, would struggle in the early years in
the event of such a system being established (ibid.).

Questioning trade openness

Turning specifically to the relationship between trade and development, the
extent to which trade openness contributes to economic growth continues
to be a source of debate. In a seminal article, Dani Rodrik and Francisco
Rodríguez (2000) question the methodologies and findings of five major studies on this area (Ben-David 1993; Dollar 1992; S. Edwards 1998; Frankel and
Romer 1999; Sachs and Warner 1995a), arguing that it is difficult to prove this
correlation. They emphasize how hard it is to isolate trade liberalization from
other aspects of trade policy, and trade-related causes from non-trade factors,
in accounting for economic growth. But their work is not a call for a return
to protectionism for developing countries, and they recognize that countries
sealed off from the rest of the international community invariably struggle to
develop and prosper. Instead, they call for more contextualized and comparative analyses of the relationship between trade and growth, and the avoidance of general and universal pronouncements on this complex subject, as is
the case in much of the relevant literature. Rodrik (1999, 2006) in particular
rejects the 'one size (or model) fits all' approach to economic development
offered by the Washington Consensus in the 1980s and 1990s (for a critical
response see Bhagwati and Srinivasan 2001). This theme is taken up in a report
by the African Trade Policy Centre (ATPC) which argues for exactly this type of
analysis, and sees particular benefit in comparing the African and Asian development experience in order to better understand the relationship between
trade policy and the economic performances of LEDCs (UNECA 2004b).

There is also increasing recognition of the limitations of markets among
both development specialists and politicians, certainly in comparison with
the heyday of the Washington Consensus. More specifically, there is greater
acceptance that markets are simply one constituent element of economic
development, and that other factors, like the availability of skilled labour,
an integrated transport infrastructure and the level of domestic savings, play
an equally significant role (see Broad 2004). Indeed, for markets to function,
they are reliant upon other development prerequisites being in place, like
stable societies, the rule of law and internationally agreed legislation on trade
and finance, and this in turn highlights the importance of the role played
by national and international institutions. The Commission on Growth and
Development (CGD), an internationally renowned think tank, contends that
participation by LEDCs in global markets has to be complemented by government intervention. Such intervention can include protectionist and diversification policies but also public investment in infrastructure, education and

health in order to attract private investment (CGD 2008: 6). For the CGD, sustained growth 'requires a long-term commitment by a country's political leaders, a commitment pursued with patience, perseverance, and pragmatism' (ibid.).

The need for flexibility

The cumulative effect of this questioning of trade openness has been a growing call for developing countries to be granted the flexibility to adapt their trade and tariff regimes to suit their particular needs, rather than simply being integrated into trade liberalization regimes. Even some northern politicians recognize that the WTO needs to tailor its development round so that this principle is clearly established (e.g., Byers 2003). Support for this particular approach is also provided by the ATPC report mentioned above which points to research showing that the Asian economic success story is not down to either trade liberalization or protectionism. Rather, it is based upon individual countries employing trade policy dynamically and pragmatically in order to support their particular development strategies, and to reflect the diverse and evolving needs of different sectors within their economies (UNECA 2004b).[8]

The UNDP (2003b) has similarly made an appeal for developing countries to be granted the flexibility and policy space to construct their own development strategies that suit their particular circumstances. In this vein, Chang and Grabel (2004) note that Hong Kong and Singapore took the free trade route to economic growth, whereas China and India achieved their rapid economic rise by pursuing a more strategic approach to economic openness. Mehdi S. Shafaeddin (2006) argues that economic growth was achieved in East Asia because the countries in the region had an established industrial base and manufacturing capacity that ensured they were equipped to take advantage of the structural reforms but also because liberalization was introduced selectively over time. This was frequently not the case in developing countries beyond this region, and Shafaeddin believes that this helps to explain their lack of sustained growth. Moreover, much depends on what is actually being traded. As the *Human Development Report 2005* notes, '[s]uccess in world trade depends increasingly on entry into higher value-added markets for manufactured goods' (UNDP 2005: 116). Thus, East Asia has more than doubled its share of world manufacturing exports since 1980, whereas the share of Latin America (with the exception of Mexico) and Africa remains limited (ibid.: 116–17).

In sum, the relationship between trade and development is a complex one. Nevertheless, it is perhaps possible to detect an emerging consensus in relation to this area. The potential of trade as an effective development strategy is widely accepted, with even a development NGO like Oxfam acknowledging that '[p]articipation in world trade has figured prominently in many of the most successful cases of poverty reduction' (2002: 8). At the same time, it is increasingly recognized that LEDCs must shape the nature of their trade policies according to their respective circumstances. Indeed, even a supporter of trade liberalization like Martin Wolf contends that developing countries should be 'able to make the policy decisions needed to promote their long-term development' (2004: 218).

Summary

- The outcome of the Doha trade round is likely to have a profound impact upon the future course of a multilateral trading system, as well as the role of the WTO.
- There is growing recognition of the complex nature of the relationship between trade and development, and that markets do not operate in a vacuum but need to be supported by public policy and stable socio-political structures.

RECOMMENDED READING

- Leading advocates of trade liberalization are: Jagdish Bhagwati, *Free Trade Today* (2006); Douglas A. Irwin, *Free Trade under Fire* (2005); and Mike Moore, *A World Without Walls* (2003).
- For critiques of free trade, see: Graham Dunkley, *Free Trade* (2004) and Ha-Joon Chang's *Kicking Away the Ladder* (2002a).
- On fair trade, see: Alex Nicholls and Charlotte Opal, *Fair Trade* (2005) and Joseph E. Stiglitz and Andrew Charlton, *Fair Trade for All: How Trade Can Promote Development* (2007).

WEBSITES

- www.unctad.org: The website for the United Nations Conference on Trade and Development.
- www.wto.org: World Trade Organization.
- For a website critical of bilateralism, see www.bilateral.org.
- www.fairtradenet: The website of FLO International, which monitors fair trade standards.

CHAPTER 7

Participation and Representation in Development

- Participatory development
- NGOs and development
- International institutions and representation
- Civil society, social capital and development

Participation and representation are at the heart of contemporary development debates, raising issues about power, self-determination, empowerment and the purpose of development. They are therefore part of the broader rethinking of development, ensuring that it is not just an economic project, but also contains important political and psychological–social dimensions. Here participation and representation are considered in relation to development in four respects. Firstly, the history of participatory development is examined, with some of the key approaches and the criticisms that they have generated outlined. Secondly, the role of NGOs within development is considered, particularly with regard to facilitating local participation. As will be shown, the diversity of NGO interventions, as well as their interactions with a range of development agencies, contributes significantly to the complexity and plurality of development (Hilhorst 2003). Thirdly, the nature of developing country representation within international intergovernmental organizations (IGOs) is explored. Fourthly, the significance of civil society and social capital for development will be discussed in relation to augmenting participation and democracy. The third and fourth sections are areas that have attracted growing interest since the early 1990s, and broaden the scope of participatory development so that the focus is not simply upon projects, but also with the wider institutional and socio-economic framework in which development takes place.

Participatory development

While the lexicon of participation had been around since the late 1940s, participatory development really took off in the mid-1970s (White 1999). This change was due to a combination of factors. It included growing dissatisfaction with existing approaches to development that were variously perceived as top-downist, western-dominated and Eurocentric (Chambers 1997). Conventional approaches attached great weight to planning, rational calculability and science, as well as the judgements of experts in the field, characteristics that are rooted in the mindset of European modernity. It meant that indigenous knowledge and expertise were frequently being marginalized within development, and for many people in the South this was reminiscent of colonialism.

Moreover, the vast amount of money that had been devoted to development was not filtering down to the poor, and many countries were actually deeper in debt as a result of the loans that they had received (Rahnema 1992). In contrast, the micro-credit schemes, like the Grameen Bank in Bangladesh, that entailed financial assistance been given directly to the poor were proving more successful (see Conclusion to this book). The emergence of participatory development was also encouraged by the limitations of the developmental state that was increasingly perceived as bureaucratic and unresponsive to the needs of its citizens. In this regard, Giles Mohan (2002) identifies a connection between the turning away from the state that participatory development entailed with the emerging neo-liberalism of the 1980s and its emphasis upon the individual and self-help.

The cumulative effect of these tendencies was that international agencies and institutions, with the support of academics, field workers and NGOs, increasingly sought to incorporate local populations into development processes. Indeed, since the mid-1980s the theory and practice of participation has become part of mainstream development. The World Bank, for example, has sanctioned investigations that explore the ways in which this process can be deepened (see Blackburn, Chambers and Gaventa 2000) and now speaks the language of 'empowerment' (e.g., World Bank 2001b).[1] While concern has been expressed about unsubstantiated claims made by its advocates (Lane 1995), participatory development has nevertheless continued to evolve and spread. This is unsurprising as participation is an attractive idea, as are associated themes like 'empowerment' and 'stakeholding' (Nelson and Wright 1995). Moreover, participation is inextricably linked with a central preoccupation of our age, namely achieving sustainability. Quite simply, sustainable development necessitates community participation.

What is participatory development?

There are numerous conceptions and variations of participatory development. Nevertheless, it is possible to detect certain common themes, notably an emphasis upon localism, self-determination, grassroots activity, empowerment and popular agency. Broadly speaking, participatory development entails involving local people at all stages in the development process, including identifying what needs to be done and the policies that need to be formulated, so that they have a greater say in the decisions that affect their lives. As Desai puts it: '[s]ince people themselves know best what they need, what they want and what they can afford, only close cooperation between project implementers and the community can lead to project effectiveness' (2000b: 117). The projects that are devised, which are increasingly NGO facilitated, can range from self-build housing programmes to micro-credit schemes. Participatory development can mean community-based organizations (CBOs) taking a key role in the decision-making processes, often in conjunction with NGOs. In contrast, radical writers emphasize the need to 'conscientize' the poor, raising awareness of their position as the basis for challenging the structures that perpetuate their poverty (see Freire 1970, 1974).

The roots of participatory development can be traced back to the emergence of what was termed 'another development' in the 1970s that emphasized self-reliance, endogenous or internal growth, and being in harmony with the environment (Potter et al. 2004). 'Another development' (later known as alternative development) in turn paved the way for 'development from below' (Chambers 1983) or bottom-up strategies (Stöhr and Taylor 1981), and the Basic Needs Approach (BNA). Rather than achieving the general economic development of societies, the BNA concentrated upon ensuring that the poor had the basic requirements for physical survival (food, clothing, shelter, clean water), as well as access to paid employment and services and the ability to participate in decision-making. The BNA was championed by the World Bank under the presidency of Robert McNamara and the ILO.

For some writers, participation is primarily about power and who is in control of development (e.g., Fals-Borda 1988). Indeed, Nelson and Wright maintain that participation 'involves shifts in power' (1995: 1). It means challenging the traditional role of international agencies and institutions within development, and exploring different approaches like collaborative planning that seeks to build policy consensus among a wide range of stakeholders and not just specialists and elites (Potter et al. 2004: 119). Furthermore, local and individual participation can help to ensure that people have a greater stake or investment in development, and in turn they are likely to have greater commitment to it. In addition, there is the psychological satisfaction that comes from active engagement and in shaping one's destiny, which potentially can enhance our feelings of self-worth and self-esteem (Rowlands 1997).

Related to the issue of power is that of knowledge. Participatory development reverses conventional ways of gathering knowledge within development, placing greater emphasis upon data collected from below and taking advantage of local insights and expertise. In *Rural Development: Putting the Last First* (1983), Robert Chambers argues that this will require development professionals unlearning much of their training in order to have a greater appreciation of indigenous knowledge (Box 7.1). Chambers played an important part in devising the Participatory Rural Appraisal (Box 7.2), the leading approach to participatory development.

Participatory development: critical perspectives

Such has been the spread of participation that some critics consider it to be a form of tyranny within development (Cooke and Kothari 2001a). And there is

Box 7.1 Robert Chambers – 'Putting the last first'

A notable critic of conventional approaches to development is Robert Chambers (1983, 1997) who has made the case for 'putting the last first', with 'the last' being constituted by the poor, the powerless and the rurally isolated. He based his work upon a study of rural communities, arguing that this philosophy is the best way of ending their persistent poverty and enabling them to achieve empowerment through the development process.

Box 7.2 Participatory approaches to development

Since the 1970s, a number of participatory approaches to development have emerged, notably the following:

Participatory Action Research (PAR)
Promoted by both academics and activists as a way of rescuing development, PAR emerged in the 1970s in Asia and Latin America. PAR was more than just another approach to development because it stressed the importance of both research and action. The goal of PAR was achieving social change through populations gaining awareness of their plight by undertaking grassroots developmental activities. For one of its founders, Orlano Fals-Borda, PAR was geared primarily to achieving people's power (1988: 2).

Participatory Rural Appraisal (PRA)
PRA, which was first tested in a few rural villages in India and Kenya in the late 1980s, emerged partly in response to the limitations of an approach known as Rapid Rural Appraisal (RRA). PRA was widely employed by development practitioners during the 1990s and has come to refer generally to participatory approaches. A leading exponent, Robert Chambers, describes PRA as 'a growing family of approaches and methods to enable local people to share, enhance and analyse their knowledge of life and conditions, and to plan, act, monitor and evaluate' (Chambers 1997: 102). PRA employs a variety of data-gathering techniques (collecting and collating oral evidence, mapping and diagramming, etc.), but underpinning the approach is the notion that local people have the ability and knowledge to determine their own development. In turn, this means that development workers conducting participatory rural appraisals must be conscious of how they interact with local people (Chambers 1997). However, the popularity of PRA has led to its commercialization, with a consultancy culture having grown up around it, and there are fears that this will undermine its original ethos (Singh 2001).

Participatory Urban Appraisal (PUA)
PUA is the application of PRA techniques and principles within urban contexts.

Participatory Poverty Assessments (PPA)
PPAs began to be employed by the World Bank in the mid-1990s, and marked a statement by this institution that it was now embracing participation. Critics argue that PPAs routinely under-represent the poor's political organizations, like trade unions and left-wing parties, and existing social protections (Craig and Porter 2006: 80).

concern that participatory development is now being employed irrespective of context and its usefulness (McGee 2002). However, the diversity of participatory development, with different approaches enabling varying degrees and types of participation, makes it difficult to critique. Furthermore, different contexts and cultures will also inform the nature of participation, as will the

Box 7.3 The Kribhco Indo-British Farming Project

In his study of the Kribhco Indo-British Farming Project (KRIBP), David Mosse (2001) found that villagers interpreted the emphasis upon participation within the development projects in terms of how it affected their dependence upon the project organizers and their perceptions of what KRIBP could deliver. As Mosse notes: '[i]t is often the case that the "local knowledge" and "village plans" produced through participatory planning are themselves shaped by pre-existing relationships' (ibid.: 32). He continues: '[r]ather than project plans been shaped by "indigenous knowledge", it is farmers who acquire and learn to manipulate new forms of planning knowledge' (ibid.). Local knowledge is therefore being shaped by participatory processes, rather than determining them.

international policy environment (Box 7.3). Consequently, the criticism of participatory development is considered here in a generic sense.

The local dimension　For participatory development to operate, and for local initiatives to be viable, there needs to be a pre-existing sense of community (Purvis and Grainger 2004). Guijt and Shah (1998a) maintain that the PRA approach to community neglects the divisions and tensions that exist within communities as a result of differences in power relations between groups. It has also been claimed that participatory approaches neglect why some people choose to participate and others do not, and how the multiple and evolving identities of individuals inform their choices (Cleaver 2001).

There is also the issue of who speaks for the local community? Achieving a fair and balanced representation of local opinion within participatory projects is difficult in societies where women and ethnic minorities are marginalized (Mosse 1994). Indeed, in some cultures, women find it difficult to become actively involved in PRA because of conventions that restrict their public roles. CBOs may also replicate these forms of discrimination through the nature of their leadership and organization. Furthermore, in some contexts there may be a high degree of deference towards local elites that deters active participation.

As well as the issue of representation, there is the challenge of ensuring the effective implementation and coordination of participatory development. Who or what is to collate the views of the different interests within communities into a coherent development policy? While NGOs increasingly perform this role, as will be discussed in the next section, coherence and coordination is sometimes lacking within the NGO sector. In some locations, the agendas and interests of NGOs can be contradictory, leading to unnecessary competition between them that is wasteful of resources (Rapley 2007: 177). It may also be the case that the donors funding NGOs have their own agendas that they want to pursue in particular countries or regions. Arguably, such complexity necessitates a body or agency to oversee the range of development activity taking place within different localities.

The emphasis upon the local within participatory development should not disguise the problems that can exist at this level, including mismanagement, lack of technical competence, parochialism and even corruption. Furthermore, the focus upon the local will not address the wider structural and institutional causes of underdevelopment that profoundly affect the lives of the poor and need to be tackled on a global scale. This forms part of a broader charge that participation is depoliticizing development by functioning simply as a technical or management approach and neglecting the issue of power (Hickey and Mohan 2004: 4). Advocates of participatory development respond that their approach has permeated international institutions, thereby helping to ensure that their policies are more in tune with the needs of local communities (Chambers 1997).

The nature of participation   Development institutions and agencies have been accused of only paying lip-service to participation. For instance, it has been claimed that PRA has become simply a rubber-stamping exercise in order to enhance the credibility of projects (Mohan 2002). Similarly, some southern governments have been criticized for publicly endorsing participatory practices simply to ensure that they continue to receive aid. In reality, many are not allowing for meaningful local and popular involvement in development planning, and some inhibit NGO activity within their countries.

For David Mosse, 'participatory approaches have proved compatible with top-down planning systems, and have not necessarily heralded changes in prevailing institutional practices of development' (2001: 17). In this vein, based on his study of health projects in Kenya, David Nyamwaya argues that 'while in theory communities are supposed to play a leading role in the health-development process, the process is still largely controlled by government and NGO development "experts" who do not allow communities to play major roles' (1997: 184). 'Development from below' therefore remains at the level of rhetoric because there is an 'implicit assumption that communities can only develop once they have assimilated specialized technical and material inputs from the outside' (ibid.: 192).[2]

Majid Rahnema (1992) contends that even some activists impose their own (often leftist) ideas upon the community that they are interacting with, rather than genuinely seeking out their views. Likewise, development specialists speak to each other and remain within their own intellectual discourses. Consequently, many development projects that are supposed to be locally inspired are in fact remarkably similar to those promoted by traditional development institutions and agencies (Rahnema 1992). For example, the participatory processes that produced the World Bank's Poverty Reduction Strategies (PRSs) frequently have a strong neo-liberal theme running through them (e.g., Cooke 2004).

In sum, despite contributing their time and labour to participatory development, the poor are having little meaningful input in its processes. Exponents of participatory development respond that approaches like PRA contain their own critically reflective practices and therefore many of these criticisms have been addressed (Chambers 1997). However, for Cooke and Kothari, this self-reflexivity is limited in scope and does not confront the nature of power relations within participatory development (2001b: 4). Encouragingly, there is growing acceptance that participatory development should not be conceptualized in a dichotomous sense as either a form of tyranny or empowerment: rather, we need to recognize the complexity of the particular issues and debates that it generates (Cooke and Kothari 2001b; Henkel and Stirrat 2001).

What is empowerment? There is also criticism of one of the key objectives of participatory development, namely that of 'empowerment'. Critics note that there is a lack of consensus over the nature of empowerment, and this is reflected in the multiple definitions that it has generated. In part, this is because underpinning empowerment is the complex and contested concept of power (see Cooke and Kothari 2001a; Craig and Mayo 1994; Rowlands 1997). For example, John Friedmann (1992) identifies different types of power in relation to households and their individual members: social, political and psychological. However, power is likely to be even more complicated than this portrayal as it operates at the macro- and micro-levels. Indeed, for Michel Foucault, power is not a fixed entity but something that circulates and is 'exercised through netlike organizations' (1980: 98).

Furthermore, there is disagreement over the level at which empowerment should be striven for. For instance, should we be concentrating upon empowering communities or whole societies? Or, perhaps we should be focusing upon particular categories of people that are often marginalized in societies, like women and the poor (Cleaver 2001)? And if we conceive of empowerment as entailing that we have more control over our lives, then perhaps it should be regarded as something that is pursued by individuals.

There is also a divergence of opinion over the types of development interventions that are required to achieve empowerment. For example, is empowerment more likely to be attained through NGOs playing an active role in the development process or through grassroots organizations? Alternatively, should empowerment be based on constructing democratic institutions and entrenching certain rights in societies? Obviously, much depends upon particular contexts but, at a minimum, empowerment would seem to necessitate local involvement in development. However, as Cooke and Kothari (2001a) have argued, involvement does not necessarily lead to empowerment because participatory approaches often only encourage or allow for limited popular participation, as we saw in the previous subsection. In turn, this raises doubts about the type of empowerment that can be achieved through participatory development. Moreover, participation in project decision-making does not address the issue of whether or not there is a need for wider structural change, and for some writers the empowerment agenda merely serves to mask the true nature of power relations (Cheater 1999).

In the light of this criticism, for many working in development, the goal of participation is increasingly defined as transformation or social transformation rather than empowerment. More specifically, a growing number of writers are now examining participation as a means of transforming existing power structures (e.g., Hickey and Mohan 2004). In this vein, participation is discussed in relation to citizenship, democratic governance and direct popular involvement, rather than just local involvement in community projects (Gaventa 2004). In other words, transformation is pursued through participatory governance. Frances Cleaver (2004), in contrast, contends that transformation must mean more than institutional design. Instead, it must also entail the transformation of everyday life so that the burdens of poverty, such as unemployment and under-nutrition, are lifted. As Cleaver notes, it is difficult for individuals to operate as active citizens when they are living at subsistence level (ibid.: 275). Thus, there is far from universal agreement over the type of transformation that we should be striving for. For example, should transformation be a political project, focused upon institutional change? Alternatively, should it be a socio-economic undertaking, involving asset redistribution and structural change? Or, perhaps transformation necessitates a combination of the two? For some commentators, there must be a series of transformations in different contexts and countries if neo-liberal globalization is to be challenged.

This discussion of empowerment and transformation highlights the fact that there are different and competing conceptions of participation. In relation to empowerment and transformation, it means that there are 'weak' and 'strong' versions of participation, which translate as 'system-maintaining' and 'system-transforming' processes (De Beer and Swanepoel 2000; Wisner 1988). Of course, such distinctions also serve to complicate our understanding and assessment of participatory development.

NGOs and development

The rise of NGOs

NGOs are not-for-profit organizations that are independent of government and business and have been at the forefront of participatory development because their mode of operation places them in close contact with local communities. They are a response to a wide array of humanitarian, economic, social, political and environmental concerns, and consequently their aims and approaches are extremely diverse. NGOs also differ with regard to their respective stakeholders, resources and influence (see Vakil 1997). In particular, there is considerable difference between international non-governmental organizations (INGOs) with worldwide programmes, like Oxfam and Save the Children, and indigenous NGOs that function at community level and implement local projects.

There has been a sharp increase in the number of NGOs since the early 1980s. The number registered in OECD countries climbed from 1,700 in 1981 to 4,000 in 1988 (OECD 1988). In particular, the number of African NGOs has risen, with many thousands of them now operating across the continent (Hearn 2007). The growth in NGO activity and influence was encouraged by the financial difficulties confronting many southern countries in the 1980s and the rise in the number of fragile states and complex emergencies in the 1990s. Furthermore, the end of the Cold War removed the military and ideological constraints that were inhibiting NGO humanitarian interventions. Lastly, media globalization has spread information about the plight of the poor in the developing world and enabled NGOs to disseminate their message, while ICTs have enhanced their internal communication so that they operate more effectively (Lindenberg and Bryant 2001).

There are numerous indications of the rise to prominence of NGOs. The strength of the Make Poverty History campaign not only did much to shape the G8 agenda at Gleneagles in July 2005, but also persuaded the UK government to allow NGOs into the negotiations for the first time and to give them space in the media centre in order to publicize their views (Schifferes 2005c). More significantly, the World Bank and UN agencies now routinely consult with NGOs as part of their policy formulation processes. In March 2009, there were 3,172 NGOs in consultative status with the UN Economic and Social Council (ECOSOC), and some 400 NGOs accredited to the Commission on Sustainable Development (CSD), a subsidiary body of ECOSOC. The World Bank has also publicly committed itself to working with NGOs in order to achieve mutually agreed goals within the Bank's programmes (e.g., World Bank 2001b, 2002, 2005b). Incorporating NGOs in this way was an important part of the World Bank's embracing of participatory development from the mid-1990s onwards. It was reflected in the fact that NGOs were participating in 50 per cent of World Bank projects in 1994, mainly as service providers (World Bank 1996a: iii). Nevertheless, there have been occasional critical voices within the IFIs who complain that NGOs are holding up policy-making processes.

The funding of NGOs

As we will see in the next chapter, NGOs like Oxfam and Save the Children are funded by private donations and foundations, but also increasingly by official government agencies. The latter, like the Department for International Development (DFID) in the UK, are directing funds through a range of not-for-profit organizations and in doing so are implementing their own development agendas and programmes. NGOs are also funded by multilateral donors and lending agencies, like the World Bank, and this type of funding increased greatly during the 1980s and 1990s, particularly for those NGOs engaged in service delivery. Indeed, 'World Bank financing of NGOs jumped by more than 300 per cent in 1989' (Craig and Porter 2006: 61).[3] The reason for this increase in funding is that NGOs were perceived to be flexible and innovative agencies, capable of responding to particular needs on the ground within developing countries, certainly in comparison with traditional institutional mechanisms like state bureaucracies,[4] although the extent and nature of this funding has led to discussion over whether NGOs can continue to be considered as independent and 'non-governmental' (Hulme and Edwards 1997). Furthermore, the service delivery role of NGOs can be potentially detrimental to states and their future modernization (Woods 2005).

Multilateral donors and northern NGOs are increasingly transferring financial resources to indigenous NGOs. It is allowing southern NGOs to take a greater role in public service delivery, but also means that they are being subjected to greater scrutiny with regard to their accountability, the quality of service that they offer and the extent to which they legitimately represent civil society (Mayhew 2005). At the beginning of the 1990s, NGOs in Africa managed less than US$1 billion in 1990 external aid; by the end of the decade, this figure had risen to nearly US$3.5 billion (ibid.: 1096). Some African governments have complained that donor money is increasingly going to the booming NGO industry, rather than directly to them and their citizens. However, other southern governments value the assistance of NGOs and help fund their activities (Riddell 2007).

NGOs and advocacy

A significant number of NGOs function as advocacy networks. Their work includes lobbying, campaigning, education and policy research as part of an attempt to raise humanitarian and development awareness. In particular, NGOs seek to influence public opinion, governments and IGOs on issues like debt relief, child labour, the nature of international trade and human rights. In the case of the latter, there has been a steady embrace of human rights-based agendas and approaches by development NGOs (see Nelson and Dorsey 2008). NGOs have been at the forefront of successful campaigns for debt relief – the Jubilee 2000 Coalition mobilized 24 million people internationally, for example – and a ban on landmines.

Advocacy-oriented NGOs seek to enhance the position of the world's poor by challenging the international economic and political structures, institutions and policies that are contributing to their marginalization. This approach is often motivated by the frustrations felt by many NGO staff working in the field, while their experience means that policy-makers listen to them (Bryer and Magrath 1999). However, NGOs are sometimes criticized for not devising a feasible alternative to the current system (Edwards and Hulme 1992: 22), and some question their right to speak for the poor. Moreover, there is concern that some NGOs are too focused on global advocacy to the exclusion of national governmental processes, especially as it is the latter that ultimately implements any policy changes (Edwards 2001b).

Initially, many SNGOs encouraged their northern counterparts to turn to advocacy because they were better placed to have an effect, due to their greater resources and closer proximity to donors (Rugendyke 2007a: 8). But, increasingly, development NGOs in the South are turning to advocacy, in part due to their unease over northern NGOs (NNGOs) speaking on their behalf. For example, groups like Focus on the Global South in Thailand, the Freedom from Debt Coalition in the Philippines and Equipo PUEBLO in Mexico have put pressure on the IMF to rethink its stabilization and restructuring policies (O'Brien et al. 2000). Furthermore, northern-based advocacy NGOs are sometimes considered to lack legitimacy because they do not have regular dealings with southern communities or SNGOs (Rugendyke 2007b: 227).

NGOs: critical debates

As will now be shown, some of the charges raised against participatory development in general apply especially to NGOs.

Accountability and representation   Unlike democratic governments, NGOs are not accountable to an electorate for their decisions and actions, and the fear is that they are too accountable to their donors (Edwards and Hulme 1995; Fox and Brown 1998). More specifically, concern is regularly expressed that NGOs are tied to donors, or to governments with whom they work. In this regard, in a book entitled *Silences in NGO Discourse: The Role and Future of NGOs in Africa* (2007), Issa G. Shivji contends that, despite their good intentions, NGOs in Africa have uncritically situated themselves within donor-driven discourses.

Furthermore, the rapid growth of NGOs, and their increasing professionalization, has raised the issue of whether they are losing touch with their roots and the poor (Desai 2002a). Some NGOs have been criticized for a lack of transparency, with concern expressed about the nature of their processes and procedures, including leadership appointments (Ebrahim 2003). It has been suggested that NGOs need to clarify their core values so that it is clear whenever they breach them (Fowler 1997).

NGOs respond that they are not like political parties seeking state power and therefore should not be judged in the same way. Moreover, indigenous NGOs emerge out of communities and are therefore likely to be fairly representative of local feeling. Nonetheless, Bebbington Hickey and Mitlin (2008) note that the failure of NGOs to address concerns about their accountability has left them vulnerable to criticism. Indeed, Mike Edwards (2008) contends that it has led to organizational self-interest becoming too dominant. In this regard, it has been observed that NGOs frequently lack exit strategies from the development projects with which they are involved (Edwards and Hulme 1995).

Another charge levelled against development NGOs is that, despite their professed commitment to partnership, many remain northern-dominated and are marginalizing the knowledge and expertise of southern branches (Mohan 2002). The headquarters of NGOs and most of their resources and staff tend to be located in the North, and they are often run from there, with southern branches performing the role of policy implementation. Similarly, indigenous or southern NGOs (SNGOs) do not exert as much influence upon development thinking and practice as their northern counterparts because of the latter's greater financial resources, public profile and access to key decision-makers (Mawdsley et al. 2002). In turn, it becomes difficult to prevent the better-known NGOs continuing to take the lion's share of any available funding. All of this helps to explain the relative lack of effective partnerships between northern and southern NGOs (Fowler 1998). But without authentic trust-based partnerships, relationships are more formal and contractual, and it follows that transaction costs between NGOs will be higher (ibid.: 146).

However, the recent expansion of SNGO activity and influence may lead to a shift of power within the NGO sector. The transformation of SNGOs has been marked by: an expansion in their numbers; improvements in their organizational capacity and professionalism; and substantial increases in their funding. Some SNGOs have grown to the extent that they have their own branches and partners in the South, and are able to make a direct appeal to potential donors (Townsend, Mawdsley and Porter 2002). All of this has raised questions about the future role and continuing relevance of NNGOs although, as Janet Townsend and her co-writers (2002) have noted, many SNGOs still feel cut off from access to development funding, knowledge and information.

Based upon her research in Senegal, Tanzania and Zimbabwe, and interviews with over one hundred local NGO directors, Sarah Michael (2004) suggests a more complex picture by highlighting the differences that exist among SNGOs. She contends that many African NGOs lack the power of their Latin American and South Asian counterparts. By power, she means 'the ability of an NGO to set its own priorities, define its own agenda and exert influence over others to achieve its ends' (ibid.: 1). Most importantly, Michael argues, this lack of power has undermined development in sub-Saharan Africa. Changing this state of affairs will require, among other things, African NGOs engaging more with the political aspects of development work, building links to the international development community and achieving financial independence from donors.

How effective are NGOs?   The organizational capacity, human resource base and technical expertise of NGOs have been questioned, especially when they have to 'scale up' their operations to deal with major World Bank projects (Edwards and Hulme 1992; Rocha 1999), while some do not monitor and evaluate projects with sufficient rigour (Desai and Potter 2002: 472). Furthermore, because NGOs are often project-oriented, they are unable to take an overview of the societies in which they are operating and consequently rarely have a national vision of development (Lewis and Opoku-Mensah 2006). Larger northern NGOs are accused of being overly bureaucratic and of displaying little evidence of innovation in project implementation. And when there is heavy

NGO involvement in particular projects or regions, it can lead to unnecessary competition between NGOs and the duplication of roles and responsibilities. This forms part of a more general concern that not enough of the funding that NGOs receive actually reaches the people who need it.

By way of reinforcing some of their claims, critics note that the development record of NGOs is an uneven one. For example, according to a study by the London School of Economics, in the ten years leading up to 2003, the number of international NGO branches operating in Africa rose by 31 per cent to 39,729, yet during this period average income per head remained static (Vasagar 2006). Clearly, there will be a range of factors contributing to this disappointing picture, but it perhaps suggests that there are limits to what NGOs can achieve. The severest critics of the development NGO sector contend that it squanders valuable resources, and some have even raised questions about how certain NGOs are using donor money. NGOs respond that they are non-profit organizations, with their staff motivated by altruism rather than personal financial gain. Nonetheless, the relationship between NGOs and donor agencies has come under close scrutiny (see Hulme and Edwards 1997).

Of course, the validity of any of these charges will be dependent upon the particular context and the NGO or NGOs concerned. Yet Edwards and Hulme note that there is growing evidence that NGOs are not performing as effectively as had been hoped in terms of poverty reduction, popular participation, flexibility and innovation, and cost-effectiveness (1995: 6). Consequently, there have been calls for NGOs to be more closely regulated through legislation, certification and codes of conduct. For Edwards and Hulme (1995), performance and accountability will determine the future role, status and even legitimacy of NGOs within development, as well as the funding that they receive. However, they and other writers (e.g., Riddell 2007) also complain about the paucity of reliable data on the impact and effectiveness of NGOs making it difficult to reach firm conclusions in relation to this area.

Neo-liberal NGOs?   Neo-liberals maintain that, because NGOs and other voluntary organizations are locally oriented, they are better placed to deal with problems on the ground than a remote and over-bureaucratic state. And critics of neo-liberalism argue that NGOs have helped to implement this philosophy by taking over functions formerly performed by the state, especially through SAPs. For this reason, neo-liberal IFIs have channelled aid through development NGOs as part of their 'New Policy Agenda' (NPA). Furthermore, to ensure that they continue to receive this funding, NGOs have adopted the language of efficiency and the performance evaluation methods favoured by their donors (Pearce 2000).

In contrast, Dorothea Hilhorst identifies what she terms 'the multiple realities' of NGOs (2003: 226). Based upon her study of a Philippine NGO, Hilhorst contends that 'NGOs may adopt particular agendas at certain interfaces, but endow them with their own meanings, while at the same time, propagating other agendas elsewhere' (ibid.). Similarly, in their relationships with funding agencies and development institutions, NGO actors deploy a multiplicity of development languages (ibid.: 220). In other words, Hilhorst emphasizes complexity, negotiation and the localization of meaning, rather than a hegemonic development discourse that NGOs must simply adhere to and propagate.

Furthermore, many within the development NGO sector consider their work to be motivated by a humanitarian rather than an ideological commitment and would therefore refute the charge that they are advancing neo-liberalism. They argue that the funding they receive from IFIs has been in the main for carrying out tasks such as community development and post-conflict reconstruction rather than structural adjustment (Potter et al. 2004). Indeed, some NGOs have simply refused to be a part of the neo-liberal project, and, where NGOs have intervened, it has not been to support adjustment programmes but to ameliorate some of their effects (Mohan et al. 2000: 172).

Nonetheless, it has been pointed out that NGOs are performing contradictory roles in helping the poor, and at the same time facilitating the withdrawal of state services for this community (Eade 2000). Moreover, it is the case that the role and status of NGOs has been enhanced with the restrictions on public spending that have accompanied neo-liberalism. And, arguably, some western-based NGOs have become too dependent upon donor funding and consequently have lost some of their independence. Furthermore, it is not only in relation to the economy and society that NGOs are accused of imposing an agenda upon the South. African governments have criticized NGOs for interfering with politics in their societies and encouraging their citizens to behave like 'westerners'.

NGOs: missionaries of development? Firoze Manji and Carl O'Coill (2002) contend the role of development NGOs in Africa marks a continuation of the work of the missionaries and voluntary organizations that collaborated in Europe's colonization of the continent during the nineteenth century. Today, in an era of globalization, with spreading conflicts, fragile states, continued impoverishment and inadequate social welfare provision, foreign NGOs have used Africa's decline to justify their work. In other words, NGOs have taken the 'missionary position', providing services and running projects that are motivated by charity, albeit expressed in the language of participation. In reality, NGOs are only making a marginal contribution to poverty alleviation, but they are undermining the struggle of African people to emancipate themselves from forms of economic, political and social oppression. If NGOs are to support African emancipation, they will have to disengage from their paternalistic role in development.

Manji and O'Coill are not alone in making a link between NGOs and colonization. For example, NGOs have been accused of being part of a 'global recolonization process' that seeks 'control over communities through funding

NGOs' (*Africa World Review* 1994: 5; see also *New African* 2005). Julie Hearn maintains that NGOs should be conceptualized as 'compradors', that is, as agents of foreign powers (Hearn 2007). Furthermore, such criticism, coupled with the fact that NGOs were overwhelmingly white and foreign-dominated, led to the deliberate 'Africanization of the NGO sector during the 1990s' with the number of local NGOs growing at nearly triple the rate of international NGOs (ibid.: 1101). This was primarily achieved by official donors funding local NGOs directly instead of channelling it though international NGOs. But as critics have noted this arrangement means that indigenous NGOs are financially dependent upon the West (Igoe and Kelsall 2005). Under these circumstances, it does not matter whether NGOs are African or foreign as the outcome is the same: namely, the continuing dependence of Africa upon the West.

In defence of NGOs

Supporters and members of NGOs defend their value by arguing that they serve many purposes. In particular, they fill the gap whenever the social welfare provision of states is inadequate, and often cut through bureaucracy to bring assistance directly to the people who need it. NGOs help to tackle poverty through distributing food and clothing, offering training and education and providing credit facilities, notably in the form of micro-credit to community groups. Some NGOs are involved in setting up schools, while others have provided teaching equipment and materials. Health-oriented NGOs provide medicines and help to run clinics and hospitals. NGOs are also a source of employment since many of them employ local people as field workers. Small-scale projects, such as boring water wells and conservation programmes, have greatly improved the quality of life in rural areas. It is for these reasons that multilateral donors and northern governments continue to fund NGOs and, because of their voluntary character, they are relatively cheap to run. They are also seen as a way of bypassing authoritarian and corrupt governments that are likely to embezzle this money or squander it by using it for their own purposes. Indeed, in parts of Latin America and Asia, NGOs have indirectly challenged such governments through their support of indigenous movements and causes (Fisher 1998).

Their comparatively small organizational size means that NGOs are frequently the first to deploy to deal with humanitarian disasters resulting from conflict or natural disasters. NGOs deliver humanitarian assistance in collaboration with UN agencies but also are able to circumvent the often time-consuming deliberations within the UN, especially when there is debate over the legitimacy of intervening in particular conflicts. Furthermore, NGOs have proved effective in publicizing humanitarian disasters like famines and large-scale population displacement through various media outlets. Within war-torn countries, they are able to provide independent monitoring of human rights abuses, and this is reflected in the increasing collaboration of human rights NGOs with the relevant UN agencies. NGOs are also playing an ever greater role in post-conflict development and reconstruction, ranging from involvement in landmine clearance to peace-building and reconciliation measures.

One of the comparative advantages claimed by NGOs is that their close cooperation with local groups gives them an informed insight into the development challenges facing southern communities. More broadly, NGOs have helped to establish participation within development, with their methods informing the approaches of other agencies and institutions. But it is important not to overestimate their capabilities, given the scale of the challenges that NGOs face in some countries and given that, despite their proliferation, they only retain a bare presence in many parts of the South. Furthermore, NGOs often have to labour under considerable constraints in the form of the guidelines and performance targets established by donors, and the controls established by states, as well as the nature of social relations within them. All of this can diminish NGO flexibility and innovation (Malena 2000). And as we saw in chapter 5, the new security era that 9/11 has ushered in is profoundly shaping the global context in which NGOs must operate (see Bebbington, Hickey and Mitlin 2008).

Ultimately, the pluralistic nature of the NGO sector, with the different types of NGOs and the multiple arenas in which they operate, means that it is difficult to make an overall assessment of its record in relation to development. As for the future, according to David Lewis, globalization and the growing challenges to the state entails that 'NGOs will need to link both local and global agendas if they are to be effective' (2002a: 522).

International institutions and representation

The spread of global governance in the form of international rules, norms and the influence of institutions is a manifestation of globalization. However, within institutions like the UN and other IGOs, poorer country representation is relatively limited, and this is despite the fact that many have been set up to promote development. It has led to calls for the United Nations system to be reformed as part of a broadening of the participatory development agenda. Indeed, for many advocates participation is fundamentally about challenging existing power relations (e.g., White 2000). Nevertheless, to date no consensus has emerged over the nature of this reform. For example, while many northern countries consider the WTO has rendered UNCTAD redundant, many southern countries insist that reform of the UN Security Council, the World Bank and the IMF should be the priority and the authority of the General Assembly enhanced. In addition, the continued willingness of states to commit themselves to international cooperation, and crucially on what terms, will be a major determinant of future reform.

World Bank and IMF reform

It is widely commented upon that developing countries do not enjoy fair representation within the Bretton Woods Institutions (BWIs). More specifically, it is claimed that there is a democratic deficit within the IMF and the World Bank (WB), especially with regard to the amount of influence that western governments are able to exert within both institutions. Their influence is a consequence of the IMF/WB's weighted voting systems, whereby voting strength is based upon the size of a country's economy and its financial contribution to these organizations. It means that the president of the World Bank is the nominee of the USA, and the director of the IMF is always a European nominee. Moreover, holding around 17 per cent of the votes, Washington can veto many issues because key decisions (e.g., constitutional matters) require an 85 per cent majority vote. In contrast, the countries of sub-Saharan Africa have only 5 per cent of the World Bank's votes.

Critics argue that both the organization of these institutions and their constitutions are outdated, reflecting the world order at the end of the Second World War. For example, the EU is over-represented, while China and India are under-represented on the board of the World Bank, relative to the size of their respective economies. Consequently, there is growing pressure to reform these IFIs so that they are more inclusive and reflect contemporary economic and political realities.

While there have been some moves to increase the quotas and voting rights of rapidly developing countries like China, India and South Korea, the nature of WB/IMF reform remains a divisive issue. Most notably, the US government has rejected calls by developing countries to give up its right to choose the president of the World Bank. During 2008, developing countries, led by Brazil, argued that, without a significant shift of power within the IFIs to allow poorer countries an equal voice, development would continue to be conducted on the basis of paternalism rather than genuine partnership between the North and the South (Stewart 2008). Rapidly growing Asian countries in particular have called for greater representation within these institutions so that their influence more fairly reflects their increasing share of the world economy.[5] There have even been calls within these countries to start disengaging from the World Bank and the IMF and to focus on developing their own regional institutions. President Luiz Inácio da Silva of Brazil also suggested in October 2007 that developing countries should set up their own alternatives to the IMF and the World Bank.

According to critics, as a result of this democratic deficit, policies emerge from the IFIs that suit the agendas of northern governments. For example, SAPs served to open up the economies of developing countries for their own companies. Critics on the Left maintain that the IFIs are simply geared to propping up an inequitable global economy in the interests of the powerful (Goldman 2005). But it is not only those on the political Left that are critical of these institutions. Some free traders have also expressed concern that the IMF and the World Bank are undermining free trade because they have become political tools for their major shareholders and are in effect pursuing their interests (Madslien 2004). Given these claims, it is perhaps not a surprise that the BWIs have also been accused of marginalizing the viewpoints emanating from the Global South. Anti-debt campaigners, for instance, have accused the WB/IMF of ignoring southern calls for them to provide grants rather than loans and to attach fewer conditions to their financial assistance (chapter 8). For all of these reasons, many commentators contend that the IMF and the World Bank are losing credibility and influence (Buira 2005).

In response to such criticism, the World Bank now articulates the language of empowerment and participation in relation to development and, as we have seen, seeks to push these themes by working with NGOs. As for the issue of representation, there are some moves afoot to give rapidly emerging economies like China and India a greater say in the running of the IMF. Moreover, the IMF has promised to increase the voting rights of the world's poorest countries by raising their number of basic votes – the votes that each of the Fund's members have, regardless of their size. However, critics have argued that the basic vote for poorer nations will need to be more than quadrupled to ensure they had fairer representation, something that many of the major powers within the IMF do not yet appear ready to accept. For Ngaire Woods (2000), if the IMF and the World Bank are to adhere to the good governance agenda that they promote, they will need to reform their own constitutional rules and decision-making practices to ensure greater representation, participation and accountability.

The UN Security Council

As we saw in chapter 5, conflict and security are becoming increasingly significant themes within development. Yet the exclusion of the Global South from key aspects of international decision-making is especially evident in the workings of the UN Security Council, with poorer countries unable to achieve permanent membership status or representation. From the perspective of southern governments, this state of affairs is all the more unacceptable, given that so many UN Security Council debates and resolutions concern the developing world (fragile states, civil and regional conflict, authoritarian regimes, etc.). Moreover, the permanent Security Council members – China, France, Russia, the UK and the US (known as the P5) – have been accused of blocking its reform because they fear their own power and global influence will be diminished. The issue of whether to grant veto power to new permanent members also continues to be divisive (Mingst and Karns 2007).

Broadening the membership of the Security Council to include greater representation of the developing world has therefore become an important issue for many southern countries, although it did not make it into the UN reform document of 2005. In part, this was due to intra-regional rivalries, with some governments unwilling to see permanent member status being extended to the so-called 'group of 4': Brazil, Germany, India and Japan. In fact, intra-regional rivalry continues to hinder the structural reform of the UN. For example, Argentina is reluctant to see Brazil secure a permanent seat; Pakistan does not want India to achieve this status, and so on. While some commentators consider regional representation as a potential solution to these tensions, in the form of the African Union and the European Union, the implementation of this type of reform still seems some way off. In fact, the UN General Assembly set up a working group on UN Security Council reform in 1993, but it has achieved little progress to date.

Civil society, social capital and development

Participatory development has wider social and political ramifications. In particular, its multiple practices are considered to contribute to civil society and the generation of social capital, and these in turn can shape the development trajectories of countries and regions.

Social capital

'Social capital' is the social fabric that knits societies together, and it has come to assume an increasingly important position within the social sciences (see Hopper 2003). The concept has been used to explain the decline in social cohesion and community values in western societies that some commentators consider is a by-product of globalization.[6] Thus, societies with good stocks of social capital are socially cohesive, with shared values and norms, a plethora of social networks and associations, and high levels of trust (Fukuyama 2001). A number of writers helped to instigate the social capital debate, although Robert Putnam's discussion of it in relation to civic decline in the USA, in a work entitled *Bowling Alone* (2000), has led the way.

Policy-makers within IFIs have been attracted by the notion that countries that are socially cohesive are likely to be more stable, enjoy greater economic growth and have better functioning governments, and hence they develop more rapidly. In practical terms, generating social capital entails encouraging civic engagement and social solidarity through local participation in networks and civic associations. These bodies are also able to contribute directly to development and poverty reduction through such schemes as microfinance programmes. Actively promoted by the World Bank Social Capital and Civil Society Working Group, the notion of 'social capital' really took hold within development from the mid-1990s onwards. Again, it reflected the World Bank's move away from the Washington Consensus and towards a post-Washington consensus (Fine 1999). For some writers, social capital has helped to broaden development's focus by adding social and institutional factors to its traditional economic agenda (Francis 2002: 88). The concept has subsequently been embraced by bodies like the OECD and the European Commission, as well as many national governments.

Social capital: critical perspectives   Social capital is criticized for a lack of conceptual clarity, reflected in the multiple definitions that it has stimulated. For many critics, it is simply too broad a concept to be of any analytical use (Fine 1999; Harriss 2002; Harriss and de Renzio 1997). As one commentator has stated, '[i]t explains everything and nothing' (Francis 2002: 89). In addition, social capital is difficult to measure or quantify, and the number of networks and associations tells us nothing about the nature and quality of the social connections. A criminal gang may have a high degree of interconnectedness, but its antisocial behaviour depletes rather than augments social capital. There is also a view that social capital cannot be generated through public policies because it evolves within societies over time. For example, the funding used by the World Bank to build social capital in Malawi and Zambia had relatively little effect as the nature of community participation in the projects was shaped by existing power and social relations (Vajja and White 2008). More broadly, many economists are sceptical that at the macro-level a clear link exists between social capital and economic growth (Field 2008).

John Harriss (2002) contends that the concept of social capital has been used by the World Bank to 'depoliticize development' and specifically to obscure existing power relations and patterns of inequality. For Harriss, social capital and related ideas like trust, participation and civil society suit global capitalism because they 'represent problems that are rooted in differences in power and class relations as purely technical matters that can be resolved outside the political arena' (ibid.: 2). Social capital therefore reinforces the status quo. In this vein, feminist writers argue that in many societies the civic engagement upon which social capital is based is highly gendered, with women facing many difficulties in participating fully in this process (Adkins 2005), while the emphasis placed upon the family to generate social capital can potentially run counter to the women's rights agenda (Molyneux 2002).

Civil society

Civil society is another contentious concept within development (e.g., Edwards 2001a; Van Rooy 2002). However, the origins or roots of civil society lie outside of development and date back to classical antiquity. Immediately prior to the European Enlightenment of the eighteenth century, and notably in the work of Thomas Hobbes and John Locke, civil society was presented as an alternative to the state of nature. Unsurprisingly, given the long history of the concept, numerous definitions of civil society have been postulated. However, civil society is viewed here as being constituted by those groups and associations that occupy the realm between the household and the state, such as trade unions and cooperatives, pressure groups, professional bodies, community groups, business associations, social movements, church groups, philanthropic organizations, academic networks and NGOs.

Building vibrant civil societies has become part of the 'good governance agenda' within development because they are seen as a way of spreading democracy and countering authoritarian states by providing individuals with a forum in which to express themselves, acting as a check upon governments.[7] Likewise, the rise of global civil society, as a result of the processes of globalization, can help to ensure that IGOs are more responsive to the views of citizens throughout the world (Kaldor 2003; Mingst and Karns 2007). For its advocates, civil society can also ease conflict within countries by providing a forum for the expression of differences, thereby helping to prevent the build up of tensions. In contrast, Alan Fowler contends that: '[i]n the short run, strengthening civil society is as likely to increase social tensions as to reduce them because more voices are better able to stake their claim of public resources and policies' (1997: 7).

Ultimately, the value of civil society rests upon the motives of the participants and groups involved, not all of whom will be governed by a sense of social responsibility and civic values. For example, NGOs will have their own goals, ideological motivations and relations to particular states, and we should therefore not regard all of them as championing civil society, which is always a danger when they are viewed generically (Cooper and Packard 2005: 136). Indeed, some studies challenge the contribution that NGOs make to civil society (e.g., Dicklitch 1998; Widner with Mundt 1998). Donors will also have their own motives for sponsoring particular NGOs and CSOs but generally do so because they further their own objectives (Francis 2002; Hulme and Edwards 1997).

As with social capital, civil society has been criticized for its broadness and, in turn, its usefulness as a development concept. David Craig and Doug Porter even question the concept of 'civil society', arguing that it is largely made up of 'professional international and local elites occupying NGO positions' (2006: 262). Other critics believe the focus upon civil society diverts attention from dealing with the inequities of international structures and the limitations of the existing state system (Mohan 2002), although some civil society groups do pursue this agenda. But, interestingly, both civil society and social capital mark a shift away from the state and therefore fit in very neatly with the neo-liberal agenda.

The most serious criticism raised against the concept of civil society is that, with its intellectual roots in European thought, it is yet another western construct that is being imposed upon the developing world. Indeed, southern governments are uneasy about the fact that the emerging global civil society, and the NGOs and transnational networks that constitute it, are markedly dominated by civic voices from the North (Edwards 2001b). With northern dominance similarly evident within IGOs, arguably the South is still being encouraged to participate in development within the parameters established by the North.

However, in the light of recent ethnographic research, there have been calls for a broader understanding of civil society, one that takes into account contextual or societal differences (see, for example, Hann and Dunn 1996). In particular, case studies undertaken in Africa suggest that dominant conceptions of civil society are increasingly contested, suggesting that we should perhaps revise the notion that the concept is simply being exported to Africa by western development donors. For example, Jean and John Comaroff (2000) explore the nature and deployment of the concept in Africa from an anthropological perspective. In particular, they examine how civil society is informed by factors such as the legacy of colonialism and the nature of politics and identity in the postcolonial state. In this vein, David Lewis (2002b) similarly presents a more nuanced view of what is taking place in Africa, identifying how local meanings are being created around the concept of civil society within different African contexts, while from a different perspective, based upon a comparative study of two Kenyan NGOs, Stephen Ndegwa (1996) challenges the association of civil society with progressive democratic forces in Africa.

Summary

- Participatory development emerged in response to the perceived limitations of conventional Eurocentric development.
- Participation and associated concepts like empowerment, social capital and civil society are now firmly a part of mainstream development, but they have generated criticism.
- NGOs have been at the forefront of participatory development, although many are increasingly turning to advocacy.
- There is concern that if the UN does not deal with the issue of developing country representation and participation, its relevance in international affairs will diminish.

RECOMMENDED READING

- Robert Chambers has written two classic works on participatory development: *Rural Development: Putting the Last First* (1983) and *Whose Reality Counts? Putting the First Last* (1997). For criticism of participatory development, see Bill Cooke and Uma Kothari (eds), *Participation: The New Tyranny?* (2001a).
- On the issue of NGO accountability, see Michael Edwards and David Hulme's *NGOs – Performance and Accountability* (1995). For funding issues and other challenges facing NGOs, see Anthony J. Bebbington et al. (eds), *Can NGOs Make a Difference?* (2008).
- For a critique of social capital, see John Harriss, *Depoliticizing Development: The World Bank and Social Capital* (2002).
- On the reform of the IFIs, see Ariel Buira (ed.), *Reforming the Governance of the IMF and the World Bank* (2005).

WEBSITES

- www.brettonwoods.org: Provides an informative overview of the role of the different IFIs.
- www.imf.org: International Monetary Fund.
- www.worldbank.org: Website for the World Bank providing access to information on social capital.
- www.dfid.gov.uk: Website for the UK Department for International Development (DFID).
- www.ids.ac.uk/ids/particp: Website of the Participation Resource Centre (Institute of Development Studies, University of Sussex) that has extensive resources on participatory development.

CHAPTER 8

Financing Development: Foreign Aid and Debt

- The debt crisis
- Dealing with debt
- Foreign aid
- Does aid work?
- The G8 Gleneagles Agreement
- Aid and debt after Gleneagles

This chapter addresses two of the most controversial areas surrounding development, and specifically the financing of development, namely foreign aid and debt. It will show how these issues have steadily gained prominence within development, as well as examine the extent to which they are interrelated. The chapter will close with an account of recent international developments in relation to both aid and debt, notably the G8 Gleneagles Agreement of July 2005.

The debt crisis

International debt has a long history, one which arguably dates back to 1823 when Mexico negotiated one of the first recorded debt arrangements.[1] In our era, what has come to be known as the debt crisis began in August 1982 when Mexico was unable to fulfil its debt repayments and suffered financial meltdown (see Díaz-Alejandro 1988, ch. 15). The crisis spread, affecting other countries in Latin America and beyond as developing nations struggled with loan repayments and with paying interest on the amount borrowed.

In Africa, debt reached crisis proportions in the mid-1980s when many states could no longer service the interest on their foreign debts. In 1985, Africa's total foreign debt was more than double the value of all its export earnings, rising to more than three times the value of its export earnings in 1987. Effectively, everything that Africa earned was accounted for by its foreign debts, a state of affairs leading to deepening underdevelopment, as well as ensuring that the sums borrowed could never be reduced. In short, Africa's debt burden was unsustainable. By 1991, Africa's total foreign debt had reached US$270 billion, entailing that debt servicing constituted an average of 21 per cent of the total export earnings of African countries (Dickenson et al. 1996: 52). However, a distinction needs to be made between sub-Saharan

Africa and the rest of Africa, with debt growing markedly in the former region between 1970 and 2002. Indeed, by 2002, sub-Saharan Africa accounted for US$210.6 billion of Africa's total foreign debt of US$295.4 billion (BBC 2005a; UNCTAD 2004a).

As we saw in chapter 1, the debt experience of countries in East Asia and South-East Asia differed from those in Latin America and Africa, due to the significant economic growth and development that many had undergone. In fact, the rapid nature of this economic growth has been cited as a contributory factor behind the Asian debt crisis that began in 1997 (chapter 1).

Explaining the debt crisis

Numerous explanations have been postulated to account for the debt problems that have beset many developing nations, and these will now be considered by discussing them in relation to four broad and interrelated themes.

(i) A legacy of colonialism   Dependency theorists consider the debt crisis has its origins in the colonial period when the European colonial powers shaped the nature of the colonial economies, and did so invariably to suit their own domestic markets. As a result, this has led to a distorted pattern of development, with developing countries often overly reliant upon a limited range of commodities and lacking the necessary diversification in order to achieve significant economic growth. African and Caribbean countries are especially vulnerable to any reduction in the international prices of primary commodities, with some countries effectively dependent upon a single commodity. For example, copper generated 98 per cent of Zambia's total export earnings during the 1980s (Potter et al. 2004: 337). This state of affairs has generated balance-of-payments deficits and in turn debt problems for many developing countries. As we saw in chapter 6, many southern governments are seeking significant improvements in the international terms of trade which would entail the industrialized North agreeing to pay more for primary commodities like agricultural produce.

(ii) Developments within the international economy   Until 1970, the debts of developing nations remained relatively small and manageable. However, during the 1960s and 1970s, southern governments began borrowing money in order to fund development projects, notably in the form of infrastructural schemes. At the same time, certain developments within the international economy began to have a detrimental impact upon the economies of developing countries and in turn contributed to their indebtedness. In particular, the oil crisis of 1973, which saw OPEC at odds with western governments over the price and supply of oil, entailed that developing countries dependent upon oil imports had to borrow money in order to continue importing this fuel, thereby exacerbating their existing debt burden. In addition, the rise in

oil prices contributed to high levels of inflation in both the developed and developing world, and a major international recession.

The decade ended with the second oil crisis in 1979, but this time western governments sought to control inflation by adopting monetarist fiscal policies that slowed down their own economies. However, this approach restricted the markets for exporters from developing nations, thereby hindering their ability to earn an income. An additional consequence of the oil crisis was to force up interest rates on debt repayments. This is because much of the increased OPEC oil revenue was invested in commercial banks, and these institutions in turn set higher interest rates on subsequent lending in order to be able to pay OPEC member states the returns on their investments. In addition, the economic problems confronting OECD countries led many of them to avoid taking on further credit and, as a result, commercial banks increasingly directed their lending strategies towards developing regions as a way of profitably employing their surplus OPEC funds (Hewitt 2000). In short, during the 1970s, developing nations were struggling to pay higher oil prices, finding it difficult to generate export earnings and having to borrow more money at high interest rates in order to alleviate their plight, all of which contributed to them spiralling further into debt.

These difficulties were exacerbated in the 1980s. Indeed, developing countries lost a considerable proportion of their income because of the collapse of commodity prices that began in the early part of the decade. It is estimated that this collapse cost Africa around US$50 billion in lost earnings between 1986 and 1990 (Oxfam 1993: 7). The slump in prices was part of a global recession which led to some northern countries adopting tariffs and merely added to the difficulties that southern countries faced in exporting their raw materials and foodstuffs. Moreover, with interest rates on borrowing continuing to rise, such was the level of debt of some southern countries that commercial banks ceased lending them new money as fears grew about the stability of the international financial system. Indeed, in the case of some African states, foreign aid became increasingly a means of servicing debt.

(iii) Structural adjustment programmes (SAPs) The neo-liberal World Bank and IMF responded to the debt crisis by insisting from the late 1970s onwards that developing countries implement SAPs in return for continuing financial assistance. By the end of the 1980s, 187 SAPs had been set up for 64 developing nations, with around 25 per cent of all WB lending now related to structural adjustment (Dickenson et al. 1996: 265). Thus, in relation to debt, lending became increasingly the preserve of these powerful IFIs rather than commercial banks. As well as being encouraged to attract more foreign investment, structural adjustment has entailed developing nations cutting back on public spending and becoming more market-oriented. It has meant allowing the market to determine prices and exchange rates and above all opening up the economies of developing nations to the global market. From the perspective of

southern governments, this has further exposed their countries to the unfairness of the existing international terms of trade. It has also made it easier for northern companies to export their products and services to the South. In contrast, many southern companies lack the productive capacity to compete, and it has led to many going out of business and made it more difficult for new firms to emerge. A study by SAPRIN (2004) of the impact of SAP-inspired trade liberalization policies upon Bangladesh, Ecuador, Ghana, Hungary, Mexico, the Philippines and Zimbabwe revealed that the increase in their imports outweighed export growth. This state of affairs merely exacerbates the budget deficits of southern countries and means that they are not earning sufficient income to cover their debt repayments.

In the case of Africa, international lending agencies, led by the IMF, responded to the debt crisis by insisting that African countries should in effect 'tighten their belts'. As a result, the conditions attached to subsequent loans included stipulations to African governments that they devalue their currencies in order to make imports more expensive and reduce domestic demand for them (thereby enhancing their balance of payments), freeze wages, spend less on social welfare, and halt (and effectively abandon) certain development projects. For their part, African governments had little alternative but to accept these demands, a move that obviously had considerable implications for their respective populations. Needless to say, the IMF has attracted considerable criticism over this issue (e.g., see Oxfam 1993).

(iv) Internal mismanagement Another factor contributing to the debt levels of some countries is that their respective governments have simply pursued inappropriate development strategies and policies. Countries have therefore been unable to maximize their export earnings, and this has made it more difficult for them to reduce their debts. In the case of Africa, George Ayittey (1992) notes that many states have under-invested in agriculture and education, with their governments preferring to build symbols of modernity, like national airlines, cement works and steel plants, as well as undertaking excessive military spending. Neo-liberals criticize the economic planning models employed by some African elites which have led to excessive bureaucracy and over-regulation. Furthermore, certain African leaders have simply squandered and embezzled a large proportion of the loans that Africa has received, enabling them to lead lavish lifestyles but leaving little to show for the debts that have been amassed. For instance, it is estimated that President Mobutu Sese Seko of Zaire and President Abacha of Nigeria each embezzled around US$5 billion (AAPPG 2006: 12).

Governing elites in many parts of the developing world are also guilty of capital flight, with money deposited in their private overseas bank accounts in Europe and the USA. Indeed, it is estimated that 70 per cent of all loans to the eight largest debtor nations in the South returned to the North in the form of capital flight (Potter 2000: 12). Some of this capital flight is wealth that has been legitimately earned by elites who simply have no faith in their own country's economy, which of course is also a comment upon their own management of these economies, but, given the sheer amount of money that this involves, inevitably some of it is illegally acquired.

Finally, and briefly, this particular explanation or theme hints at some of the different theoretical perspectives on debt. Thus, for neo-liberals, debt is invariably due to country-specific factors, while dependency theorists take a more systemic approach.

Dealing with debt

The measures required to tackle the enormous debt burdens of some developing countries has generated considerable debate. However, alleviating debt is made more difficult by the fact that indebted countries often owe money to different sources. For example, the poorest countries in sub-Saharan Africa owe money to international organizations (mainly the IMF, the WB and the ADB), to private sector lenders and to rich country governments, with the latter constituting around 80 per cent of the debt. In contrast, according to UNCTAD (2006a), 'private commercial bank lending accounts for much of the external debt of middle-income developing countries', such as those in Latin America (ibid.: 5).

Developing countries must service their debt through the income gained from their export earnings. While some states will seek to undertake further external borrowing in order to meet their debt repayments, and respond to internal demands for development, this invariably leads to a cycle of deepening debt that is difficult to break free from. An additional strategy is to restrict imports but, given that trade liberalization has dominated the international agenda since the 1980s, this has simply not been an option for southern governments. Another alternative is to attract foreign investment. However, the record of the South is mixed in this area, with parts of Africa largely being bypassed by global flows of FDI, a fact that also goes some way to account for their continuing reliance upon foreign aid. For these reasons, there has been a growing call for more drastic action to be taken to deal with debt.

Debt relief

For many southern governments and anti-debt groups, such as the Jubilee 2000 coalition, debt reduction and cancellation in the case of countries with an unsustainable burden is the most direct way to tackle the global debt crisis. They argue that many of the causes of debt are unfair. In particular, they consider debt to be a product of how the international economy is structured (terms of trade) and operates (neo-liberalism), and it means that southern countries are at a considerable disadvantage in their dealings with the North. Debt cancellation is also justified on the grounds that, in servicing their debts over many years, developing countries have already paid an enormous amount of money in interest repayments to their creditors, and in most cases many times more than the original sums that were borrowed (Corbridge 2002b: 477). More importantly, there are the human consequences of debt and specifically the reduction in social welfare and education provision that it invariably entails, a problem that is likely to become ever more acute if aid flows continue to decline in real terms. Moreover, the future development of southern countries is greatly impeded by debt, and it means that they are restricted in their ability to tackle poverty and related problems, like population growth, conflict and environmental harm.[2] Finally, countries that remain in a state of indebtedness do not make for good trading partners and are unlikely to be attractive to foreign investors. Quite simply, it is not in the North's own economic and financial interests for countries in the South to remain in this condition. In this vein, Susan George (1992) argues that debt is responsible for, among other things, deforestation in the South, international drugs trafficking and illegal immigration into northern countries.

However, debt cancellation has attracted criticism. It is pointed out that, if the debts of the poorest countries in the world are cancelled, then other poor and indebted countries will seek the same treatment. Indeed, countries that have missed out on either debt cancellation or reduction may consider this to be unfair and feel less obliged to carry on repaying their debts. Furthermore, countries that have benefited from debt relief may be tempted to build up their debts once again in the hope that history will be repeated. It is for this reason that many anti-debt advocates insist that debt remission must be a one-off event (e.g., Dent and Peters 1999).

From a different perspective, if debt cancellation is carried out on a wide scale, it could have significant repercussions for the international economy. It is argued that IFIs need to continue to collect the interest repayments from existing loans in order to fund future lending. It is also claimed that countries that have had their debts cancelled or reduced will be viewed as bad debtors and are likely to find it difficult to secure loans and attract investment in the future. However, Dent and Peters (1999) have responded to this particular contention, arguing that the debt reduction deals negotiated for southern countries under the Brady Plan (see p. 188) did not lead to them suffering a subsequent decline in investment.

Other critics insist that debt cancellation is an implicit statement that poor countries are unable to manage their own affairs. It therefore smacks of paternalism and may even serve to reinforce stereotypical images of the South, while, for neo-liberals, debt is a regular feature of individual and societal activity and a natural part of the development process that countries incur during their early development before reducing their indebtedness as they mature (Beenstock 1984: 242). We should therefore cease thinking of debt as an aberration. Moreover, paying off their debts can provide an incentive for indebted countries to pursue rapid export-driven economic growth, as well as encourage financial and economic discipline in the future. From this view-point, debt and more specifically debt repayment, can enable countries to take a significant step on the path to development and self-reliance.

Highly Indebted Poor Countries (HIPC) initiative

There have been numerous international initiatives to deal with the debt crisis. In 1989, for example, the so-called Brady Plan sought to facilitate debt-reduction agreements between developing states and their commercial bank creditors through such measures as extending repayment periods and incorporating IMF and World Bank financial support. However, to date the most comprehensive attempt on the part of the international community to alleviate debt has been the Highly Indebted Poor Countries (HIPC) initiative. Unveiled by the WB and the IMF in 1996, it aims to reduce the debt burden of countries through debt relief programmes. The HIPC initiative was enhanced in 1999 so that debt relief was increased and more closely linked to the effectiveness of local poverty reduction strategies.

The IMF and the WB establish the criteria for participation in this initiative, notably measuring the sustainability of a country's debt to determine whether or not it is entitled to assistance. Debt relief is also dependent upon the country pursuing 'good governance' as defined by the WB and the IMF, which usually entails undertaking macro-economic reform to maintain economic stability, devising a poverty reduction strategy and reducing corruption. Critics of the HIPC initiative consider the time it takes to qualify for debt relief is too long, and the criteria established by the IMF/WB are too strict and should be revised to allow more countries to qualify for debt relief. In particular, countries plagued by internal conflict have little chance of meeting their assessment criteria.

A study commissioned by the WB Independent Evaluation Group (WBIEG) reported in 2006 that, since its previous evaluation of the HIPC initiative in 2003, there had been reduction of US$19 billion of debt, which had halved debt ratios for 18 countries. However, in eight of these countries, the debt ratios have come to once again exceed HIPC thresholds (WBIEG 2006: vii). Interestingly, the report finds that 'debt reduction alone is not a sufficient instrument to affect the multiple drivers of debt sustainability', which will require a range of additional measures, like improvements in export diversification and fiscal management, 'measures that fall outside the ambit of the HIPC Initiative' (ibid.).

Thus, in the period leading up to the G8 Gleneagles Summit, debt and the effectiveness of debt relief were much-debated issues. Meanwhile, even countries that had been through HIPC and related initiatives were still estimated to be paying around US$2.5 billion to service their remaining debts. Indeed, Africa's total external debt in 2003 had risen to US$231.4 billion from US$190.2 billion in 1990 (ADB 2006: 14). Moreover, many HIPC countries in sub-Saharan

Africa were still paying more in debt repayments to international development institutions than they were spending on health and education (Williams 2004).

Foreign aid

Aid has generated numerous controversies but, before examining them, it is important to understand both the history of the subject, as well as the different forms that aid can take.

A brief history of aid

The origins of aid can be traced back to the British Colonial Development Act of 1929, which provided loans and grants to colonial governments and aimed to integrate the colonies more fully into the metropolitan economy (UNCTAD 2006a). In fact, aid provision has often been driven by motives other than development and humanitarianism, most notably during the Cold War and especially following decolonization, when it was seen by the major powers as a means of maintaining influence and securing allies within the developing world.

Aid in its contemporary guise emerged in 1948 with the Marshall Plan to rebuild war-torn Europe but arguably a more significant moment occurred in 1970 when the UN General Assembly passed Resolution 2626. This resolution established that the richer countries should allocate 0.7 per cent of their GNI (gross national income) to overseas aid – before 2001 the GNI was called GNP (gross national product) by the World Bank – a figure that was to be attained by 1975. However, developed nations have a poor track record in relation to this target, with most failing to attain it each year. In 2007, for example, only Denmark, Luxembourg, Norway, Sweden and the Netherlands exceeded this target (OECD 2008). Indeed, the cumulative aid shortfall was estimated to be over US$3.1 trillion in 2006 (IBON International 2007). In fact, aid levels have generally been in decline since the mid-1980s, with the proportion of rich-world GNP declining from 0.3 to 0.2 per cent in the 1990s (Sachs 2005b: 213). This pattern reflected the ideological acceptance of market-based solutions among governments in the North, with SAPs and similar conditions increasingly attached to the aid that developing countries received. Aid contraction was also evidence of economic globalization, with a greater emphasis being placed upon FDI, MNCs and trade in facilitating development. Indeed, between 1990 and 2006, private capital flows to developing countries increased tenfold and exceeded official development assistance (ODA); i.e., aid that is provided by governments and international agencies (WDI 2008: 318).

However, from the start of this century, the international community appeared to recommit itself to development aid by signing up to the MDGs to reduce world poverty. But even with the aid increases established at Gleneagles in 2005 (discussed on p. 201), on current trajectories, many rich nations will not be devoting 0.7 per cent of their GNP in overseas aid by 2015. Furthermore, there are growing concerns that donors will respond to the global financial crisis by reducing their aid budgets.

As for the history of the debates that have surrounded aid, a report published in 1998 by the World Bank entitled *Assessing Aid: What Works, What Doesn't, and Why* generated notable comment (see Hermes and Lensik 2001). It contended that development aid is able to foster economic growth and reduce poverty when recipient countries have achieved effective governance, especially in the area of economic policy and management. The report therefore made the case for 'selectivity', whereby countries wishing to be eligible to receive aid had to meet specific conditions with regard to these areas. Since then, there has also been a greater focus upon improving political governance, especially with regard to tackling corruption and unstable institutions. In contrast, advocacy groups and charities like Reality of Aid (2006) and Oxfam (2006) insist that aid should focus exclusively on poverty reduction.

In the recent period, increasing emphasis is also being placed upon enhancing aid effectiveness within international development. In particular, greater attention is being devoted to the notion of 'country ownership', whereby recipient governments and their respective citizens take greater control of aid and development within their countries (see p. 192). This shift is reflected in international donors and recipient governments signing up to this agenda in the *Paris Declaration on Aid Effectiveness* at a summit organized by the OECD in March 2005.

The evolving nature of aid provision is reflected in the fact important new non-northern donors have emerged, notably China, but also other countries like India and Saudi Arabia (see Six 2009). For example, in 2008, India provided more than £300 million (US$500 million) to poorer countries (BBC 2011). Indeed, the Indian government has debated whether it wants to continue to receive aid from countries like the UK. The rise of new donors raises the issue of whether they will undermine the international consensus on poverty reduction and aid effectiveness by pursuing their own agendas (Harmer and Cotterrell 2005). However, Richard Manning (2006) does not consider the new donors represent a major challenge to this consensus and will offer greater choice to developing countries. Our attention, he argues, should be directed towards encouraging the new donors to commit to the MDGs and to participate more in the multilateral system.

The profile of aid also continually changes, with some sectors and regions supported more than others at any particular moment. For instance, broadly speaking, there has been a decline in aid to agricultural projects, while aid provision for health has experienced the highest increase in aid commitments. The latter reflects the devastating impact that infectious diseases like HIV/AIDS are having upon many developing societies. In fact, donor support for basic health, population and reproductive health has increased from US$3.5 billion in 2000 to US$11.9 billion in 2008 (Reality of Aid 2010: 164). In the case of agriculture, there has been a long-term downward trend in donor agriculture investments as a percentage of sector-allocated aid, falling from 17 per cent in the mid-1980s to only 6 per cent in 2006–7 (ibid.: 166). As we saw in chapter 5, there has also been a rise in aid provision in relation to security. For instance, the UK will increase spending on this area from £1.8 billion in 2010 to £3.8 billion in 2014–15 (DFID 2011: 3). The so-called 'securitization of aid' also accounts for many of the regional shifts in aid spending in the recent period. In other words, those regions that are receiving increased aid tend to be the ones where 'fragile' and strategically important states are located, such as Afghanistan and Pakistan.

The different types of foreign aid

There are many different types and sources of aid. As well as the ODA provided by governments and international agencies, there is also aid provided by CSOs and NGOs. Aid includes one-off emergency and humanitarian relief in the event of disasters and severe resource or commodity shortages. Indeed, emergency relief in the form of food aid is accounting for a growing proportion of the global aid budget (Barrett and Maxwell 2005). At the other end of the spectrum are the major development projects geared to contributing to the long-term economic development of a country – which can include debt relief – and preventing cyclical problems, like drought and famine.

In reality, the different types of aid are often interconnected. Dealing with famine, for example, will require food parcels as well as the provision of seeds and ensuring adequate water supplies for the long term. Most long-term aid is in the form of concessional loans and grants, either as bilateral or multilateral aid. The latter comes from several countries and is often distributed through international institutions such as the WB and the UN agencies. Bilateral aid can take the form of direct government-to-government transfer of capital, goods or services, including technical cooperation (Burnell 1997), although critics argue that this type of assistance does not always filter down to the poor (Hanlon 2004).

Non-governmental aid comes from international charities and aid agencies, like Oxfam, Save the Children and UNICEF. This type of aid is funded by private donations and government contributions, and is less likely to have conditions attached to it. Non-governmental aid is often targeted at completing specific projects, such as improving sanitation and building water wells in rural areas, with a strong emphasis upon local participation in project design and implementation. NGOs also provide professional support and technical expertise – although their knowledge-gathering processes have attracted criticism (see Samoff and Stromquist 2001).

In contrast, tied aid, which can be in the form of either bilateral or multilateral aid, entails the recipient country giving assurances that it will spend the aid on goods and services from the donor country or a group of selected countries and/or allow them unfettered access to their domestic market. Tied aid is therefore a form of conditionality because it decrees that aid should be used in specified ways. As we saw in the discussion on SAPs, conditionality entails the attachment of conditions to aid, including the implementation of economic and political reforms. Conditionality has generated considerable research and discussion (e.g., Koeberle et al. 2005) but, as we will see below, it has also attracted criticism.

There is pressure to move away from tied aid and conditionality from aid groups, and also from some donor governments via the OECD. This pressure is the result of numerous factors but includes the perceived failure of aid in its current guise to facilitate substantive development, especially in Africa. It has led some donors to promote a *New Aid Agenda* that emphasizes notions of 'partnership' and 'ownership' in relation to aid as a means of enhancing aid effectiveness (see OECD 2009). Indeed, in 2001, the Development Assistance Committee (DAC) of the OECD agreed, with some exceptions, on a recommendation to untie ODA to LEDCs, which was extended in 2008 to all of the 39 HIPC countries (www.oecd.org/department).

However, the *2006 Reality of Aid Report* found that 'donors are still largely paying lip-service to the principles of "local ownership" of development' (Reality of Aid 2006: 2). More than 36 per cent of aid remained tied in 2004, and this figure does not include an estimated 72 per cent of undeclared tied US aid (ibid.). This pattern was also subsequently detected by the *2008 Reality of Aid Report*. It concluded that recent donor/government agreements, like the 2005 Paris Declaration, had done little to change the unequal nature of the traditional donor–recipient relationship. In short, both tied aid and the use of policy-based conditionalities by donors continues (Reality of Aid 2008).

This disappointing picture is reflected in a growing critical literature on the issues of ownership and conditionality in relation to aid. For instance, an edited book by Alf Morton Jerve, Shimomura and Skovsted Hansen, entitled *Aid Relationships in Asia* (2007), explores Japanese and Nordic aid relationships in various Asian countries, examining aid ownership and partnership at the implementation level. In particular, they deconstruct the concept of 'ownership' by focusing upon aid relationships from the perspective of the recipient. Likewise, based on their study of policy-making in eight African countries, Paolo de Renzio, Whitfield and Bergamaschi (2008), while acknowledging the importance of country contexts, nevertheless identify certain recurring themes behind weak ownership. It includes fragmented planning processes as a result of donor proliferation which in turn has led to aid-dependent states becoming engaged in a permanent and burdensome negotiation process with donors over almost all areas of development. As a result, the recipient governments are denied the space to determine their own policy preferences (ibid.: 3).

It is also the case that the interrelationships between aid, conditionality and ownership have been complicated by the global financial crisis. As an OECD report highlighted in 2009, testing economic conditions makes it more difficult to maintain traditional conditionality frameworks. Nevertheless, the OECD report outlines strategies to reduce aid conditionality still further and to enhance recipient ownership of aid policies (OECD 2009). However, in relationship to ownership, it has been pointed out that country systems and capacity are not uniform, and we need to take into account the current capacity constraints of some states (Koeberle et al. 2005: 16).

Finally, it is important to note that there is often a difference between the headline aid level (i.e., how much OECD countries give as ODA) and how much is actually received in the recipient country. This is because the provision of aid invariably generates a range of costs, such as consultant, equipment and administrative costs, which can significantly reduce the amount of aid that is actually received in the country for which it is intended.

Does aid work?

A recurring debate surrounding aid concerns its effectiveness. However, this point is difficult to determine, given that there are different types of aid, a plethora of associated projects and programmes, multiple ways of measuring effectiveness and a lack of high quality data on aid impact (Riddell 2007: 379). Furthermore, the extent to which there has been indigenous participation in the formation of an aid programme will significantly determine the level of local commitment to it and in turn its future prospects. Factors that are unrelated to aid will also affect how countries develop – such as the nature of the international economy and the form of governance within the recipient country – as well as arguably determine the effectiveness of aid. Further complicating matters is that aid will be employed within a range of contexts and countries. For example, a common view is that aid is least effective when employed within fragile states, and this is despite a recent study suggesting it can have positive impacts in such states if the provision is based upon close engagement with local authorities and communities (see Manor 2007).

Aid: critical perspectives

Beyond general concerns about the harm caused by fluctuating aid levels and the lack of a mechanism for ensuring that aid provision is governed by the needs of the recipients, the role of aid in development has been criticized in other ways.

Wasted aid   Critics point to the amount of aid that has been embezzled, with direct government-to-government aid considered to be especially susceptible to corruption because of the lack of controls operating upon the recipient government. Moyo (2010) argues that aid leads to resource competition that foments conflict and diminishes social capital. She also contends that aid has discouraged private enterprise and the export sector in Africa. For critics, aid encourages state-owned enterprises that tend to be heavily subsidized and lacking in dynamism. Indeed, critics argue, the only real growth that aid has contributed to within developing nations has been in the form of burgeoning bureaucracies (Bauer 1972). The cumulative effect of these tendencies has been that a large amount of money has been wasted on inappropriate development projects, with many subsequently being abandoned. Moreover, the aid industry as a whole is expensive, with money being spent on running international branches and offices, the salaries of consultants and campaigning activity generally. In fact, much of this activity and spending takes place within donor countries rather than in developing countries.

Given that in 2006 total official foreign aid since 1970 stood at just under US$2.3 trillion, critics have questioned what this vast outlay has actually achieved (IBON International 2007). If aid was an effective development strategy, then it surely would have yielded more tangible results in Africa and elsewhere in the developing world. Indeed, it is argued that some African states are in certain respects worse off now than they were at the time of independence (Dowden 2005).[3] And it is this lack of perceived success that helps to explain why 'aid fatigue' is becoming increasingly prevalent within many northern donor countries.

Aid undermines indigenous authority   Critics argue that aid can be harmful to the recipient's sense of self-esteem and in turn discourage self-reliance and initiative (Dowden 2005). Moreover, aid can erode indigenous authority and governance. In particular, when countries become dependent upon aid, the respect of citizens for their governments is inevitably diminished. For example, the plethora of NGO branches, international charities and UN agencies dotted across the African continent is a visible reminder to Africans of the shortcomings of their respective states. Furthermore, if you have low expectations of your government, then your demands upon it are likely to be minimal. In turn, this serves to weaken the social contract between government and the governed. Arguably, continuing external assistance also reduces the need for the governments of developing societies to improve. Indeed, development aid can serve to prop up unpopular, authoritarian and even corrupt regimes (Walle 2005). In sum, aid can work to inhibit 'good governance' within developing societies, and this may be contributing to the disproportionate number of fragile states within Africa.

To counter this tendency, international charities and aid agencies are increasingly focusing upon advocacy work and operating as NGOs. This approach enables them to put pressure upon the governments of developing societies, which includes encouraging their citizens to be more demanding of their own governments. However, NGOs have been accused of imposing their own agendas and ideologies upon developing societies (chapter 7). For example, it is often claimed that they are encouraging Africans to behave as western citizens. Others argue that NGOs have an innate resistance to market-based and private sector solutions, which in some instances may be preferable. In short, there is a fine line between advocating and preaching. For these reasons, tensions can emerge between aid agencies and indigenous authorities. In 2005, for instance, Niger's president, Mamadou Tandja, accused aid agencies of exaggerating his country's food crisis, portraying it as famine when it was chronic malnutrition, in order to raise their own profile and funds (Astier 2006).

Trade rather than aid   For neo-liberals, a better alternative to aid in facilitating development, one which avoids accumulating high levels of debt, is through countries pursuing sound economic policies, establishing good trading relations and adhering to market disciplines (Bauer 1972). In particular, the focus upon aid diverts attention from the vital role that trade can play in development. The spectacular economic growth enjoyed by China, India, South Korea and Taiwan is cited as evidence to substantiate this point. In the case of China and India, their economic growth has enabled substantial (albeit uneven) reductions in poverty in a remarkably short space of time, something that opponents of aid put down to their implementation of free market reforms. China has been actively pursuing an 'open door' trading policy with the outside world, whereas India has been cutting back on excessive bureaucracy and fostering enterprise.[4] There has also been a greater emphasis upon pursuing the trade route to development in many Latin American countries, reflected in the steady increase in private capital flows since the early 1990s. Thus, for trade advocates, aid can never serve as a substitute for the powerful wealth-generating mechanisms that markets facilitate (Easterly 2006; Stewart 2006b).

However, it is debatable whether economic growth can ever be reduced to a single factor like the market. Economic development invariably requires numerous constituent elements, including in some cases the provision of aid. The latter is especially necessary for those countries that are struggling to realize their full productive capacity, whether this is in the form of agricultural production, resource exploitation, the lack of an integrated transport infrastructure, an inchoate educational system, or some other fetter holding back their development. Indeed, some writers stress that internal factors, such as labour productivity, a diversified economy and the level of domestic savings, are a more important determinant of development than externally generated forces, such as markets and trade (Ingham 1995: 333).

Lastly, another line of argument often raised by trade supporters is that aid artificially protects developing societies. In turn, this ensures that they remain uncompetitive because there is little incentive for them to be entrepreneurial and to adapt to global market conditions. From this perspective, aid discourages reform and merely perpetuates the underdevelopment of developing countries.

Self-interest, conditionality and aid imperialism   Another criticism of aid is that much of it is driven by self-interest on the part of donors. For example, the aid provision of northern governments may be informed by factors like concern over their country's international reputation, domestic political pressures, commercial and strategic interests, and even colonial guilt. While for the Left, because so much assistance is in the form of loans, aid perpetuates forms of dependency, thereby ensuring that developing countries are tied into the international capitalist system (Hayter 1971). It is presented as a charitable gesture on part of the North and packaged to convince southern nations of the advantages of remaining within this system, but in reality aid functions to preserve the status quo and establish economic relationships that benefit the donors themselves (Petras and Veltmeyer 2004).

Donor governments are best able to push for favourable economic arrangements with recipients through bilateral aid. It also enables them to exert diplomatic and political influence because they can always threaten to withhold aid if a country acts against their interests. For instance, the American and British governments withheld aid to Sudan in the early 1990s because of its support for Saddam Hussein during the Kuwait crisis. Likewise, according to the *Reality of Aid 2006 Report*, aid spending since 9/11 has largely focused on the foreign policy priorities of donors in the Global War on Terror, with some US$20 billion of US assistance going to strategically important countries between 2002 and 2004 (IBON Foundation 2007). Indeed, for critics, the conditions that donor countries attach to bilateral aid ensure that the aid relationships are inequitable and imperialistic (see Browne 2006). As we saw above, the structural adjustment conditions attached to securing new loans from the World Bank and IMF have created real hardships for citizens in many parts of the Global South.

An important consequence of donors pursuing their own interests is that aid is not necessarily directed to the poorest countries but to where those interests are best served. Indeed, the nature and amount of aid that a developing country receives is dependent upon a range of variables, not simply upon need. If need alone were the consideration, then Sierra Leone, one of the poorest countries in Africa, would receive more financial aid than Kenya, one of the continent's richer countries. However, Kenya actually receives 11 per cent of its GNP in the form of ODA, while for Sierra Leone the figure is only 8 per cent (Dickenson et al. 1996: 299). On a global scale, less than half of all ODA is received by the 65 poorest countries (Riddell 2007: 358).

There can be problems with donor conditionality, even when it is genuinely geared to promoting development. Firstly, there are numerous instances of recipient governments accepting aid and not actually implementing the conditions (Kanbur 2000; Killick et al. 1998). In Kenya, pressure from foreign donors led President Daniel arap Moi's government to agree to improve economic and political governance, including holding multi-party elections in 1992. But, as the IMF and the WB acknowledge, corruption, patronage and human rights abuses continued, so did the provision of foreign aid. Secondly, the economic record of the Washington Consensus conditionalities has been dismissed as 'uninspiring', with Latin American countries experiencing a reduction in their economic growth rates following their implementation (Singh 2004: 82). In contrast, Joseph Hanlon (2004) points to examples in Mozambique where it has proved possible and efficient simply to give money directly to the poor without conditions. Thirdly, recipient countries are always likely to resent having conditions imposed upon them. And, as we have seen, there are claims that SAPs are primarily an attempt on the part of the West to mould the economies and societies of developing countries and specifically to encourage their westernization.

Continuing the latter theme, William Easterly (2006) contends that western aid efforts have had a negligible impact because they are based on the premise that the West knows best, thereby excluding local knowledge and expertise. For Easterly, the blame lies with the aid bureaucrats within international organizations and aid agencies such as the IMF, the WHO, UNICEF and the UN Children's Agency. He labels these figures the 'Planners' because of their proclivity to over-plan and design grandiose and inappropriate schemes from afar, like SAPs and the MDGs. In the case of the latter, he argues that goals which are designed to motivate rarely lead to anything concrete and practical. Instead, he favours greater reliance upon 'Searchers'; these are figures on the ground who operate in a pragmatic and ad hoc way to solve specific problems. Further, their resourcefulness is more suited to functioning in a market and indeed they will seek to utilize the market in order to get by. Easterly therefore favours aid resources going to local groups that are geared to achieving specific goals, such as building a school in a particular village (Stewart 2006b: 6).

However, directing resources towards smaller local groups and experts working in the field has its own attendant difficulties. In particular, it is difficult to monitor their activities and ensure accountability. Moreover, the turn to localism means that aid provision is more fragmented, making the coordination of strategy difficult to achieve and potentially paving the way for unnecessary competition among the plethora of charities, aid agencies and local groups. For this reason, senior figures within UNCTAD are looking to replace current aid arrangements and practices with the creation of a central UN agency (UNCTAD 2006b). Of course, for Easterly, such a body would merely perpetuate the influence of the Planners within development.

The case for aid

Advocates of aid argue that it is most successful when its aims and objectives are targeted and measurable. They point to aid-backed successes in relation to immunization campaigns against diseases like polio and measles, which they claim have saved countless lives and, in particular, reduced infant mortality (Sachs 2005a). In the case of polio, aid provision (and of course medical advances) have helped to ensure that it is close to being eradicated, and it follows on from the worldwide eradication of smallpox during the second half of the last century. More generally, the quality of life for millions of others living in impoverished countries has improved as a result of the setting up of schools, the provision of drainage and sanitation, and the guarantee of clean water supplies, all of which frequently have an aid component.

Aid also plays a vital role in emergency relief, helping to alleviate human suffering brought about by extreme conditions and disasters, like drought, flooding, famine, conflict and the spread of disease. Indeed, without aid, very often countless more lives would be lost as a result of such catastrophes. Moreover, in order to try and prevent a repetition of some of these human and natural disasters, the provision of long-term aid can help to address these matters, most notably the poverty that frequently lies behind many of them (Lawson 2005), while, on a global level, it is of benefit to us all that regions and societies are peaceful and stable, and that countries are not damaging the environment in order to meet everyday subsistence levels (Degnbol-Martinussen and Engberg-Pedersen 2003). Aid is therefore an implicit acknowledgement that we live in an interdependent world. Furthermore, because there is a redistributive element to aid, it marks an acceptance on the part of northern countries that it needs to be a more equitable world. At the same time, the interaction between different peoples, countries and regions that aid relationships necessitate can help to foster international understanding and inter-cultural dialogue. Finally, aid advocates emphasize the genuine humanitarian motives that lie behind aid provision. For example, the governments of Sweden, Denmark, Finland and the UK have all declared that they have a moral duty to alleviate poverty in the developing world (Riddell 2007: 140).

Supporters of aid generally do not deny the role that trade can play in the development process but maintain that developing societies often require financial assistance in order to be able to compete in global markets. This funding can be used to help build transport systems or to expand the pool of skilled labour through investment in education and training, or some similar measure. Moreover, aid will continue to be necessary while the international terms of trade remain the same, ensuring that the debts of the developing world continue to spiral.

Jeffrey Sachs (2005b) contends that, when the debt repayments of developing countries are taken into account, the amount of development aid they receive is small. For example, the average amount of real development aid given to each citizen in sub-Saharan Africa was just US$12 (£6.37) in 2002. Nick Dearden, director of the Jubilee Debt Campaign, argues that in 2008 developing countries were still giving US$5 in debt repayments to the North for every US$1 they get back in aid (Seager 2008). Indeed, Sachs (2005a) maintains that too little aid has been given to make a difference, and this half-hearted approach to aid is not only inhibiting the development of LEDCs but also damaging the case for aid – although some aid supporters acknowledge that this is also harmed when the wrong policies are pursued (e.g., Pronk 2004).

Unsurprisingly, aid advocates reject the charge of imperialism that is made in relation to conditionality. If aid is not to be wasted or embezzled, then attaching conditions that seek to improve transparency, accountability and economic management is unavoidable. Jan Pronk (2004) stresses that, for the catalytic potential of aid to be realized, there is little point in using it to reward countries that have already attained desirable development goals; rather, it should be employed to encourage countries to pursue such goals. It follows that, if development is about enhancing human security, freedom and well-being, then it is appropriate to make aid provision conditional upon developing countries pursuing the type of governance necessary to achieve this end. Indeed, it may even include empowering civil society groups so that they are able to contribute to this process. In this vein, Max Lawson (2005) cites the example of Malawi where Oxfam has funded education groups that monitor whether schools receive the equipment promised to them in government budgets and then present their findings to parliament and the media.

Aid and development: a complex relationship

Thus, the extent to which aid can catalyze, or indeed stifle, development is disputed (see Pronk et al. 2004; Tarp 2000). Aid supporters point to countries where foreign aid has been instrumental in generating economic growth. For example, aid is considered to have encouraged political governance reform within Mozambique that has led to peace, stability and growth after years of conflict (Arndt, Jones and Tarp 2006).[5] However, further evidence of the uneasy relationship between aid and development can be gleaned from a study by Tony Killick and Mick Foster (2007), who note how large aid inflows often have the unintended effect of disadvantaging producers of tradeable goods within developing societies. In this regard, critics point to instances where emergency food aid has served to drive down prices for local farmers and increase dependency. For instance, the drought aid that Kenya received in the 1990s is considered to have destroyed production in many parts of the country (Astier 2006).

Within development circles, there is growing recognition of the complex nature of the aid–development dynamic (e.g., Pronk et al. 2004). Based upon a study of 88 aid-recipient countries, Easterly (2003) found, in the vast majority of cases, no discernible relationship between foreign aid and economic growth. Others argue that aid effectiveness is dependent upon context and, specifically, governments having established a sound macro-economic policy environment through fiscal, monetary and trade policies (Burnside and Dollar 2000), although this linkage has been challenged (Rajan and Subramaniam 2005). Of course, this is to focus upon development simply as economic growth and to ignore its other dimensions. Moreover, as we have seen, not all aid is directed towards growth. In this regard, aid fungibility is emphasized – namely, that it provides recipients with resources that can be employed in a range of ways, a condition that also adds to the difficulty of measuring the impact of aid.

Irrespective of these particular debates, considerable attention continues to be devoted to enhancing aid effectiveness by focusing upon impact evaluation, as well as its management, delivery and coordination (e.g., Banerjee 2007). For example, because of the lack of coordination among donors, many of the demands that they place upon recipients are duplicated resulting in excessive bureaucracy and inefficiency. Tanzania, for example, produces 2,400 reports for aid donors every year (Tran 2008). In the mid-1990s, the Mozambican Ministry of Health alone was doing the same for over 400 donors (Wuyts 1996). Furthermore, coordination has been made even more difficult by the proliferation in the number of aid donors, a development that has contributed to the fragmentation of aid flows (Acharya, de Lima and Moore 2006).

The G8 Gleneagles Agreement

The G8 summit held at Gleneagles in July 2005 attracted enormous international publicity, with more than a billion people watching Live8, and the meeting itself the focus of the campaigning efforts of the *Make Poverty History* campaign. However, it is important to recognize that the Gleneagles Summit and the decisions taken were not made in isolation, but were part of a broader reform effort, particularly in relation to changing the global aid architecture. While Glenagles focused upon the amount of aid and how it was delivered, as we saw above there were other processes at work – like the Paris Declaration – that were addressing the conditions over its use, especially in relation to questions of ownership and conditionality.

Along with a decision to achieve universal access to anti-HIV drugs in Africa by 2010, the main outcome of the Gleneagles deal covered the areas of aid, debt and trade (Box 8.1).

Gleneagles and debt

The G8 finance ministers agreed upon the Multilateral Debt Relief Initiative (MDRI) to broaden debt relief. There would be a 100 per cent cancellation of debts owed to the IMF, WB and the African Development Fund (ADF), an affiliate to the African Development Bank (ADB), initially for 18 countries, but the agreement could eventually include up to 43 countries and cost US$55 billion (£31bn). The eighteen countries designated to benefit from this debt relief

---

Box 8.1 G8 Summit results in relation to aid, debt and trade

- The G8 agreed a US$50bn (£28.8bn) boost to aid.
- EU members pledged to reach a collective aid target of 0.56 per cent of GDP by 2010, and 0.7 per cent by 2015.
- The debts of the 18 poorest countries were to be cancelled.
- The summit signalled the need for a new deal on trade, especially in relation to ending agricultural subsidies.

Box 8.2 Debt cancellation at Gleneagles

The G8 countries agreed to the debt cancellation of the following countries:

Benin	Bolivia	Burkina Faso
Ethiopia	Ghana	Guyana
Honduras	Madagascar	Mali
Mauritania	Mozambique	Nicaragua
Niger	Rwanda	Senegal
Tanzania	Uganda	Zambia

---

qualified under the HIPC initiative (Box 8.2). Of this debt, about 70 per cent was owed to the WB, while the rest was owed to the IMF and the ADB. This proposal was later endorsed by these institutions, largely because the G8 was able to confirm that their future lending capacity would not be reduced as a result of losing income from debt repayments and debt interest. In particular, the WB and its subsidiary the IDA were assured that additional resources would be made available to them to cover the costs of the MDRI.

The wider significance of this debt deal is that it is viewed as an essential step to achieving the MDGs – although campaigners at the time insisted a further 35 countries would require debt relief to meet its poverty targets. The debt cancellation countries can now devote money that would previously have been spent on servicing their debts to development projects. For example, the West African state of Benin, which without the Gleneagles Agreement would have had to pay US$7.7 billion in debt interest in 2006, was able to spend this money on health and education, as well as supporting one of its main industries, the cotton industry (Stewart 2006a).

The main criticism of this policy was that it did not go far enough, with African countries at Gleneagles calling for debt relief for all of Africa. Moreover, concerns have continued to be expressed by debt relief campaign groups about the conditions attached to the Gleneagles deal, notably that in order to receive debt relief, countries had to attain the HIPC Completion Point, a test that could include accepting forms of budget control, privatization and trade liberalization. There are also numerous countries that were left off the original debt relief deal because they failed to meet the HIPC criteria. An additional shortcoming of the Gleneagles deal is that arguably it does not recognize the complex nature of debt, in particular, that some debtor countries are not making repayments simply to the IMF and the WB but also to other sources, such as regional development banks like the Inter-American Development Bank. Gleneagles therefore does not provide for complete debt cancellation.

Gleneagles and aid

The second major aspect of the Gleneagles deal was a commitment by the G8 to increase aid to US$130 billion a year by 2010, which constitutes an extra US$50 billion globally above 2004 levels, with half of it going to Africa, thereby doubling the aid to the continent. It also meant that by 2010 the wealthiest countries would be giving collectively 0.36 per cent of their income in aid. Many NGOs, while welcoming the fulfilment of the promised debt cancellation, were less impressed by the progress made in relation to aid, with some viewing the initial G8 aid pledge as disappointing, marking a restatement of existing commitments. Moreover, they noted that a quarter of the promised aid increase was to come from non-G8 sources, while some governments were engaging in double accounting, counting the money spent on debt relief, including debt cancellation deals for Iraq and Nigeria, as part of their aid budget.

Gleneagles and trade

One of the central tenets of the Gleneagles deal reached by G8 ministers was for 'an ambitious and balanced conclusion' to the Doha Round of global trade talks. This was seen as the best way of making trade work for Africa and to increase African countries' integration into the global economy. Indeed, G8 finance ministers regard trade as having even greater potential to generate income growth and development for poorer nations than aid. However, as we saw in chapter 6, the Doha 'development' round of trade talks stalled. Some developing countries are therefore concerned that without, as they see it, fairer trade agreements, they will have little prospect of achieving development through trade.

Aid and debt after Gleneagles

The Gleneagles Summit aroused considerable hope because the G8 leaders signed up to a series of concrete measures rather than simply making statements of principle, as is so often the case at these events. Subsequently, however, it proved difficult to raise the funding necessary to ensure that the G8 fulfilled its commitments. In 2008, it appeared that the commitment by G8 countries to pledge an additional US$50 billion in aid by 2010 would fall short by as much as US$30 billion, while the EU was a long way off achieving a collective spending target of 0.7 per cent of national income by 2015 (Blanchflower 2008). In April 2010, the OECD announced in its annual assessment of development assistance that the shortfall was in line to be US$18 billion against the 2005 commitments (OECD 2010). These shortfalls reflect a wider international trend, with the OECD reporting that aid to the developing world decreased in the two years following Gleneagles (OECD 2008). In 2007, for example, overall aid totalled US$103.7bn (£51.8bn), a fall of 8.4 per cent in real terms, which also reflected the fact that the G8 debt cancellation was complete and could no longer be counted as part of their aid budget (ibid.).

Many commentators believe that 'aid fatigue' is the underlying reason for the decline, resulting from a growing perception that aid is ineffective and is being used to promote the agendas of donor institutions (Robinson and Tarp

2000). Indeed, conditionality has continued to be a divisive issue since the Gleneagles Summit. In this regard, in September 2006 the UK government threatened to withhold £50 million (US$94 million) from the World Bank unless it displayed a more flexible approach in relation to countries that did not meet its requirements to privatize key industries and liberalize their economies, arguing that this merely delayed help to the poor.

Finally, an emerging trend in relation to aid is the increase in substantial private donations from major corporations, foundations and even internet firms. According to the World Bank, over US$1 trillion in private funds was invested in developing countries in 2007; in 2002 the figure was US$174 billion (Schifferes 2008). Unfortunately, the flow of private funds is unevenly spread, with relatively better-off countries like Brazil and China receiving the bulk of this funding, while poor countries in sub-Saharan Africa receive very little (ibid.).

Development specialists increasingly believe it is better to direct aid to the local level – such as NGOs working on the ground, micro-credit and loans to civil society, self-help community development and poverty programmes – as this is the best way of acknowledging diversity and ensuring that aid is targeted at the people who really need it. But all of this does not mean that the state and public aid are being displaced. Indeed, northern governments are employing ODA to deal with the threats associated with globalization, like terrorism, drugs trafficking, international crime and global environmental decline. Furthermore, sovereignty remains an important international principle, and it means that to operate within a developing country NGOs require the permission of the respective government and have to abide by its terms.

As for debt, some development NGOs and debt relief groups are concerned about 'debt fatigue'. While debt relief was a defining issue for the UK chairmanship of the G8 during 2005, it will struggle to retain its place at the top of the international agenda as issues like terrorism and the environment become more prominent, and other countries take over the stewardship of the G8. There may also be a sense of self-satisfaction on the part of richer countries, who may feel that they have done enough to alleviate hardship within developing nations. But from the perspective of the anti-debt movement, encouraged by the Gleneagles deal, they are seeking to take their agenda to a new level and make an even more fundamental attack upon debt. The target of some campaigners is to challenge the legitimacy of some debts, arguing that they were entered into by corrupt and authoritarian regimes, like Mobutu Sese Seko in Zaire and Ferdinand Marcos in the Philippines, who wasted the money or siphoned away into Swiss bank accounts, and in many instances IFIs colluded in this process (Jubilee Debt Campaign 2008).

Summary

- The debt crisis that took off in the 1980s had a long history and was the product of multiple factors.
- Writers who are sceptical about aid argue that it has a poor record when it comes to generating economic growth, which they invariably contend is the best way of reducing poverty.
- The G8 Gleneagles Summit established substantive foreign aid and debt commitments, although some governments are accused of counting the money spent on debt relief as part of their aid budget.

RECOMMENDED READING

- Stuart Corbridge presents a useful overview of a range of perspectives on the debt crisis in *Debt and Development* (1993).
- For an informative work on aid, see Roger Riddell's *Does Foreign Aid Really Work?* (2007).

WEBSITES

- www.jubilee2000uk.org: Website of the Jubilee 2000 coalition.
- www.commissionforafrica.org: For access to its Commission for Africa's report *Our Common Interest* (2005) which urges wealthy nations to double their aid to Africa.
- www.g8.gov.uk: For access to the G8 Gleneagles Summit documents.
- www.devinit.org/realityofaid: For up-to-date reports and analysis on aid.

CHAPTER 9

Sustainable Development

- Development and the global environment
- Globalization, development and the environment
- Global governance and the environment
- Sustainable development

This chapter investigates the nature of the interrelationship between development and the environment within the context of globalization. It will also consider the evolution of global environmental governance (GEG), assessing its effectiveness in relation to environmental protection. The chapter then evaluates the main international response to environmental decline: the concept of sustainable development. As will be shown, these areas generate important questions that lie at the heart of development–environment nexus.

Development and the global environment

Concern about the impact of development and other human practices upon the global environment has steadily grown in the post-war period. A notable landmark was the publication of Rachel Carson's *Silent Spring* in 1962 that highlighted the extent to which the insecticide DDT was leading to a reduction in biodiversity. A decade later, in a work commissioned by the Club of Rome entitled *The Limits to Growth* (1972), D. H. Meadows and her co-writers argued that current resource use and emissions will lead to a rapid decline in both industrial growth and the human population before 2100. Two years later, E. F. Schumacher, in *Small is Beautiful* (1974), published an influential critique of contemporary economics, condemning it for neglecting people and generating environmental destruction. In addition to these important publications, a growing number of environmental movements emerged in many parts of the world from the 1960s onwards.

Development agencies and institutions have also become increasingly environmentally oriented, reflected in the setting up of international commissions and conferences, including the creation by the UN of the influential World Commission on Environment and Development (WCED) in 1983 (see p. 218). Out of these different bodies have emerged numerous reports on the condition of the global environment. For example, in 2007 a major UNEP report, entitled *Global Environment Outlook 4 – Environment for Development*, warned

LLYFRGELL COLEG MENAI LIBRARY

that the failure of governments to address properly environmental issues like deforestation, biodiversity loss, desertification, pollution and climate change, was putting humanity at risk (UNEP 2007). At the same time, there is growing international awareness of the interrelationship between the global economy and the environment. This was evident in the Stern Review that was published by the UK government in October 2006 and made the economic case for acting immediately to reduce the impact of global warming.

But the most worrying statement on the condition of the global environment emanated from the Intergovernmental Panel on Climate Change (IPCC), the leading international scientific authority on climate change, in a series of reports that it published during 2007. The IPCC warned that earlier predictions have underestimated the rate at which the temperature of the planet is rising. In essence, carbon dioxide emissions from the burning of fossil fuels like coal and oil, as well as other 'greenhouse gases' like methane and nitrous oxide, are warming the earth's atmosphere by forming a layer that is preventing heat radiated from the earth from escaping (Willis 2005: 160). Furthermore, the IPCC view reflected the growing acceptance by many in the scientific community that the effects of global warming will not necessarily be gradually felt, but rather will be in the form of sudden and intense spurts of essentially unpredictable climactic activity (National Research Council 2002). In sum, all the indicators suggest that, as the century progresses, the physical global environment will become a more unstable place.

Furthermore, it is widely accepted that the developing world, and in particular Africa, will bear the brunt of climate change and other forms of environmental degradation. While the extent to which the global climate is changing continues to be a source of contestation, there is now virtual consensus that it is changing and will have profound implications for development in the future. In this vein, the UNDP's (2006) Human Development Report entitled *Beyond Scarcity: Power, Poverty and the Global Water Crisis*, concludes that, while the effects of global climate change will vary from country to country in Africa, especially within sub-Saharan Africa, a number of broad consequences can be predicted. These include the following:

- rising sea levels as a result of melting glaziers will reduce access to fresh water;
- an increased risk of floods and droughts owing to more extreme and unstable weather patterns;
- an increase in extreme poverty and malnutrition as water supplies become less stable;
- climate change will have the greatest and most damaging impact upon agriculture and rural development, increasing unpredictability and risk in these areas (UNDP 2006).

The UNDP restated this position in its next Human Development Report, entitled *Fighting Climate Change: Human Solidarity in a Divided World* (2007), arguing that to deal with climate change developed countries will have to cut their carbon emissions by 80 per cent by 2050. Regions like sub-Saharan Africa are especially vulnerable because they have limited water infrastructures and hence have more difficulty in dealing with unpredictable weather patterns, particularly irregular and erratic rainfall. Climate change and other forms of environmental degradation, therefore, have the potential to reverse any development advances that have been made in these regions.

Continuing this theme of the differential impacts of climate change across the Global South, it follows that environmental issues do not just operate at the global level but are played out at the national and local levels. It is also the case that the interconnected causes and experiences of environmental degradation affect some people within different countries and communities much more than others. Put another way, those profiting from environmental degradation are not simply the West or the North, but governments and local elites in poor countries, while those that lose out are not just the South, but particular people within the South.[1] In turn, this diversity of experiences raises the matter of environmental justice. Indeed, the environmental justice movement (EJM) has consistently emphasized the connection between environmental problems and social inequities, highlighting how low-income and minority communities invariably bear a disproportionate burden when it comes to living with environmental decline (Pellow and Brulle 2005).

However, environmental justice is a complex and deeply contested concept (see Low 1999; Schlosberg 1999, 2009). One reason for the complexity is that it raises the difficult issue of intergenerational justice – we arguably have an obligation to future generations to tackle climate change, for example – as well as that of our relationship to other species. For David Schlosberg (2009), environmental justice is a multidimensional concept because it deals with issues about distribution, recognition, participation and the capability of communities and individuals to function and flourish in society. But further complicating the debates surrounding environmental justice is that the EJM and the environmental movement are distinct movements with a history of tension between them. For example, the EJM has accused the environmental movement of neglecting socio-economic issues like racism and elitism in relation to the environment and of valuing the natural world over people (see Sandler and Pezzullo 2007).

Most development specialists acknowledge the complex interrelationships that exist between development, poverty and the natural environment. For example, it is difficult for the poor to think of the condition of the planet and the plight of future generations when faced with an everyday struggle for survival (Elliott 1999). Piers Blaikie contends that the need to survive can lead to a 'desperate ecocide' (1985: 138).[2] However, the economic development required to achieve poverty reduction can often place excessive demands upon the environment. Yet, without development, it is likely that many people in developing societies will migrate to the North, and this also has environmental costs.

Box 9.1 The costs of China's rapid development

China is repeatedly cited as a major cause of global warming through its pursuit of rapid economic development. Between 1997 and 2007 the Chinese economy tripled in size, and crucially coal, of which China has a plentiful amount, constitutes two-thirds of the energy that has powered its dash-for-growth policy. The lightly regulated Chinese coal industry has grown dramatically, with hundreds of new coal-fired power stations being built. It has led to coal production doubling to more than 1.2 billion tonnes per year and a dramatic rise in electricity generation.

However, an OECD report published in 2007 concluded that the environmental degradation caused by China's spectacular economic growth was not only harming the health of a large proportion of its population but also holding back the country economically (Vidal 2007b). Based upon an 18-month investigation, the OECD report highlights the number of working days lost through environmentally related illnesses, especially those associated with air and water pollution, such as respiratory problems and diarrhoea, respectively. Dealing with these illnesses also places a further financial strain upon China's inchoate health services. The Worldwatch Institute estimates that air pollution cost the country more than US$63 billion (£31 billion) in 2004 (Watts and Vidal 2007a: 23). It is also anticipated that China's pollution levels and generally poor environmental record will put off some consumers in other countries, especially in relation to food and food-based products (Vidal 2007b).

However, questions continue to be raised about how deeply the environmental agenda has penetrated development thinking and practice. For W. M. Adams (2001), the disciplines of environmental and development studies remain as curiously apart as ever, and greatly in need of integration and coordination. Further complicating matters, as will be shown below (p. 213), is the fact that it is possible to detect different perspectives on the relationship between development and environment in southern and northern governments. Southern countries resent the ways in which the regulatory regimes that make up GEG place restrictions upon their ability to develop, something that their northern counterparts never had to face (Shahin 1999). Adding to their sense of injustice is the fact that northern countries continue to expel most of the world's carbon dioxide emissions, although the economic rise of China (see Box 9.1) complicates this picture because during 2007 it became the world's largest emitter of greenhouse gases (Vidal 2007a).[3]

Finally, environmental concerns look set to gain in importance within development studies as the century progresses. This is because there are few tangible signs of a reduction in the tendencies and practices contributing to environmental degradation, such as consumerism and current consumption patterns, global population growth, the expansion of world trade and the use of fossil fuels and 'industrial' technologies. Indeed, contemporary human practices are encouraging predictions of resource conflict, environmental refugees, and the abandonment of development projects. Of course, there remain dissenting voices. For instance, the economist Wilfred Beckerman (2003) maintains that the claims made about resource shortages and environmental decline are unfounded.

Globalization, development and the environment

Arguably, globalization adds further complexity to the already intricate relationship that exists between development and the environment. Indeed, the environmental degradation caused by some forms of development is perhaps the ultimate manifestation of globalization because it readily transcends national borders. What has been termed 'the globalization of environmental hazards' entails that any harm done to the environment in one part of the world will have potentially catastrophic effects for other regions (Middleton 2003). Thus, the deforestation of the Amazonian rainforests in Latin America can have a detrimental environmental impact upon the African continent, especially with regard to the temperature levels and the number of droughts experienced there. In turn, this creates the conditions in which development can take place.

However, the exact nature of the relationship between globalization and the environment remains contested. As will now be shown, while critics of globalization see it as causing environmental harm, its advocates point to the benefits that it can bring to the environment.

Globalization and environmental harm

Many critics of globalization view it as primarily an economic phenomenon. It entails the growth of world trade and the greater movement of goods and peoples across the globe, causing environmental harm in the form of increased pollution and carbon dioxide emissions, as well as using up limited resources (Hines 2000). As James Gustave Speth, has observed, 'since 1960 the size of the world economy has doubled and then doubled again' (2003: 2). From this perspective, globalization is the antithesis of sustainable development, serving to preclude its realization. Indeed, Martin Khor (2001a) maintains that globalization is a competing paradigm to sustainable development, and this accounts for the difficulty in implementing the environmental treaties agreed upon at international summits. More specifically, globalization is the model promoted by the more powerful northern countries, but it is also what most of us are contributing to during the course of our daily lives. In this regard, for some writers, the very forces and processes generating globalization, like industrialism, capitalism, rationalism, science and progress, are harmful to the environment (Held et al. 1999).

For radical critics, what we are confronted with is capitalist globalization, and it is leading to the commodification and privatization of natural resources, like water and land. It means that environmental objectives have to compete with the principle of profit maximization. In his book *The Enemy of Nature: The End of Capitalism or the End of the World?* (2007), Joel Kovel argues that this system is leading to an ecological crisis because it is motivated by an endless drive for expansionism irrespective of the environmental effects. It is a system that is therefore beyond reform, and instead we need a society based on socialist and ecological principles. However, Kovel's critics argue that environmental decline cannot simply be reduced to a monocausal explanation, albeit one as powerful as that of capitalism.

Some writers articulate the notion of neo-liberal globalization, and emphasize how it is throwing countries and regions together more closely than ever before and generating greater competition between them. In other words, by establishing free trade internationally, it creates a never-ending concern among businesses and governments that their counterparts in other countries are not pursuing the same environmental standards in order to make themselves more competitive. As a result, it puts pressure upon countries to reduce their own environmental standards to those with the poorest record (Pacheco-Vega 2006). It can also lead to an environmental 'race to the bottom', whereby companies relocate to countries with lower environmental standards because of the prospect of cheaper production costs. Furthermore, with globalization eroding national borders, it is now much easier for companies to relocate. In most instances, this means firms moving to poorer countries – so-called 'pollution havens' – and emitting their pollution there because such countries generally lack the resources to enforce rigorous regulatory regimes (Gallagher 2004).[4]

Of course, there may be some southern governments that see maintaining relatively weak environmental regulatory regimes as a way of attracting foreign investment into their countries. Nevertheless, there is general concern within developing countries about the harm being done to local environments as a result of their becoming home to some of the world's major polluters (Clapp 2002). However, a number of studies suggest that non-environmental factors, like tax incentives, cheaper labour and the prospect of new markets, exert greater influence upon the investment decisions of companies than the extent of environmental regulation within a country (e.g., Janicke, Binder and Monch 1997; Van Beers and Van den Bergh 1997; Wheeler 2002).

In *Localization: A Global Manifesto* (2000), Colin Hines contends that, if we are to move away from the relentless competition ushered in by globalization and aid the environment, we must focus upon localization. This approach is based upon the fostering of cooperative practices at a local level, but also the dissemination of what he terms a 'supportive internationalism', 'where the flow of ideas, technologies, information, culture, money and goods has, as its end goal, the protection and rebuilding of local economies worldwide' (ibid.: 256). For Hines, if we follow this route, it will reduce the environmental harm caused by our current global practices and at the same time enhance the quality of our lives.

The case for environmental globalization

Advocates of globalization naturally stress its environmental benefits. They argue that participation in global markets is the most effective way for developing countries to achieve economic growth and poverty reduction and this in turn can aid the environment. In other words, by moving beyond subsistence level, it becomes easier to think of future generations and to pursue sustainable development (Bhagwati 2004; Wolf 2004). Countries will also be able to invest their increasing wealth in environmentally friendly technologies and in cleaning up the environment (Legrain 2002: 244).

Free traders consider that the emphasis upon self-sufficiency within environmentalism undermines comparative advantage. As we saw in chapter 6, they argue that the latter encourages specialization and more efficient production, and therefore benefits the environment. In this regard, some of the forces driving globalization, such as ICTs, rapid transportation and MNCs, contribute to the effective functioning of comparative advantage by allowing production to be truly globalized. Indeed, many MNCs locate the different parts of their production process to the countries and regions of the world where they can be most effectively produced. In contrast, a concern of some southern producers is that the spread of localism in the North, including the growth of farmers' markets and local food distribution networks, is hindering their ability to sell their goods in northern markets (Willis 2005: 170).

As a result of their greater wealth and productive capacity, MNCs are in a position to pursue higher environmental standards than local companies, and this includes globally disseminating through their firms the most advanced environmental technologies. Furthermore, under globalization, companies must seek to universalize standards and best practice because knowledge of environmental harm caused by a particular branch or outlet can soon spread and tar the image of the whole organization. Indeed, in an image-obsessed era, a reputation for corporate responsibility is also good for business. Moreover, popular concern over the environment has ensured that selling eco-friendly goods and services has become profitable and can help companies to increase their market share (Clapp and Dauvergne 2005). For supporters of globalization, profit maximization and the environment are therefore not incompatible.

Another aspect of globalization that is claimed to benefit the environment concerns the growth of global governance. In comparison with nation-states, institutions like the UN are considered to be better placed to deal with the environmental challenges that lie ahead. The latter are able to take a cosmopolitan perspective on the environment, whereas the former invariably approach environmental issues from the perspective of their national interests, making it difficult to achieve effective international cooperation (see p. 216).[5] From a practical perspective, global institutions can facilitate the relocation of resources to regions suffering from environmental hardships, like famine and drought. These institutions are also able to enforce international environmental standards. Indeed, global governance reinforces the notion of global and transnational accountability for harm done to the environment, although critics argue that international institutional mechanisms and processes for ensuring transnational environmental accountability remain inchoate (Park 2005).

Nevertheless, some environmentalists welcome the diminution of national sovereignty that is considered to be a function of globalization (see chapter 10) because many advocate the 'greening of sovereignty', whereby the notion of what is sovereign in international law is extended to non-state actors like international institutions and ordinary citizens.[6] Challenges to the predominance of the nation-state within international affairs will also strengthen environmental concepts, such as the 'global commons'. In this vein, there is an increasing tendency within international law to view natural resources as being held in trusteeship or stewardship by states, rather than simply being owned by them (Sand 2004). In addition, the globalization of environmental hazards has the potential to undermine the nation-state's role as protector of its citizens. As we saw in New Orleans in the aftermath of Hurricane Katrina, even the world's wealthiest nation can struggle to provide welfare provision, basic amenities and security for its citizens against the forces of nature. Accelerated environmental decline can therefore undermine the social contract between the state and its citizens and suggests that states will have to widen their conceptions of national security, placing greater emphasis upon international environmental cooperation (Trittin 2004).

Advocates of globalization argue that the global dissemination of ICTs may enable us to rethink contemporary work patterns, ensuring more video conferencing and working from home and, crucially, less environmentally harmful commuting. Meanwhile, environmental NGOs and scientific network communities, whose work and activities are sustained by ICTs, are helping to disseminate knowledge about the environment and raising public awareness of environmental issues. Indeed, the expertise that these bodies possess is increasingly acknowledged, with more and more of them being incorporated into international environmental regimes.

It is claimed that the shift to technology driven post-industrial economies and away from resource-intensive industrial modes of production will have obvious environmental benefits. This type of argument forms part of the ecological modernization thesis (see Mol and Spaargaren 2000; Spaargaren, Mol and Buttel 2000). But it is most often viewed as an environmental 'Kuznets curve'. Named after the economist Simon Kuznets (1955), it contends that the pollution levels of developing countries increase as they develop, but start to diminish steadily once these societies move into a less energy-intensive, post-industrial stage.

Global governance and the environment

From a development perspective, the different types of trans-boundary environmental degradation present enormous challenges. It has led to numerous international conferences, conventions and treaties that have created environmental regulatory regimes on areas ranging from biodiversity to climate change.[7] In particular, the 1972 UN Stockholm Conference on the Human Environment established that the environment was a legitimate area of concern for both national and international governance (Caldwell 1996). This change was reflected in the setting up of the UN Environment Programme (UNEP) in 1973. Since then, there have been a number of key moments in the evolution of GEG:

The Rio Earth Summit of 1992

The Rio Earth Summit confirmed the place of sustainable development on the international agenda but also highlighted how multilateral environmental agreements (MEAs) can serve this end. It was organized by the United Nations Conference on Environment and Development (UNCED) in Rio de Janeiro in 1992, and 176 countries attended. At this summit, world leaders signed five agreements on a range of issues designed to protect the planet, such as the prevention of species extinction, deforestation and climate change (see Box 9.2). The summit also saw the Global North and the South outline different approaches towards development and the environment. Southern governments argued that their pursuit of sustainable development necessitated revising the international terms of trade so that they can escape from their indebtedness and from having to prioritize servicing their debts. In contrast, northern governments saw the dissemination of green technologies, especially within the developing world, as the most effective way of meeting environmental challenges. However, the North did acknowledge their particular responsibility for the environmental crisis as a result of industrializing first, and this forms one of the principles of the Rio Declaration.

Box 9.2 The Rio Earth Summit Agreements

- The Rio Declaration: While it is not legally binding upon its signatories, the declaration nevertheless establishes 27 principles that are designed to guide environmental behaviour.
- The Framework Convention on Climate Change: This convention was a compromise solution to end the deadlock at UNCED over climate change. As a result, it is a relatively ineffective convention that established no legally binding commitments on the part of industrialized countries to stabilize their carbon dioxide emissions.
- The Convention on Biological Diversity: This convention aimed to protect the earth's biological wealth through a combination of new conservation programmes and the promotion of sustainable exploitation of wild habitats. It was signed by 156 countries and came into force in 1993.
- The Statement of Principles on Forests: This established guidelines for countries to follow in their policies on natural forest conservation and exploitation. However, this non-binding statement did not establish any limits with regards to deforestation.
- Agenda 21: This established a sustainable development programme for the twenty-first century. All the countries agreed to formulate a detailed national sustainable development strategy (NSDS) incorporating the efforts of both their national governments and local authorities. In particular, chapter 28 of this document, entitled Local Agenda 21 (LA21), encourages local governments to facilitate community involvement in environmental decision-making processes.

As for what was achieved at this summit, many development writers point to Agenda 21 as the most significant outcome (see Box 9.2), with 7,000 LA21s initiated by local groups in over 110 countries by the end of 2001 (Sacquet 2005). But overall, the Rio Earth Summit is viewed as a disappointment by environmentalists who identify an economic growth and ecological moderni- zation agenda behind many of the Rio Declaration's statement of principles (Pelling 2002). Furthermore, no binding agreements were reached on impor- tant issues like population control and the transfer of technologies and fund- ing from the developed to the developing world. From the perspective of many NGOs attending the summit, there was crucially no attempt to rethink the relationship between development and environment, and in a sense UNCED merely confirmed that it was going to be 'business as usual' (ibid.: 288).

The Kyoto Protocol

Of the principal environmental treaties, the Kyoto Accord signed in 1997 has attracted the most international attention. This treaty, which came into force in February 2005, aims to curb the air pollution blamed for global warming, demanding that countries cut their emissions of carbon dioxide and other greenhouse gases. By 2005, some 141 countries had ratified the treaty, and in doing so they pledged to cut their greenhouse gas emissions – that account for 55 per cent of total emissions – by 5.2 per cent by 2012. A major shortcoming of the Kyoto Protocol is that rapidly developing economies like China, India and Brazil remain outside the framework and were not immediately required to meet specific targets. Most seriously, the US government pulled out of Kyoto in 2001, challenging some of the scientific evidence behind the agreement and claiming that the changes it would necessitate would be too expensive to implement. Despite the fact that the US is the world's largest polluter, Washington also justified its non-intervention by noting that China and India were not part of the agreement and this provided them with an unfair com- petitive advantage in the international economy. The US has received wide- spread condemnation for its unilateral approach to this issue. In its defence, the US government has argued it will continue to innovate and invest in new technologies in order to meet the challenge of global warming.

For many environmentalists, the Kyoto Protocol is too limited in its ambi- tion, and the target of 5.2 per cent will be insufficient to tackle global warm- ing. From the perspective of the signatories, a number have admitted that they will struggle to meet their legally binding Kyoto commitments, with some experiencing an increase in rather than a reduction in their emission levels. In 2005, Canada's greenhouse gas emissions were 20 per cent higher than in 1990. Irrespective of the difficulties that they were facing in meet- ing these reductions, 157 countries agreed to extend the Kyoto agreement at the UN climate change conference in Montreal in December 2005. When its first phase expires in 2012, the expressed intention is that the next Kyoto phase will see developed countries undertake even harsher cuts in green-house gas pollution – although no specific targets were agreed upon at this conference. Similarly, while there was discussion at the Montreal confer-ence about developing countries pursuing voluntary targets for emissions reductions, the actual role that they would play in the new phase of Kyoto remained unclear.

The World Summit for Sustainable Development of 2002

Another notable UN event was the World Summit for Sustainable Development, held in Johannesburg in 2002. In relation to the environment, a number of rel-atively minor proposals on energy were agreed at the summit, including the removal of lead in petrol and the promotion of energy-efficient technologies. The Kyoto Protocol also received a boost when Russia announced that it would ratify the treaty. It ensured that sufficient large-scale producers of greenhouse gases were signed up to the Accord for it to be brought into effect in 2005. However, governments failed to agree on specific targets to boost the share of global energy produced from renewable sources like wind and solar power, largely because the US and certain oil-producing countries were opposed to them. As a result, the summit action plan simply called on countries to increase substantially the global share of renewable energy. And even the meaning of the term 'renewable' was disputed during the summit, with some countries arguing that hydroelectric schemes and nuclear power should be included under this heading. Likewise, while governments agree to cut signifi-cantly by 2010 the rate at which plants and animals were becoming extinct, no specific targets were set. Many activists and campaign groups condemned the plan of action produced by this summit, arguing that a major opportunity to help both the planet and the poor was squandered at Johannesburg.

Global governance and the environment: what has been achieved?

As for what has been achieved from all this international environmental activ-ity and governance, it is in truth a mixed picture. There has been considerable progress over the depletion of the stratospheric ozone layer by chlorofluoro-carbons (CFCs) and other gases, with measures such as the 1987 Montreal Protocol having done much to help protect the ozone layer (Barrow 2004). But with environmental issues, the results have generally been disappointing. Despite the conventions and statements of principle agreed upon at the Earth Summit in Rio, the extinction trends in animals and plants have continued more or less in the same manner as in the pre-Rio period. Likewise, in 2002, ten years after Rio, the global rate of tropical rainforest destruction was 1 per cent per year, the same level as it was in 1992. Desertification, nitrogen pollution, marine protection and the management of toxic substances are other areas where environmental regimes have achieved only scant success. Moreover, a

> **Box 9.3 MDGs Goal 7: Ensure environmental sustainability**
> - **Target 1:** Integrate the principles of sustainable development into country policies and programmes and reverse the loss of environmental resources.
> - **Target 2:** Reduce biodiversity loss, achieving, by 2010, a significant reduction in the rate of loss.
> - **Target 3:** Halve, by 2015, the proportion of the population without sustainable access to safe drinking water and basic sanitation.
> - **Target 4:** Achieve, by 2020, a significant improvement in the lives of at least 100 million slum-dwellers.

persistent criticism of summits and international institutions is that, in focusing upon 'green' issues (rural, agricultural and wildlife concerns), they pay insufficient attention to brown agenda issues, such as pollution, air quality and housing, that are problems particularly affecting people living in urban and industrial areas (see Forsyth 2002).

The UN Millennium Development Goals are a useful indicator of how the international community is faring in relation to the environment. The environmental targets are included in Goal 7 (see Box 9.3). However, broadly speaking, world leaders tend not to focus upon these targets, especially sanitation, preferring instead to prioritize health, education and poverty. Critics argue that this is a misguided approach because environmental concerns underpin all of these issues. For example, it will never be possible to tackle health matters effectively in countries with high levels of pollution and unclean water. Likewise, land degradation holds back the economies of developing societies, thereby hindering poverty alleviation and investment in education. In 2008, the UN reported the progress that had been made with regard to the environmental targets, but conceded that: more than one third of the growing urban population in developing countries live in slum conditions, with nearly one in four using no form of sanitation; the number of species threatened with extinction is rising rapidly; nearly a billion people lack safe sources of drinking water; and immediate action is needed to contain rising carbon dioxide emissions (UNMDG 2008: 41, 39, 42, 36).

How effective are international summits?

There is an ongoing debate about whether international summits are an effective mechanism for tackling development and environment issues. Their sheer size, and the range of different and competing interests involved, makes consensus-building and effective policy formulation difficult to achieve. And many governments seemingly view summits as occasions to promote their respective national interests. Consequently, the conventions and agreements emerging from summits tend to be statements of intent, rather than legally binding targets. Moreover, the success of summits is closely linked to the extent to which the major powers support the decisions arrived at. Lastly, MNCs and TNCs have proved very effective at lobbying governments, both in the run up to summits and in the proceedings during them, raising concerns that the views of national electorates are being marginalized.

However, summits do mark a coming together of the international community to deal with global problems. They provide a forum for dialogue between governments and the chance to resolve differences and establish common international norms, practices and values. And without summits, countries will have even greater autonomy to pursue their own national agendas, ensuring that the fate of the environment and other vital matters lie simply within any voluntary initiatives they may wish to undertake. Summits also ensure that the environment and development remain high on the international agenda by attracting considerable worldwide publicity and media attention. Moreover, they provide opportunities for environmentalists and other campaigners to exert pressure upon governments and companies to act in an ethical and environmentally sensitive manner. For example, over 30,000 members of NGOs participated in the Global Forum that paralleled the Rio Earth Summit in 1992. Summits have also been credited for disseminating the concept of sustainable development throughout the international community (Baker 2006: 213).

The GEG balance sheet

Effective global environmental governance is being hindered by the voluntarist nature of existing environmental regimes, with countries being selective about their participation and continuing to pursue their national interest over such matters. It has also meant that environmental treaties generally lack strong compliance mechanisms and contain widely varying verification and monitoring processes. At the same time, countries are struggling to meet relatively modest environmental targets for agreements like the Kyoto Protocol, and this despite an emphasis upon incorporating incentives into environmental regimes in order to encourage compliance. Even today, therefore, global environmental governance remains fairly inchoate and uncoordinated.

In this regard, the findings of the UNDP's Human Development Report (*Beyond Scarcity*, 2006) concluded that to date the efforts to help developing countries adapt to the impacts of climate change have been 'woefully inadequate'. In focusing upon reducing greenhouse gas emissions, the international community has failed to provide the investment that would enable LEDCs to undertake adaptation projects in response to climate change. Christian Aid and other NGOs believe MEDCs need to set up a 'global fighting fund' of some £50 billion per annum in order to help LEDCs adapt to climate change (Adam 2007). For example, because Africa is heavily reliant upon rain-fed agriculture, its farmers require financial and technical assistance in order to change the nature of crop production, including the introduction of new crop varieties more suited to changeable rainfall patterns.

The current piecemeal arrangements that constitute contemporary GEG will therefore struggle to deal with the serious environmental challenges that lie ahead. It is also widely recognized that the UNEP struggles to drive the environmental agenda forward because it lacks the authority, mandate and financial autonomy to do so (Biermann and Bauer 2005: 259). Indeed, the UN Secretary-General's High Level Panel in a 2006 report proposed: the upgrading of the UNEP with improved resources and a renewed mandate; the clustering of the UN's (over 700) environment conventions; and the strengthening of the Global Environment Facility (GEF) as the major financial mechanism for global environmental initiatives.

Some commentators advocate the 'greening' of the major international institutions, like the World Bank, IMF and the WTO, so that they lead the way on the environment (Tran 2007). But critics counter that these institutions are propping up a global economic system that encourages the pursuit of profit rather than sustainable development (Ward and Brack, 2000). For this reason, others seek the establishment of an environmental equivalent to the WTO, namely a World Environment Organization (WEO) (Esty and Ivanova 2003). In contrast, Marc Williams (2001) contends that the significance of the environment is now acknowledged within the world trading system, and environmental concerns are now factored into the different rounds of trade negotiations held by the WTO.

In sum, the complexities and contested nature of international environmental politics ensures that reforming GEG is difficult to achieve. Moreover, any attempt to do so must take into account the different agendas and capacities of national governments. At the same time, many states are also pursuing their own unilateral measures to combat environmental decline and achieve sustainable development. Further complicating matters is the fact that an environmental agenda has been incorporated into the policy-making processes of many regional organizations and groupings, notably the EU and NAFTA (see Chasek, Downie and Welsh Brown 2006). Lastly, alongside the institutional dynamics of GEG, there is increasingly a civil society input into environmental decision-making processes in the form of industry groups, local communities, NGOs and environmental networks. GEG is therefore a multilateral and multilevel phenomenon.

Sustainable development

Sustainable development underpinned the WCED's influential 1987 Brundtland Report that did much to popularize the concept (see Box 9.4). It is founded upon a number of mutually reinforcing economic, social and environmental objectives that must be integrated into the policies and practices that we pursue (Dalal-Clayton and Bass 2002: 12). For its advocates, sustainable development is viewed as a way of bridging the divide between economic growth and environmental sustainability that informed development, debates in the 1970s (Hettne 2008: xvii). It acknowledges that without economic development the Global South will be condemned to perpetual

---

Box 9.4 The Brundtland Report and sustainable development

Named after its Chair, the former prime minister of Norway, Gro Harlem Brundtland, and entitled Our Common Future, the influence of this report is evidenced by the fact that its definition of sustainable development continues to be widely used. It defined sustainable development as: 'development that meets the needs of the present without compromising the ability of future generations to meet their own needs' (WCED 1987: 43). Arguably, part of the attraction of this definition lies with its broadness and lack of policy prescription, thereby allowing countries to pursue their own conceptions of sustainable development.

Another notable feature of this report is its underlying optimism. It argues that if we pursue sustainable development, which would entail, among other things, improvements in international cooperation, technology usage and resource conservation, our common future can be 'prosperous, just and secure' (WCED 1987: 363). Critics contend that the Brundtland Report remains rooted within the economic growth model tradition. Indeed, the WCED considers economic growth to be the best way of eradicating poverty, which is portrayed as the major obstacle to attaining sustainable development, and even explores the rates and types of growth that should be striven for. But crucially the report maintains that economic growth should not be achieved at the expense of the environment: it must be environmentally sensitive and sustainable, especially with regard to resource usage (ibid.: 52–4).

---

underdevelopment, but this has to be balanced with the protection of environmental resources.

Sustainable development also incorporates certain normative principles or behavioural guidelines, as well as a concern with social justice in the form of poverty alleviation and gender equality. It is also motivated by a concern with the plight of future generations and other species (see Adams 2001; Lafferty and Langhelle 1999; Meadowcroft 1997), while some writers emphasize social inclusivity and community participation (Blewitt 2008a). Consequently, sustainable development has been conceived of as a moral, not a market, concept (Jacobs 1990) and has been described as marking a 'paradigm shift' (Koenig 1995: 2). For radical environmentalists, however, the incorporation of economic growth into mainstream sustainable development negates any notion that it is an ecological concept, although Susan Baker contends that the different models of sustainable development 'share the common belief that there are ultimate, biophysical limits to growth' (2006: 212).

For some writers, the absence of a universal model of sustainable development is not a shortcoming as they regard it as a political concept, like 'democracy' and 'liberty', which functions as an agent of societal change (Baker 2006; Jacobs 1991). Moreover, multiple understandings and conceptualizations of sustainable development allow for the input of local knowledge and expertise. And in reality such pluralism is inevitable as there will be a range of factors shaping the sustainable development strategies pursued by countries, such as access to resource endowments, population sizes, land mass, technological capacity, and cultural and political influences (Redclift 2002). Indeed, governments will have differing capacities to implement sustainable development policies, dependent upon their infrastructure and national governance processes and institutions. Sustainable development should therefore reflect the particular conditions of the countries, cultures or other local contexts in which it is being implemented, especially as these conditions will evolve and change. In addition, these societies will be informed by external influences, including the policies of international authorities, global and transnational cultures, migration patterns and the investment strategies of MNCs. In other words, sustainable development can only ever be a guiding principle rather than a universally prescribed set of policies.

However, sustainable development remains a contested concept, one that has generated a range of approaches and perspectives from, among others, deep ecologists, eco-socialists and eco-feminists, as well as economists, anthropologists and politicians. Lack of space precludes a detailed exposition of these different positions (for such an analysis, see Adams 2001; Baker 2006; Blewitt 2008b); rather, they will be discussed as part of two broad approaches to sustainable development.[8]

Weak sustainable development

This view favours reliance upon technology, economic growth and the effective management of resources as the best way of achieving sustainable development. This position has been prominent within the sustainable development debate, with the WCED operating within this tradition, for example. Arguably, a common theme of this approach is that of optimism. There is a belief in our innate capacity to develop the necessary technological innovations to meet the environmental challenges that lie ahead, but also in human ingenuity in general (e.g., Simon 1981). Indeed, economists generally resent the restrictions that more rigorous models of sustainable development impose upon economic growth and place their faith in the free operation of market mechanisms like price changes to deal with future environmental problems. For example, David Pearce believes attaching a monetary value to the environment will help us stop treating natural resources as if they were free (Pearce, Markandya and Barbier 1989).

The main charge against the weak sustainable development is that it fails to grasp the complex interconnections between patterns of human behaviour and the earth's ecosystems and, in turn, the extent of environmental decline. It is therefore unwise, critics argue, to continue with growth-based models and to rely upon the prospect of future technological innovations, which may or may not emerge. In this regard, even the mainstream Rio Declaration established the 'precautionary principle': namely that, when there are threats of serious or irreversible environmental damage, lack of full scientific evidence should not be used to prevent action to protect the environment (Principle 15 on Environment and Development).

Strong sustainable development

Writers operating from this tradition are more radical and question the continued reliance upon the market within mainstream sustainable development. Their starting point is that ecological constraints entail that current patterns of economic growth cannot be sustained. Instead, sustainable development is promoted at a grassroots level with local contexts, knowledges and participation all prioritized. Consequently, there is an emphasis upon the pursuit of autarky (economic self-sufficiency) and the empowerment of local people in this approach. For Herman Daly (1992), we must seek to build a 'steady state economy', one that allows time for both renewable resources to regenerate and for natural systems to break down the pollutants that we emit. However, the 'limits to growth' thesis has been criticized for underplaying the potential of technology and technological developments to overcome some of the physical limits to growth (Baker 2006: 18).

For deep ecologists, the existing economic order needs to be replaced by ecologically sustainable belief and knowledge systems (Naess 1973). In other words, we need to move away from current dominant patterns of human behaviour and pursue values and lifestyles that are in harmony with nature. However, this perspective is often criticized as being, at least at this juncture, politically impractical. Not only is there is little sign of the international economic system being replaced, but at this stage even restricting economic growth would create enormous political problems for any government.

Criticism of sustainable development

What is sustainable development?   Concern has been expressed about the lack of consensus surrounding the concept of sustainable development. At least seventy-two definitions of sustainable development have been identified and, with countries pursuing their own conceptions of it with varying degrees of rigour, there is a danger of the concept being rendered meaningless (Rogers, Jalal and Boyd 2008: 23). One writer has gone as far as to suggest that sustainable development is effectively anything that one wants it to be (O'Riordan 1995). In turn, this pluralism makes it difficult to establish universal environmental standards or to determine progress. For this reason, it has been suggested that we need more rigorous concepts and clearly defined and identifiable principles underpinning sustainable development (Ben-Eli 2007), whereas Blake Ratner (2004) believes the way forward lies with an ongoing 'dialogue of values' between interest groups, ranging from governments to citizens. Nevertheless, advocates of sustainable development argue that established and rigorous strategies do exist, and development specialists spend a great deal of time analysing and seeking to enhance them (see Dalal-Clayton and Bass 2002). Moreover, the EU and the OECD have devised sets of sustainable development indicators in order to measure progress.

Too growth oriented   Some environmentalists contend that economic development rather than environmental sustainability is the dominant discourse
within the concept of sustainable development (Banerjee 2003). If this is true,
it means that the intellectual origins of development in eighteenth-century
notions of modernity and material progress are imbuing sustainable development. Critics argue that this tendency is reflected in the continuing preoccupation within development circles with the GNP achieved by countries. From
an ecological perspective, GNP is a crude indicator of the nature of economic
growth and development, providing no indication of the extent of the environmental damage and other costs that have been sustained in achieving such
growth. For this reason, Kirk Hamilton and John Dixon (2003), among others,
discuss the possibility of a green GNP that will take into account factors like
environmental decline and resource pollution when measuring national
income accounts (see also Repetto 1992).

However, despite such initiatives, for many in the environmental movement it remains the case that there is simply insufficient emphasis within
the discourse of sustainable development upon reducing ecological harm
and limiting growth (Jacob 1994). Consequently, some ecologists have simply
given up on the concept of sustainable development.

Who decides?   There is also the broader issue of who is determining policy at
a national level in relation to sustainable development. To date, for example,
the growth in the number of LA21s has arguably not led to the widespread
dissemination of sustainable development best practice at national and
international levels (Dalal-Clayton and Bass 2002: 13). Are national policy-
making processes within countries allowing for full public participation and
consultation? To what extent are the decision-makers in a position to balance
considerations of long-term sustainability with more immediate demands for
decent or high standards of living within their societies? Are there mechanisms for ascertaining any connections between governing elites and polluter
companies? Of course, for countries that receive a substantial proportion of
their income from pollution-generating industries, the pursuit of sustainable
development will be even more of a challenge. In this vein, Bruno and Karliner
(2002) identify a number of companies that are employing the rhetoric of sustainable development in order to enhance their green credentials and profit
margins, but are not actually implementing it in any meaningful way. All of
this has led Michael Redclift to question whether sustainable development is
achievable 'without increased democratization at all levels of society' (2002:
277). Conversely, the emphasis upon the local within sustainable development can often lead to the postponement of the difficult and substantive decisions that need to be made at the national level (Purvis and Grainger 2004).

North–South perspectives   From the perspective of many people in the South,
while the North was freely able to pursue, and enjoy the benefits of, economic

growth-based development, the condition of the planet dictates that they must now pursue sustainable development. Many see sustainable development as eroding their autonomy because it insists that the natural resources of developing countries are part of a common project in which all the citizens of the world have an interest (Soto 1992: 694). Moreover, the governments and peoples of developing societies are expected to nurture and protect these assets for the good of humankind (Elliott 2004: 171). At the same time, the North continues to diminish a vital component of the global commons, namely its climate system. On the grounds of consistency, as well as for the sake of the planet, this would seem to necessitate an erosion of the North's autonomy and specifically the curtailment of northern consumption patterns and lifestyles. But to the frustration of many citizens in the South, this has not happened.

Northern governments respond that they are taking measures to reduce their carbon dioxide emissions through more efficient energy usage and the use of alternative energy sources. Moreover, from the perspective of many in the North, their interest and involvement in natural resource management in the South cannot fairly be portrayed as an unhelpful and alien intrusion. For example, built in to recent environmental initiatives and treaties are forms of assistance for developing societies, notably in the form of technology transfers and financial aid, in order that they may better conserve their natural resources. Similarly, recent environmental agreements have given developing countries a degree of leeway when it comes to meeting their international environmental responsibilities, especially in relation to different timescales, and even exempted them from some agreements like the Kyoto Protocol. This approach has coalesced into a principle known as 'common but differentiated responsibilities' (CBDR) that has been incorporated into international environmental agreements and documents, notably the Rio Declaration. Underpinning this principle is the notion that both MEDCs and LEDCs have a common cause to safeguard the earth's resources, but also that they have differing capacities to do so. It also entails recognition of the varying degree to which countries have contributed to environmental decline. For its supporters, therefore, sustainable development seeks to transcend the North–South divide. However, what constitutes 'common but differentiated responsibilities' is often a source of contestation amongst governments, particularly when environmental treaties are being negotiated.

Sustainable development is not enough   The most serious charge raised against sustainable development is that it is an inadequate response to contemporary environmental threats. Concern is expressed about the lack of successful NSDSs nearly twenty years after the Rio Earth Summit (Dalal-Clayton and Bass 2002). More fundamentally, ecologists argue it is impossible to pursue economic development that is not harmful to the earth's ecosystem as such activity invariably leads to resource depletion and pollution.

Consequently, mainstream sustainable development has been described as 'a sham' because it ignores the fact that the earth's natural self-regulating systems are incompatible with the expansionary nature of industrial society (Richardson 1997: 57). We must therefore focus solely upon the pursuit of ecological sustainability and end our preoccupation with economic development.

In this regard, the leading UK scientist James Lovelock, noted for developing the Gaia hypothesis, maintains that in place of sustainable development we need a well-planned sustainable retreat from development. For Lovelock, the earth's natural ecosystems are not designed to be employed simply as farmland but are there to sustain the climate and the chemistry of the planet (Kirby 2004). We must therefore end immediately natural habitat destruction. Likewise, he maintains that we need to achieve the cessation of fossil fuel consumption as quickly as possible. Accompanying this retreat, we need to place our faith in high-level technology, including nuclear energy, which produces considerably fewer carbon dioxide emissions than fossil fuels (ibid.). Of course, as Lovelock's critics have noted, there remains the important and unresolved matter of how to deal with the radioactive waste that is produced by nuclear energy.

W. M. Adams concludes his book *Green Development* by arguing that sustainable development marks 'the beginning of the process, not the end', and should be viewed as 'a statement of intent, not a route-map' (2001: 383). The concept acknowledges that countries and peoples will continue to pursue development, and that economic growth remains integral to this process, but at the same time account must be taken of the finite and in some cases diminishing environmental resources. However, Paul Raskin and his co-authors (2002) argue for a 'great transition' that would see the emergence of a 'new sustainability paradigm', one that would rethink the concept of progress.

Conclusion: global sustainable development

Sustainable development has now to be understood within the context of globalization and environmental decline. If globalization is diminishing the autonomy of nation-states and increasing their vulnerability to global economic developments, then this will potentially make it more difficult for them to implement coherent and effective national sustainable development strategies. This point especially applies to developing countries as they are considered to be more vulnerable to these processes. This new reality therefore has to be factored into future sustainable development approaches. As Dalal-Clayton and Bass have observed, 'the impacts of globalization have been weakly addressed in strategies for sustainable development so far, and there is a particularly urgent need for a new approach to the international dimension of national strategies (2002: 23). Likewise, if we are moving into a period of accelerated environmental decline, as is being predicted by various international scientific authorities, the dominant conception of sustainable development, which combines environmental, social and economic objectives, may have to be rethought so that the first of these is prioritized. In other words, if sustainable development is to remain relevant, it must continue to be an evolving concept and reflect the changes that are taking place in the world. This includes ensuring that local, national, regional and international sustainable development strategies are designed in ways that meet these global challenges.

Summary

- Since the 1980s, the environment has come to assume a key position within the discourse of development, coalescing around the concept of sustainable development.
- The track record of international institutions in dealing with the environment is an uneven one, and considerable attention is now been devoted to the reform of GEG.
- Given the multiple conceptions and practices of sustainable development, the usefulness of the term has been questioned.
- In response to the criticism that sustainable development has attracted, the principles of common responsibility and differentiated obligations have been incorporated into the concept.

RECOMMENDED READING

- On sustainable development, see: W. M. Adams, *Green Development* (2001); Jennifer Elliott, *An Introduction to Sustainable Development* (1999); Susan Baker, *Sustainable Development* (2006); and Michael Redclift, *Sustainable Development: Exploring the Contradictions* (1987).
- For an up-to-date and informative analysis of the condition of the global environment, see the UNEP's *Global Environment Outlook 4: Environment for Development* (2007).
- For essential reports on sustainable development, see the WCED's *Our Common Future* (1987) and the World Bank's *Sustainable Development in a Dynamic World: Transforming Institutions, Growth and Quality of Life* (2003).
- For a work exploring the interrelationship between globalization and the environment, see James Gustave Speth (ed.), *Worlds Apart: Globalization and the Environment* (2003); and for the nature of GEG, see Daniel C. Esty and Maria H. Ivanova (eds), *Global Environmental Governance* (2002).

WEBSITES

- www.unep.org: Site of the United Nations Environment Programme, the leading environmental agency within the United Nations system.
- www.ipcc.ch: The website for the Intergovernmental Panel on Climate

Change from where it is possible to get access to its much discussed assessment reports.

- www.foe.org: Site of the Friends of the Earth, the leading environmental NGO.
- www.worldwatch.org: Environmental research organization carrying out independent research into climate change and its human and economic costs but also providing information on how to build sustainable societies.

CHAPTER 10

Globalization and Development

- Approaching globalization
- Globalization and the developmental state
- Globalization and development
- Globalization and the network society
- Globalizing cities and uneven development
- Globalization, cosmopolitanism and development

As has been stressed throughout this book, development in the contemporary period must be understood within the context of more intensive forms of global interconnectedness that we have come to call 'globalization'. This final chapter explores in more detail the complex interrelationship between globalization and development.[1] But given the enormity of his subject, the focus will simply be upon the key issues and debates surrounding this relationship, including: the impact of globalization upon the developmental state; the network society and development; globalizing cities and patterns of inequality and development; and whether globalization is leading to greater economic convergence or divergence between the North and the South. It will be argued that, in determining the impact of globalization upon development, much rests upon our conception of globalization and the nature of global interconnectedness. In essence, it is dependent upon whether we conceive of globalization as a process or a project. It will also be claimed that any impact globalization is having upon development is contingent upon the nature of the interaction between its different processes and particular societies, and this in turn reinforces the notion that we need to view development in the plural (see Hopper 2006, 2007). Of course, in order to be able to undertake this investigation, we need to be clear about what we mean by globalization, and it is to this matter that this chapter will now turn.

Approaching globalization

Despite the considerable debate that globalization has stimulated, and the myriad of definitions and descriptions that have been postulated by writers seeking to encapsulate and explain it, three broad approaches to this subject, or waves of analysis, have emerged.

First-wave approaches

First-wave theorists of globalization – variously termed 'globalizers', 'strong globalizers', 'globalists' and 'hyperglobalizers' – consider contemporary developments and global processes to be constituting a new phase in human history (see Greider 1997; Guéhenno 1995; Julius 1990; Ohmae 1990; Wriston 1992). They delineate the emergence of an integrated global economy, based upon open markets and the breaking down of national borders, a development that has been aided by the spread of ICTs and advances in transportation. From their perspective, production is a global process, evident in the growing volume of international trade, the greater mobility of capital, information and people, increased levels of FDI, and the heightened importance of MNCs and TNCs. In relation to development, increasing global economic interdependence is the overarching context in which developing countries must operate, and this has obvious implications for their ability to shape their own destiny, as will be discussed below.

Second-wave approaches

Among second-wave theorists, often labelled 'sceptics', there exists a range of perspectives that are highly critical of the globalizers' thesis. For example, many on the Left deny globalization constitutes a new epoch, viewing it simply as a further expansion of international capitalism, and for this reason seek to resist it (Burbach et al. 1997; Petras and Veltmeyer 2001; Sklair 2002). Other critics, like Paul Hirst and Grahame Thompson (1996, 2000), highlight the 'myths' that have become associated with globalization. Based upon their research, they maintain that the world economy is far from being genuinely 'global'. Trade, investment and financial flows are concentrated in a triad of Europe, Japan and North America and look likely to remain so; they therefore contend it is more appropriate to talk of 'triadization' rather than globalization. Hirst and Thompson acknowledge certain developments in the flows of trade, people, finance and capital investment across societies in the contemporary period, but point to historical precedents such as the period 1870–1914 when they claim the world economy was even more internationalized than it is in our own time. Hirst and Thompson therefore conclude that contemporary trends can best be described as a process of economic internationalization, rather than fully developed globalization.

Third-wave approaches

There is considerable diversity of opinion among third-wave theorists of globalization. It includes writers like Anthony Giddens (1990) and James Rosenau (1997) who have been identified as *transformationalists* (see Held et al. 1999). Writers from this tradition stress the unprecedented nature of current

economic, political and cultural flows and levels of global interconnectedness as a result of the combined forces of modernity (Held et al. 1999: 10).
Globalization is therefore not just motored by capitalism but by industrialization, the nation-state, technological and scientific developments and critical
thinking. From this position, globalization is seen as a powerful, complex
and essentially indeterminate and open-ended transformative force or process responsible for massive change within societies and world order (ibid.:
7). This particular approach therefore raises the issue of the relationship
between globalization and modernity, which is a recurring theme within
the globalization literature. Put simply, if modernity and globalization are
interrelated, then, given the European origins of modernity, should globalization be understood as primarily a western project? In short, is globalization
westernization? If this is the case, and globalization is indeed providing the
context in which developing countries must operate, then it follows that the
nature of their development is likely to be significantly shaped by the West.
And this returns us to a claim addressed in chapter 2, namely that development for some writers has always been a profoundly Eurocentric and western-
dominated project.[2]

However, as mentioned above, there is more to the third-wave analysis of
globalization than just the transformationalist approach. For example, Colin
Hay and David Marsh make the case for avoiding conceptualizing globalization as a causal process having specific effects and instead they emphasize
fluidity, multiple processes, contingency, resistance and contestation, arguing globalization is that which needs to be explained (2001: 6). It is a stance
that hints at the unevenness of globalization. Furthermore, rather than viewing globalization as an abstract or general phenomenon, within third-wave
thinking, greater importance is attached to how human agents negotiate and
contribute to globalizing processes within particular contexts (see Holton
2005; Hopper 2007). This in turn adds to the significance of our perceptions
of globalization and the dominant ideas and rhetoric surrounding it. In this
regard, Angus Cameron and Ronen Palan (2004), in their analysis of the discourse of globalization, stress the influence that conventional narratives are
able to exert upon individuals, governments and businesses. In other words,
there is an ideational dimension to globalization that can indeed lead to it
having particular effects, and in doing so it becomes a self-fulfilling prophecy.

Having outlined the major approaches to globalization, attention will now
turn to the possible impact that its processes are having upon one of the key
development institutions in the post-war period, namely, the developmental
state.

Globalization and the developmental state

The 'developmental state' refers to those states which evolved in the post-
war era of decolonization geared to the promotion of development in their

societies through planning and government intervention, rather than leaving it to some 'spontaneous' dynamic, like the market. The Global South used to be heavily populated with developmental states, but since the late 1970s it has been in decline, accompanied by much discussion about 'the crisis of the developmental state'. During this time, the governments of many LEDCs have sought to redefine the relationship between the state and the economy with the intention of expanding the role of the market and private enterprise. It has been achieved by 'rolling back' the state through privatization and deregulation. This transition has been largely down to external pressures from agencies like the IMF and World Bank who have been pushing their neo-liberal agenda (Rivero 2001). But it is also due to growing internal dissatisfaction with the economic performance of developmental states, with the charges ranging from excessive bureaucracy and stifling entrepreneurship to elite mismanagement and even corruption. Moreover, as we saw in chapter 5, there has been a rise in the number of 'fragile states' in the recent period, and this in turn has served to erode the quality of life enjoyed by their respective citizens.

The end of the developmental state?

For first-wave theorists, globalization is undermining the state within both the developing and developed worlds, mainly by restricting the autonomy of national governments to pursue independent economic and political management. In particular, the growing power of international financial markets makes it difficult for countries to pursue policies that run counter to the logic of international capital. This point even applies to mature industrialized countries like the UK, as demonstrated on so-called 'Black Wednesday' (16 September 1992), when the British government was forced to withdraw the pound from the European Exchange Rate Mechanism (ERM) in the face of hostile market speculation. In this vein, globalizing forces are considered to be responsible for the shift from Keynesianism and structuralist theories of economic development and planning in both the North and the South to monetarism, with the role of government increasingly confined to ensuring that their countries are able to participate in the world economy. Some globalizers even anticipate that globalization will lead to the demise of the nation-state (e.g., Ohmae 1990). At the very least, it will make it difficult for governments to perform their traditional role as protector of their citizens, especially in the area of social welfare provision.

Globalizers believe that globalization creates particular challenges for the developmental state. They point to the increased influence of globalizing forces such as MNCs, markets and IGOs upon development. In the case of MNCs, which now constitute roughly half of the world's one hundred largest economies, governments of developing countries struggle to resist their demands as they rely upon the investment and jobs that they provide. Similarly, the globalization of capitalist markets is considered to encourage common ways of organizing economic and social life – a tendency with obvious implications for the ability of countries to steer their own path to development (Berger and Dore 1996). In addition, the World Bank and the IMF have imposed particular development strategies like SAPs upon countries, while the WTO has established global trade regimes that are intended to be binding upon countries. Governments have responded to these globalizing forces and pressures by setting up regional organizations like MERCOSUR (Southern Cone Common Market) in Latin America and the Southern African Development Community (SADC). In short, they have been pooling their sovereignty to ensure that they remain significant players on the global stage. It means that development is increasingly shaped by global and regional frameworks, rather than national contexts.

Sceptical perspectives

For second-wave theorists, if globalization does not exist, then it follows that states are likely to be in a healthier condition than can be found in the accounts of globalizers. Moreover, many sceptics maintain that the state and sovereignty remain powerful forces within world politics (e.g., Hirst and Thompson 1996, 2000). In this regard, the nature of international law and legislative processes ensure that international institutions find it difficult to encroach upon the sovereignty of countries. Indeed, for many writers, the world is still shaped by an international nation-state system – a system of inter nation-state exchanges – rather than globalization (Featherstone 1990: 6). As for the turning away from Keynesianism and other managed or government-led approaches to economic development and planning, arguably this is as much to do with ideology and the passing popularity, at least within governance circles, of neo-liberalism as it is with globalization. It is also the case, sceptics argue, that globalization can be politically expedient for governments. Often, political leaders will cite globalization as the cause of their respective country's lack of economic growth and development as a means of deflecting attention away from their own performance.

Second-wave theorists also question the extent to which the development of LEDCs and MEDCs is informed by globalization. Sceptics maintain that, in general, governments retain sufficient autonomy to pursue substantive national economic and political management (Box 10.1). This is reflected in the steady growth in their powers and functions since 1945, especially in the areas of social welfare provision and education (see Dunn 1995; Holton 1998; Mann 1997). While some governments are now seeking to introduce an element of privatization into their welfare states, notably in relation to health and pensions, levels of public spending have not in general declined. Moreover, MNCs have to abide by national regulatory frameworks, and it is nation-states that set up institutions like the UN and the WTO, for which nation-statehood is a criterion for membership. In this vein, while global markets are powerful, the terms upon which they operate are ultimately established by governments.

> **Box 10.1 The return of the developmental state?**
>
> Beyond debates about the impact of globalization, since the early 1990s the develop-
> mental state has attracted renewed interest for the following reasons:
>
> - the growing disillusionment with neo-liberalism and resentment of the hardships caused by
>   structural adjustment;
> - increased recognition that markets require effective states if they are to function properly
>   (e.g., World Bank 1997);
> - the view that developmental states, not open markets, were primarily responsible for the
>   East Asian economic 'miracle' has gained increasing support (chapter 1);
> - criticism of some participatory approaches to development and the role performed by NGOs
>   (chapter 7);
> - the developmental state allows LEDCs to retain some autonomy and control, and to avoid
>   simply leaving their fate to the workings of the global market (Gilpin 2001);
> - with the rise in the number of fragile states, an effective and stable developmental state
>   is now seen as a mechanism for enhancing human security (see Fritz and Rocha Menocal
>   2007).
>
> However, David Batley (2002) does not believe these factors will necessarily result in
> the state becoming the lead agent in development again. Rather, it reflects a growing
> concern within development about creating the right institutional conditions within
> which markets and citizens can flourish (ibid.: 138).

Third-wave perspectives

Given the diversity of third-wave approaches to globalization, unsurprisingly, there are a range of perspectives concerning the impact it is having upon the developmental state. A useful starting point from this perspective would be to examine the nature of the interaction between globalizing processes and particular countries. Such studies would, for example, be able to determine the extent to which the discourse surrounding globalization is informing development strategies within particular societies and also provide more nuanced accounts of the effects of globalization that acknowledge its unevenness and complexity. In this regard, this type of analysis is likely to reveal that richer industrialized countries are better able to stand up to the forces of globalization than developing countries (Gritsch 2005; Rudra 2002). In this vein, national sovereignty is neither absolute nor passing; rather, it is more accurate to think of it as a condition that is increasingly 'negotiated' on the international stage between, on the one hand, national governments with varying degrees of power and influence and, on the other, a range of non-state actors – a negotiation that occurs within different contexts. In short, from this perspective, we need to take a contextualizing approach to globalization if we are to understand its influence upon development and the developmental state.

Globalization and development

While the extent of globalization is contested, there is nevertheless widespread agreement that significant changes are afoot within the international economy. Most notable among these changes is that the number of countries and people participating in the global marketplace has risen dramatically in recent decades. Globalizing processes, like the IT revolution and advances in transportation, have changed the nature of trade, finance and industry and contributed greatly to this expansion. However, the growth and spread of the international economy is also due to developments that have little direct relationship to globalization, such as the decision of the Chinese authorities to pursue an 'open door' trading policy with the rest of the world. Likewise, the end of the Cold War, the collapse of communism in Eastern Europe, the discrediting of state-planning and the East Asian economic 'miracle' have all contributed to the growth of the world economy.

For some commentators, the ever-expanding world economy has been accompanied by a growing acceptance on the part of the international community of a market-based or neo-liberal approach to capitalism and development. This approach is not simply founded upon economies being open to trade and investment, it also favours an efficient (i.e., limited) state that allows a greater role for the private sector and insists upon government confining itself to pursuing sound economic policy by keeping inflation and budget and trade deficits within reasonable limits. Advocates of this model maintain that it has led to the growth of world trade and this in turn has contributed to a rise in average incomes and material living standards, including within the developing world (Bhagwati 2004; Wolf 2004). They argue that countries which have actively participated in this trade, like Japan, South Korea and China, have enjoyed considerable economic growth, with the wealth generated 'trickling down' to poorer groups within their respective societies and hence contributing to the general prosperity of all. Moreover, it means the economic disparities between countries and regions are diminishing, and there is now greater uniformity among them as they adjust to and are shaped by the dictates of global capitalism. It is noted, for example, that the economies of Latin America and East Asia increasingly resemble the economies of industrial countries of the North.

The view of globalizers

Many globalizers maintain that a defining feature of greater global economic interdependence has been the tendency for production to shift to the developing world. This movement is a consequence of higher wage levels in MEDCs, and hence higher production costs, and the fact that ICTs make it relatively easy for MNCs to relocate much of their production to developing societies where labour costs are cheaper. At the same time, they are able to maintain their communication links with offices, branches and outlets in the industrialized North. MNCs have therefore become truly global enterprises and production has been globalized in the process. Globalists argue that this is not only reflected in the massive migration of capital from major OECD countries to low-cost production sites in the developing world, but also in the emergence of a new international division of labour involving the transfer of manufacturing industry from the North to the NICs of East Asia and Latin America. This transformation presents obvious challenges for existing industries in the developed world and helps to explain the shift to the 'service economy' in the North, a process that has entailed more and more people leaving manufacturing and going to work in service industries.

However, the North also faces a growing challenge from the South in the service sector, notably in areas like banking, software development and accounting, as a result of the increasing tendency for global companies to outsource work. Many are choosing to go to India which is leading the way in business process outsourcing (invoicing or billing, payroll, IT support, etc.), reflected in the setting up of a plethora of call/contact centres within the country (Schifferes 2007a). In particular, Bangalore, the capital of the South Indian state of Karnataka, has become known as the Silicon Valley of India because it is at the heart of the country's IT boom. As well as being the world's leading exporter of IT services – it is expected to earn US$60 billion from these services in 2010 – India now has its own major outsourcing companies (Schifferes 2007b). Moreover, both India and China are now investing heavily overseas, particularly in the West where companies are being bought up. The cumulative effect of these developments has been the transformation of the Indian economy, which by 2008 was growing at more than 9 per cent per annum, and it is hoped that this economic growth can provide the basis for tackling poverty within the country. Similarly, China has a growing relationship with sub-Saharan Africa that in terms of trade and investment is challenging traditional western hegemony in Africa (Kaplinsky, McCormick and Morris 2010).

Cumulatively, these developments are leading workers in the North to become increasingly concerned about their own wage levels and job security. But these changes are also informing everyday life within the South, with more and more rural migrants moving into urban areas to take advantage of these new employment opportunities. Anthony Brewer speculated in the early 1990s that 'perhaps it is the centre, not the periphery, which now has most to lose from participation in the capitalist world system' (1990: 284). For other writers, the globalization of production is blurring core/periphery relations and it follows the North–South division (Held et al. 1999; Kiely 1998). In short, globalization has contributed to the demise of the 'Third World'.

Globalization and development: critical responses

However, for critics of globalization, such views ignore the actual condition and state of underdevelopment of many LEDCs, particularly in Africa where some states are displaying signs of economic decline. As we saw in the Introduction, many writers maintain that economic inequalities both within and between states have increased under contemporary globalization (e.g.,

Nayyar 2003; Stiglitz 2003; also see UNDP 1999). In this regard, writers on the Left are especially critical of trickle-down theory, and detect little evidence that the wealth being generated by increasing world trade is filtering down to the poor within developing countries. Rapid economic development in India, for example, has seen a burgeoning middle class – anticipated to reach 300 million by 2010 – but poverty levels remain high, with an estimated 300 million Indians living on less than US$1 a day in 2007. They maintain that we should not be surprised by all of this as what we are dealing with is capitalist globalization, which is primarily about the pursuit of profit maximization. Leslie Sklair contends that 'capitalism produces a distorted form of development globally, where it produces any development at all' (1994: 165).

Many within the anti-globalization movement condemn what they regard as the lack of international regulation and control of globalization. This is leading, they argue, to developing countries being exposed to the often unfair and unethical practices of MNCs, with their workers having to endure poor labour standards and working conditions, a state of affairs not helped by the fact that the ILO lacks substantive enforcement powers (Amoore 2005). Indeed, the greater mobility of capital has not been matched by the greater mobility of labour. Moreover, the lack of effective governance of world capital and financial markets means that LEDCs are vulnerable to any downturns in commodity prices for their products, as well as to economic recessions in our more globally connected world. Of course, from the perspective of advocates of globalization, greater regulation of the world economy will serve to reduce world trade, and this in turn will reduce average incomes in the developing world.

Sceptics also reject the notion that we are witnessing a new international division of labour, facilitated by globalizing technologies and processes. They note that many poorer countries in the developing world simply lack the productive capacity and infrastructure to diversify and shift to manufacturing and service sectors and hence continue to be reliant upon the export of primary products. Nor can they rely upon MNCs moving into their countries and regions and providing this productive capacity and infrastructure. This is because, according to Hirst and Thompson (1996), genuinely global or transnational companies are relatively rare. Based upon their research, they argue that most companies are nationally based, if for no other reason than it is costly to relocate. From their perspective, this in turn raises doubts about the extent to which production has been globalized. Moreover, many commentators detect the persistence of national forms of capitalism, ranging from the state-centred conceptions of capitalism practised by some 'Asian tiger' economies to the social democratic mixed economies that can be found in Europe (see Boyer and Drache 1996). If they are correct, then it challenges the notion of a universal market-based or neo-liberal global capitalism. And these points form part of the questioning of the existence of a global economy articulated by many sceptics (e.g., Garrett 1998; Jones 1995; Watson 2001).

Globalization, complexity and development

In reality, the relationship between globalization and development is likely to be more complex and uneven than both globalizers and their critics allow. For instance, their respective positions on the issue of whether globalization is leading to greater convergence or divergence between the North and the South neglect the extent of the economic disparities that exist within these blocs, both between countries as well as within them. Moreover, determining whether this diversity is due to globalization or other factors will require a contextualizing approach that examines what is taking place within particular countries and societies and the nature of the engagement with globalizing processes. To add to the complexity, what is arguably underpinning many of the disputes surrounding globalization is a basic disagreement over whether it is a process or a specific (neo-liberal capitalist) project (Nederveen Pieterse 2001: 152). Of course, in reality, it is almost certainly a combination of both. While neo-liberalism has undoubtedly facilitated the global spread of trade and finance, many writers on globalization maintain that it both pre-dates neo-liberalism and includes important non-economic dimensions. And it is to some of these other dimensions that this chapter will now turn.

Globalization and the network society

As well as contributing to globalization, ICTs are widely considered to have significant implications for development and developing nations, in particular (e.g., see Pejout 2010). From the globalist perspective, new ICTs are leading to more intensified forms of global interconnectedness. As is well known, global communication has been aided by a number of technological advances in the contemporary period, notably the internet, e-mail, fax, mobile phones and text messaging have all made it much easier to communicate with different parts of the world. The internet is providing unprecedented access to information and has resulted in a rise in the international exchange of data. In addition, there has been considerable progress in relation to telecommunications infrastructure, with the effective globalization of fibre-optic cables and satellite and digital technologies facilitating social and cultural interaction across borders, regions and continents. Furthermore, digital technology constitutes a major leap forward for global communication since digitization is able to translate information into a universal binary code, making it possible to covert information between different communication media and then transmit it via digital networks. Similarly, broadband technology enables greater data traffic capacity and is being introduced at such a rate that it is considered to be one of the fastest ever expanding technologies: worldwide, the number of broadband connections took off during 2004, reaching around 100 million towards the end of that year (BBC 2004c). In 2010, half a billion households worldwide had access to the internet (ITU 2010).

All of the above has meant an increase in worldwide data flows and voice traffic. In this regard, a major contributor to the increase in voice traffic has been mobile phones, which have enjoyed a dramatic growth in both owner-ship and usage since the 1990s. In June 2006, the two billionth GSM (Global System for Mobile Communications) phone was connected. Interestingly, the recent dramatic expansion increase in GSM connections now means that mobile phones are the first communication technology to have more users in the developing world than the developed world. In 2010, according to the ITU, while the mobile cellular market was reaching saturation levels in MEDCs, the developing world increased its share of mobile subscriptions from 53 per cent of total mobile subscriptions in 2005 to 73 per cent in 2010 (ITU 2010). This development has at least in part been brought about because mobile phone companies are designing affordable products for these newly emerging and potentially huge markets. Mobile phone technology also offers additional benefits for poorer nations. For instance, the Worldwatch Institute has argued that mobile phones will help to narrow the information gap that exists between developed and developing societies. In particular, 3G or third-generation mobile telecommunications provides internet access, enabling the less well-off to make wireless connections to the Web without having to purchase PCs (BBC 2003b). There were an estimated 940 million subscriptions worldwide to 3G services in 2010 (ITU 2010).

However, sceptics like Hirst and Thompson (1996) question the impact of these technologies and regard the development of the telegraph (introduced in 1837) and underground cable to be a pivotal moment in the history of international communication. For Tom Standage, this was the 'Victorian Internet', which ensured that '[a]ttitudes to everything from newsgathering to diplomacy had to be completely rethought' (1998: 1). Writers who are sceptical about some of the more extreme claims made by globalizers do not deny that recent developments in information and communication tech-nologies are shaping the ways in which we communicate with each other but stress this is an evolutionary process, rather than a revolution. In this regard, with the exception of the rapidly industrializing countries in East Asia that are indeed integrating into global communication and informa-tion networks at a remarkable pace, world telephone distribution patterns have remained relatively unchanged for a hundred years (Tehranian and Tehranian 1997).

Similarly, sceptics argue that we need to acknowledge the ways in which national societies can shape global and transnational phenomena, both with regards to technology but also in relation to other areas of social and eco-nomic life, like markets. For example, in *The Global Internet Economy* (2004), a series of studies devoted to studying the evolution of the internet especially in relation to business, the common theme that emerges is the different ways in which it is evolving in particular societies, reflecting the specific conditions within those countries, such as national systems of law and regulation. It leads the editor to conclude that, despite the title of the book, 'the global Internet economy has not yet arrived!' (Kogut 2004: 437). Such findings also serve to balance claims that national governments are unable to control or influence the Internet and that the primary consequence of advances in global ICTs is the enhancement of the power of MNCs and TNCs to the detriment of national sovereignty (Schiller 1995).

The global digital divide

'The global digital divide' refers to inequalities of access to and usage of ICTs on an international scale. Thus, while at the turn of the millennium the information and communication revolution had firmly taken hold in the North, many people in the South remained largely untouched by it. Indeed, as the former South African President Thabo Mbeki observed towards the end of the last millennium: '[o]ver half of humankind has never dialled a phone number' (Lynch 1997: 253). For sceptics, the persistence of such a divide chal-lenges the concept of global communication. It also undermines the ability of global technologies to act as a catalyst for development. In this regard, Africa is less endowed with both ICTs and supporting infrastructure compared to industrialized regions in the North, entailing that many African states and peoples are not as integrated into global information and communication networks as their northern counterparts. However, there have been attempts to address this matter, notably the construction of an undersea fibre-optic cable around the whole continent that is intended to transform high-speed communications within Africa and to integrate it into the international telecommunications network.

Determining the nature of the global digital divide, if indeed it actually exists, is made more difficult by the fast pace of change in the ICT sector. For example, according to the ITU, the total number of texts or Short Message Service (SMS) sent globally tripled between 2007 and 2010, from an estimated 1.8 trillion to 6.1 trillion (ITU 2010). Moreover, access to mobile networks has grown to the extent that at the end of 2010 it was available to 90 per cent of the world's population (ibid.). This has a number of potentially significant implications for development. For example, mobile phones have seen some interesting innovations in the recent period, such as in mobile banking and saving (e.g., M-PESA – a branchless banking service) and similar schemes in Tanzania, Kenya and Afghanistan.

In relation to the internet, worldwide the number of internet users doubled between 2005 and 2010. Indeed, in 2010, the number of internet users sur-passed the two billion mark, of which 1.2 billion were in developing countries (ITU 2010). Of course, population levels are higher in the South than in the North. Indeed, 71 per cent of the population in MEDCs are online, but only 21 per cent of the population in LEDCs are online (ibid.). In particular, there are still too few people on the internet in Africa. Internet usage is also uneven in

Africa, with the majority of users based in South Africa. By the end of 2010, internet user penetration in Africa had reached 9.6 per cent, which was some way behind the developing country average of 21 per cent – the global average was 30 per cent (ibid.). More broadly, 15.8 per cent of LEDCs had internet access in 2010, compared to 65.6 per cent in MEDCs (ibid.).

The Global South now has a significant share of fixed (wired) broadband subscriptions: in 2010 it accounted for an estimated 45 per cent of global subscriptions. But again Africa still lags behind in this area, accounting for less than 1 per cent of this figure. Moreover, fixed broadband subscriptions in developing countries remain low at 4.4 subscriptions per 100 people compared to 24.6 in developed countries (ibid.).

Overall, while improvements in access to ICTs need to continue, especially with regard to the continuing broadband divide and Internet access in Africa, there are some signs of the diminution of the global digital divide. However, according to the UN body, the International Telecommunication Union (ITU), worldwide statistics on ICTs may not be entirely reliable. This is largely due to the inadequate data-gathering mechanisms and procedures of some developing nations. Indeed, when presented with ITU research, some LEDC governments have occasionally been surprised by the number of people that were online within their own countries (BBC 2003b). In turn, it may mean that the global digital divide may not be as wide as is often claimed.

Irrespective of concerns about the reliability of data, improved access to the new technologies is widely seen as vital for developing societies. It is hoped that some of them will be able to skip or at least speed up stages of their development, especially as information (knowledge) and communication (networking) are key sources of wealth generation in the contemporary period (see Castells 1996). Indeed, some Latin American governments consider a post-industrial mode of development, one based upon information technology, the service sector and a knowledge-based economy, to be a way of breaking free from their role as a producer of commodities.

For the preceding reasons, the ownership of intellectual property rights in relation to information technology and knowledge, notably the WTO-administered Agreement on Trade-Related Aspects of Intellectual Property Rights (TRIPS), which seeks to establish intellectual property standards for the global knowledge economy, has become a much contested issue. Peter Drahos and John Braithwaite (2002) believe that current rules concerning intellectual property are the product of coercion by developed countries (specifically the US and to a lesser extent the EU) and powerful corporations who directly benefit from a state of affairs that they describe as 'information feudalism'. Copyrights, patents and trademarks have protected layout designs, as well as restricted access to computer software programmes and the algorithms that underpin digital technologies, resulting in many developing societies struggling to pay fees and royalties on these informational resources. In short, such intellectual property regimes have the potential to generate new forms of inequality and hinder development in the South by reducing their access to new sources of information and knowledge.

An additional problem confronting many states in the developing world is that the World Wide Web is an English-language dominated phenomenon. In December 2003, at the opening of the first UN summit on the digital divide, the former Secretary-General, Kofi Annan, argued that, with 70 per cent of websites in English 'local voices' were being crowded out. There are also regular complaints from developing countries that much of the content of the Web is American as a result of the dominance of US web servers and search engines, and that the USA has unilateral control of the internet's domain name and addressing systems in the form of a corporation known as ICANN (Internet Corporation for Assigned Names and Numbers). However, there are starting to be changes in relation to some of these areas, most notably the fact that other languages are emerging on the internet. For example, the Chinese Web has significantly expanded as a result of the dramatic growth in internet usage in China. According to the government-run China Internet Network Information Centre, the country's online population is doubling every six months, and by the end of 2004 it had more than 20 million broadband subscribers (Twist 2004). Indeed, in 2010, China was the largest internet market in the world, with more than 420 million internet users (ITU, 2010).

We should also not overlook the considerable efforts being undertaken to narrow the global digital divide. For example, the One Laptop Per Child campaign has led to the development of the sub-US$100 clockwork laptop computer. Similarly, a handheld battery-operated alternative to PCs, the Simputer (short for 'simple computer') has been designed in India. In this vein, the open-source movement provides services and information as public rather than private goods (and hence without charge), such as the Linux operating system and OpenOffice (which provide free alternatives to systems offered by Microsoft), its own browser Firefox, as well as the online encyclopaedia, Wikipedia. Of particular importance is the fact that the World Bank and the UN are seeking to tackle the digital divide and spread ICTs to developing countries – with the UN attempting to connect every village in the world to the internet by 2015 – although progress is slow, especially with regards to who will pay for the construction of the information and communication infrastructures.

Globalizing cities and uneven development

As a result of global urbanization, for the first time in history more than half of the world's population are now living in cities. Moreover, this figure is expected to increase from 3.3 billion people in 2008 to over 5 billion by 2030, with most of the growth taking place in developing countries. Within development studies, cities and urbanization have long been important areas of concern but are now increasingly discussed in relation to globalization, with many commentators classifying the major cities of the contemporary world, notably London, New York, Paris and Tokyo, as global cities. However, the terminology of this subject area is contested. Writers such as King (1990) and Sassen (2001) employ the term 'global city', but other writers variously discuss 'world cities' (Knox 2002), 'global city-regions' (Scott 2001), megacities and even 'transnational urbanism' (Smith 2001). Here, the notion of globalizing cities will be employed to indicate that cities other than the four mentioned are becoming important global sites with extensive worldwide connections. In this regard, globalizing cities should not just be associated with the North. Indeed, in the case of the USA, the size of the domestic market means that American cities can remain nationally oriented in their connections. Arguably, only New York and Miami can be considered as globalizing cities and are so due to their particular locations and histories (Taylor 2003).

Globalizing cities also expresses the unevenness of globalization and reminds us that it is a process or set of processes (Marcuse and van Kempen 2000). In fact, globalizing cities are engaged in a mutually dependent relationship with globalization. Their development has been aided by globalizing forces, including electronic communication technologies, migration and an emerging global economy, but at the same time they are driving globalization by operating as its financial centres. However, in relation to development, the impact of globalizing cities has been both uneven and complex, as will now be shown.

Global urban networks

A characteristic feature of globalizing cities is their increasing global reach and the density of their worldwide connections, which is reflected in the formation of a plethora of global networks (see Taylor 2003). In fact, globalizing cities, aided by ICTs, are considered to be the nodal points of cross-border networks (Castells 1996; Sassen 2002). However, this development is contributing to social polarization in some cities, as global networkers often reside and work within gated communities sealed off from other city dwellers. Protected by extensive surveillance, an increasing feature of urban design, these communities are contributing to the privatization of public spaces within urban areas – a process that has been described as 'splintering urbanism' (Graham and Marvin 2001). Initially part of the urban landscape in some Latin American countries, South Africa and parts of the USA, gated communities have come to be a feature of many European cities and in some cities in East Asia (Atkinson and Blandy 2007; Glasze, Webster and Frantz 2005). Of course, ICTs are also facilitating the growth of creative industries within many inner cities, particularly in the areas of media, design and internet services, many of which are globally oriented (Hutton 2008). But this too is generating its own forms of social separation, with media enclaves or cyberdistricts emerging in some European and North American cities. Manuel Castells (1993) believes 'the informational city', as he terms it, results in the primary urban dualism of our time, namely the division between a connected cosmopolitan elite and unconnected locals; the former is shaping city life, while the latter is largely excluded from such developments.

Globalizing cities and the world economy

Saskia Sassen (2000, 2001) contends global cities have become transnational centres of financial and service activity. In a world of decentralized economic activity and hypermobile capital, they are the places where economic and financial power is located. Their growth has been aided by deregulation and privatization, as well as the creation of worldwide neo-liberal regimes in trade, information and financial services. Other writers share her view that these urban developments are the product of the evolution of capitalism (e.g., Clark 2003). However, while many of these globalizing cities are generating enormous wealth, it is not evenly shared. Those people working in international finance and the high-status service sector (lawyers, computer programmers, etc.) have enjoyed a considerable rise in their income and unprecedented levels of conspicuous consumption, whereas those in the low-status sector (cleaners, janitors, security guards, etc.) have not. As a result, economic inequalities are growing, along with levels of social deprivation, so that low-income city areas are becoming even more marginalized. Indeed, in many respects the position of lower income groups has deteriorated through the casualization of labour markets that has accompanied the shift to post-industrialism within many globalizing cities. Levels of socio-economic inequality are also increased by another feature of globalization, namely increased global migration, with globalizing cities invariably the destination of the world's economic migrants. Continuing the theme of inequality, many writers on this area have commented that urban elites in the South have more in common with their counterparts in the North in terms of lifestyles and consumption patterns than they do with their fellow city-dwellers. This is confirmed by the UN–Habitat's *State of the World's Cities Report 2006/7* (2007) which has highlighted how the urban poor in developing countries are now in many respects worse off than their rural counterparts, with slums in cities becoming effectively human dumping grounds (see also M. Davis 2006).

Globalizing cities, influence and inequality

The cumulative effect of the trends mentioned above has been to enhance the power and influence of globalizing cities, and in some instances this has arguably led to a degree of detachment from the countries in which they are located (Taylor 2003). It has certainly led them to outstrip other cities within their respective countries; Marseilles is declining because of the growing economic power and status of Paris, for example (Sassen 2001). Indeed, John Rennie Short (2004) maintains that the discourse of globalizing is providing much of the momentum behind these cities and shaping their socio-spatial development in the process. Thus, they are projecting their global credentials by competing for the right to host mega-events like the Olympics, putting on urban events like international festivals, positioning themselves as centres of cultural cosmopolitanism, signing up internationally renowned architects and attracting the super-rich. Moreover, recent research is indicating that even those cities that are not yet established global cities, like Bangkok, Manila, Sydney and Johannesburg, are globalizing in important ways through a combination of global market forces and transnational and local agents (Mark Amen et al. 2006).

There is, therefore, a view that globalizing cities are more in tune in with the flows and mobilities of globalization than nation-states. Consequently, globalizing cities are considered to offer their inhabitants an alternative to the nation-state, both in terms of sources of authority and identity. More broadly, they are seen as an important element of the trend towards multi-level governance, which is itself a reflection of the erosion of national sovereignty. However, Brenner (1998) take a contrary view, suggesting that states are promoting their cities in order to attract capital investment. But whether or not it is due to deliberate policy, globalizing cities, such as Johannesburg, Mumbai, São Paulo and Shanghai, are certainly serving as gateways to the global economy for their respective countries (Segbers 2007). As for the civic leaders and administrators within these cities, they are engaged in an ongoing struggle to attract foreign investment and consequently are devising strategies to demonstrate that their particular city is world class (ibid.).

Some writers articulate the notion of a global hierarchy of world cities (e.g., Friedmann 1994), and the processes of globalization may well be reinforcing this hierarchy. This is because there is a wide divergence between cities with regard to the extensity and intensity of their global connections and their engagement in global networks, and this in turn is contributing to their disparities in economic wealth. Sassen (2001), in particular, has emphasized how global economic power is increasingly concentrated in London, New York and Tokyo to the extent that they have become the command centres of the global economy. In short, São Paulo, Mexico City and Lagos may compete with London, New York and Tokyo to be global cities, but there remain considerable differences between them.

Globalizing cities and sustainable development

Finally, the environmental impact of globalizing cities is also attracting concern, especially with regard to their impact upon global warming, with attention being directed towards achieving sustainable development in these urban areas (see Beatley and Wheeler 2004). However, Luciana Melchert (2005) argues that, in their attempt to become global cities, Third World metropolitan cities like Beijing and São Paulo are relegating issues of sustainability in order to attract MNCs and banks. These cities are undergoing a massive spatial and environmental transformation because of the verticalization and densification of land use which is creating its own local environmental stresses, including diminishing green sites and increasing levels of atmospheric pollution. She argues that their approach is motivated by the sense that they are in competition with one another, when they should be recognizing their interdependency and incorporating environmental innovations that are available through global networks and cooperation. But irrespective of environmental considerations, the rapid growth of globalizing cities, as well as the complex nature of their interconnectedness with global economic processes, is placing a strain upon conventional urban planning methods. For some cities, this is also raising considerable resource issues.

Globalization, cosmopolitanism and development

This final section will consider an additional way in which globalization is arguably informing development, namely that it is changing our relationship with 'distant others'. Underpinning this idea is the conceptualization of globalization as marking a new stage or epoch in the organization of time and space. David Harvey (1989), for example, views this change to be a form of 'time–space compression', whereby space is eroded or shrunk due to modern developments (such as jet air travel), new information and communication technologies, and changing economic and social processes. Similarly, Anthony Giddens (1990) articulates the notion of 'time–space distanciation' to describe the 'disembedding' of relationships and personal contacts from particular localities or contexts, entailing that social relations are 'stretched' across distances and extending our phenomenal worlds from the local to the global. With regard to development, this entails that we are now more aware of the plight of others in different parts of the world. At the same time, advances like the global media, ICTs and jet transportation ensure that the world seems a much smaller place, and we are sharing it with the rest of humankind. In short, because these 'others' no longer seem so geographically distant, and we can no longer plead ignorance of their plight, there is arguably greater onus upon us to alleviate their condition. This is perhaps one reason why ethical and moral debates are receiving increased attention within development studies and geography (see Potter 2001; Smith 2000; Lee and Smith 2004).

However, this thesis can be overstated. This is because poverty and underdevelopment can invariably be found within our own societies, even when we live in advanced industrial countries, and yet many of us will show little inclination to do anything directly and substantively to tackle this problem. To want to aid 'distant others', we must therefore have a predisposition to do so. Interestingly, there may be some evidence that the processes of globalization are contributing to this end. There is a burgeoning literature exploring the potential of aspects and manifestations of globalization to engender cosmopolitan attitudes (e.g., Beck 2000, 2002; Hopper 2006, 2007).[3] And if it is the case that more and more of us are increasingly able to think beyond our local and particular concerns, then this has potentially positive implications for development.

But before we can consider such implications, it is necessary to establish the possible linkages between globalization and cosmopolitanism. One such linkage lies with the greater flows of people, culture, music and other media that are rapidly traversing the globe, ensuring that our societies are increasingly penetrated by cultures from around the world, leading to increased cultural hybridization and the formation of multiple allegiances and identities and arguably the diminution of national cultures (see Nederveen Pieterse 2004), while ICTs enable the formation of global networks and the chance to communicate regularly with people of other countries. Jet air transportation makes it easier for us to travel to different parts of the world, and a burgeoning global tourist industry has encouraged us to do so (Telfer and Sharpley 2007).[4] While media images ensure that we have greater access to and information about the trouble spots of the world without even having to leave the comfort of our own homes. All of this provides us with the opportunities to think and act beyond our local and national boundaries and to empathize with the plight of those in other societies.

Evidence that more and more of us are becoming concerned with development issues can be seen in the popularity of the Live Aid concerts and the Make Poverty History campaign, as well as the growth of the global environmental movement. Everyday cosmopolitanism is apparent in the boycotting of some fast food chains and coffee houses for alleged or proven unethical practices, as well as the growth of fair trade sales and recycling in many societies. Likewise, a growing number of pressure groups and NGOs are scrutinizing the external ethical dealings of national governments, especially in relation to foreign policy, arms contracts, the environment and trade with the developing world. For some writers, the huge growth in the number of NGOs is evidence of an evolving global civil society (e.g., Kaldor 2003). All of this may also indicate an emerging global consciousness, something that Roland Robertson considers to be integral to globalization, and he coins the term 'globality' to describe 'the circumstance of extensive awareness of the world as a whole, including the species aspect of the latter' (1992: 78). Such an attitude is likely to be necessary to tackle the issues associated with globalization, like environmental decline, global health scares, population growth, people trafficking, and international crime and terrorism. Global risks require cosmopolitan thinking and solutions, especially as national governments will often pursue national agendas. For Ulrich Beck (1999), our 'world risk society' must by necessity be a cosmopolitan place.

In sum, certain globalizing processes may be encouraging some people to think and act in a more cosmopolitan manner. And if this is the case then it may help to halt and even reverse the growing fatigue with the aid industry and development more generally that has been detected by some commentators.

However, the association between globalization and cosmopolitanism is far from universally accepted. Critics argue that it is not necessarily the case that people will become more cosmopolitan simply because they are encountering other cultures and societies more regularly. James Hunter and Joshua Yates (2002) identify what they term 'parochial cosmopolitans': people, especially business people, who travel widely but essentially remain within the 'protective bubble' of their own culture, which prevents them from properly experiencing indigenous cultures. Moreover, being on the move, as Ulf Hannerz has noted, 'is not enough to turn one into a cosmopolitan' (1990: 241). In this vein, much of the tourist industry is geared to ensuring clients enjoy relaxing and safe holidays, which entails confining them to artificial enclaves and in so doing limits meaningful encounters with 'the locals'. More fundamentally, the cosmopolitan opportunities that globalizing processes facilitate can actually serve to reinvigorate national identities, especially when, as is often the case with migration and media flows, they are perceived as threats to national traditions and ways of life. Finally, recent international conflicts would suggest both the persistence of 'traditional' non-cosmopolitan attitudes and that the media and communication revolution has not diminished our capacity to essentialize other peoples and cultures.

Conclusion

As this chapter has revealed, the relationship between globalization and development is complex, largely because both are contested and multidimensional phenomena. Globalization, for instance, consists of economic, political, cultural, social and environmental dimensions, to mention but a few. But our understanding of the nature of this relationship will be enhanced if we move beyond general accounts of globalization and employ a contextualizing approach. In doing so, it will reveal the diverse and uneven ways that globalizing processes are impacting upon development in regions and societies throughout the world.

Summary

- Development in the contemporary period must be understood within the context of more intensive forms of global interconnectedness that we have come to call 'globalization'.
- However, globalization is a complex, contested, multidimensional and uneven phenomenon, which makes it difficult to determine its impact upon the different aspects of development.
- The concept of the network society is undermined by the persistence of a global digital divide, although the latter is displaying signs of diminishing.
- The processes of globalization are contributing to disparities in development and inequality, both within globalizing cities and between them.

RECOMMENDED READING

- Globalization has generated a vast literature, but key works are by: Anthony Giddens, *The Consequences of Modernity* (1990); David Held et al., *Global Transformations* (1999); Paul Hirst and Grahame Thompson, *Globalization in Question* (1996); Roland Robertson, *Globalization: Social Theory and Global Culture* (1992); and Jan Aart Scholte, *Globalization: A Critical Introduction* (2005).
- The journal *Globalizations* regularly deals with different aspects of development in relation to globalization.
- For writers who believe that the different aspects of globalization make a positive contribution to development, see Jagdish Bhagwati, *In Defence of Globalisation* (2004), and Martin Wolf, *Why Globalisation Works* (2004).
- Notable critics of globalization, at least in its current guise, are Leslie Sklair, *Globalization: Capitalism and its Alternatives* (2002), and Joseph Stiglitz, *Globalisation and its Discontents* (2002).
- On cities and globalization, see Neil Brenner and Roger Keil (eds), *The Global Cities Reader* (2005), and Peter J. Taylor, *World City Network* (2003).

WEBSITES

- www.warwick.ac.uk/csgr: Website for the Centre for the Study of Globalization and Regionalization at the University of Warwick, UK.
- www.lboro.ac.uk/gawc: Website for the University of Loughborough's Globalization and World City Research Group.
- www.globalcitiesdialogue.org: The Global Cities Dialogue is a worldwide network of cities which are interested in creating an information society free of digital divide and based on sustainable development.

Conclusion: Development – Future Trajectories

- What has development actually achieved?
- In defence of development
- Development: future trajectories

As well as synthesizing the key themes and arguments of this work, the intention is now to take stock in relation to development, considering its contemporary condition and future trajectories, as well as returning to the post-development contention that it has reached the end of the road. It will be argued that, while many post-development interventions are insightful, there nevertheless persists within the development project a legitimate normative concern to reduce poverty and inequality and enhance human freedoms. Furthermore, this project should not only be persisted with but also adapted to our globalizing era and looming environmental problems.

What has development actually achieved?

The halting progress towards achieving the UN Millennium Development Goals, and indeed the perceived necessity of creating such goals, has formed part of a wider questioning of the record of development. Despite the emergence of an extensive development industry (IFIs, NGOs, academic scholarship, etc.) in the post-war period and the vast amount of money devoted to development projects, the lack of notable improvement on the part of many developing countries has raised questions about the role and effectiveness of this industry. Moreover, as we saw in the Introduction, decades of development have not been able to diminish global inequality and may have exacerbated aspects of it.

In addition, numerous development theories have been espoused from modernization theory through to neo-liberalism, yet few states could be said to adhere to their respective models of development. As a result, the credibility of such theories is brought into question, along with the explanations, predictions and solutions that they provide. Such perceptions are reinforced by the fact that these theories often struggle to account for the sheer range of development experiences. Schuurman (1993) has noted that dependency theory in particular, which positions itself as a critique of development, struggles to explain and encapsulate such diversity.[1] Indeed, as we saw earlier in this work, the Global South is now a much more heterogeneous place. More generally, some practitioners have come to view development theory as an irrelevance, contributing little or nothing to their everyday experiences and practices on the ground (Edwards 1989).

The preceding points all relate to disputes over the effectiveness of development. But as we have seen, post-development writers believe that development is really about knowledge and power (see Crush 1995), more specifically, that development is rooted in European Enlightenment notions of progress, science, rationalism and capitalism, which has resulted in many countries in the South pursuing models of economic development often unsuited to their own needs and resources. In some cases, this pursuit has contributed to their debt burden, while development *per se*, has provided the opportunity and justification for international institutions like the World Bank and the IMF to intervene and shape these societies. Some radical commentators consider development to be simply a contemporary form of western imperialism, enhancing the power of countries and corporations of the North while marginalizing the views and interests of people in the South, a tendency reinforced by the creation of 'the Third World'. In sum, development has been a universalizing project and, as such, is the antithesis of pluralism and local expression of diversity.

There is also the important matter of the damage that has been done to the environment in the pursuit of development. For environmentalists, much of the responsibility for environmental degradation lies with the values that lie at the heart of the development project, notably notions of progress, science and materialism. With experts predicting that environmental decline will accelerate as we move further into the millennium, it raises questions about both the feasibility and wisdom of pursuing development.

Of course, what greatly adds to the difficulty in critically evaluating 'development' is the lack of consensus over its nature and purpose. As we saw in the Introduction, there is a great deal of ambiguity surrounding this complex, contested and multidimensional phenomenon – or phenomena if we view it in the plural. For example, is development a long-term historical process or more accurately viewed as a contemporary post-1945 project? Moreover, is the purpose of development to achieve social and economic transformation? If so, what type of change is development seeking to achieve? Is it the creation of more equitable societies and/or a fairer and more just global order? Alternatively, should the primary concern of development be the pursuit of individual empowerment and the enhancement of human dignity? And, from a radical perspective, is development primarily about ameliorating the worst excesses of capitalism? As we have seen, much rests upon who has the power to determine what development should be. While the most straightforward way of determining development effectiveness is to assess whether development agencies meet their stated targets, as we saw in the Introduction, writers like Alan Thomas (2000) are critical about the reduction of development to practice.

In defence of development

Some of the charges outlined in the previous section are regularly raised against development. However, in the case of many of them, there is a degree of reductionism at work that fails to acknowledge the extent of the diversity that exists within development. For example, advocates of structuralism and dependency theory would contest the notion that these approaches are part of mainstream development. Furthermore, from their perspective, the rejection of development theories should really entail rejection of those mainstream approaches that have exerted real influence, which since the 1980s has been neo-liberalism.

The broader response to the above charges is that they conceptualize development as a static enterprise, ignoring the ways in which it has evolved, especially in the recent period. In this regard, advocates of development point to the shift away from neo-liberal SAPs on the part of IFIs towards a greater emphasis on poverty reduction strategies. While critics may doubt the strength of commitment to the strategies of the part of the IFIs, it nevertheless reflects a response to criticism of mainstream development approaches, as does the more general shift within development to more locally based and participatory approaches, accompanied by targeted funding. More generally, it is pointed out that development is no longer viewed as an exclusively economic and market-oriented phenomenon, although of course these remain important themes. Even within development economics, there is growing recognition that non-market institutions, like CSOs, can contribute productively to the development process. Moreover, within development studies, quality-of-life issues are increasingly informing conceptualizations of development. In short, development entails more than just material standards of living and includes having sufficient leisure time, feeling secure, free expression, being healthy and receiving a decent education.

Further evidence that development studies is an evolving and reflexive discourse can be gleaned from the fact that it has fully incorporated into its area of analysis many of the most significant contemporary issues and trends, including globalization, global governance and the global environment. In the case of the latter, and in response to the charge of environmental vandalism raised against the development industry, development theorists and practitioners point to the shift towards sustainable development within their discipline. An enormous amount of effort and research is now devoted to the issue of sustainability, and indeed it has become part of the rethinking of development.

People working in development maintain that the project has a moral purpose: it constitutes a genuine attempt to alleviate poverty and improve the lives of the poor throughout the world. Moreover, development and associated improvements in standards of living remain a genuine aspiration for many people throughout the world and is not simply an agenda that is imposed upon them. And in countries where a lack of economic development persists, this cannot simply be blamed upon the development industry as there will often be internal forces and factors contributing to this condition. In addition, some of the different branches of development have encouraged improvements in governance in a number of countries, albeit for varying motives and with uneven effects, as we saw in chapter 5. Nevertheless, the pursuit of greater security and freedom as well as increased political participation is another aspiration of citizens throughout the world as the revolutions in the Middle East and North Africa in 2011 would seem to demonstrate.

As for the often repeated charges of Eurocentrism and western dominance, there is now greater acceptance that development is not simply confined to the South, but also continues to be pursued in the North. For instance, notions of empowerment, participation, inclusion and localization, which are increasingly discussed in relation to development in the South, have proved attractive to citizens and policy-makers in the North (see Jones 2000). But there are other signs that the West's dominance of development may be weakening. For example, the rising economic power of many Asian countries has led to calls in the region for the setting up of Asian financial institutions, as well as the reform of the UN Security Council to reflect more fairly the shift in the balance of economic power.[2] In turn, this forms part of a broader discussion of the extent to which the twenty-first century will be a multipolar world, one that is no longer simply dominated by Washington. At the same time, some commentators detect an erosion of western cultural identity as a result of challenges ranging from multiculturalism to postmodernism, and with it a decline in western cultural hegemony (e.g., Friedmann 1999), and there is even discussion about whether the West should be learning from the East. More generally, there is now growing acceptance that there can be multiple modernities and different paths to development. All of this may indicate that, as we move further into the new millennium, development and development institutions will no longer simply be shaped by the North, although the place of Africa, Latin America and the Middle East in these debates and power shifts remains a moot point. In sum, development does not take place within a power vacuum, but crucially power may be becoming more dispersed in the twenty-first century.

Finally, there remains the question of what is the alternative to development? What would its critics, such as post-development writers, like to see in its place? Unless we are willing to accept current levels of global inequality and poverty, the onus would seem to be upon them to provide viable alternatives to development. And, as we saw in chapter 2, there are potential limitations to the post-development reliance upon grassroots participation and social movements. Of equal seriousness is the fact that occasionally there surfaces within the post-development literature a sense that not much needs to be done. For example, Marshall Sahlins observes that poverty is a 'social status' and hence 'the invention of civilization' (1997: 19). Similarly, Escobar

(1995a) emphasizes the role that development specialists played in constructing poverty in Colombia, and how in doing so they designated the country as being in need of development.

However, in their antithesis to development, some post-development writers perhaps overlook the tangible everyday experiences of the poor. In short, in seeking to break from the mental construct of development, they underplay the physical reality of poverty and inequality (Simon 1998; Sylvester 1999). Furthermore, dispensing with development does not mean that the problems that led to its emergence in the first place will disappear as well. But to date, while post-development has raised significant critical questions of development and, in doing so, encouraged practitioners and theorists to reassess the work that they are engaged in, few practicable alternative proposals have emanated from this tradition. In a certain sense, therefore, post-development is perpetuating the status quo (Nederveen Pieterse 2001: 107). Moreover, until such time as any alternatives do emerge, the place of development on the agenda of the international community appears relatively secure. Of course, this should not lead to complacency, and we should remain critically reflexive, continually seeking to enhance the development project and adapting to ever-changing conditions. And it is to this matter that the remainder of this book will now turn.

Development: future trajectories

The following, often interconnected, areas and issues are likely to receive increasing attention within development during the course of this century, and do much to influence its future trajectory.

Globalization

As we have seen, whether or not globalization undermines development is a contested point. However, there is a little dispute that globalization introduces additional complexity into development. For example, globalization and the greater mobility of our age can serve to disrupt the course of development within countries. The rapid spread of the credit crisis that began in the USA in August 2007 is an obvious instance of this new reality, destabilizing national economies throughout the world and highlighting the extent to which they are now interconnected (IMF 2008). Many developing countries experienced a reduction in foreign aid and investment as the global credit crisis took hold. Likewise, in response to the crisis, some OECD governments reviewed their immigration quotas in order to protect domestic jobs, but such a move hurts developing countries that rely upon the remittances sent home by their citizens working abroad.

As we saw in chapter 10, aspects of globalization are considered to be challenging the role of the state within development. From the perspective of globalizers, governments are struggling to pursue national economic management in the face of a powerful global market and the rapid movement of capital around the world. Further, globalization is considered to introduce other (non-state) actors, such as MNCs, international institutions and NGOs, into the development process, adding to the complexity of policy coordination and implementation. At the same time, public utilities and other areas that were formerly the preserve of states have been privatized and deregulated in many developing countries and are now run by private companies. And with developing economies having to operate under conditions shaped by powerful capitalist markets, it raises the question of who or what is determining development.

For some writers, it places the onus of responsibility for poverty alleviation on the individual and is therefore in accord with the approach championed by neo-liberals (Judson 1993). In addition, the decline of the state raises problems for writers advocating a rights-based approach to development because traditionally the state has operated as a protector of our rights (Maxwell 1999).[3] It has led to renewed interest in neo-dependency approaches but also in the developmental state with calls for its capacity to be rebuilt (Mohan 2002: 53). Indeed, for Craig and Porter, real empowerment entails 'enabling the state to do its job by making sure it has the resources' (2006: 262).

From a broader perspective, what type of world order are globalizing processes helping to build and will it be conducive to development in the future (Hettne, Inotai and Sundras 1999; Nederveen Pieterse 2000a)? In this regard, what type of global governance is required to generate equitable development so that global poverty and inequality can be reduced? Will the emerging global civil society of networks and activists, which is another manifestation of globalization, bring about a cultural change in prevailing attitudes towards development and the environment? Most importantly, in what ways, if at all, can globalization be utilized to facilitate development?

Environmental decline and global sustainable development

Arguably, the major factor shaping development as the twenty-first century progresses will be global environmental decline. Obviously, there is much debate over the extent and pace of environmental change; nevertheless, we are entering uncharted territory. Global environmental degradation will therefore inform key development issues and debates, some of which are likely to be the following:

- The nature and operability of sustainable development. What are the prospects of achieving a universal or global conception of sustainable development?
- Can the market be relied upon to achieve sustainable development? Or, should we be simply slowing down or reversing economic growth, and moving away from economic models of development?

- What role should technology play in development?
- Is the current system of GEG capable of dealing with climate change?
- Do we require a WEO, or equivalent, to enforce environmental agreements?
- Does establishing the necessary environmental regimes to halt environmental decline necessitate a revived role for the developmental state?
- What, if any, measures need to be taken to address anticipated global population growth in the twenty-first century?

Global environmental decline will in turn exacerbate the issue of resource shortages. Indeed, climate change is considered to be contributing to the growing world food crisis. Moreover, the escalating cost of some commodities and resources, notably food and energy, threatens to reverse many of the advances in development of recent years. Developing countries that are net importers of food like Egypt, Kenya and Jamaica will particularly struggle with increased prices, as will the urban poor who are unable to grow their own food (Thurston 2003: 52). There is also concern that countries will increasingly resort to subsidies, protectionism and biofuels to deal with their energy concerns. The spread of biofuels is exacerbating the food crisis resulting in spiralling food prices, which is causing considerable hardship for the poor in both the developed and developing worlds. In June 2008, the UN Secretary-General, Ban Ki-moon, informed the UN Food Summit that world food production must rise by 50 per cent by 2030 to meet increasing demand. Already the rising price of food is creating considerable nutritional difficulties in some countries which has led to food riots in places like Cairo and Haiti.

Wealthier countries and corporations are currently engaged in a 'land grab' in Africa and elsewhere in the developing world, buying up millions of hectares of agricultural land in developing countries in an effort to safeguard their own long-term food supplies. Moreover, increased competition over resources is likely to lead to more and more resource-based conflicts, ranging from so-called 'water wars' to the form of energy nationalism that Moscow has been pursuing of late. Resource-based conflict will merely contribute to the growing number of fragile states that exist in the developing world, and in turn ensure that governance remains a key issue within development (chapter 5).

Global governance reform

The reform of international governmental institutions will receive increasing attention as attempts are made to address their widely perceived democratic deficit, especially within the WB, the IMF and the UN Security Council. For developing countries, as we saw in chapter 7, the current system of global governmental architecture contains a major imbalance of power, reflecting the fact that much of it was devised immediately after the Second World War.

It is also widely recognized that the UN system as a whole, with its plethora of agencies and programmes and their often overlapping mandates and bureaucracies, needs to be streamlined and more effectively coordinated. Indeed, this was one of the findings in the 2006 report by the Kofi Annan-convened High Level Panel on UN Reform, which was co-chaired by three prime ministers (Black 2006). For example, the panel reported that there were 17 countries in which the UNDP not only lacked the authority to regulate other agencies but was actually in competition with them. The report also identified global environmental governance as an area that particularly needed to be enhanced, especially with regard to improving the funding for global environmental initiatives and coordinating the numerous UN environmental conventions and regimes. Meanwhile, environmentalists have been calling for: the authority and powers of the UNEP to be bolstered; for the UN to adopt a more integrated and rigorous conception of sustainable development; and for environmental security to be given greater priority by the UN Security Council (Barnett 2001; Dalby 2002; Hopper forthcoming).

For some critics, global governance in its current guise is excessively focused upon trade, open markets and the smooth running of the international economy, often at the expense of human development and the environment. Indeed, there is a degree of dissension among international institutions themselves over development strategy, with the WTO and the IMF favouring a market-oriented approach, whereas organizations like UNCTAD and the UNDP are more focused upon its human and social dimensions. In fact, the latter have put forward proposals on how the WTO and the world trade regime need to be reformed along these lines (see UNCTAD 2004b and UNDP 2003b, respectively). Reflecting this complexity, the World Bank appears to be steadily shifting from its free-market position towards greater emphasis upon poverty reduction, equitable growth and acknowledging the role of the state in the development process, and this is increasingly placing it at odds with the IMF and the WTO (Nederveen Pieterse 2001; Wade and Veneroso 1998). But irrespective of these particular institutional debates over trade, if producers in developing countries continue to struggle to export their goods, and existing patterns of global poverty and inequality persist, the call for changes to the international terms of trade from the South will become increasingly vociferous.

The issue of trade

However, as we have seen, the nature of international trade is one of the most controversial issues within development (chapter 6). Indeed, the protracted nature of the Doha Trade Round is ample evidence of the challenges a multilateral trading system can face when national interests remain such a powerful motivating force. Establishing a collectively agreed trade framework is made all the more difficult by the fact that developing countries are belatedly playing an increasing role in international trade negotiations. Often they act collectively, but there is also divergence among them, dependent upon the nature and condition of their own economies and how they see their interests being best served. Moreover, trade talks have become international media events, attracting protestors from throughout the world, ranging from anti-globalizers to South Korean rice farmers, and creating an atmosphere that is not always conducive to reasoned debate. While the actual influence of protest groups upon policy formulation is difficult to determine, there is little doubt that they have helped to stir up popular opposition to trade liberalization and globalization.

Looking to the future, there are other factors likely to have an influence upon the future course of the multilateral trading system. Firstly, an aspect of trade-related governance that will have to be addressed concerns how to deal with the anticipated hikes in the price of primary commodities and natural resources. These markets are likely to become increasingly unpredictable and in turn to have a destabilizing effect upon the international economy. Secondly, the spread of trade rules to services, employment, health and safety, and the environment is raising concerns that this is infringing upon national sovereignty and governmental control over these areas. Thirdly, these and other trade-related matters will be played out within the context of the growing economic power and influence of Asia, something that is reflected in China and India's increasing involvement in Africa (see Boardman 2007; Winters and Yusuf 2007). The likely consequences of these developments are difficult to predict.

Human-centred development

Within development studies, debate continues over the nature of the relation-ship between theory and practice, as well as the relative merits of macro- and micro-level perspectives of development. In this regard, both post-development and alternative development writers have contributed significantly to the case for localizing and particularizing development (Ferguson 1998). Beyond the benefits that it brings to indigenous peoples, an additional advantage of local-based development is that attached to it is an attractive vocabulary, notably that of empowerment, participation and inclusion. Given the negative asso-ciations that development has accrued, this is not an insignificant point, especially within the context of growing evidence of aid fatigue on the part of some northern countries.

Microfinance-led development

One way of encouraging local development that looks set to continue has been through micro-credit finance (Rhyne 2001). This initiative was developed by the Grameen (village) bank, which was set up in Bangladesh in 1976 by Muhammad

Yunus. It is based upon the provision of small loans being given to the poor in developing countries without collateral, who would otherwise be unlikely to receive traditional bank loans. The Grameen initiative began with an agricultural focus, but it has now extended into areas like irrigation and fisheries. Today it has more than 7 million borrowers and has spread to more than 40 countries. Indeed, it is being replicated even in advanced industrialized countries like the UK and the USA, and hence is an example within development of the North learning from the South (Rogaly and Roche 1998). These loans are often less than US$100, but they provide targeted financial assistance, with microfinance providers retaining close contact with the communities in which they operate. While critics argue that the poor often struggle to repay these loans, from the perspective of the recipients it provides them with direct funding, rather than having to rely upon its dispersal through various development agencies. It also gives them greater control over how it is employed and without this finance many would have little prospect of setting up their own businesses (Rutherford 2000). In short, it enables the poor to be entrepreneurial.

Some commentators have argued that establishing successful enterprises requires more than just small loans, notably investment in management training and marketing expertise (ibid.). Others do not see it as a coherent or long-term solution to poverty because it does not address the deeper structural issue of the nature of the international economy. Nevertheless, microfinance is now a widely employed approach to poverty alleviation, including by the World Bank (Ledgerwood 1999). The Grameen model has inspired many thousands of micro-lenders throughout the world, and there are signs that the internet will greatly expand this form of social lending, enabling more people to participate either as lenders or clients. For its advocates, microfinance is the ultimate form of grassroots participation in development.

Gender issues

One of the most notable features of the Grameen initiative is that 97 per cent of its borrowers are women.[4] In turn, this has increased the numbers benefiting from microfinance because women have proved extremely adept at spreading the finance, and any benefits it has generated, to their households and wider families (Remenyi and Quinones 2000; Todd 1996). Moreover, in some societies microfinance has enhanced the autonomy and status of women within these families, with some writers crediting the scheme with reducing domestic violence against women. However, this latter point is context specific. In some countries, greater access to credit has merely added to women's workload – they are responsible for raising the loans and meeting their repayments – without altering gender relations within the household (Kabeer 2001). Furthermore, in countries like Sri Lanka, there is evidence of male resentment against this scheme because it is perceived as challenging traditional gender roles (Dissanayake 2006).

Of course, for feminists, challenging patriarchal structures in this way is exactly what is required if the position and life experiences of women are to be improved. But irrespective of the different positions over this particular issue, it is safe to predict that strategies designed to reduce gender inequality will continue to be an important development theme. According to the High Level Panel on UN Reform, it is an area that also needs to be addressed at an institutional level as the UN has been weak on gender issues. It recommended a single UN agency for gender to consolidate the work of the three existing agencies (Black 2006).

Global taxation

In the early 1970s, the economist James Tobin (1974) proposed that financial transactions should be taxed – from between 0.25 and 0.1 per cent for each transaction – as a way of curbing financial speculation and thereby introducing greater stability into international financial markets. Subsequently, the notion that the revenues raised could go towards measures designed to alleviate poverty began to gain support. Indeed, it is now estimated that a levy of 0.25 per cent upon contemporary financial transaction levels would raise US$250 billion per annum (Potter et al. 2004: 169). The Brandt Commission (1977–83) essentially concurred with this approach in its two reports (see Brandt 1980 and 1983) in which it recommended the transfer of resources from the North to the South in order to accelerate development in the latter.

The idea of a global tax has attracted renewed interest in the recent period. This is because the volume of global financial transactions has risen significantly, due to economic globalization and the liberalization of international financial markets. In the 1990s, daily foreign exchange transactions reached US$1 trillion per day. Consequently, a relatively low rate of taxation has the potential to raise an enormous amount of money for development purposes (Raffer 1998; Watchel 2000). In fact, a taxation level of below 0.01 per cent would still generate substantial revenues without significantly distorting the international economy, and at the same time this figure may be more acceptable to companies and traders (Henderson 2000: 79).

This type of taxation may also help to reduce the instability that arises from global financial speculation (Haq, Kaul and Grunberg 1996). In particular, it may help to reduce the rate at which capital is taken in and out of countries, a phenomenon that, as we saw in chapter 1, many commentators believe contributed to the Asian financial crisis of 1997. In 2010, in response to the global financial crisis, there were renewed calls for a global bank levy and a financial transaction tax.

In this vein, as a way of tackling environmental decline, some commentators argue for taxes being imposed on the use of global goods like air and water. It would mean companies and individuals paying an environmental tax when using air or maritime transport, a measure that may serve to reduce usage levels. The money raised could then be devoted to the environment, with some policy-makers arguing that it should be allocated to funding a World Environmental Organization (e.g., Trittin 2004).

Needless to say, these forms of taxation are always likely to generate considerable opposition from the international business community, and, given the influence that its members exert upon governments, the future implementation of such measures is far from certain. In addition, this type of Keynesian/ redistributive response goes against the grain of the current neo-liberal orthodoxy. Indeed, neo-liberals have highlighted the difficulties of implementing and enforcing such schemes, although advocates of a Tobin tax contend that electronic markets make it possible to monitor every trade. Other critics claim that businesses will engage in forms of tax avoidance, including relocating to regions that do not impose such forms of taxation. And ultimately, they argue, it will merely serve to reduce the flows of capital, including into developing countries. Nevertheless, a greater emphasis upon the reduction of global poverty and inequality within development may help to revive the faith of people in the South in this project (Gardner and Lewis 1996). Moreover, it may be the case that a Tobin-type tax is needed to counteract the reductions in aid budgets of a growing number of MEDCs.

Conclusion

In conclusion, and contrary to much of the preceding discussion, we should not overlook the fact that existing themes and approaches currently dominating development will continue at least for the foreseeable future. This includes neo-liberalism continuing to inform the development strategies of the leading IFIs and many national governments, despite the fact that the World Bank, for example, has become more oriented towards tackling the human consequences of underdevelopment. In short, the view that poverty alleviation is best attained through the pursuit of market-based, export-driven economic growth persists within development. Moreover, this mindset will continue to compete with the recent and emerging themes mentioned above, helping to ensure that development remains an evolving, contested and ultimately complex phenomenon. But, arguably, many of the above areas need to receive attention, if only to ensure that development continues to be relevant. This is because some commentators are detecting not only aid fatigue but also a sense that development may be running out of steam in the light of the disappointments and controversies that continue to surround it (Haines 2000; Harcourt 1997; Hettne 1995). However, development in essence is concerned with how we as human beings lead our lives, or at least aspire to live them, as well as our relationship with other species and the environment. Such all-too-human concerns are likely to ensure not only the continuing relevance of development but that it remains a valid and legitimate enterprise.

RECOMMENDED READING

- For an overview of a range of potential global taxes, including the Tobin tax, see Howard Watchel's article entitled 'The Mosaic of Global Taxes' (2000).
- On microfinancing, see Joe Remenyi and Ben Quinones (eds), *Microfinance and Poverty Alleviation* (2000).
- On the future impact of global warming, see Mark Lynas, *Six Degrees: Our Future on a Hotter Planet* (2007).

WEBSITES

- www.waronwant.org/tobintax: For information on the Tobin tax.
- www.stampoutpoverty.org: Campaigns for a stamp duty on currency transactions as part of the Tobin tax network.
- www.grameen-info.org: For the Grameen bank's own website.
- www.fairtradenet: The website of FLO International, which monitors fair trade standards.
- www.fairtrade.org.uk: Website of the Fairtrade Foundation, the UK fair trade labelling initiative.

Notes

INTRODUCTION: UNDERSTANDING DEVELOPMENT

1 There is also little point in covering ground that has been covered comprehensively and indeed excellently elsewhere (e.g., Elliott 1999; Potter et al. 2004; Willis 2005).

2 However, Gilbert Rist (2002) identifies the roots of western thought on development in the work of Aristotle and Saint Augustine.

3 In contrast, Cowen and Shenton (1996) trace the origins of development thinking to a critique of progress that some European thinkers, such as Auguste Comte and the Saint-Simonians, articulated in response to the social upheavals being generated by industrialization.

4 Rist (2002) maintains that interest in underdevelopment, and in particular concern about the plight of what today we call the South, pre-dates Truman's speech.

5 Trusteeship has been defined as: 'The intent which is expressed, by one source of agency, to develop the capacities of another' (Cowen and Shenton 1996: p. x).

6 More recently, the South has come to be described as the 'Global South'. The UNDP initiative of 2003, *Forging a Global South*, has helped promote this concept by seeking to encourage South–South cooperation (UNDP 2003b). Furthermore, aspects of globalization – such as migration, global cities, transnational capitalism and the network society – have disrupted the traditional North–South distinction, with areas of poverty found in the North, and areas of affluence existing in the South (see Dirlik 2007).

7 Martin Wolf (2000) maintains that global inequality and the proportion of the world's population in extreme poverty declined in the 1980s and 1990s. Robert Hunter Wade (2003) contends that the opposite is the case and is critical of how institutions like the World Bank determine poverty and income inequality. In particular, Wade questions the measurements of how many people live below the international poverty line, and the data on which it is based, arguing that these estimates 'contain a large margin of error' (2004b: 571).

8 For a critique of Sen's work, see Corbridge (2002a).

CHAPTER 1 THEORIZING DEVELOPMENT

1 Latin American countries had gained their independence in the nineteenth century. However, many remained closely tied to Europe and the basic colonial relationship, whereby they exported primary goods and imported European manufactured products, arguably persisted until the pursuit of import-substitution industrialization by some Latin American governments in the 1950s (see Gwynne and Kay 2004; Kirby 2003; Munck 2003).

2 Berger (1994) also points to the close ties between elites in the developing and developed worlds, arguing that together they form an international class structure that further undermines the notion of a discrete Third World. Bill Warren (1980) makes a similar claim, arguing that 'Third Worldism' has been an ideology promoted by postcolonial governments for their own political ends.

3 However, since 1945, the concept of the Third World has served as a rallying point and source of solidarity for developing countries facilitating, for example, bloc voting in the UN (Merriam 1988).

4 However, John Toye presents a different take on this point, arguing that Prebisch and ECLA were concerned about the problems generated by ISI, especially in relation to the creation of artificial industries through tariff protection (2003: 23).

5 The term 'neo-colonialism' is often credited to Ghana's first president, Kwame Nkrumah. In *Neo-Colonialism: The Last Stage of Imperialism* (1965), he argues that: 'The essence of neo-colonialism is that the state which is subject to it is, in theory, independent, and has the trappings of international sovereignty. In reality its economic system and thus its internal policy is directed from the outside.' Beyond the economic realm, neo-colonialism is detected in the cultural legacy of the Europeans in the form of languages and models of government, in their tendency to intervene in the political affairs of their former colonies (e.g., there was western involvement in the overthrow of Nkrumah's government) and in the defence agreements signed at the time of independence that led to former colonies becoming caught up in the Cold War.

6 However, Ha-Joon Chang (2003b) maintains that industrial advancement, rather than macro-economic stability, was the main priority of East Asian countries.

CHAPTER 2 APPROACHING DEVELOPMENT

1 Culture, for example, has very much returned to the development debate. See recent publications by: Allen 2000; Huntington and Harrison 2000; Schech and Haggis 2000, 2002; Tucker 1996.

2 Harrison continues this theme in a co-edited volume with Samuel Huntington entitled *Culture Matters* (2000). See also an essay by David Landes entitled 'Culture Makes Almost All the Difference' in the same volume for a further contribution to this thesis.

3 However, Wolfgang Sachs, a leading post-development writer, does acknowledge that development has changed since Truman's speech in 1949, becoming a shapeless, 'amoeba-like concept' that continues to spread everywhere 'because it connotes the best of intentions' (1992: 4). Similarly, Gustavo Esteva (1992) has mapped the process of conceptual inflation that development has undergone.

4 However, in a later essay, Escobar (2002) seeks to clarify his position, arguing that he is interested in exploring how poverty has been problematized within development discourse and associated with the Third World.

CHAPTER 3 HEALTH, EDUCATION AND POPULATION

1 Countries and regions also respond to contemporary demographic challenges in different ways. For instance, the relatively more open immigration policy of the United States means that it is better placed than the EU and Japan to deal with the problems that are associated with an ageing population.

2 For a counter-view to the neo-Malthusian thesis, see Julian Simon, *Population Matters* (1990). Simon presents a more optimistic portrayal of population growth, identifying its potential advantages for societies.

3 Rupert Hodder (2000) notes that at the Rio UNCED Conference in 1992, many developing countries sought to relegate the significance of population growth as a development issue.

4 However, Betsy Hartmann (1997) believes that the push for women's empowerment is still primarily based on family planning and that to address this matter seriously would require challenging the status quo.

5 Murray Last (1999) is more critical of development health organizations, especially their global orientation which is embodied in the goal of 'health for all'. Instead, he argues for a more locally oriented approach to health, one that incorporates local insights and knowledge. For Last, this has the additional benefit of providing people with a degree of power and control over their own lives.

CHAPTER 4 GENDER AND DEVELOPMENT

1 For analysis of the representations of women within development, and some of the 'gender myths' and 'feminist fables' that have come to be associated with this subject, see Jackson and Pearson (1998) and Cornwall, Harrison and Whitehead (2007), respectively.
2 For case studies of women's development experiences in Africa, Asia and Latin America, along with consideration of context-specific gender and development issues, see Momsen and Kinnaird (1993) and Afshar (1985).
3 However, Wieringa (1994) has criticized the practical/strategic distinction, arguing women's needs change over time and are dependent upon context and who is defining them. It is therefore impossible to distinguish between practical and strategic needs.
4 In this vein, Uma Kothari (2002) has observed that more needs to be done to bring together the discourses of feminism and postcolonialism (see also Gandhi 1998).

CHAPTER 5 CONFLICT, SECURITY AND DEVELOPMENT

1 For example, Charles Ukeje (2008) contends that aspects of globalization are fuelling social and political instability in many states in West Africa.
2 However, Caroline Thomas (2007) maintains that globalization necessitates the state playing an important mediating role between global processes and local outcomes.
3 For a defence of human security, see Jolly and Basu Ray (2006).
4 Monty G. Marshall and Ted Robert Gurr in *Peace and Conflict 2005* adopt a similar line to that taken by the HSRP. Their report emphasizes the security gains that have been achieved as a result of a range of agencies engaging seriously in peace-building activities, but also warns that half of the world's countries are facing serious problems that will require international attention (Marshall and Gurr 2005: 2).
5 In reality, the distinction between peacekeeping and peace-building is often blurred. For example, facilitating fair and free elections, training civil and military personnel, rooting out corruption and reforming judicial and legal systems can be tasks undertaken by both peacekeepers and peace-builders. Furthermore, countries undergoing post-conflict development can relapse into violence. For Michèle Griffin (2005), given the complexity of contemporary conflicts, we should stop distinguishing between conflict and post-conflict states and instead pursue a multidimensional approach to intervention by simultaneously implementing a range of strategies.

CHAPTER 6 TRADE AND DEVELOPMENT

1 Academics tend to employ terms like 'outward orientation', 'openness' and even 'open and outward-oriented economies' rather than trade liberalization and free trade. Here all of these terms will be used interchangeably.
2 Free traders do not make such a claim, given that it may put off northern countries from pursuing trade liberalization. Indeed, writers like Martin Wolf (2004) insist the developed world has nothing to fear from 'openness' because ultimately what matters to an economy is not the cheapness of labour but its level of productivity, and this tends to be higher in the North.

3 Free traders stress that countries actively encouraging trade (e.g., in South-East Asia) have diversified beyond producing just raw materials and moved into manufacturing and other areas (Irwin 2005; Krueger 1997).

4 Free traders respond to this charge by arguing that trade liberalization helps to improve market access and reduce trade-distorting subsidies in agriculture. It also argues that the world food crisis was deepened by countries like Russia adopting protectionist measures and restricting its food exports.

5 However, critics argue that by accepting its 'single undertaking' mandate when they join the WTO, whereby they have to comply with all agreements, developing countries now lose much of the SDT they have previously enjoyed.

6 However, the correlation between trade and development is far from straightforward as share of world trade does not necessarily reveal how LEDCs are faring in the global economy. As Doyle (2006) has noted, despite the increasing trade that developing countries as a whole are engaged in, their actual share of global GDP has fallen in the last thirty years.

7 However, this figure conceals considerable diversity within Africa, with different countries and regions engaging in particular ways and to varying degrees with foreign markets. For example, selling manufactured goods has become a significant part of the economies of Mauritius and Tunisia. See S. Bora, A. Bouët and D. Roy (2007) for an analysis of the complexity of African trading relationships with the rest of the world.

8 As was discussed in chapter 1, it is now widely accepted that there is no single East Asian economic development model. However, Douglas Irwin maintains that common elements can be found in the different countries of the region, including macro-economic stability, reliance on private enterprise and market competition, investment in human capital, and export-oriented policies (2005: 183).

CHAPTER 7 PARTICIPATION AND REPRESENTATION IN DEVELOPMENT

1 However, Anthony Bebbington et al. (2007) contend that commitments to empowerment in World Bank texts are not always readily translated into practice within Bank-funded projects.

2 This is not an uncommon tale. For example, see Michael D. Woost, 'Alternative Vocabularies of Development? "Community" and "Participation" in Development Discourse in Sri Lanka' (1997).

3 The World Bank funds NGOs indirectly via developing country governments, and this generally entails NGOs having to work with these governments.

4 By the end of the 1990s, however, some donor reviews of NGO-sector funding began expressing concern that NGOs were not fulfilling expectations (e.g., World Bank NGO Unit Social Development 1998). Moreover, some studies have thrown doubt upon the ability of NGOs to perform the resource-allocating functions of states (e.g., Dicklitch 1998; Kiondo 1995).

5 The global recession is likely to exacerbate tensions because it is predicted to mark a shift in the economic balance of power with developing economies, led by China and India, accounting for more than 50 per cent of world GDP by 2013 once the lower cost of living in poorer countries is taken into account (Elliott 2008).

6 It is the changes associated with globalization that are considered to diminish social capital and community life, notably increased geographical mobility and familial instability, greater individualism and privatization, the spread of the market, increasing commodification and commercialization, and growing inequality (Hopper 2003).

7 There are differing conceptions of 'good governance'. For example, the World Bank arguably seeks the formation of liberal states that support private entrepreneurship and a

free-market economy (Crawford 2006). Moreover, the notion of civil society operating as a counterweight to authoritarian states must be weighed against the existence of many fragile states in the South (Whaites 2000).

CHAPTER 8 FINANCING DEVELOPMENT: FOREIGN AID AND DEBT

1 While this discussion of debt will focus upon the South, it is increasingly a problem for the North, with some writers anticipating a first-world debt crisis (Pettifor 2006). For example, the US National Debt reached US$9.4 trillion during 2008.
2 However, some writers argue that it is the pursuit of development that has led many southern countries to accumulate debt (e.g., George 1989).
3 In response to this charge, aid advocates maintain that instances of African decline are due to a range of factors and cannot simply be blamed upon aid.
4 As we saw in chapter 1, critics of neo-liberalism emphasize the role that non-market factors have played in Asia's development, while aid advocates believe the considerable financial support that South Korea, Taiwan and other countries in the region received after the Second World War laid the foundations for their subsequent economic growth (Stewart 2006b: 6).
5 Critics are not so sure, variously arguing in relation to this area that: aid is of limited use in facilitating conflict resolution (Macrae 2001); there is little prospect of aid fostering development in the midst of conflict; and there is a strong likelihood that it will be wasted under such conditions (Dowden 2005).

CHAPTER 9 SUSTAINABLE DEVELOPMENT

1 I am indebted to one of this book's anonymous reviewers for this point.
2 Critics respond that the relationship between poverty and environmental destruction is more complex than this thesis allows for and will ultimately be determined by context (Dobson 2000).
3 Beijing responds that when population sizes are taken into account, the USA remains the world's biggest CO_2 emitter. China, with a population of 1.3 billion, releases approximately 4,762 kg of carbon dioxide per person, while for the USA the figure is roughly 19,277 kg per person (Watts and Vidal 2007: 23).
4 The issue of pollution havens has generated a considerable literature, including writers who deny their existence (Letchumanan 2000); others who argue that developing countries are tightening their environmental regulatory regimes (Mani and Wheeler 1998); and some who maintain that pollution is increasingly being relocated between developed countries (Repetto 1995).
5 Defenders of the role of states within GEG argue that they have a more informed understanding of their local environments than remote international institutions. Indeed, the latter often introduce policies only after they have been tried and tested at a national level (Tews and Busch 2002). Moreover, it is governments that in the main implement international environmental agreements.
6 However, as Karen T. Litfin has noted, the greening of sovereignty is an uneven, variegated and contested process, and 'its ultimate trajectory is by no means certain' (1998: 23).
7 Academics and policy-makers now devote considerable effort to analysing the nature and effectiveness of environmental regimes (e.g., Breitmeier, Young and Zurn 2006).
8 For an informative article that maps the many perspectives on sustainable development, see Hopwood, Mellor and O'Brien (2005). They classify the different approaches to sustainable development: status quo, reform and transformation.

CHAPTER 10 GLOBALIZATION AND DEVELOPMENT

1 Reflecting this complexity, Gilbert Rist has speculated upon whether globalization has replaced development (2002: 249). Globalization is also considered to undermine geography, notably by unsettling the relationship between space and place, and location and economic development (O'Brien 1992), although geographers dispute this contention (see Johnston, Taylor and Watts 2002; Murray 2006; Potter et al. 2004).

2 Anthony Giddens, while acknowledging that globalization is 'one of the fundamental consequences of modernity', challenges the association of globalization with westernization, arguing that the former 'introduces new forms of world interdependence' (1990: 175).

3 Cosmopolitanism is understood here to mean: '1a of or from or knowing many parts of the world. b consisting of people from many or all parts. 2 free from national limitations and prejudices' (*Concise Oxford Dictionary*, 8th edn, 1991: 260).

4 Quicker travel, ICTs and the diminution of national borders also make it easier for international agencies to coordinate and implement their responses to humanitarian emergencies.

CONCLUSION: DEVELOPMENT – FUTURE TRAJECTORIES

1 However, as we saw in chapter 1, advocates of dependency theory would counter this charge by pointing to the work of dependency theorists like Fernando Henrique Cardoso who emphasized the importance of contextualization and of taking into account particular historical processes in understanding development and underdevelopment.

2 An indication of the future is perhaps evident in the intensification of trade and investment patterns between China and many African countries. From the perspective of the latter, China means conditionality-free investment, although in many instances it also means Chinese workers being brought in to run the new plants and businesses that are being set up on the African continent.

3 However, rights-based development is not without its critics. For some writers, it is part of a broader problem within development, namely that of its alleged Eurocentric bias (Mohan and Holland 2001).

4 Within the formal banking system of many developing societies, women tend to struggle to secure loans because of their generally low earnings.

Bibliography and References

AAPPG (2006), *The Other Side of the Coin: The UK and Corruption in Africa*, A Report by the AAPPG, March 2006, www.africaappg.org.uk (accessed 10/4/11).

Abu-Lughod, J. L. (1989), *Before European Hegemony: The World-System, 1250–1350*, Oxford: Oxford University Press.

Acharya, A., de Lima, A. T. F. and Moore, M. (2006), 'Proliferation and Fragmentation: Transaction Costs and the Value of Aid', *Journal of Development Studies* 42(1): 1–21.

Adam, B. (2007), 'Climate Change Will Hit Poorest Hardest, Say UN Scientists', *The Guardian*, 6 April, p. 6.

Adams, W. M. (2001), *Green Development*, 2nd edn, London: Routledge.

ADB (2006), *African Development Report 2006*, Oxford: Oxford University Press.

Addison, T. (2004), 'The Global Economy, Conflict Prevention, and Post-Conflict, Recovery', *World Institute for Development Economics Research*, www.wider.unu.edu (accessed 14/9/08).

Adkins, L. (2005), 'Social Capital: The Anatomy of a Troubled Concept', *Feminist Theory* 6(2): 195–211.

Adorno, T. (1991), *The Culture Industry*, London: Routledge.

Africa World Review Editorial (1994), 'NGOs and the Recolonization Process', *Africa World Review* (theme issue), London: Africa Research and Information Bureau.

Afshar, H. (ed.) (1985), *Women, Work and Ideology in the Third World*, London: Tavistock.

Afshar, H. (ed.) (1996), *Women and Politics in the Third World*, London: Routledge.

Agarwal, B. (1997a), 'Bargaining and Gender Relations Within and Beyond the Household', *Feminist Economics* 3(1): 1–51.

Agarwal, B. (1997b), 'The Gender and Environment Debate: Lessons from India', in N. Visvanathan et al. (eds), *The Women, Gender and Development Reader*, London: Zed Books, pp. 68–75.

Agrawal, A. (1995), 'Dismantling the Divide between Indigenous and Scientific Knowledge', *Development and Change* 26: 413–49.

Ahmed, A. (1995), 'Ethnic Cleansing: A Metaphor for Our Time', *Ethnic and Racial Studies* 18(1): 2–25.

Akyüz, Y. (2003), *Developing Countries and World Trade*, London: UNCTAD/Zed Books.

Alavi, A. (2007), 'African Countries and the WTO's Dispute Settlement Mechanism', *Development Policy Review* 25(1): 25–42.

Albrow, M. (1996), *The Global Age*, Cambridge: Polity.

Allen, T. (2000), 'Taking Culture Seriously', in T. Allen and A. Thomas (eds), *Poverty and Development into the 21st Century*, Oxford: Oxford University Press, pp. 443–65.

Amin, S. (1974), *Accumulation on a World Scale: A Critique of the Theory of Underdevelopment*, New York: Monthly Review Press.

Amin, S. (1976), *Unequal Development: Social Formations at the Periphery of the Capitalist System*, Brighton: Harvester Press.

Amoako, K. Y. (2004), 'World Trade Liberalization Still Excludes Africa', *FT.com, Financial Times*, 23 November, www.new.ft.com/cms (accessed 29/06/08).

Amoore, L. (ed.) (2005), *The Global Resistance Reader*, London: Routledge.

Amsden, A. H. (1992), *Asia's Next Giant: South Korea and Late Industrialization*, new edn, Oxford: Oxford University Press.

Amsden, A. H. (2001), *The Rise of 'The Rest': Challenges to the West From Late-Industrialising Economies*, Oxford: Oxford University Press.

Annan, K. (2005), *In Larger Freedom: Towards Development, Security and Human Rights for All*, A/59/2005, UNGA: New York.

Apter, D. E. (1965), *The Politics of Modernization*, Chicago: University of Chicago Press.

Apthorpe, R. (1985), 'Pleading and Reading Agricultural Development Policy: Small Farm, Big State and the "Case of Taiwan"', in R. Grillo and A. Rew (eds), *Social Anthropology and Development Policy*, London: Tavistock.

Apthorpe, R. (1986), 'Development Policy Discourse', *Public Administration and Development* 6: 377–89.

Apthorpe, R. and Gasper, D. (eds) (1996), *Arguing Development Policy: Frames and Discourses*, London: Frank Cass.

Arce, A. and Long, N. (eds) (2000), *Anthropology, Development and Modernities*, London: Routledge.

Arndt, C., Jones, S. and Tarp, F. (2006), 'Aid and Development: The Mozambican Case'. Paper presented at the AERC Biannual, Nairobi, May 2006.

Ashford, L. (2001), 'New Population Policies: Advancing Women's Health and Rights', *Population Reference Bureau* 56(1), March, www.prb.org (accessed 12/5/10).

Astier, H. (2006), 'Can Aid Do More Harm than Good?', *BBC News Online*, 1 February, www.bbcnews.co.uk (accessed 13/3/08).

Athreya, B. (2002), 'Women in the Global Economy', in V. Desai and R. B. Potter (eds), *The Companion to Development Studies*, London: Arnold, pp. 342–6.

Atkinson, R. and Blandy, S. (eds) (2007), *Gated Communities*, London: Routledge.

Ayittey, G. (1992), *Africa Betrayed*, London: Macmillan.

Azar, E. (1990), *The Management of Protracted Social Conflict: Theory and Cases*, Aldershot: Dartmouth.

Baker, S. (2006), *Sustainable Development*, London: Routledge.

Balassa, B. (1971), 'Trade Policies in Developing Countries', *American Economic Review* 61: 178–87.

Balassa, B. (1981), *The Newly Industrializing Countries in the World Economy*, Oxford: Pergamon.

Balassa, B. (1982), 'Development Strategies and Economic Performance', in B. Balassa et al., *Development Strategies in Semi-Industrial Economies*, Baltimore: Johns Hopkins University Press.

Ballentine, K. and Nitzschke, H. (2006), 'Beyond Greed and Grievance: Policy Lessons from Studies in the Political Economy of Armed Conflict', in R. Picciotto and R. Weaving (eds), *Security and Development*, London: Routledge, pp. 159–86.

Ballentine, K. and Sherman, J. (eds) (2003), *The Political Economy of Armed Conflict*, London: Lynne Rienner.

Bamford, D. (2007), 'UN leader Asks for Increased Aid', *BBC News Online*, 2 July, www.bbcnews.co.uk (accessed 3/9/07).

Banerjee, A. V. (2007), *Making Aid Work*, Cambridge, MA: MIT Press.

Banerjee, A. V., Bénabou, R. and Mookherjee, D. (eds) (2006), *Understanding Poverty*, Oxford: Oxford University Press.

Banerjee, S. B. (2003), 'Who Sustains Whose Development? Sustainable Development and the Reinvention of Nature', *Organization Studies* 24(1):143–80.

Baran, P. (1957), *The Political Economy of Growth*, New York: Monthly Review Press.

Barber, B. (1996), *Jihad vs. McWorld*, New York: Ballantine.

Barnett, J. (2001), *The Meaning of Environmental Security*, London: Zed Books.

Barnett, J. and Adger, N. (2005), 'Security and Climate Change: Towards an Improved Understanding', *Human Security and Climate Change*, Oslo, 21–23 June, www.gechs.org/holmen (accessed 7/9/08).

Barnett, M. and Weiss, T. G. (eds) (2008), *Humanitarianism in Question*, Ithaca: Cornell University Press.

Barrett, C. B. and Maxwell, D. G. (2005), *Food Aid After Fifty Years*, London: Routledge.

Barrett, H. (2006), *Health and Development*, London: Routledge.

Barrow, C. (2004), *Environmental Management and Development*, London: Routledge.

Batley, R. (2002), 'The Changing Role of the State in Development', in V. Desai and R. B. Potter (eds), *The Companion to Development Studies*, London: Arnold, pp. 135–9.

Bauer, P. T. (1972), *Dissent on Development*, Boston: Harvard University Press.

Bauer, P. T. (1976), 'Western guilt and Third World poverty', *Quadrant* 20(4): 13–22.

Bauer, P. T. (1981), *Equality, the Third World and Economic Delusion*, London: Methuen.

Bauer, P. T. (1984), *Reality and Rhetoric: Studies in the Economics of Development*, London: Weidenfeld and Nicolson.

Bayart, J.-F. (1991), 'Finishing with the Idea of the Third World: The Concept of the Political Trajectory', in J. Manor (ed.), *Rethinking Third World Politics*, Harlow: Longman, pp. 51–71.

Baylis, J., Smith, S. and Owens, P. (eds), *The Globalization of World Politics*, Oxford: Oxford University Press.

BBC (2003a), 'Jobs "Key" to Middle East Growth', *BBC News Online*, 19 September, www.bbcnews.co.uk (accessed 5/5/10).

BBC (2003b), 'Digital Divide Figures are "Flawed"', *BBC News Online*, 29 January, www.bbcnews.co.uk (accessed 7/1/08).

BBC (2004a), 'UN Warns of Population Explosion', *BBC News Online*, 15 September, www.bbcnews.co.uk (accessed 8/9/09).

BBC (2004b), 'India Population "to be Biggest"', *BBC News Online*, 18 April, www.bbcnews.co.uk (accessed 8/9/09).

BBC (2004c), 'Global Broadband Keeps Climbing', *BBC News Online*, 6 January, www.bbcnews.co.uk (accessed 12/10/08).

BBC (2005a), 'World Bank and IMF Back Debt Deal', *BBC News Online*, 26 September, www.bbcnews.co.uk (accessed 3/8/06).

BBC (2005b), 'World Population "to Rise by 40%"', *BBC News Online*, 25 February, www.bbcnews.co.uk (accessed 8/9/09).

BBC (2006a), 'Fragile States Risk Instability', *BBC News Online*, 14 September, www.bbcnews.co.uk (accessed 20/11/07).

BBC (2006b), 'Conflict "Wipes Out" Global Aid', *BBC News Online*, 25 October, www. bbcnews.co.uk (accessed 23/12/07).

BBC (2007a), 'World "Losing Fight against Aids"', *BBC News Online*, 23 July, www. bbcnews.co.uk (accessed 30/9/07).

BBC (2007b), 'Millennium Goals: In Statistics', *BBC News Online*, 5 September, www. bbcnews.co.uk (accessed 30/9/07).

BBC (2008), 'UN forces "Stretched to Limits"', *BBC News Online*, 31 July, www.bbc-news.co.uk (accessed 13/9/08).

BBC (2010), 'China Faces Growing Gender Imbalance', *BBC News Online*, 11 January, www.bbcnews.co.uk (accessed 9/5/10).

BBC (2011), 'Who, What, Why: Why Does the UK Give Aid to India?', *BBC News Online*, 1 March, www.bbcnews.co.uk (accessed 10/4/11).

Beall, J., Goodfellow, T. and Putzel, J. (2006), 'Introductory Article: On the Discourse of Terrorism, Security and Development', *Journal of International Development* 18(1): 51–67.

Beatley, T. and Wheeler, S. M. (eds) (2004), *The Sustainable Urban Development Reader*. London: Routledge.

Bebbington, A. J., Hickey, S. and Mitlin, D. C. (eds) (2008), *Can NGOs Make a Difference?*, London: Zed Books.

Bebbington, A., Lewis, D., Batterbury, S., Olson, E. and Shameem Siddiqi, M. (2007), 'Of Texts and Practices: Empowerment and Organizational Cultures in World Bank-funded Rural Development Programmes', *Journal of Development Studies* 43(4): 597–621.

Beck, U. (1999), *World Risk Society*, Cambridge: Polity.

Beck, U. (2000), *What is Globalization?*, Cambridge: Polity.

Beck, U. (2002), 'The Cosmopolitan Perspective: Sociology in the Second Age of Modernity', in S. Vertovec and R. Cohen (eds), *Conceiving Cosmopolitanism*, Oxford: Oxford University Press, pp. 61–85.

Beck, U., Giddens, A. and Lash, S. (1995), *Reflexive Modernization*, Cambridge: Polity.

Beckerman, W. (2003), *A Poverty of Reason*, Oakland, CA: The Independent Institute.

Beckford, G. (1972), *Persistent Poverty: Underdevelopment in Plantation Economies of the Third World*, New York: Oxford University Press.

Beenstock, M. (1984), *The World Economy in Transition*, 2nd edn, London: George Allen and Unwin.

Bellamy, A. J., Williams, P. and Griffin, S. (2004), *Understanding Peacekeeping*, Cambridge: Polity.

Bello, W. (1995), 'Export-Led Development in East Asia: A Flawed Model', in R. Ayres (ed.), *Development Studies*, Dartford: Greenwich University Press, pp. 342–54.

Ben-David, D. (1993), 'Equalizing Exchange: Trade Liberalization and Income Convergence', *Quarterly Journal of Economics* 108(3): 653–79.

Ben-Eli, M. (2007), 'Defining Sustainability', *Resurgence* 244: 12–14.

Berger, M. (1994), 'The End of the Third World', *Third World Quarterly* 15(2): 257–75.

Berger, S. and Dore, R. (eds) (1996), *National Diversity and Global Capitalism*, Ithaca: Cornell University Press.

Berman, M. (1983), *All That Is Solid Melts Into Air*, London: Verso.

Bhagwati, J. (2004), *In Defence of Globalisation*, Oxford: Oxford University Press.

Bhagwati, J. (2006), *Free Trade Today*, Princeton: Princeton University Press.

Bhagwati, J. and Panagariya, A. (2001), 'The Truth about Protectionism', *Financial Times*, 29 March.

Bhagwati, J. and Srinivasan, T. N. (2001), 'Outward-Orientation and Development: Are Revisionists Right?', in D. Lal and R. Snape (eds), *Trade, Development and Political Economy: Essays in Honour of Anne Krueger*, London: Palgrave.

Biermann, F. and Bauer, S. (eds) (2005), *A World Environmental Organization*, Aldershot: Ashgate.

Binns, T. (1994), *Tropical Africa*, London: Routledge.

Binns, T. (2002), 'Dualistic and Unilinear Concepts of Development', in V. Desai and R. B. Potter (eds), *The Companion to Development Studies*, London: Arnold, pp. 75–80.

Black, R. (2006), 'Panel to Recommend a Simplified UN', *BBC News Online*, 8 November, www.bbcnews.co.uk (accessed 23/11/07).

Black, R. and White, H. (eds) (2006), *Targeting Development: Critical Perspectives on the Millennium Development Goals*, London: Routledge.

Blackburn, J., Chambers, R. and Gaventa, J. (2000), *Mainstreaming Participation in Development*, OED Working Paper Series No. 10, Washington, DC: World Bank.

Blaikie, P. (1985), *The Political Economy of Soil Erosion in Developing Countries*, London: Longman.

Blanchflower, K. (2008), 'Aid to Developing World Falls for Second Year', *Guardian Online*, 4 April, www.guardian.co.uk (accessed 18/4/08).

Blewitt, J. (ed.) (2008a), *Community, Empowerment and Sustainable Development*, Totnes: Green Books.

Blewitt, J. (2008b), *Understanding Sustainable Development*, London: Earthscan.

Blomström, M. and Hettne, B. (1984), *Development Theory in Transition*, London: Zed Books.

Boardman, H. (2007), *Africa's Silk Road: China and India's New Economic Frontier*, Washington, DC: World Bank.

Bøås, M. and Jennings, K. M. (2007), '"Failed States" and "State Failure": Threats or Opportunities?', *Globalizations* 4(4): 475–85.

Bongaarts, J. (1997), 'The Role of Family Planning Programmes in Contemporary Fertility Transitions', in G. W. Jones, R. M. Douglas, J. C. Caldwell and R. M. D'Souza (eds), *The Continuing Demographic Transition*, New York: Oxford University Press, pp. 422–43.

Booth, D. (1985), 'Marxism and Development Sociology: Interpreting the Impasse', *World Development* 13: 761–87.

Bora, S., Bouët, A. and Roy, D. (2007), 'The Marginalization of Africa in World Trade', *International Food Policy Research Institute*, www.ifpri.org/pubs/ib/rb07.asp (accessed 29/6/08).

Borger, J. (2008), 'Darfur Peacekeepers Struggling to Cope', *Guardian Online*, 12 September, www.guardian.co.uk (accessed 19/9/08).

Bornschier, V. (2005), *Culture and Politics in Economic Development*, London: Routledge.

Boseley, S. (2006), '"Terrible Silence" over Mbeki's Record on AIDS', *Guardian Online*, 19 August, www.guardian.co.uk (accessed 19/10/06).

Boseley, S. (2008), 'Mbeki Aids Denial "Caused 300,000 Deaths"', *Guardian Online*, 26 November, www.guardian.co.uk (accessed 6/6/10).

Boserup, E. (1993[1965]), *The Conditions of Agricultural Growth*, London: Earthscan.

Boserup, E. (2007[1970]), *Woman's Role in Economic Development*, London: Earthscan.

Bowden, R. (2002), 'Young People, Education and Development', in V. Desai and R. B. Potter (eds), *The Companion to Development Studies*, London: Arnold, pp. 405–9.

Boyer, R. and Drache, D. (eds) (1996), *States against Markets*, London: Routledge.

Bracking, S. (1999), 'Structural Adjustment: Why it Wasn't Necessary and Why it Didn't Work', *Review of African Political Economy* 26(80): 207–26.

Brahimi, L. (2000), *Report of the Panel on United Nations Peace Operations* (A/55/305), UN General Assembly Security Council, www.un.org/peace/reports (accessed 14/9/08).

Brainard, L. and Chollet, D. (eds) (2007), *Too Poor for Peace?*, Washington, DC: Brookings Institution Press.

Brandt Commission (1980), *North–South: A Programme for Survival*, London: Pan.

Brandt Commission (1983), *Common Crisis: North–South Cooperation for World Recovery*, London: Pan.

Breitmeier, H., Young, O. R. and Zurn, M. (2006), *Analyzing International Environmental Regimes*, Cambridge, MA: MIT Press.

Bremner, J., Haub, C., Lee, M., Mather, M. and Zuehlke, E. (2009), 'World Population Highlights 2009', *Population Reference Bureau* 64(3), www.prb.org (accessed 11/5/10).

Brenner, N. (1998), 'Global Cities, Glocal States: Global City Formation and State Territorial Restructuring in Contemporary Europe', *Review of International Political Economy* 5(1): 1–37.

Brenner, N. and Keil, R. (eds) (2005), *The Global Cities Reader*, London: Routledge.

Brewer, A. (1990), *Marxist Theories of Imperialism: A Critical Survey*, 2nd edn, London: Routledge.

Bristow, M. (2007), 'Has China's One-Child Policy Worked?', *BBC News Online*, 20 September, www.bbcnews.co.uk (accessed 29/9/07).

Broad, R. (2004), 'The Washington Consensus Meets the Global Backlash: Shifting Debates and Policies', *Globalizations* 1(2): 129–54.

Brohman, J. (1996), *Popular Development: Rethinking the Theory and Practice of Development*, Oxford: Blackwell.

Brookfield, H. (1975), *Interdependent Development*, London: Methuen.

Brown, E. (1996), 'Deconstructing Development: Alternative Perspectives on the History of an Idea', *Historical Geography* 22(3): 33–9.

Brown, O., Halle, M., Peña Moreno, S. and Winkler, S. (eds) (2007), *Trade, Aid and Security*, London: Earthscan.

Browne, S. (2006), *Aid and Influence*, London: Earthscan.

Brune, N. and Garrett, G. (2005), 'The Globalization Rorschach Test: International Economic Integration, Inequality and the Role of Government', *Annual Review of Political Science*, vol. 8.

Bruno, K. and Karliner, J. (2002), *earthsummit.biz: The Corporate Takeover of Sustainable Development*, Oakland: Food First Books.

Brydon, L. and Chant, S. (1989), *Women in the Third World*, Aldershot: Elgar.

Bryer, D. and Magrath, J. (1999), 'New Dimensions of Global Advocacy', *Nonprofit and Voluntary Sector Quarterly* 28(4): 168–77.

Buchan, J. and Dovlo, D. (2004), *International Recruitment of Health Workers to the UK: A Report for DFID*, www.healthsystemsrc.org/publications/reports (accessed 30/5/10).

Buira, A. (ed.) (2005), *Reforming the Governance of the IMF and the World Bank*, London: Anthem Press.

Burbach, R. et al. (1997), *Globalization and its Discontents*, London: Pluto.

Burnell, P. (1997), *Foreign Aid in a Changing World*, Buckingham: Open University Press.

Burnell, P. (ed.) (2000), *Democracy Assistance: International Co-operation for Democratization*, London: Frank Cass.

Burnside, C. and Dollar, D. (2000), 'Aid, Policies and Growth', *American Economic Review* 90: 847–68.

Byers, S. (2003), 'Can the WTO Work for the Poorest?', in P. Griffith (ed.), *Rethinking Fair Trade*, London: Foreign Policy Centre, pp. 55–8.

Caldwell, L. (1996), *International Environmental Policy*, Durham, NC: Duke University Press.

Cameron, A. and Palan, R. (2004), *The Imagined Economies of Globalization*, London: Sage.

Cardoso, F. H. (1977), 'The Consumption of Dependency Theory in the United States', *Latin American Research Review* 12(3): 7–24.

Cardoso, F. H. and Faletto, E. (1979[1969]), *Dependency and Development in Latin America*, California: University of California Press.

Carroll, R. and Boseley, S. (2004), 'The Greatest Catastrophe', *Guardian Unlimited*, 10 December, www.guardian.co.uk (accessed 9/6/10).

Carson, R. (1962), *Silent Spring*, St Louis: Houghton Mifflin.

Castells, M. (1993), 'European Cities, the Information Society and the Global Economy', in A. Gray and J. McGuigan (eds), *Studying Culture*, London: Arnold.

Castells, M. (1996), *The Rise of the Network Society*, vol. 1, Oxford: Blackwell.

CGD (2008), *The Growth Report: Strategies for Sustained Growth and Inclusive Development*, Commission on Growth and Development, www.growthcommission.org (accessed 23/6/08).

Chambers, R. (1983), *Rural Development: Putting the Last First*, London: Longman.

Chambers, R. (1997), *Whose Reality Counts? Putting the First Last*, London: ITDG Publishing.

Chambers, R. (2005), *Ideas for Development*, London: Earthscan.

Chang, H.-J. (2002a), *Kicking Away the Ladder: Development Strategy in Historical Perspective*, London: Anthem Press.

Chang, H.-J. (2002b), 'Breaking the Mould: An Institutionalist Political Economy Alternative to the Neo-liberal Theory of the Market and the State', *Cambridge Journal of Economics* 26(5): 539–59.

Chang, H.-J. (ed.) (2003a), *Rethinking Development Economics*, London: Anthem Press.

Chang, H.-J. (2003b), 'The East Asian Development Experience', in H.-J. Chang (ed.), *Rethinking Development Economics*, London: Anthem Press, pp. 107–24.

Chang, H.-J. (2003c), *Globalization, Economic Development and the Role of the State*, London: Zed Books.

Chang, H.-J. (2003d), 'Trade and Industrial Policy Issues', in H.-J. Chang (ed.), *Rethinking Development Economics*, London: Anthem Press, pp. 257–76.

Chang, H.-J. (2007), *Bad Samaritans*, London: Random House.

Chang, H.-J. and Grabel, I. (2004), *Reclaiming Development*, London: Zed Books.

Chant, S. (2000), 'Men in Crisis? Reflections on Masculinities, Work and Family in Northwest Costa Rica', *European Journal of Development Research* 12(2): 199–218.

Chant, S. and Gutmann, M. C. (2000), *Mainstreaming Men into Gender and Development*, Oxford: Oxfam.

Chant, S. and Gutmann, M. C. (2005), '"Men-streaming" Gender? Questions for Gender and Development Policy in the Twenty-first century', in M. Edelman and A. Haugerud (eds), *The Anthropology of Development and Globalization*, Oxford: Blackwell, pp. 240–9.

Chasek, P. S., Downie, D. L. and Welsh Brown, J. (2006), *Global Environmental Politics*, 4th edn, Boulder, CO: Westview Press.

Chatterjee, D. K. and Scheid, D. E. (eds) (2003), *Ethics and Foreign Intervention*, Cambridge: Cambridge University Press.

Cheater, A. (ed.) (1999), *The Anthropology of Power: Empowerment and Disempowerment in Changing Structures*, London: Routledge.

Chen, S. and Ravallion, M. (2008), 'The Developing World is Poorer than We Thought, but No Less Successful in the Fight against Poverty', *World Bank Report*, 26 August, www.worldbank.org (accessed 17/4/11).

Cho, G. (1995), *Trade, Aid and Global Interdependence*, London: Routledge.

Chomsky, N. (2000), *Rogue States*, London: Pluto.

CHS (2003), *Human Security Now*, New York: Commission on Human Security, www.humansecurity–chs.org/finalreport/ (accessed 8/9/08).

Clapham, C. (2002), 'The Challenge to the State in a Globalized World', *Development and Change* 33(5): 775–95.

Clapp, J. (2002), 'What the Pollution Havens Debate Overlooks', *Global Environmental Politics* 2(2): 1–19.

Clapp, J. and Dauvergne, P. (2005), *Paths to a Green World: The Political Economy of the Global Environment*, Cambridge, MA: MIT Press.

Clark, D. (2003), *Urban World/Global City*, London: Routledge.

Clarke, C. (2002), 'The Latin American Structuralists', in V. Desai and R. B. Potter (eds), *The Companion to Development Studies*, London: Arnold, pp. 92–6.

Cleaver, F. (2001), 'Institutions, Agency and the Limitations of Participatory Approaches to Development', in B. Cooke and U. Kothari (eds), *Participation: The New Tyranny?*, London: Zed Books, pp. 35–55.

Cleaver, F. (2004), 'The Social Embeddedness of Agency and Decision-making', in S. Hickey and G. Mohan (eds), *Participation: From Tyranny to Transformation?*, London: Zed Books, pp. 271–7.

Cleaver, K. and Schreiber, G. (1994), *Reversing the Spiral: The Population, Agriculture and Environment Nexus in Sub-Saharan Africa*, Washington, DC: World Bank.

Clegg, S., Redding, G. S. and Carte, M. (eds) (1990), *Capitalism in Contrasting Cultures*, Amsterdam: Walter de Gruyter & Co.

Clifford, J. (1992), 'Travelling Cultures', in L. Grossberg, C. Nelson and P. Treichler (eds), *Cultural Studies*, London: Routledge, pp. 96–116.

Clifton, D. and Gell, F. (2001), 'Saving and Protecting Lives by Empowering Women', in C. Sweetman (ed.), *Gender, Development and Humanitarian Work*, Oxford: Oxfam, pp. 8–18.

Cloke, P., Crang, P. and Goodwin, M. (eds) (2005), *Introducing Human Geographies*, 2nd edn, London: Hodder Arnold.

Coale, A. J. and Hoover, E. M. (1958), *Population Growth and Economic Development in Low-Income Countries*, Princeton, NJ: Princeton University Press.

Cohen, J. L. (1995), *How Many People Can the Earth Support?*, New York: W. W. Norton.

Collier, P. (2000), 'Doing Well Out of War: An Economic Perspective', in M. Berdal and D. M. Malone (eds), *Greed and Grievance: Economic Agendas in Civil Wars*, Boulder: Lynne Rienner, pp. 91–111.

Collier, P. (2007), *The Bottom Billion*, Oxford: Oxford University Press.

Collier, P. and Hoeffler, A. (1998), 'On Economic Causes of Civil War', *Oxford Economic Papers* 50: 563–73.

Collier, P. and Hoeffler, A. (2004a), *The Challenge of Reducing the Global Incidence of Civil War*, Copenhagen: Copenhagen Consensus Papers.

Collier, P. and Hoeffler, A. (2004b), 'Conflicts', in B. Lomborg (ed.), *Global Crises, Global Solutions*, Cambridge: Cambridge University Press, pp. 129–56.

Collier, P. and Hoeffler, A. (2004c), 'Greed and Grievance in Civil War', *Oxford Economic Papers* 56(4): 563–95.

Collier, P. and Sambanis, N. (eds) (2005), *Understanding Civil War*, vols 1 and 2, Washington, DC: World Bank.

Collier, P., Guillaumont, P., Guillaumont, S. and Gunning, J. W. (1997), 'Redesigning Conditionality', *World Development* 25(9) (Sept.): 1399–407.

Collier, P., Elliot, L., Hegre, H., Hoeffler, A., Reyna-Quirol, M. and Sambanis, N. (2003), *Breaking the Conflict Trap*, Washington, DC: World Bank and Oxford University Press.

Comaroff, J. and Comaroff, J. L. (eds) (2000), *Civil Society and the Political Imagination in Africa: Critical Perspectives*, Chicago: University of Chicago Press.

Cooke, B. (2004), 'The Managing of the (Third) World', *Organization* 11(5): 603–29.

Cooke, B. and Kothari, U. (eds) (2001a), *Participation: The New Tyranny?*, London: Zed Books.

Cooke, B. and Kothari, U. (2001b), 'The Case for Participation as Tyranny', in B. Cooke and U. Kothari (eds), *Participation: The New Tyranny?*, London: Zed Books, pp. 1–15.

Cooper, A. (2006), *World Issues: Fair Trade?*, London: Aladdin.

Cooper, F. (2002), *Africa Since 1940: The Past of the Present*, Cambridge: Cambridge University Press.

Cooper, F. and Packard, R. (2005), 'The History and Politics of Development Knowledge', in M. Edelman and A. Haugerud (eds), *The Anthropology of Development and Globalization*, Oxford: Blackwell, pp. 126–39.

Corbridge, S. (1993), *Debt and Development*, Oxford: Blackwell.

Corbridge, S. (ed.) (1995), *Development Studies: A Reader*, London: Edward Arnold.

Corbridge, S. (1998a), 'Beneath the Pavement Only Soil: The Poverty of Post-Development', *Journal of Development Studies* 34(6): 138–48.

Corbridge, S. (1998b), 'Development Ethics: Distance, Difference, Plausibility', *Ethics, Place and Environment* 1(1): 35–53.

Corbridge, S. (2002a), 'Development as Freedom: The Spaces of Amartya Sen', *Progress in Development Studies* 2(3): 183–217.

Corbridge, S. (2002b), 'Third World Debt', in V. Desai and R. B. Potter (eds), *The Companion to Development Studies*, London: Arnold, pp. 477–80.

Cornia, G. A. (ed.) (2005) *Inequality, Growth, and Poverty in an Era of Liberalization and Globalization*, Oxford: Oxford University Press.

Cornia, G. A. and Court, J. (2001), *Inequality, Growth and Poverty in the Era of Liberalization and Globalization – A Policy Brief*, Helsinki: UNU/WIDER.

Cornwall, A. (1997), 'Men, Masculinity and Gender in Development', *Gender and Development* 5(2): 8–13.

Cornwall, A. and White, S. C. (2000), 'Introduction: Men, Masculinities and Development – Politics, Policies and Practices', *IDS Bulletin* 31(2): 1–6.

Cornwall, A., Harrison, E. and Whitehead, A. (eds) (2007), *Feminisms in Development*, London: Zed Books.

Cowen, M. P. and Shenton, R. W. (1996), *Doctrines of Development*, London: Routledge.

Craig, G. and Mayo, M. (1994), *Community Empowerment*, London: Zed Books.

Craig, D. and Porter, D. (2006), *Development Beyond Neoliberalism?*, London: Routledge.

Crawford, G. (2006), 'The World Bank and Good Governance: Rethinking the State or Consolidating Neo-liberalism?', in A. Paloni and M. Zanardi (eds), *The IMF, World Bank and Policy Reform*, London: Routledge, pp. 115–41.

Crewe, E. and Harrison, E. (1998), *Whose Development? An Anthropology of Aid*, London: Zed Books.

Croll, E. and Parkin, D. (1992), 'Anthropology, the Environment and Development', in E. Croll and D. Parkin (eds), *Bush Base, Forest Farm: Culture, Environment and Development*, London: Routledge.

Crush, J. (ed.) (1995), *Power of Development*, London: Routledge.

Cvetkovich, A. and Kellner, D. (eds) (1997), *Articulating the Global and the Local*, Boulder, CO: Westview.

DAC (2008), 'Evaluating Conflict Prevention and Peacebuilding Activities', *Organization for Economic Co-operation and Development*, www.oecd.org/dac/conflict (accessed 14/9/08).

Dalal-Clayton, B. and Bass, S. (2002), *Sustainable Development Strategies*, London: Earthscan.

Dalby, S. (2002), *Environmental Security*, Minneapolis: University of Minnesota Press.

Dale, R. (2004), *Development Planning: Concepts and Tools for Planners, Managers and Facilitators*, London: Zed Books.

Dalla Costa, M. (1995), *Paying the Price: Women and the Politics of International Economic Strategy*, London: Zed Books.

Daly, H. (1992), *Steady-State Economics*, London: Earthscan.

Dannreuther, R. (2007), *International Security*, Cambridge: Polity.

Davids, T. and van Driel, F. (2001), 'Globalization and Gender: Beyond Dichotomies', in F. J. Schuurman (ed.), *Globalization and Development Studies*, London: Sage, pp. 153–75.

Davidson, B. (1992), *The Black Man's Burden: Africa and the Curse of the Nation-State*, London: James Currey.

Davis, E. (2006), 'The Death of the WTO's Doha Talks', *BBC News Online*, 25 July, www.bbcnews.co.uk (accessed 19/11/06).

Davis, M. (2006), *Planet of the Slums*, London: Verso.

De Beer, F. and Swanepoel, H. (eds) (2000), *Introduction to Development Studies*, 2nd edn, Oxford: Oxford University Press.

De Souza, R.-M., Williams, J. S. and Meyerson, F. A. B. (2003), 'Critical Links: Population, Health, and the Environment', *Population Bulletin* 58(3).

Degnbol-Martinussen, J. and Engberg-Pedersen, P. (2003), *Aid*, London: Zed Books.

Demeny, P. and McNicoll, G. (1998), *The Earthscan Reader in Population and Development*, London: Earthscan.

Dent, M. and Peters, B. (1999), *The Crisis of Poverty and Debt in the Third World*, Aldershot: Ashgate.

Desai, V. (2002a), 'Role of Non-governmental Organizations (NGOs)', in V. Desai and R. B. Potter (eds), *The Companion to Development Studies*, London: Arnold, pp. 495–9.

Desai, V. (2002b), 'Community Participation in Development', in V. Desai and R. B. Potter (eds), *The Companion to Development Studies*, London: Arnold, pp. 117–21.

Desai, V. and Potter, R. B. (eds) (2002), *The Companion to Development Studies*, London: Arnold.

Devereux, S. and Maxwell, S. (2001), *Food Security in Sub-Saharan Africa*, London: ITDG Publishing.

DFID (2006) 'Eliminating World Poverty: Making Governance Work for the Poor', White Paper Cm 6876, Department for International Development, London: HMSO.

DFID (2011), *Annual Report & Resource Accounts 2009–10*, Third Report of Session 2010–11, Vol. 1, London: HMSO.

Díaz-Alejandro, C. F. (1988), *Trade, Development and the World Economy: Selected Essays of Carlos F. Díaz-Alejandro* (ed. A. Velasco), Oxford: Blackwell.

Dicken, P. (2003), *Global Shift: Reshaping the Global Economic Map in the 21st Century*, 4th edn, London: Sage.

Dickenson, J. et al. (1996), *A Geography of the Third World*, 2nd edn, London: Routledge.

Dicklitch, S. (1998), *The Elusive Promise of NGOs in Africa: Lessons from Uganda*, New York: St Martins.

Di John, J. (2007), 'Oil Abundance and Violent Political Conflict: A Critical Assessment', *Journal of Development Studies* 43(6): 961–86.

Dirlik, A. (2007), 'Global South: Predicament and Promise', *The Global South* 1(1 and 2): 12–23.

Dissanayake, S. (2006), 'Sri Lanka Banks on Poorest Women', *BBC News Online*, 6 April, www.bbcnews.co.uk (accessed 21/03/08).

Dixon, C. (1999), 'The Pacific Asian Challenge to Neoliberalism', in D. Simon and A. Närman (eds), *Development as Theory and Practice: Current Perspectives on Development and Development Co-operation*, Harlow: Longman, pp. 205–29.

Dobson, A. (1990), *Green Political Thought*, London: Routledge.

Dobson, A. (2000), 'Sustainable Development and the Defence of the Natural World', in K. Lee, A. Holland and D. McNeill (eds), *Global Sustainable Development in the 21st Century*, Edinburgh: Edinburgh University Press, pp. 49–61.

Dodds, K. (2002), 'The Third World, Developing Countries, the South, Poor Countries', in V. Desai and R. B. Potter (eds), *The Companion to Development Studies*, London: Arnold, pp. 3–7.

Dollar, D. (1992), 'Outward-oriented Developing Economies Really Do Grow more Rapidly: Evidence from 95 LDCs, 1976–1985', *Economic Development and Cultural Change* 40(3): 523–44.

Dollar, D. (2007), 'Globalization, Poverty, and Inequality since 1980', in D. Held and A. Kaya (eds), *Global Inequality*, Cambridge: Polity, pp. 73–103.

Dollar, D., and Kraay, A. (2001), 'Growth is Good for the Poor', Development Research Group Draft (March), World Bank: Washington, DC.

Dollar, D. and Kraay, A. (2002a), 'Spreading the Wealth', *Foreign Affairs* 81(1): 120–33.

Dollar, D., and Kraay, A. (2002b), 'Trade, Growth, and Poverty', Development Research Group, Draft, July, World Bank: Washington, DC, pp. 1–34.

Dowden, R. (2005), 'Aid "Is Not Solution" for Africa', *BBC News Online*, 24 June, www.bbcnews.co.uk (accessed 19/11/05).

Doyle, M. (2006), 'Can Aid Bring an End to Poverty?', *BBC News Online*, 4 October, www.bbcnews.co.uk (accessed 29/11/06).

Drahos, P. and Braithwaite, J. (2002), *Information Feudalism*, London: Earthscan.

Dresner, S. (2002), *The Principles of Sustainability*, London: Earthscan.

Drinkwater, M. (1992), 'Cows Eat Grass Don't They? Evaluating Conflict over Pastoral Management in Zimbabwe', in E. Croll and D. Parkin (eds), *Bush Base, Forest Farm: Culture, Environment and Development*, London: Routledge.

Duffield, M. (2001), *Global Governance and the New Wars*, London: Zed Books.

Duffield, M. (2007), *Development, Security and Unending War*, Cambridge: Polity.

Dunkley, G. (2004), *Free Trade: Myth, Reality and Alternatives*, London: Zed Books.

Dunn, J. (ed.) (1995), *Contemporary Crisis of the Nation-State?*, Oxford: Blackwell.

Eade, D. (2000), *Development, NGOs and Civil Society*, Bloomfield, CT: Kumarian Press.

Easterly, W. (2003), 'Can Foreign Aid Buy Growth?', *Journal of Economic Perspectives*, 17(3): 23–48.

Easterly, W. (2006), *The White Man's Burden*, Oxford: Oxford University Press.

Easterly, W. and Levine, R. (1997), 'Africa's Growth Tragedy: Policies and Ethnic Divisions', *Quarterly Journal of Economics* 112(4): 1203–50.

Ebrahim, A. (2003), *NGOs and Organizational Change*, Cambridge: Cambridge University Press.

ECIPE (2007), 'Africa and World Trade', *European Centre for International Political Economy*, www.ecipe.org (accessed 27/6/08).

Eckes, A. E., Jr and Zeiler, T. W. (2003), *Globalization and the American Century*, Cambridge: Cambridge University Press.

Economist, The (2001), *Globalisation*, London: Profile.

Edelman, M. (1999), *Peasants Against Globalization: Rural Social Movements in Costa Rica*, Stanford: Stanford University Press.

Edelman, M. and Haugerud, A. (eds) (2005), *The Anthropology of Development and Globalization*, Oxford: Blackwell.

Edwards, M. (1989), 'The Irrelevance of Development Studies', *Third World Quarterly* 11(1): 116–36.

Edwards, M. (2001a), 'The Rise and Rise of Civil Society', *Developments: The International Development Magazine* 14(2): 5–7.

Edwards, M. (2001b), 'Introduction', in M. Edwards and J. Gaventa (eds), *Global Citizen Action*, Boulder, CO: Lynne Rienner, pp. 1–16.

Edwards, M. (2008), 'Have NGOs "Made a Difference"? From Manchester to Birmingham with an Elephant in the Room', in A. J. Bebbington et al. (eds), *Can NGOs Make a Difference?*, London: Zed Books, pp. 38–52.

Edwards, M. and Hulme, D. (eds) (1992), *Making a Difference: NGOs and Development in a Changing World*, London: Earthscan.

Edwards, M. and Hulme, D. (eds) (1995), *NGOs – Performance and Accountability*, London: Earthscan.

Edwards, S. (1998), 'Openness, Productivity and Growth: What Do We Really Know?', *Economic Journal* 108: 383–98.

Ehrlich, P. R. and Ehrlich, A. H. (1990), *The Population Explosion*, New York: Simon & Schuster.

Eisenstadt, S. N. (eds) (2002), *Multiple Modernities*, New Brunswick: Transaction.

Eisenstadt, S. N. (2003), *Comparative Civilizations and Multiple Modernities*, Vols 1 and 2, Leiden: Brill.

Elliott, J. A. (1999), *An Introduction to Sustainable Development*, 2nd edn, London: Routledge.

Elliott, J. A. (2002), 'Development as Improving Human Welfare and Human Rights', in V. Desai and R. B. Potter (eds), *The Companion to Development Studies*, London: Arnold, pp. 45–9.

Elliott, L. (2004), *The Global Politics of the Environment*, 2nd edn, Basingstoke: Palgrave.

Elliott, L. (2008), 'Developing World Set to Overtake the West, PWC Argues', *Guardian Online*, 31 October, www.guardian.co.uk (accessed 13/02/09).

Elson, D. (1991), 'Structural Adjustment: Its Effect on Women', in T. Wallace and C. March (eds), *Changing Perceptions: Writings on Gender and Development*, Oxford: Oxfam.

Elson, D. (ed.) (1995a), *Male Bias in the Development Process*, 2nd edn, Manchester: Manchester University Press.

Elson, D. (1995b), 'Gender Awareness in Modeling Structural Adjustment', *World Development* (special issue on gender, adjustment and macroeconomics) 23(11): 1851–68.

Elson, D. and Pearson, R. (1981), '"Nimble Fingers Make Cheap Workers": An Analysis of Women's Employment in Third World Export Manufacturing', *Feminist Review* 7: 87–107.

Emmanuel, A. (1972), *Unequal Exchange: A Study of the Imperialism of Trade*, New York: Monthly Review Press.

England, R. S. (2005), *Aging China*, London: Praeger.

Eriksen, T. H. (ed.) (2003), *Globalisation: Studies in Anthropology*, London: Pluto.

Escobar, A. (1995a), *Encountering Development: The Making and Unmaking of the Third World*, Princeton, NJ: Princeton University Press.

Escobar, A. (1995b), 'Imagining a Post-Development Era', in J. Crush (ed.), *Power of Development*, London: Routledge, pp. 211–27.

Escobar, A. (2002), 'The Problematization of Poverty: The Tale of Three Worlds and Development', in S. Schech and J. Haggis (eds), *Development: A Cultural Studies Reader*, Oxford: Blackwell, pp. 79–92.

Esteva, G. (1987), 'Regenerating People's Space', *Alternatives* 10(3): 125–52.

Esteva, G. (1992), 'Development', in W. Sachs (ed.), *The Development Dictionary: A Guide to Knowledge as Power*, London: Zed Books, pp. 6–25.

Esteva, G. and Prakash, M. S. (1998), *Grassroots Post-Modernism: Remaking the Soil of Cultures*, London: Zed Books.

Esty, D. C. and Ivanova, M. H. (eds) (2002), *Global Environmental Governance*, New Haven, CN: Yale School of Forestry and Environmental Studies.

Esty, D. C. and Ivanova, M. H. (2003), 'Toward a Global Environmental Mechanism', in J. G. Speth (ed.), *Globalisation and the Environment*, London: Island Press, pp. 67–82.

Etzioni, A. (2004), 'A Self-restrained Approach to Nation-building by Foreign Powers', *International Affairs* 80(1): 1–17.

Evans, A. (1992), 'Statistics', in L. Ostergaard (ed.), *Gender and Development: A Practical Guide*, London: Routledge.

Evans, P. B., Rueschemeyer, D. and Skocpol, T. (eds) (1985), *Bringing the State Back In*, Cambridge: Cambridge University Press.

Fabian, J. (1983), *Time and the Other: How Anthropology Makes its Object*, New York: Colombia University Press.

Fairtrade Foundation (2010), *The Great Cotton Stitch-Up*, A Fairtrade Foundation Report, November 2010, www.fairtrade.org.uk.

Fals-Borda, O. (1988), *Knowledge and People's Power*, New Dehli: Indian Social Institute.

FAO (2008), *The State of Food Insecurity in the World 2008*, www.fao.org/docrep/011/i0291e/io291e00.pdf (accessed 3/10/09).

Faria, J. R., León-Ledesma, M. A. and Sachsida, A. (2006), 'Population and Income: Is There a Puzzle?', *Journal of Development Studies* 42(6): 909–17.

Fearon, J. (2002), 'Why Do Some Civil Wars Last So Much Longer than Others?', *Journal of Peace Research* 41(3): 275–301.

Featherstone, M. (ed.) (1990), *Global Culture*, London: Sage.

Featherstone, M. (1995), *Undoing Culture*, London: Sage.

Ferguson, A. (1998), 'Resisting the Veil of Privilege: Building Bridge Identities as an Ethico-politics of Global Feminisms', *Hypatia: Special Issue. Border Crossings: Multicultural and Feminist Challenges to Philosophy*, Part 2, 13(3): 95–114.

Ferguson, J. (1994), *The Anti-Politics Machine: 'Development', Depoliticization, and Bureaucratic Power in Lesotho*, Minneapolis: University of Minnesota Press.

Ferguson, J. (2005), 'Anthropology and Its Evil Twin: "Development" in the Constitution of a Discipline', in M. Edelman and A. Haugerud (eds), *The Anthropology of Development and Globalization*, Oxford: Blackwell, pp. 140–53.

Field, J. (2008), *Social Capital*, 2nd edn, London: Routledge.

Fine, B. (1999), 'The Developmental State Is Dead – Long Live Social Capital?', *Development and Change* 30: 1–19.

Finkle, J. L. (1995), 'The Cairo Conference on Population and Development: A New Paradigm?', *Population and Development Review* 21(2): 223–60.

Firebaugh, G. (2003) *The New Geography of Global Income Inequality*, Harvard: Harvard University Press.

Fisher, J. (1998), *Non Governments: NGOs and the Political Development of the Third World*, West Hartford: Kumarian Press.

FLO (2007), 'An Inspiration for Change', *Fairtrade Labelling Organizations International Annual Report 2007*, www.fairtrade.net (accessed 23/8/08).

Folbre, N. (1986), 'Hearts and Spades: Paradigms of Household Economics', *World Development* 14(2): 245–55.

Font, M. (2001), 'The Craft of a New Era: The Intellectual Trajectory of Fernando Henrique Cardoso', in M. Font (ed.), *Charting a New Course: The Politics of Globalization and Social Transformation: Fernando Henrique Cardoso*, Lanham, MD: Rowman & Littlefield, pp. 1–34.

Foong-Khong, Y. (2001), 'Human Security: A Shotgun Approach to Alleviating Human Misery?', *Global Governance* 7(3): 231–6.

Forsyth, T. (2002), 'The Brown Environmental Agenda', in V. Desai and R. B. Potter (eds), *The Companion to Development Studies*, London: Arnold, pp. 294–7.

Fortanier, F. (2005), *Networking for Development*, London: Routledge.

Foucault, M. (1980), *Power/Knowledge: Selected Interviews and Other Writings*, Brighton: Harvester Wheatsheaf.

Foulkes, I. (2006), 'World Health Care Deficit Warning', *BBC News Online*, 6 April (accessed 28/5/10).

Fowler, A. (1997), *Striking a Balance*, London: Earthscan.

Fowler, A. F. (1998), 'Authentic NGDO Partnerships in the New Policy Agenda for International aid: Dead-end or Light Ahead?', *Development and Change* 29: 137–59.

Fox, J. (2005), 'Advocacy Research and the World Bank: Propositions for Discussion', in M. Edelman and A. Haugerud (eds), *The Anthropology of Development and Globalization*, Oxford: Blackwell, pp. 306–12.

Fox, J. A. and Brown, L. D. (eds) (1998), *The Struggle for Accountability: The World Bank, NGOs, and Grassroots Movements*, Cambridge, MA: MIT Press.

Francis, P. (2002), 'Social Capital, Civil Society and Social Exclusion', in U. Kothari and M. Minogue (eds), *Development Theory and Practice: Critical Perspectives*, pp. 71–91.

Frank, A. G. (1967), *Capitalism and Underdevelopment in Latin America*, New York: Monthly Review.

Frankel, J. and Romer, D. (1999), 'Does Trade Cause Growth?', *American Economic Review* 89(3): 379–99.

Freire, P. (1970), *Pedagogy of the Oppressed*, New York: The Seabury Press.

Freire, P. (1974), *Education for Critical Consciousness*, London: Sheed and Ward.

Friedman, J. (1999), 'The Hybridization of Roots and the Abhorrence of the Bush', in M. Featherstone and S. Lash (ed.), *Spaces of Culture*, London, Sage, pp. 230–56.

Friedman, T. L. (1999), *The Lexus and the Olive Tree: Understanding Globalization*, New York: Farrar, Straus and Giroux.

Friedmann, J. (1992), *Empowerment: The Politics of Alternative Development*, Oxford: Blackwell.

Friedmann, J. (1994), 'Where We Stand: A Decade of World City Research', in P. Knox and P. J. Tayor (eds), *World Cities in a World-System*, Cambridge: Cambridge University Press.

Friedmann, J. and Weaver, C. (1979), *Territory and Function: The Evolution of Regional Planning*, London: Edward Arnold.

Fritz, V. and Rocha Menocal, A. (2007), 'Developmental States in the New Millennium: Concepts and Challenges for a New Aid Agenda', *Development Policy Review* 25(5): 531–52.

Fukuyama, F. (2001), 'Social Capital, Civil Society and Development', *Third World Quarterly* 22: 7–20.

Fukuyama, F. (2004), *State-Building*, Ithaca, NY: Cornell University Press.

Furedi, F. (1997), *Population and Development*, Cambridge: Polity.

Furley, O. (ed.) (1995), *Conflict in Africa*, London: I. B. Tauris.

Furtado, C. (1963), *The Economic Growth of Brazil*, Los Angeles: University of California Press.

Furtado, C. (1964), *Development and Underdevelopment*, Los Angeles: University of California Press.

Furtado, C. (1969), *Economic Development in Latin America*, Cambridge: Cambridge University Press.

Gallagher, K. P. (2004), *Free Trade and the Environment*, Palo Alto, CA: Stanford University Press.

Gandhi, L. (1998), *Postcolonial Theory: A Critical Introduction*, Edinburgh: Edinburgh University Press.

Gardner, K. and Lewis, D. (1996), *Anthropology, Development and the Post-Modern Challenge*, London: Pluto.

Gardner, K. and Lewis, D. (2005), 'Beyond Development?', in M. Edelman and A. Haugerud (eds), *The Anthropology of Development and Globalization*, Oxford: Blackwell, pp. 352–9.

Gareis, S. B. and Varwick, J. (2005), *The United Nations*, Basingstoke: Palgrave.

Garnaut, R. (1998), 'The East Asian Crisis', in R. H. McLeod and R. Garnaut (eds), *East Asia in Crisis: From Being a Miracle to Needing One?*, London: Routledge, pp. 3–27.

Garrett, G. (1998), 'Global Markets and National Politics', *International Organization* 52(4): 787–824.

Gatter, P. (1993), 'Anthropology in Farming Systems Research: A Participant Observer in Zambia', in J. Pottier (ed.), *Practising Development*, London: Routledge.

Gaventa, J. (2004), 'Towards Participatory Governance: Assessing the Transformative Possibilities', in S. Hickey and G. Mohan (eds), *Participation: From Tyranny to Transformation?*, London: Zed Books, pp. 25–41.

George, S. (1989), *A Fate Worse Than Debt*, Harmondsworth: Penguin.

George, S. (1992), *The Debt Boomerang*, London: Pluto.

Gereffi, G. (2004), 'Is Wal-Mart Good for America?', *Frontline PBS Interview*, 16 November, www.pbs.org/wgbh/pages/frontline/shows/walmart/ (accessed 8/4/11).

Gereffi, G. (2007), *The New Offshoring of Jobs and Global Development*, Geneva: International Labour Organization.

Gereffi, G., Humphrey, J. and Sturgeon, T. (2005), 'The Governance of Global Value Chains', *Review of International Political Economy* 12(1): 78–104.

Gereffi, G., Spener, D. and Blair, J. (eds) (2002), *Free Trade and Uneven Development: The North American Apparel Industry after NAFTA*, Philadelphia: Temple University Press.

Gerschenkron, A. (1962), *Economic Backwardness in Historical Perspective*, Cambridge, MA: The Belnap Press.

Gibson, C. C., Andersson, K., Ostrom, E. and Shivakumar, S. (2005), *The Samaritans Dilemma*, Oxford: Oxford University Press.

Giddens, A. (1990), *The Consequences of Modernity*, Cambridge: Polity.

Giddings, B., Hopwood, B. and O'Brien, G. (2002), 'Environment, Economy and Society: Fitting Them Together into Sustainable Development', *Sustainable Development* 10: 187–96.

Gilpin, R. (2001), *Global Political Economy*, Princeton: Princeton University Press.

Glasze, G., Webster, C. and Frantz, K. (2005), *Private Cities*, London: Routledge.

Glewwe, P. and Hall, G. (1998), 'Are Some Groups More Vulnerable to Macroeconomic Shocks than Others? Hypothesis Tests Based on the Panel Data from Peru', *Journal of Development Economics* 56: 181–206.

Goetz, A. M. (ed.) (1997), *Getting Institutions Right for Women in Development*, London: Zed Books.

Goetz, A. M. (1998), 'Mainstreaming Gender Equity to National Development Planning', in C. Miller and S. Razavi (eds), *Missionaries and Mandarins*, London: UNRISD, pp. 42–86.

Goldman, M. (2005), *Imperial Nature*, New Haven: Yale University Press.

Gould, W. (2006), *Population and Development*, London: Routledge.

Graham, S. and Marvin, S. (2001), *Splintering Urbanism*, London: Routledge.

Greenaway, D. and Milner, C. (2002), 'Trade and Industrial Policy in Developing Countries', in V. Desai and R. B. Potter (eds), *The Companion to Development Studies*, London: Arnold, pp. 196–201.

Greenpeace (2007), 'Carving up the Congo', *Greenpeace*, www.greenpeace.org (accessed 12/12/08).

Greider, W. (1997), *One World, Ready or Not: The Manic Logic of Global Capitalism*, London: Penguin.

Greig, A., Hulme, D. and Turner, M. (2007), *Challenging Global Inequality*, Basingstoke: Palgrave.

Greig, A., Kimmel, M. and Lang, J. (2000), 'Men, Masculinities and Development: Broadening our Work towards Gender Equality', *Gender in Development Monograph Series* 10, New York: UNDP.

Griffin, M. (2005), 'Where Angels Fear to Tread: Trends in International Intervention', in R. Wilkinson (ed.), *The Global Governance Reader*, London: Routledge, pp. 190–203.

Grillo, R. D. (1997), 'Discourses of Development: The View from Anthropology', in R. D. Grillo and R. L. Stirrat (eds), *Discourses of Development: Anthropological Perspectives*, Oxford: Berg, pp. 1–34.

Grillo, R. D. (2002), 'Anthropologists and Development', in V. Desai and R. B. Potter (eds), *The Companion to Development Studies*, London: Arnold, pp. 54–8.

Grillo, R. D. and Stirrat, R. L. (eds) (1997), *Discourses of Development: Anthropological Perspectives*, Oxford: Berg.

Gritsch, M. (2005), 'The Nation-State and Economic Globalization: Soft Geo-politics and Increased State Autonomy?', *Review of International Political Economy* 12(1): 1–25.

Guéhenno, J.-M. (1995), *The End of the Nation-State*, Minneapolis: University of Minnesota Press.

Guijt, I. and Kaul Shah, M. (eds) (1998), *The Myth of Community: Gender Issues in Participatory Development*, Rugby: ITDG Publishing.

Guijt, I. and Kaul Shah, M. (1998a), 'Waking up to Power, Conflict and Process', in I. Guijt and M. Kaul Shah (eds), *The Myth of Community*, Rugby: ITDG Publishing, pp. 1–23.

Gupta, A. and Ferguson, J. (1997), *Culture, Power, Place: Explorations in Critical Anthropology*, Durham: Duke University Press.

Gwynne, R. N. and Kay, C. (eds) (2004), *Latin America Transformed: Globalization and Modernity*, 2nd edn, London: Arnold.

Haines, R. (2000), 'Development theory', in F. De Beer and H. Swanepoel (eds), *Introduction to Development Studies*, 2nd edn, Oxford: Oxford University Press, pp. 31–60.

Hallak, J. and Poisson, M. (2005), 'Ethics and Corruption in Education: An Overview', *Journal of Education for International Development* 1(1): 1–16.

Hamilton, K. and Dixon, J. D. (2003), 'Measuring the Wealth of Nations', *Environmental Monitoring and Assessment* 86(1–2): 75–89.

Hanlon, J. (2004), 'It Is Possible to Just Give Money to the Poor', in J. P. Pronk et al. (eds), *Catalysing Development?*, Oxford: Blackwell, pp. 181–9.

Hann, C. and Dunn, E. (eds) (1996), *Civil Society: Challenging Western Models*, London: Routledge.

Hannerz, U. (1990), 'Cosmopolitans and Locals in World Culture', in M. Featherstone (ed.), *Global Culture*, London: Sage, pp. 237–51.

Hannerz, U. (2003), 'Several Sites in One', in T. H. Eriksen (ed.), *Globalisation: Studies in Anthropology*, London: Pluto, pp. 18–38.

Haq, M. ul, Kaul, I. and Grunberg, I. (1996), *The Tobin Tax: Coping with Financial Volatility*, New York: Oxford University Press.

Harcourt, W. (1997), 'The Search for Social Justice', *Development* (editorial feature) 40(1): 5–11.

Hardin, G. (1993), *Living within Limits: Ecology, Economics, and Population Taboos*, New York: Oxford University Press.

Hargroves, K. and Smith, M. H. (eds) (2005), *The Natural Advantage of Nations: Business Opportunities, Innovation and Governance in the 21st Century*, London: Earthscan.

Harmer, A. and L. Cotterrell (2005), *Diversity in Donorship: The Changing Landscape of Official Humanitarian Aid*, Humanitarian Project Group Report, September 2005, London: ODI.

Harper, R. (2005), 'The Social Organization of the IMF's Mission Work', in M. Edelman and A. Haugerud (eds), *The Anthropology of Development and Globalization*, Oxford: Blackwell, pp. 323–33.

Harris, N. (1986), *The End of the Third World: Newly Industrializing Countries and the Decline of an Ideology*, Harmondsworth: Penguin.

Harrison, L. E. (2000), *Underdevelopment is a State of Mind: The Latin American Case*, updated edn, Lanham: Madison Books.

Harrison, L. E. and Huntington, S. P. (eds) (2000), *Culture Matters*, New York: Basic Books.

Harrison, P. (1993), *The Third Revolution: Population, Environment, and a Sustainable World*, London: Penguin.

Harriss, J. (2002), *Depoliticizing Development: The World Bank and Social Capital*, London: Anthem Press.

Harriss, J. and de Renzio, P. (1997), '"Missing Link" or Analytically Missing? The Concept of Social Capital: An Introductory Biographic Essay', *Journal of International Development* 9(7): 919–37.

Hartmann, B. (1997), 'Women, Population and the Environment: Whose Consensus? Whose Empowerment?', in N. Visvanathan et al. (eds), *The Women, Gender and Development Reader*, London: Zed Books, pp. 293–302.

Harvey, D. (1989), *The Condition of Postmodernity*, Oxford: Blackwell.

Harvey, D. (2005), *A Brief History of Neoliberalism*, Oxford: Oxford University Press.

Harvey, L. D. D. (2000), *Global Warming: The Hard Science*, Harlow: Pearson.

Hay, C. and Marsh, D. (eds) (2001), *Demystifying Globalization*, Basingstoke: Palgrave.

Hayek, F. A. (1971[1944]), *The Road to Serfdom*, London: Routledge.

Hayter, T. (1971), *Aid as Imperialism*, Harmondsworth: Penguin.

Hearn, J. (2007), 'African NGOs: The New Compradors?', *Development and Change* 38(6): 1095–110.

Heertz, N. (2004), *The Debt Threat*, New York: Harper Collins.

Held, D. (2004), *Global Covenant*, Cambridge: Polity.

Held, D. and Kaya, A. (eds) (2007), *Global Inequality*, Cambridge: Polity.

Held, D., McGrew, A., Goldblatt, D. and Perraton, J. (1999), *Global Transformations*, Cambridge: Polity.

Helleiner, E. (2006), 'Reinterpreting Bretton Woods: International Development and the Neglected Origins of Embedded Liberalism', *Development and Change* 37(5): 943–67.

Helleiner, G. (1992), 'The IMF, the World Bank and Africa's Adjustment and External Debt Problems: An Unofficial View', *World Development* 20(6): 779–92.

Henderson, H. (2000), 'Life beyond Global Economic Warfare', in J. Nederveen Pieterse (ed.), *Global Futures: Shaping Globalization*, New York: Zed Books, pp. 63–82.

Henkel, H. and Stirrat, R. (2001), 'Participation as Spiritual Duty; Empowerment as Secular Subjection', in B. Cooke and U. Kothari (eds), *Participation: The New Tyranny?*, London: Zed Books, pp. 168–84.

Hermes, N. and Lensik, R. (2001), 'Changing the Conditions for Development Aid: A New Paradigm?', *Journal of Development Studies* 37(6): 1–16.

Hettne, B. (1995), *Development Theory and the Three Worlds: Towards an International Political Economy of Development*, 2nd edn, Harlow: Longman.

Hettne, B. (2002), 'Current Trends and Future Options in Development Studies', in V. Desai and R. B. Potter (eds), *The Companion to Development Studies*, London: Arnold, pp. 7–12.

Hettne, B. (ed.) (2008), *Sustainable Development in a Globalized World*, Palgrave: Basingstoke.

Hettne, B., Inotai, A. and Sundras, O. (eds) (1999), *Globalism and the New Regionalism*, London: Macmillan.

Hewitt, T. (2000), 'Half a Century of Development', in T. Allen and A. Thomas (eds), *Poverty and Development into the 21st Century*, Oxford: Oxford University Press, pp. 289–308.

Hewitt, T. Johnson, H. and Wield, D. (eds) (1992), *Industrialization and Development*, Oxford: Oxford University Press and the Open University.

Hickey, S. and Mohan, G. (eds) (2004), *Participation: From Tyranny to Transformation?*, London: Zed Books.

Hilhorst, D. (2003), *The Real World of NGOs: Discourses, Diversity and Development*, London: Zed Books.

Hines, C. (2000), *Localization: A Global Manifesto*, London: Earthscan.

Hirshman, M. (1995), 'Women and Development: A Critique', in M. H. Marchand and J. L. Parpart (eds), *Feminism/Postmodernism/Development*, London: Routledge, pp. 42–55.

Hirst, P. and Thompson, G. (1996), *Globalization in Question*, Cambridge: Polity.

Hirst, P. and Thompson, G. (2000), 'Global Myths and National Policies', in B. Holden (ed.), *Global Democracy: Key Debates*, London: Routledge, pp. 47–59.

Hobart, M. (1993), *An Anthropological Critique of Development*, London: Routledge.

Hodder, R. (2000), *Development Geography*, London: Routledge.

Holt-Giménez, E. and Patel, R. (2009), *Food Rebellions! Crisis and the Hunger for Justice*, Oxford: Pambazuka Press.

Holton, R. J. (1998), *Globalization and the Nation-State*, Basingstoke: Macmillan.

Holton, R. J. (2005), *Making Globalization*, Basingstoke: Palgrave.

Holzgrefe, J. L. and Keohane, R. O. (eds) (2003), *Humanitarian Intervention: Ethical, Legal and Political Dilemmas*, Cambridge: Cambridge University Press.

Hoogvelt, A. (1982), *Third World in Global Development*, London: Macmillan.

Hoogvelt, A. (1997), *Globalization and the Postcolonial World*, London: Macmillan.

Hopper, P. (2003), *Rebuilding Communities in an Age of Individualism*, Aldershot: Ashgate.

Hopper, P. (2006), *Living with Globalization*, Oxford: Berg.

Hopper, P. (2007), *Understanding Cultural Globalization*, Cambridge: Polity.

Hopper, P. (forthcoming), *Global Environmental Politics*, Cambridge: Polity.

Hopwood, B., Mellor, M. and O'Brien, G. (2005), 'Sustainable Development: Mapping Different Approaches', *Sustainable Development* 13: 38–52.

Horsman, M. and Marshall, A. (1995), *After the Nation-State: Citizens, Tribalism and the New World Disorder*, London: Harper Collins.

Hout, W. and Robison, R. (eds) (2009), *Governance and the Depoliticization of Development* London: Routledge.

HSRP (2005), *Human Security Report 2005: War and Peace in the 21st Century*, Oxford: Oxford University Press.

HSRP (2007), *Human Security Brief 2007*, www.humansecurityreport.info (accessed 10/9/08).

HSU (2008), 'Building Peace', *Human Security at the United Nations – Newsletter 2*, (Winter), www.ochaonline.un.org/humansecurity (accessed 4/9/08).

Hull, T. H. (1990), 'Recent Trends in Sex Ratios at Birth in China', *Population and Development Review* 16(1): 63–83.

Hulme, D. and Edwards, M. (eds) (1997), *NGOs, States and Donors: Too Close for Comfort?*, Basingstoke: Macmillan.

Human Rights Watch/Asia (1996), *Death by Default: A Policy of Fatal Neglect in China's State Orphanages*, New York: Human Rights Watch.

Hunt, J. (2004), 'Gender and Development', in D. Kingsbury et al. (eds), *Key Issues in Development*, Basingstoke: Palgrave, pp. 243–65.

Hunter, J. D. and Yates, J. (2002), 'In the Vanguard of Globalization: The World of American Globalizers', in P. L. Berger and S. P. Huntington (eds), *Many Globalizations*, Oxford: Oxford University Press, pp. 323–57.

Huntington, S. P. and Harrison, L. E. (eds) (2000), *Culture Matters*, New York: Basic Books.

Hurrell, A. (2001), 'Global Inequality and International Institutions', *Metaphilosophy* 32(1–2): 4–57.

Hutchful, E. and Aning, K. (2004), 'The Political Economy of Conflict', in A. Adebajo and I. Rashid (eds), *West Africa's Security Challenges*, Boulder, CO: Lynne Rienner.

Hutton, T. A. (2008), *The New Economy of the Inner City*, London: Routledge.

IBON Foundation (2007), *The Reality of Aid 2006: Focus on Conflict, Security and Development*, London: Zed Books.

IBON International (2007), *Primer on Development and Aid Effectiveness*, www.international.ibon.org (accessed 3/5/08)

ICG (2007a), 'Zimbabwe', *International Crisis Group*, www.crisisgroup.org. (accessed 13/10/09).

ICG (2007b), 'Zimbabwe: A Regional Solution?', *International Crisis Group: Africa Report No. 132*, 18 September, www.crisisgroup.org (accessed 13/10/09).

IDC (2006), *Conflict and Development: Peacebuilding and Post-conflict Reconstruction*, House of Commons International Development Committee, London, HC 923–1, 25/10/06.

Igoe, J. and Kelsall, T. (eds) (2005), *Between a Rock and a Hard Place: African NGOs, Donors and the State*, Durham, NC: Carolina Academic Press.

ILO (2003), 'Facts on Women at Work', Geneva: International Labour Organization, www.ilo.org/public/english/region/budapest/download/womenwork.pdf (accessed 4/08/09).

IMF (2008), *World Economic Outlook April 2008: Housing and the Business Cycle*, www.news.bbc.co.uk (accessed 10/4/08).

Ingham, B. (1995), *Economics for Development*, London: McGraw-Hill.

IPFA (1995), *Excessive Force: Power, Politics and Population Control*, Washington, DC: IFPA.

Irwin, D. A. (2005), *Free Trade under Fire*, 2nd edn, Princeton: Princeton University Press.

ITU (2010), *The World in 2010: ICT Facts and Figures*, www.itu.int/ITU–D/ict/ (accessed 12/4/11).

Jackson, C. and Pearson, R. (eds) (1998), *Feminist Visions of Development: Gender Analysis and Policy*, London: Routledge.

Jacob, M. (1994), 'Toward a Methodological Critique of Sustainable Development', *Journal of Developing Areas* 28: 237–52.

Jacobs, M. (1990), *Sustainable Development: Greening the Economy*, London: Fabian Society.

Jacobs, M. (1991), *The Green Economy: Environment, Sustainable Development and the Politics of the Future*, London: Pluto.

Jahan, R. (1995), *The Elusive Agenda: Mainstreaming Women in Development*, London: Zed Books.

Jameson, F. (1984), 'Postmodernism, or the Cultural Logic of Late Capitalism', *New Left Review* 146: 53–92.

Janicke, M., Binder, M. and Monch, H. (1997), '"Dirty Industries": Patterns of Change in Industrial Countries', *Environmental and Resource Economics* 9: 467–91.

Jaquette, J. S. and Summerfield, G. (eds) (2006), *Women and Gender Equity in Development Theory and Practice*, Durham: Duke University Press.

Jeffery, R. and Basu, A. M. (eds) (1997), *Girls' Schooling, Women's Autonomy and Fertility Change in South Asia*, New Delhi: Sage.

Jiang, L. and Hardee, K. (2009) 'How Do Recent Population Trends Matter to Climate Change?', *Population Action International*, April, www.populationaction.org (accessed 11/5/10).

Johnson, H. G. (1964), *Money, Trade and Economic Growth*, London: Allen and Unwin.

Johnson, H. G. (1971), 'A Word to the Third World: A Western Economist's Frank Advice', *Encounter* 37.

Johnston, J. (2002), 'Consuming Global Justice: Fair Trade Shopping and Alternative Development', in J. Goodman (ed.), *Protest and Globalisation: Prospects for Transnational Solidarity*, Annandale: Pluto, pp. 113–36.

Johnston, R. J., Taylor, P. J. and Watts, M. J. (eds) (2002), *Geographies of Global Change: Remapping the World*, Oxford: Blackwell.

Jolly, R. and Basu Ray, D. (2006), *The Human Security Framework and National Development Reports*, UNDP, www.origin-hdr.undp.org/en/media/HumanSecurity (accessed 14/10/08).

Jones, P. S. (2000), 'Why Is it All Right to Do Development "Over There" but Not "Here"? Changing Vocabularies and Common Strategies of Inclusion across "First" and "Third" Worlds', *Area* 32(2): 237–41.

Jones, R. J. B. (1995), *Globalization and Interdependence in the International Political Economy*, London: Pinter.

Jordan, L. and van Tuijl, P. (eds) (2006), *NGO Accountability: Politics, Principles and Innovations*, London: Earthscan.

Jubilee Debt Campaign (2008), *Unfinished Business*, www.jubileedebtcampaign.org. uk (accessed 12/6/08).

Judson, F. (1993), 'The Making of Central American National Agendas under Adjustment and Restructuring', *Labour, Capital and Society* 26(2): 148–80.

Julius, D. (1990), *Global Companies and Public Policy*, London: Pinter.

Junne, G. and Verkoren, W. (eds) (2005), *Postconflict Development: Meeting New Challenges*, London: Lynne Rienner.

Justino, P., Litchfield, J. and Whitehead, L. (2003), *The Impact of Inequality in Latin America*, Poverty Research Unit at Sussex, Working Paper No. 21, www.sussex. ac.uk/Users/PRU

Kabeer, N. (1994), *Reversed Realities: Gender Hierarchies in Development Thought*, London: Verso.

Kabeer, N. (2001), 'Conflicts over Credit: Re-evaluating the Empowerment Potential of Loans to Women in Rural Bangladesh', *World Development* 29(1): 63–84.

Kaldor, M. (2001), *New and Old Wars*, Cambridge: Polity.

Kaldor, M. (2003), *Global Civil Society*, Cambridge: Polity.

Kaldor, M. (2007), *Human Security*, Cambridge: Polity.

Kanbur, R. (2000), 'Aid, Conditionality and Debt in Africa', in F. Tarp (ed.), *Foreign Aid and Development*, London: Routledge, pp. 409–22.

Kanbur, R. and Lustig, N. (1999), *Why Is Inequality Back on the Agenda?*, Washington, DC: World Bank.

Kanji, N., Tan, S. F. and Toulmin, C. (2007[1970]), 'Introduction: Boserup Revisited', in E. Boserup, *Woman's Role in Economic Development*, London: Earthscan, pp. v–xxvi.

Kaplinsky, R. (2005), *Globalization, Poverty and Inequality*, Cambridge: Polity.

Kaplinsky R., McCormick, D. and Morris, M. (2010), 'Impacts and Challenges of a Growing Relationship between China and Sub-Saharan Africa', in V. Padayachee (ed.), *The Political Economy of Africa*, London: Routledge, pp. 389–409.

Karam, A. M. (2000), 'Feminist Futures', in J. Nederveen Pieterse (ed.), *Global Futures: Shaping Globalization*, London: Zed Books, pp. 175–86.

Kay, C. (1989), *Latin American Theories of Development and Underdevelopment*, London: Routledge.

Keen, D. (2008), *Complex Emergencies*, Cambridge: Polity.

Kelly, A. (2011), 'How Can We Achieve Development Goals if We Ignore Human Rights?', *Guardian Online*, 28 February, www.guardian.co.uk (accessed 16/4/11).

Kent, M. M. and Yin, S. (2006), 'Controlling Infectious Diseases', *Population Bulletin*, 61(2).

Keynes, J. M. (1936), *The General Theory of Employment, Interest and Money*, Cambridge: Harcourt.

Khor, M. (2001a), 'Globalisation and Sustainable Development: The Choices before Rio+10', *International Review for Environmental Strategies* 2(2) (Winter).

Khor, M. (2001b), *Rethinking Globalization*, London: Zed Books.

Khor, M. (2003), 'Globalization, Global Governance and Development', in H.-J. Chang (ed.), *Rethinking Development Economics*, London: Anthem Press, pp. 523–44.

Kiely, R. (1998), 'Introduction: Globalisation, (Post-)modernity and the Third World', in R. Kiely and P. Marfleet (eds), *Globalisation and the Third World*, London: Routledge, pp. 1–22.

Kiely, R. (1999), 'The Last Refuge of the Noble Savage? A Critical Account of Post-Development', *European Journal of Development Research* 11(1): 130–55.

Kiely, R. and Marfleet, P. (eds) (1998), *Globalisation and the Third World*, London: Routledge.

Killick, A. (1990), 'Whither Development Economics?' *Economics* 26(2): 294–8.

Killick, T. with Gunatilaka, R. and Mar, A. (1998), *Aid and the Political Economy of Policy Change*, London: Routledge.

Killick, T. (2002a), 'Aid Conditionality', in V. Desai and R. B. Potter (eds), *The Companion to Development Studies*, London: Arnold, pp. 480–4.

Killick, T. (2002b), *Responding to Inequality*, Inequality Briefing Paper No. 3, London: DFID and ODI.

Killick, T. and Foster, M. (2007), 'The Macroeconomics of Doubling Aid to Africa and the Centrality of the Supplyside', *Development Policy Review* 25(2): 167–92.

King, A. D. (1990), *Global Cities*, London: Routledge.

Kingsbury, D., Remenyi, J., McKay, J. and Hunt, J. (2004), *Key Issues in Development*, Basingstoke: Palgrave.

Kiondo, A. (1995), 'When the State Withdraws: Local Development, Politics, and Liberalization in Tanzania', in P. Gibbon (ed.), *Liberalized Development in Tanzania*, Uppsala: Nordiska Afrikainstitutet.

Kirby, A. (2004), 'World "Appeasing" Climate Threat', *BBC News Online*, 3 June, www.bbcnews.co.uk (accessed 24/11/06).

Kirby, P. (2003), *Introduction to Latin America: Twenty-First Century Challenges*, London: Sage.

Klak, T. (2002), 'World-systems Theory: Cores, Peripheries and Semi-peripheries', in V. Desai and R. B. Potter (eds), *The Companion to Development Studies*, London: Arnold, pp. 107–12.

Klein, N. (2000), *No Logo*, London: Flamingo.

Knight, J., Weir, S. and Woldehanna, T. (2003), 'The Role of Education in Facilitating Risk-Taking and Innovation in Agriculture', *Journal of Development Studies* 39(6): 1–22.

Knox, P. L. (2002), 'World Cities and the Organisation of Global Space', in R. J. Johnson, P. J. Taylor and M. J. Watts (eds), *Geographies of Global Change*, 2nd edn, Oxford: Blackwell, pp. 328–39.

Koeberle, S., Bedoya, H., Silarsky, P. and Verheyen, G. (eds) (2005), *Conditionality Revisited: Concepts, Experiences, and Lessons*, Washington, DC: World Bank.

Koenig, D. (1995), 'Sustainable Development: Linking Global Environmental Change to Technology Cooperation', in O. P. Dwivedi and D. K. Vajpeyi (eds), *Environmental Politics in the Third World: A Comparative Analysis*, Westport, CN: Greenwood Press.

Kogut, B. (ed.) (2004), *The Global Internet Economy*, London: MIT Press.

Kothari, U. (2002), 'Feminist and Postcolonial Challenges to Development', in U. Kothari and M. Minogue (eds), *Development Theory and Practice*, Basingstoke: Palgrave, pp. 35–51.

Kothari, U. (2005), 'From Colonial Administration to Development Studies: A Postcolonial Critique of the History of Development Studies', in U. Kothari (ed.), *A Radical History of Development Studies*, London: Zed Books, pp. 47–66.

Kovel, J. (2007), *The Enemy of Nature: The End of Capitalism or the End of the World?*, 2nd edn, New York: Zed Books.

Krier, J.-M. (2005), *Fair Trade in Europe 2005*, Brussels: Fair Trade Advocacy Office.

Krueger, A. O. (1997), 'Trade Policy and Economic Development: How We Learn', *American Economic Review* 87: 1–22.

Krugman, P. (1994), 'The Myth of the Asia's Miracle', *Foreign Affairs* 73(6) (Nov./Dec.): 62–79.

Kuznets, S. (1955), 'Economic Growth and Income Inequality', *American Economic Review* 45(1): 1–28.

Lafferty, W. (ed.) (2004), *Governance for Sustainable Development*, Edward Elgar: Cheltenham.

Lafferty, W. and Langhelle, O. (eds) (1999), *Towards Sustainable Development*, London: Macmillan.

Lal, D. (1983), *The Poverty of Development Economics*, London: IEA.

Lancaster, C. (1999), *Aid to Africa. So Much to Do, So Little Done*, Chicago: University of Chicago Press.

Lancaster, C. (2007), *Foreign Aid*, Chicago: University of Chicago Press.

Lancet, The (2008), 'Human Security Approach for Global Health', vol. 372: 13–14, 5 July, www.thelancet.com (accessed 26/8/08).

Landes, D. (2000), 'Culture Makes Almost All the Difference', in L. E. Harrison and S. P. Huntington (eds), *Culture Matters*, New York: Basic Books, pp. 2–13.

Lane, J. (1995), 'NGOs and Participatory Development: The Concept in Theory Versus the Concept in Practice', in N. Nelson and S. Wright (eds), *Power and Participatory Development*, London: IT Publications, pp. 181–91.

Large, J. and Sisk, T. D. (eds) (2006), *Democracy, Conflict and Human Security*, Stockholm: International IDEA.

Lash, S. and Lury, C. (2007), *Global Culture Industry: The Mediation of Things*, Cambridge: Polity.

Last, M. (1999), 'Understanding Health', in T. Skelton and T. Allen (eds), *Culture and Global Change*, London: Routledge, pp. 70–83.

Lawson, M. (2005), 'Aid to Africa "Must be Doubled"', *BBC News Online*, 24 June, www.bbcnews.co.uk (accessed 23/11/05).

Lazreg, M. (1988), 'Feminism and Difference: The Perils of Writing as a Woman on Women in Algeria', *Feminist Issues* 14(1): 81–107.

Lederach, J. (1997), *Building Peace: Sustainable Reconciliation in Divided Societies*, Washington, DC: US Institute of Peace.

Ledgerwood, J. (1999), *Microfinance Handbook*, Washington, DC: World Bank.

Lee, R. and Smith, D. M. (eds) (2004), *Geographies and Moralities*, Oxford: Blackwell.

Legrain, P. (2002), *Open World: The Truth about Globalisation*, London: Abacus.

Letchumanan, R. (2000), 'Testing the Pollution Haven Hypothesis', in P. Könz et al. (eds), *Trade, Environment and Sustainable Development*, Geneva: ICTSD, pp. 339–74.

Lewis, D. (2002a), 'Non-Governmental Organizations: Questions of Performance and Accountability', in V. Desai and R. B. Potter (eds), *The Companion to Development Studies*, London: Arnold, pp. 519–23.

Lewis, D. (2002b), 'Civil Society in African Contexts: Reflections on the Usefulness of a Concept', *Development and Change* 33(4): 569–86.

Lewis, D. (2005), 'Individuals, Organizations and Public Action: Trajectories of the 'Non-governmental' in Development Studies', in U. Kothari (ed.), *A Radical History of Development Studies*, London: Zed Books, pp. 200–21.

Lewis, D. and Opoku-Mensah, P. (2006), 'Moving Forward Research Agendas on International NGOs: Theory, Agency and Context', *Journal of International Development* 18: 665–75.

Lewis, D. and Wallace, T. (2000), *New Roles and Relevance: Development NGOs and the Challenge of Change*, Bloomfield, CT: Kumarian Press.

Lewis, W. A. (1955), *The Theory of Economic Growth*, London: George Allen and Unwin.

Leys, C. (1996), *The Rise and Fall of Development Theory*, Oxford: James Currey.

Lim, L. (1983), 'Capitalism, Imperialism and Patriarchy: The Dilemma of Third World Women Workers in Multinational Factories', in J. Nash and M. P. Fernandez-Kelly (eds), *Women, Men and the International Division of Labor*, Albany: SUNY Press, pp. 70–91.

Lim, L. (1990a), 'Women's Work in Export Factories: The Politics of a Cause', in I. Tinker (ed.), *Persistent Inequalities: Women and World Development*, Oxford: Oxford University Press.

Lim, L. (1990b), 'Labour Organization among Women Workers in Multinational Export Factories in Asia', *Journal of Southeast Asia Business* 6(4): 1–8.

Lim, L. (1996), *More and Better Jobs for Women*, Geneva: ILO.

Lim, L. (2004), 'China Fears Bachelor Future', *BBC News Online*, 5 April, www.bbc. co.uk (accessed 20/10/06).

Lindahl-Kiessling, K. and Landberg, H. (eds) (1997), *Population, Economic Development and the Environment*, Oxford: Oxford University Press.

Linden, E. (1996), 'The Exploding Cities of the Developing World', *Foreign Affairs* (Jan./Feb.): 52–65.

Lindenberg, M. and Bryant, C. (2001), *Going Global: Transforming Relief and Development NGOs*, Bloomfield, CT: Kumarian Press.

Lindsey, B. (2003), 'Grounds for Complaint? Understanding the "Coffee Crisis"', Washington, DC: Cato Institute, www.cato.org (accessed 7/8/08).

Litfin, K. T. (ed.) (1998), *The Greening of Sovereignty in World Politics*, Cambridge, MA: MIT Press.

Little, I. (1979), 'An Economic Renaissance', in W. Galenson (ed.), *Economic Growth and Structural Change in Taiwan*, Ithaca: Cornell University Press.

Little, I. (1982), *Economic Development: Theory, Policy and International Relations*, New York: Basic Books.

Little, I., Scitovsky, T. and Scott, M. (1970), *Industry and Trade in Some Developing Countries: A Comparative Study*, London: Oxford University Press.

Lockheed, M. E., Jamison, D. and Lau, L. (1980), 'Farmer Education and Farm Efficiency: A Survey,' *Economic Development and Cultural Change* 29(1): 37–76.

Long, N. and Long, A. (eds) (1992), *Battlefields of Knowledge: The Interlocking of Theory and Practice in Social Research and Development*, London: Routledge.

Low, N. (ed.) (1999), *Global Ethics and Environment*, London: Routledge.

Lowe, L. and Lloyd, D. (eds) (1997), *The Politics of Culture in the Shadow of Capital*, Durham: Duke University Press.

Luck, E. C. (2006), *UN Security Council*, London: Routledge.

Lutz, W., Sanderson, W. C. and Scherbov, S. (eds) (2004), *The End of World Population Growth in the 21st Century*, London: Earthscan.

Lynas, M. (2007), *Six Degrees: Our Future on a Hotter Planet*, London: Fourth Estate.

Lynch, K. (2004), *Rural–Urban Interaction in the Developing World*, London: Routledge.

Lynch, M. D. (1997), 'Information Highways', in Y. Courrier and A. Large (eds), *World Information Report 1997/98*, Paris, UNESCO, pp. 258–303.

Lyon, P. (1995), 'The End of the Cold War in Africa', in O. Furley (ed.), *The Conflict in Africa*, London: I. B. Tauris, pp. 171–82.

MacDonald, T. H. (2007), *The Global Human Right to Health*, Oxford: Radcliffe Publishing.

MacFarlane, N. S. (2002), *Intervention in Contemporary World Politics*, Oxford: Oxford University Press.

MacFarlane, N. S. and Foong-Khong, Y. (2006), *Human Security and the UN: A Critical History*. Bloomington: Indiana University Press.

Macrae, J. (2001), *Aiding Recovery?*, London: Zed Books.

Madslien, J. (2004), 'IMF and the World Bank: Is Reform Underway?', *BBC News Online*, 22 July, www.bbcnews.co.uk (accessed 28/11/05).

Malena, C. (2000), 'Beneficiaries, Mercenaries, Missionaries and Revolutionaries: Unpacking NGO Involvement in World Bank-financed Projects', *IDS Bulletin* 31(3): 19–34.

Malone, D. and Nitzschke, H. (2004), 'Economic Agendas in Civil Wars: What We Know, What We Need to Know', WIDER Discussion Paper No. 2005/07, Helsinki: WIDER.

Malthus, T. (1798), *An Essay on the Principle of Population*, ed. A. Flew, Harmondsworth: Penguin (1982).

Mani, M. and Wheeler, D. (1998), 'In Search of Pollution Havens? Dirty Industry in the World Economy, 1960–1995', *Journal of Environment and Development* 7(3): 215–47.

Manji, F. and O'Coill, C. (2002), 'The Missionary Position: NGOs and Development in Africa', *International Affairs* 78(3): 567–83.

Mann, M. (1997), 'Has Globalization Ended the Rise and Rise of the Nation-State?', *Review of International Political Economy* 4(3): 472–96.

Manning, R. (2006), 'Will "Emerging Donors" Change the Face of International Co-operation?', *Development Policy Review* 24(4): 371–85.

Manor, J. (ed.) (2007), *Aid That Works*, Washington: World Bank.

Manuel, G. and Posluns, M. (1974), *The Fourth World: An Indian Reality*, Don Mills: Collier Macmillan Canada.

Manzo, K. (2003), 'Africa in the Rise of Rights-based Development', *Geoforum* 34(4): 437–56.

Marchand, M. H. and Parpart, J. L. (eds) (1995), *Feminism/Postmodernism/Development*, London: Routledge.

Marcus, G. and Fischer, M. (1986), *Anthropology as Cultural Critique: An Experimental Moment in the Human Sciences*, Chicago: University of Chicago Press.

Marcuse, P. and van Kempen, R. (eds) (2000), *Globalizing Cities*, Oxford: Blackwell.

Mark Amen, M., Archer, K. and Martin Bosman, M. (eds) (2006), *Relocating Global Cities*, Lanham: Rowman & Littlefield.

Marshall, M. G. and Gurr, T. R. (2005), *Peace and Conflict 2005*, Center for International Development and Conflict Management, College Park, MD: University of Maryland.

Martinussen, J. (1997), *Society, State and Market: A Guide to Competing Theories of Development*, London: Zed Books.

Masina, P. (ed.) (2001), *Rethinking Development in East Asia: From Illusory Miracle to Economic Crisis*, Copenhagen: NIAS.

Massey, D. (2007), *World City*, Cambridge: Polity.

Mawdsley, E., Townsend, J., Porter, G. and Oakley, P. (2002), *Knowledge, Power and Development Agendas: NGOs North and South*, Oxford: INTRAC.

Maxwell, S. (1999), 'What Can We Do with a Rights-based Approach to Development?', ODI Briefing Paper 1999 (3), London: ODI, www.odi.org.uk (accessed 9/2/08).

Mayhew, S. H. (2005), 'Hegemony, Politics and Ideology: The Role of Legislation in NGO–Government Relations in Asia', *Journal of Development Studies* 41(5): 727–58.

Mayoux, L. (1998), 'Gender Accountability and NGOs: Avoiding the Black Hole', in C. Miller and S. Ravazi (eds), *Missionaries and Mandarins*, London: UNRISD, pp. 172–93.

McAslan, E. (2002), 'Social Capital and Development', in V. Desai and R. B. Potter (eds), *The Companion to Development Studies*, London: Arnold, pp. 139–43.

McCoy, D., Chand, S. and Sridhar, D. (2009), 'Global Health Funding: How Much, Where it Comes from and Where it Goes', *Health Policy and Planning* 24(6): 407–17.

McGee, R. (2002), 'Participating in Development', in U. Kothari and M. Minogue (eds), *Development Theory and Practice: Critical Perspectives*, Basingstoke: Palgrave, pp. 92–116.

McGourty, C. (2009), 'Global Crisis to Strike by 2030', *BBC News Online*, 19 March, www.bbcnews.co.uk (accessed 23/3/09).

McGrane, B. (1989), *Beyond Anthropology*, New York: Colombia University Press.

McGreal, C. (2006a), 'Mbeki Urged to Sack Ally over HIV Views', *Guardian Online*, 7 September, www.guardian.co.uk (accessed 19/10/06).

McGreal, C. (2006b), 'South Africa Ends Long Denial over AIDS Crisis', *Guardian Online*, 30 November, www.guardian.co.uk (accessed 1/12/06).

McGrew, A. and Poku, N. K. (eds) (2007), *Globalization, Development and Human Security*, Cambridge: Polity.

McIlwaine, C. (1997), 'Fringes or Frontiers? Gender and Export-oriented Development in the Philippines', in C. Dixon and D. Drakakis-Smith (eds), *Uneven Development in Southeast Asia*, Aldershot: Ashgate, pp. 100–23.

McIlwaine, C. (2002), 'Perspectives on Poverty, Vulnerability and Exclusion', in C. McIlwaine and K. Willis (eds), *Challenges and Change in Middle America*, London: Pearson, pp. 82–109.

McKay, A. (1997), 'Poverty Reduction through Economic Growth: Some Issues', *Journal of International Development* 9(4): 665–73.

McKay, J. (2004), 'Crises in Africa, Asia and Latin America: Lessons and Wider Implications', in D. Kingsbury et al., *Key Issues in Development*, Basingstoke: Palgrave, pp. 124–63.

McLeod, R. H. and Garnaut, R. (eds) (1998), *East Asia in Crisis: From Being a Miracle to Needing One?*, London: Routledge.

McMichael, P. (2004), *Development and Social Change*, 3rd edn, Thousand Oaks: Pine Forge Press.

Meadowcroft, J. (1997), 'Planning, Democracy and the Challenge of Sustainable Development', *International Political Science Review* 20: 167–90.

Meadows, D. H., Meadows, D. L., Randers, J. and Behrens, W. W. (1972), *The Limits to Growth*, London: Pan Books.

Mehmet, O. (1995), *Westernizing the Third World: The Eurocentricity of Economic Development Theories*, London: Routledge.

Meier, G. M. and Stiglitz, J. E. (eds) (2000), *Frontiers of Development Economics: The Future in Perspective*, New York: World Bank and Oxford University Press.

Melchert, L. (2005), 'The Age of Environmental Impasse? Globalization and Environmental Transformation of Metropolitan Cities', *Development and Change* 36(5): 803–23.

Mercer, C. (2002), 'NGOs, Civil Society and Democratization: A Critical Review of the Literature', *Progress in Development Studies* 2: 5–22.

Merriam, A. H. (1988), 'What Does "Third World" Mean?', in J. Norwine and A. Gonzalez (eds), *The Third World: States of Minds and Being*, London: Unwin-Hyman, pp. 15–22.

Michael, S. (2004), *Undermining Development: The Absence of Power among Local NGOs in Africa*, Oxford: James Currey.

Middleton, N. (2003), *The Global Casino*, 3rd edn, London: Hodder Arnold.

Mies, M. (1986), *Patriarchy and Accumulation on a World Scale*, London: Zed Books.

Milanovic, B. (2005), *Worlds Apart: Measuring International and Global Inequality*, Princeton: Princeton University Press.

Milanovic, B. (2007), 'Globalization and Inequality', in D. Held and A. Kaya (eds), *Global Inequality*, Cambridge: Polity, pp. 26–49.

Miller, C. and Razavi, S. (eds) (1998), *Missionaries and Mandarins: Feminist Engagement with Development Institutions*, London: UNRISD.

Miller, D. (ed.) (1995), *Acknowledging Consumption*, London: Routledge.

Mingst, K. A. and Karns, M. P. (2007), *The United Nations in the 21st Century*, 3rd edn, Boulder, CO: Westview Press.

Mohan, G. (2002), 'Participatory Development', in V. Desai and R. B. Potter (eds), *The Companion to Development Studies*, London: Arnold, pp. 49–54.

Mohan, G. and Holland, J. (2001), 'Human Rights and Development in Africa: Moral Intrusion or Empowering Opportunity?', *Review of African Political Economy* 88: 177–96.

Mohan, G., Brown, E., Milward, B. and Zack-Williams, A. B. (2000), *Structural Adjustment: Theory, Practice and Impacts*, London: Routledge.

Mohanty, C. T. (1991), 'Under Western Eyes: Feminist Scholarship and Colonial Discourses', in C. T. Mohanty, A. T. Russo and L. Torres (eds), *Third World Women and the Politics of Feminism*, Indianapolis: Indiana University Press, pp. 51–80.

Mol, A.P.J. (2003), *Globalization and Environmental Reform: The Ecological Modernization of the Global Economy*, Cambridge, MA: MIT Press.

Mol, A. P. J. and Spaargaren, G. (2000), 'Ecological Modernization Theory in Debate: A Review', *Environmental Politics* 9(1): 17–49.

Molyneux, M. (2002), 'Gender and the Silences of Social Capital: Lessons from Latin America', *Development and Change* 33(2): 167–88.

Molyneux, M. (2007), 'The Chimera of Success: Gender *Ennui* and the Changed International Policy Environment', in A. Cornwall et al. (eds), *Feminisms in Development*, London: Zed Books, pp. 226–40.

Momsen, J. H. (2004), *Gender and Development*, London: Routledge.

Momsen, J. H. and Kinnaird, V. (eds) (1993), *Different Places, Different Voices: Gender and Development in Africa, Asia and Latin America*, London: Routledge.

Moore, M. (2001), 'Empowerment at Last?', *Journal of International Development* 13: 321–9.

Moore, M. (2003), *A World Without Walls: Freedom, Development, Free Trade and Global Governance*, Cambridge: Cambridge University Press.

Morris, J. (2003), 'The Argument for Free Trade', *BBC News Online*, 12 February, www.bbcnews.co.uk (accessed 2/11/06).

Morton Jerve, A., Shimomura, Y. and Skovsted Hansen, A. (eds) (2007), *Aid Relationships in Asia: Exploring Ownership in Japanese and Nordic Aid*, Basingstoke: Palgrave.

Moser, C. (1993), *Gender Planning and Development: Theory, Practice and Training*, London: Routledge.

Mosley, P., Harrigan, J. and Toye, J. (1995), *Aid and Power*, 2nd edn, Vol. 1, London: Routledge.

Mosse, D. (1994), 'Authority, Gender and Knowledge: Theoretical Reflections on the Practice of Participatory Rural Appraisal', *Development and Change* 25(3): 497–526.

Mosse, D. (2001), '"People's Knowledge", Participation and Patronage: Operations and Representations in Rural Development', in B. Cooke and U. Kothari (eds), *Participation: The New Tyranny?*, London: Zed Books, pp. 16–35.

Moyo, D. (2010), *Dead Aid*, London: Penguin.

MSF (2010), *No Time to Quit: HIV/Aids Treatment Gap Widening in Africa*, Brussels: Médecins Sans Frontières.

Munck, R. (2003), *Contemporary Latin America*, Basingstoke: Palgrave.

Munkler, H. (2005), *The New Wars*, Cambridge: Polity.

Munslow, B. (2002), 'Complex Emergencies and Development', in V. Desai and R. B. Potter (eds), *The Companion to Development Studies*, London: Arnold, pp. 444–8.

Munslow, B. and Ekoko, F. (1995), 'Is Democracy Necessary for Sustainable Development?', *Democratisation* 2: 158–78.

Murray, W. E. (2006), *Geographies of Globalization*, London: Routledge.

Naess, A. (1973), 'The Shallow and the Deep, Long-Range Ecology Movement', *Inquiry* 16: 95–100.

Naicker, S., Plange-Rhule, J., Tutt, R. C. and Eastwood, J. B. (2009), 'Shortage of Health Care Workers in Developing Countries – Africa', *Ethnicity & Disease* 19: 60–4.

Naipaul, S. (1985), 'A Thousand Million Invisible Men: The Myth of the Third World', *The Spectator*, 18 May: 9–11.

Narayan, U. (1998), 'Essence of Culture and a Sense of History: A Feminist Critique of Cultural Essentialism', *Hypatia*, Special Issue – Border Crossings: Multicultural and Postcolonial Feminist Challenges to Philosophy, Part 1, 13(2): 86–107.

National Research Council (2002), *Abrupt Climate Change: Inevitable Surprises,* Washington, DC: National Academies Press.

Nayyar, D. (2003), 'Globalization and Development', in H.-J. Chang (ed.), *Rethinking Development Economics*, London: Anthem Press, pp. 61–82.

Ndegwa, S. N. (1996), *The Two Faces of Civil Society: NGOs and Politics in Africa*, West Hartford, CT: Kumarian Press.

Nederveen Pieterse, J. (1992), 'Emancipation, Modern and Post-Modern', in J. Nederveen Pieterse (ed.), *Emancipation, Modern and Post-Modern*, London: Sage, pp. 5–43.

Nederveen Pieterse, J. (2000a), 'After Post-Development', *Third World Quarterly* 21(2): 175–91.

Nederveen Pieterse, J. (ed.) (2000b), *Global Futures: Shaping Globalization*, London: Zed Books.

Nederveen Pieterse, J. (2001), *Development Theory*, London: Sage.

Nederveen Pieterse, J. (2004), *Globalisation and Culture*, Lanham, MD: Rowman & Littlefield.

Nelson, P. J. and Dorsey, E. (2008), *New Rights Advocacy: Changing Strategies of Development and Human Rights NGOs*, Washington, DC: Georgetown University Press.

Nelson, N. and Wright, S. (eds) (1995), *Power and Participatory Development*, London: IT Publications.

New African (2005), 'NGOs: What are They Really Doing in Africa?', *New African* 443, (August/September 2005): 12–15.

Newman, S. (1991), 'Does Modernization Breed Ethnic Conflict?', *World Politics* 43(3): 451–78.

Nicholls, A. and Opal, C. (2005), *Fair Trade*, London: Sage.

Nkrumah, K. (1965), *Neo-Colonialism: The Last Stage of Imperialism*, London: Nelson.

Norwine, J. and Gonzalez, A. (eds) (1988), *The Third World: States of Minds and Being*, London: Unwin-Hyman.

Nyamwaya, D. O. (1997), 'Three Critical Issues in Community Health Development Projects in Kenya', in R. D. Grillo and R. L. Stirrat (eds) (1997), *Discourses of Development: Anthropological Perspectives*, Oxford: Berg, pp. 183–202.

Nye, J. S., Jr. (2002), *The Paradox of American Power*, Oxford: Oxford University Press.

Nyerere, J. K. (1967a), *The Arusha Declaration*, Dar es Salaam: Government Printer.

Nyerere, J. K. (1967b), *Education for Self-Reliance*, Dar es Salaam: Government Printer.

O'Brien, R. (1992), *Global Financial Integration: The End of Geography*, London: Pinter.

O'Brien, R., Goetz, A. M., Scholte, J. A., and Williams, M. (2000), *Contesting Global Governance*, Cambridge: Cambridge University Press.

Ocampo, J. A. and Taylor, L. (1998), 'Trade Liberalization in Developing Economies: Modest Benefits but Problems with Productivity Growth, Macro Prices, and Income Distribution', *The Economic Journal* 108(453): 1523–46.

OECD (1988), *The Role of Non-government Organizations*, Paris: OECD.

OECD (2007), 'Africa and International Trade', www.oecd.org/dataoecd/53/48/39759627 (accessed 6/4/11).

OECD (2008), 'Debt Relief is Down: Other ODA Rises Slightly', press release 4 April, www.oecd.org/dataoecd/27/55/40381862 (accessed 6/4/11).

OECD (2009), *Policy Ownership and Aid Conditionality in the Light of the Financial Crisis*, Paris: OECD.

OECD (2010), 'Development Aid Rose in 2009 and Most Donors Will Meet 2010 Aid Targets', www.oecd.org/document/11/0,3746,en_2649_34447_44981579 (accessed 10/4/11).

Ohmae, K. (1990), *The Borderless World*, London: Collins.

Olivier de Sardan, J.-P. (2005), *Anthropology and Development*, London: Zed Books.

Ong, A. (1999), *Flexible Citizenship: The Cultural Logics of Transnationality*, Durham, NC: Duke University Press.

Öniş, Z. and Şenses, F. (2005), 'Rethinking the Emerging Post-Washington Consensus', *Development and Change* 36(2): 263–90.

O'Riordan, T. (ed.) (1995), *Environmental Science for Environmental Management*, London: Longman.

Østergaard, L. (ed.) (1992), *Gender and Development: A Practical Guide*, London: Routledge.

Oxfam (1993), *Africa: Make or Break. Action for Recovery*, Oxford: Oxfam.

Oxfam (2002), *Rigged Rules and Double Standards*, Oxford: Oxfam.

Oxfam (2006), *Kicking the Habit*, Briefing Paper 96, www.oxfam.org (accessed 12/6/08).

Pacheco-Vega, R. (2006), 'Book Review of Kevin Gallagher's *Free Trade and the Environment: Mexico, NAFTA and Beyond*', *Global Environmental Politics* 6(1): 125–6.

Packenham, R. A. (1998), *The Dependency Movement: Scholarship and Politics in Development Studies*, new edn, Harvard: Harvard University Press.

Palma, G. (2003), 'The Latin American Economies during the Second Half of the Twentieth Century – from the Age of "ISI" to the Age of "The End of History"', in H.-J. Chang (ed.), *Rethinking Development Economics*, London: Anthem Press, pp. 125–51.

Parfitt, T. (2002), *The End of Development*, London: Pluto.

Paris, R. (2001), 'Human Security: Paradigm Shift or Hot Air', *International Security*, 26(2): 87–102.

Park, S. (2005), 'Book Review of Michael Mason's *The New Accountability: Environmental Responsibility across Borders*', *Global Environmental Politics*, 5(4): 130–1.

Parkins, C. (1996), 'North–South Relations and Globalization after the Cold War', in C. Bretherton and G. Ponton (eds), *Global Politics: An Introduction*, Oxford: Blackwell, pp. 49–73.

Parpart, J. (1995), 'Postmodernism, Gender and Development', in J. Crush (ed.), *Power of Development*, London: Routledge, pp. 253–65.

Parpart, J. (2002), 'Gender and Empowerment: New Thoughts, New Approaches', in V. Desai and R. B. Potter (eds), *The Companion to Development Studies*, London: Arnold, pp. 338–42.

Parpart, J. (2007), 'Gender, Power and Governance in a Globalizing World', in A. McGrew and N. K. Poku (eds), *Globalization, Development and Human Security*, Cambridge: Polity, pp. 207–19.

Parpart, J., Rai, S. and Staudt, K. (eds) (2002), *Rethinking Empowerment: Gender and Development in a Global/Local World*, London: Routledge.

Patrick, S. (2006), 'Weak States and Global Threats: Fact or Fiction?', *The Washington Quarterly* 29(2): 27–53.

Peake, L. and Alissa Trotz, D. (2002), 'Feminism and Feminist Issues in the South', in V. Desai and R. B. Potter (eds), *The Companion to Development Studies*, London: Arnold, pp. 334–8.

Pearce, D., Markandya, A. and Barbier, E. B. (1989), *Blueprint for a Green Economy*, London: Earthscan.

Pearce, F. (2010), *Peoplequake: Mass Migration, Ageing Nations and the Coming Population Crash*, London: Eden Project.

Pearce, J. (2000), 'Development, NGOs, and Civil Society: The Debate and its Future', in D. Eade and J. Pearce (eds), *Development, NGOs and Civil Society*, Oxford: Oxfam, pp. 15–43.

Pearson, R. (1998), '"Nimble Fingers" Revisited: Reflections on Women and Third World Industrialization in the Late Twentieth Century', in C. Jackson and R. Pearson (eds), *Feminist Visions of Development*, London: Routledge, pp. 171–88.

Pearson, R. (2000), 'Rethinking Gender Matters in Development', in T. Allen and A. Thomas (eds), *Poverty and Development into the 21st Century*, Oxford: Oxford University Press, pp. 383–402.

Pearson, R. (2005), 'The Rise and Rise of Gender and Development', in U. Kothari (ed.), *A Radical History of Development Studies*, London: Zed Books, pp. 157–79.

Pearson, R. (2007), 'Reassessing Paid Work and Women's Empowerment: Lessons from the Global Economy', in A. Cornwall et al. (eds), *Feminisms in Development*, London: Zed Books, pp. 201–13.

Peet, R. (2003), *Unholy Trinity: The IMF, World Bank and the WTO*, London: Zed Books.

Peet, R., with Hartwick, E. (1999), *Theories of Development*, New York: The Guildford Press.

Pejout, N. (2010), 'Africa and the "Second New Economy"', in V. Padayachee (ed.), *The Political Economy of Africa*, London: Routledge, pp. 231–44.

Pelling, M. (2002), 'The Rio Earth Summit', in V. Desai and R. B. Potter (eds), *The Companion to Development Studies*, London: Arnold, pp. 284–9.

Pellow, D. N. and Brulle, R. J. (eds) (2005), *Power, Justice, and the Environment: A Critical Appraisal of the Environmental Justice Movement*, Cambridge, MA: MIT Press.

Petras, J. and Veltmeyer, H. (2001), *Globalization Unmasked*, London: Zed Books.

Petras, J. and Veltmeyer, H. (2004), 'Age of Reverse Aid: Neo-liberalism as Catalyst of Regression', in J. P. Pronk et al., *Catalysing Development*, Oxford: Blackwell, pp. 63–75.

Pettifor, A. (2006), *The Coming First World Debt Crisis*, Basingstoke: Palgrave.

Pew Research Center (2008), 'The Chinese Celebrate Their Roaring Economy, As They Struggle With Its Costs', *Pew Global Attitudes Project*, 22 July, www.pewglobal.org (accessed 13/4/11).

Phani Kumar, P. (2010), 'China's One-Child Policy Little Enforced – and Set to End', *MarketWatch*, 18 March, www.marketwatch.com (accessed 13/4/11).

Phani Kumar, P. (2011), 'China Reportedly Considering Two-child Policy', *MarketWatch*, 8 March, www.marketwatch.com (accessed 13/4/11).

Picciotto, R. and Weaving, R. (eds) (2006), *Security and Development*, London: Routledge.

Picciotto, R., Olonisakin, F. and Clarke, M. (2007), *Global Development and Human Security*, New Brunswick: Transaction.

Poku, N. K. (2002), 'Global Pandemics: HIV/AIDS', in D. Held and A. McGrew (eds), *Governing Globalization*, Cambridge: Polity, pp. 111–26.

Poku, N. K. (2005), *AIDS in Africa: How the Poor are Dying*, Cambridge: Polity.

Porter, D., Allen, B. and Thompson, G. (1991), *Development in Practice: Paved with Good Intentions*, London: Routledge.

Porter, G. (1999), 'Trade Competition and Pollution Standards: "Race to the Bottom" or "Stuck at the Bottom"?', *Journal of Environment and Development* 8(2): 133–51.

Potter, G. A. (2000), *Deeper than Debt*, London: Latin America Bureau.

Potter, R. B. (2001), 'Geography and Development of Core and Periphery?', *Area* 33: 422–7.

Potter, R. B., Binns, T., Elliott, J. A. and Smith, D. (2004), *Geographies of Development*, 2nd edn, Harlow: Pearson Education.

Prebisch, R. (1950), *The Economic Development of Latin America and Its Principal Problems*, New York: UN.

Preston, P. W. (1996), *Development Theory: An Introduction*, Oxford: Blackwell.

Pronk, J. P. (2004), 'Aid as a Catalyst', in J. P. Pronk et al., *Catalysing Development? A Debate on Aid*, Oxford: Blackwell, pp. 1–19.

Pronk, J. P. et al. (2004), *Catalysing Development? A Debate on Aid*, Oxford: Blackwell.

Prügl, E. and Lustgarten, A. (2006), 'Mainstreaming Gender in International Organizations', in J. S. Jaquette and G. Summerfield (eds), *Women and Gender Equity in Development Theory and Practice*, Durham: Duke University Press, pp. 53–70.

Pugh, J. (2002), 'Local Agenda 21 and the Third World', in V. Desai and R. B. Potter (eds), *The Companion to Development Studies*, London: Arnold, pp. 289–93.

Purvis, M. and Grainger, A. (eds) (2004), *Exploring Sustainable Development: Geographical Perspectives*, London: Earthscan.

Putnam, R. (1995), 'Bowling Alone: America's Declining Social Capital', *Journal of Democracy* 6: 65–78.

Putnam, R. (2000), *Bowling Alone: The Collapse and Revival of American Community*, New York: Simon and Schuster.

Radcliffe, S. A. (2005), 'Rethinking Development', in P. Cloke et al. (eds), *Introducing Human Geographies*, 2nd edn, London: Hodder Arnold, pp. 200–10.

Radcliffe, S. A. (ed.) (2006), *Culture and Development in a Globalizing World*, London: Routledge.

Radford, T. (2002), 'World Health "Threatened by Obesity"', *Guardian Online*, 18 February, www.guardian.co.uk (accessed 9/10/05).

Raffer, K. (1998), 'The Tobin Tax: Reviving a Discussion', *World Development* 26(3): 529–38.

Rahnema, M. (1992), 'Participation', in W. Sachs (ed.), *The Development Dictionary*, London: Zed.

Rahnema, M. with Bawtree, V. (eds) (1997), *The Post-Development Reader*, London: Zed Books.

Rai, S. M. (2002), *Gender and the Political Economy of Development*, Cambridge: Polity.

Rajan, R. G. and Subramaniam, A. (2005), *What Undermines Aid's Impact on Growth*, IMF Working Paper No. 05/126, Washington, DC: IMF.

Ramsbotham, O., Woodhouse, T. and Miall, H. (2005), *Contemporary Conflict Resolution*, 2nd edn, Cambridge: Polity.

Randel, J., German, T. and Ewing, D. (eds) (2000), *The Reality of Aid*, London: Earthscan.

Rapley, J. (2004), *Globalization and Inequality*, Boulder: Lynne Rienner.

Rapley, J. (2007), *Understanding Development: Theory and Practice in the Third World*, Boulder, CO: Lynne Rienner.

Raskin, P., Banuri, T., Gallopin, G., Gutman, P., Hammond, A., Kates, R. and Swart, R. (2002), *Great Transition: The Promise and Lure of the Times Ahead*, Boston, MA: Stockholm Environment Institute.

Rathgeber, E. (1990), 'WID, WAD, GAD: Trends in Research and Policy', *Journal of Developing Areas* 24: 489–502.

Ratner, B. D. (2004), '"Sustainability" as a Dialogue of Values: Challenges to the Sociology of Development', *Sociological Inquiry* 74(1): 59–69.

Raynolds, L. T., Murray, D. and Wilkinson, J. (eds) (2007), *Fair Trade: The Challenges of Transforming Globalization*, London: Routledge.

Reality of Aid (2006), *2006 Report – Facts and Figures*, www.devinit.org/realityofaid (accessed 3/9/08).

Reality of Aid (2008), *The Reality of Aid 2008, Aid Effectiveness: 'Democratic Ownership and Human Rights'*, Quezon City: IBON Books.

Reality of Aid (2010), *The Reality of Aid 2010*, www.realityofaid.org/reports (accessed 10/4/11).

Redclift, M. R. (1987), *Sustainable Development: Exploring the Contradictions*, London: Routledge.

Redclift, M. R. (2002), 'Sustainable Development', in V. Desai and R. B. Potter (eds), *The Companion to Development Studies*, London: Arnold, pp. 275–8.

Reed, D. (ed.) (1992), *Structural Adjustment and the Environment*, London: Earthscan.

Reilly, N. (2008), *Women's Human Rights*, Cambridge: Polity.

Reimann, C. (2002), 'Engendering the Field of Conflict Management: Why Gender Does Not Matter! Thoughts from a Theoretical Perspective', in M. Braig and S. Wolte (eds), *Common Ground or Mutual Exclusion: Women's Movements and International Relations*, London: Zed Books.

Remenyi, J. V. and Quinones, B. (eds) (2000), *Microfinance and Poverty Alleviation*, London: Pinter.

Renzio, P. de, Whitfield, L. and Bergamaschi, I. (2008), *Reforming Foreign Aid Practices*, Briefing Paper, June, www.globaleconomicgovernance.org (accessed 9/4/11).

Repetto, R. (1992), 'Earth in the Balance Sheet: Incorporating Natural Resources in National Income Accounts', *Environment* 34(7): 13–20.

Repetto, R. (1995), *Jobs, Competitiveness and Environmental Regulation: What Are the Real Issues?*, Washington, DC: World Resources Institute.

Reynolds, J. (2007), 'Chinese Challenge One-Child Policy', *BBC News Online*, 25 May, www.bbcnews.co.uk (accessed 29/9/07).

Rhyne, E. (2001), *Mainstreaming Microfinance*, Bloomfield, CN: Kumarian Press.

Ricardo, D. (1817), *On the Principles of Political Economy and Taxation*, London: Penguin (reprinted 1971).

Richards, P. (1993), 'Cultivation: Knowledge or Performance?', in M. Hobart (ed.), *An Anthropological Critique of Development*, London: Routledge, pp. 61–78.

Richardson, D. (1997), 'The Politics of Sustainable Development', in S. Baker, M. Kousis, D. Richardson and S. Young (eds), *The Politics of Sustainable Development*, London: Routledge, pp. 43–60.

Richey, L. A. (2000), 'Gender Equality and Foreign Aid', in F. Tarp (ed.), *Foreign Aid and Development*, London: Routledge, pp. 247–70.

Riddell, R. C. (2007), *Does Foreign Aid Really Work?*, Oxford: Oxford University Press.

Rigg, J. (1997), *Southeast Asia*, London: Routledge.

Rigg, J. (2002), 'The Asian Crisis', in V. Desai and R. B. Potter (eds), *The Companion to Development Studies*, London: Arnold, pp. 27–32.

Rigg, J. (2003), *Southeast Asia*, 2nd edn, London: Routledge.

Rigg, J. (2007), *An Everyday Geography of the Global South*, London: Routledge.

Righter, R. (2009), 'China's Future will be Hobbled by Old Age', *Times Online*, 3 August, www.timesonline.co.uk (accessed 9/5/10).

RIIA (2005), 'The Globalization of Security', Chatham House Briefing Paper 05/02, www.chathamhouse.org.uk (accessed 3/10/08).

Riles, A. (2005), 'The Network Inside Out', in M. Edelman and A. Haugerud (eds), *The Anthropology of Development and Globalization*, Oxford: Blackwell, pp. 262–7.

Risse, M. (2005), 'How does the Global Order Harm the Poor?', *Philosophy and Public Affairs* 33(4): 349–76.

Rist, G. (2002), *History of Development: From Western Origins to Global Faith*, 2nd edn, London: Zed Books.

Ritzer, G. (1993), *The McDonaldization of Society*, London: Sage.

Rivero, O. de (2001), *The Myth of Development*, London: Zed Books.

Robertson, R. (1992), *Globalization: Social Theory and Global Culture*, London: Sage.

Robertson, R. (1995), 'Glocalization: Time–Space and Homogeneity–Heterogeneity', in M. Featherstone, S. Lash and R. Robertson (eds) (1995), *Global Modernities*, London: Sage, pp. 25–44.

Robey, B., Rutstein, S. and Morris, L. (1993), 'The Fertility Decline in Developing Countries', *Scientific American* 269 (December 1993).

Robinson, S. and Tarp, F. (2000), 'Foreign Aid and Development: Summary and Synthesis', in F. Tarp (ed.), *Foreign Aid and Development*, London: Routledge, pp. 1–14.

Rocha, J. (1999), 'San Francisco Libre: Giving it One More Try', *Envio* 210–11: 36–46.

Rocheleau, D., Thomas-Slayter, B. and Wangari, E. (eds) (1996), *Feminist Political Ecology: Global Issues and Local Experiences*, London: Routledge.

Rodrik, D. (1997), *Has Globalization Gone Too Far?*, Washington, DC: Institute for International Economics.

Rodrik, D. (1999), *The New Global Economy and Developing Countries: Making Openness Work*, Washington DC: Overseas Development Council.

Rodrik, D. (2006), 'Goodbye Washington Consensus, Hello Washington Confusion?', *Journal of Economic Literature* XLIV: 973–87.

Rodrik, D. and Rodríguez, F. (2000), 'Trade Policy and Economic Growth: A

Skeptic's Guide to the Cross-National Evidence', in B. S. Bernanke and K. S. Rogoff (eds), *NBER Macroeconomics Annual 2000*, Cambridge, MA: MIT Press, pp. 261–325.

Roe, E. (1995), 'Critical Theory, Sustainable Development and Populism', *Telos* 103: 149–62.

Rogaly, B. and Roche, C. (1998), *Learning from South–North Links in Microfinance*, Oxford: Oxfam.

Rogers, B. (1980), *The Domestication of Women: Discrimination in Developing Societies*, London: Kogan Page.

Rogers, P. P., Jalal, J. F. and Boyd, J. A. (2008), *An Introduction to Sustainable Development*, London: Earthscan.

Rosenau, J. (1997), *Along the Domestic–Foreign Frontier*, Cambridge: Cambridge University Press.

Rosenthal, E. (2000), 'Rural Flouting of One-Child Policy Undercuts China's Census', *New York Times*, 14 April, p. A10.

Ross, M. (2003), 'The Natural Resource Curse: How Wealth Can Make You Poor', in I. Bannon and P. Collier (eds), *Natural Resources and Violent Conflict*, Washington, DC: World Bank.

Rostow, W. W. (1960), *The Stages of Economic Growth: A Non-Communist Manifesto*, Cambridge: Cambridge University Press.

Roudi-Fahimi, F. and Kent, M. M. (2007), 'Challenges and Opportunities – The Population of the Middle East and North Africa', *Population Reference Bureau*, 62(2), www.prb.org (accessed 9/5/10).

Rowlands, J. (1997), *Questioning Empowerment*, Oxford: Oxfam.

Rudra, N. (2002), 'Globalization and the Decline of the Welfare State in Less-Developed Countries', *International Organization* 56(2): 411–45.

Rugendyke, B. (2007a), 'Lilliputians or Leviathans? NGOs as Advocates', in B. Rugendyke (ed.), *NGOs as Advocates for Development in a Globalising World*, London: Routledge, pp. 1–14.

Rugendyke, B. (2007b), 'Making Poverty History?', in B. Rugendyke (ed.), *NGOs as Advocates for Development in a Globalising World*, London: Routledge, pp. 222–32.

Rutherford, K. R. (2008), *Humanitarianism under Fire: The US and UN Intervention in Somalia*, Bloomfield, CT: Kumarian Press.

Rutherford, S. (2000), *The Poor and Their Money*, London: Oxford University Press.

Sachs, J. (2000), 'South Africa as the Epicenter of HIV/AIDS: Vital Political Legacies and Current Debates', *Current Issues in Comparative Education* 3(1): 52–6.

Sachs, J. (2005a), 'Why Aid Does Work, *BBC News Online*, 11 September, www.bbc.co.uk/news (accessed 3/11/06).

Sachs, J. (2005b), *The End of Poverty*, London: Penguin.

Sachs, J. and Warner, A. (1995a), 'Economic Reform and the Process of Global Integration', *Brookings Papers on Economic Activity* 1: 1–118.

Sachs, J. and Warner, A. (1995b), 'Natural Resources and Economic Growth', Development Discussion Paper 517a, Cambridge, MA: Harvard Institute for International Development.

Sachs, W. (ed.) (1992), *The Development Dictionary: A Guide to Knowledge as Power*, London: Zed Books.

Sachs, W. and Santarius, T. (eds) (2007), *Fair Future*, London: Zed Books.

Sacquet, A.-M. (2005), *World Atlas of Sustainable Development*, London: Anthem Press.

Safa, H. (1995), *The Myth of the Male Breadwinner: Women and Industrialization in the Caribbean*, Boulder, CO: Westview.

Sahlins, M. (1997), 'The Original Affluent Society', in M. Rahnema with V. Bawtree (eds), *The Post-Development Reader*, London: Zed Books, pp. 1–21.

Said, E. (1995), *Orientalism*, Harmondsworth: Penguin.

Saith, A. (2006), 'From Universal Values to Millennium Development Goals: Lost in Translation', *Development and Change* 37(6): 1167–99.

Samoff, J. and Stromquist, N. P. (2001), 'Managing Knowledge and Storing Wisdom? New Forms of Foreign Aid?', *Development and Change* 32: 631–56.

Sample, I. (2009), 'World Faces "Perfect Storm" of Problems by 2030', *Guardian Online*, 18 March, www.guardian.co.uk (accessed 19/3/09).

Sánchez-Rodríguez, R. (2006), 'Fernando Henrique Cardoso', in D. Simon (ed.), *Fifty Key Thinkers on Development*, London: Routledge, pp. 61–7.

Sand, P. H. (2004), 'Sovereignty Bounded: Public Trusteeship for Common Pool Resources?', *Global Environmental Politics* 4(1): 47–71.

Sandler, R. and Pezzullo, P. C. (eds) (2007), *Environmental Justice and Environmentalism: The Social Justice Challenge to the Environmental Movement*, Cambridge, MA: MIT Press.

SAPRIN (2004), *Structural Adjustment: The SAPRI Report*, London: Zed Books.

Sapsford, D. (2002), 'Smith, Ricardo and the World Marketplace', in V. Desai and R. B. Potter (eds), *The Companion to Development Studies*, London: Arnold, pp. 70–4.

Sardar, Z. (1998), *Postmodernism and the Other: The New Imperialism of Western Culture*, London: Pluto.

Sardar, Z. and Wyn Davies, M. (2002), *Why Do People Hate America?*, Cambridge: Icon Books.

Sardar, Z., Nandy, A. and Davies, M. (1993), *Barbaric Others: A Manifesto on Western Racism*, London: Pluto.

Sassen, S. (2000), *Cities in a World Economy*, 2nd edn, Thousand Oaks, CA: Pine Forge Press.

Sassen, S. (2001), *The Global City*, 2nd edn, Princeton: Princeton University Press.

Sassen, S. (ed.) (2002), *Global Networks, Linked Cities*, New York: Routledge.

Schech, S. and Haggis, J. (2000), *Culture and Development: A Critical Introduction*, Oxford: Blackwell.

Schech, S. and Haggis, J. (eds) (2002), *Development: A Cultural Studies Reader*, Oxford: Blackwell.

Schifferes, S. (2005a), 'World Bank Rediscovers Inequality', *BBC News Online*, 20 September, www.bbc.co.uk/news (accessed 11/10/06).

Schifferes, S. (2005b), 'Final Round for Global Trade Talks', *BBC News Online*, 21 December, www.bbc.co.uk/news (accessed 1/5/08).

Schifferes, S. (2005c), 'Can G8 Be Considered a Success?', *BBC News Online*, 8 July, www.bbc.co.uk/news (accessed 10/8/08).

Schifferes, S. (2007a), 'Globalisation Shakes the World', *BBC News Online*, 21 January, www.bbc.co.uk/news (accessed 8/4/08).

Schifferes, S. (2007b), 'Multinationals Lead India's IT Revolution', *BBC News Online*, 24 January, www.bbc.co.uk/news (accessed 8/4/08).

Schifferes, S. (2008), 'Poor Countries Get US$1 trillion', *BBC News Online*, 10 June, www.bbc.co.uk/news (accessed 10/4/11).

Schiller, H. I. (1995), 'The Global Information Highway', in J. Brook and I. A. Boal (eds), *Resisting the Virtual Life: The Culture and Politics of Information*, San Francisco: City Lights Press.

Schlosberg, D. (1999), *Environmental Justice and the New Pluralism*, Oxford: Oxford University Press.

Schlosberg, D. (2009) *Defining Environmental Justice: Theories, Movements, and Nature*, Oxford: Oxford University Press.

Scholte, J. A. (2005), *Globalization: A Critical Introduction*, 2nd edn, Basingstoke: Palgrave.

Schumacher, E. F. (1974), *Small is Beautiful: A Study of Economics as if People Mattered*, London: Abacus.

Schuurman, F. (ed.) (1993), *Beyond the Impasse: New Directions in Development Theory*, London: Zed Books.

Schuurman, F. (2000), 'Paradigms Lost, Paradigms Regained? Development Studies in the Twenty-First Century', *Third World Quarterly* 21: 7–20.

Scott, A. J. (ed.) (2001), *Global City-Regions*, Oxford: Oxford University Press.

Seager, A. (2008), 'West is Urged to Cancel Further US$400bn of Poor Countries' Debt', *Guardian Online*, 16 May, www.guardian.co.uk (accessed 17/5/08).

Seager, A. (2009), 'World Bank Calls on West to Help Relieve Trillion Dollar Drain on World's Poor', *Guardian Online*, 22 June, www.guardian.co.uk (accessed 14/7/10).

Seal, R. and Manson, K. (2008), 'Why are Mothers Still Dying in Childbirth?', *Guardian Online*, 28 September, www.guardian.co.uk (accessed 31/5/10).

Segbers, K. (ed.) (2007), *The Making of Global City Regions*, Baltimore: Johns Hopkins University Press.

Seitz, J. L. (2008), *Global Issues*, 3rd edn, Oxford: Blackwell.

Sen, A. (1981), *Poverty and Famines*, Oxford: Clarendon Press.

Sen, A. (1987), *On Ethics and Economics*, Oxford: Blackwell.

Sen, A. (1989), 'Food and Freedom', *World Development* 17: 769–81.

Sen, A. (2001), *Development as Freedom*, Oxford: Oxford University Press.

Sen, A. (2008[1990]), 'More than 100 Million Women are Missing', in S. Chari and S. Corbridge (eds), *The Development Reader*, London: Routledge, pp. 432–41.

Sen, G. and Grown, K. (1987), *Development, Crises and Alternative Visions: Third World Women's Perspectives*, New York: Monthly Review Press.

Sen, G., Germain, A. and Chen, L. (eds) (1994), *Population Policy Reconsidered*, Harvard: Harvard University Press.

Shafaeddin, M. S. (2006), 'Trade Liberalization and Economic Reform in Developing Countries: Structural Change or De-industrialization?', in A. Paloni and M. Zanardi (eds), *The IMF, World Bank and Policy Reform*, London: Routledge, pp. 162–90.

Shahin, M. (1999), 'Trade and Environment: How Real is the Debate?', in G. Sampson and W. Bradnee Chambers (eds), *Trade, Environment and the Environment*, Tokyo: United Nations Press, pp. 35–64.

Shani, G., Sato, M. and Pasha, M. K. (eds) (2007), *Protecting Human Security in a Post-9/11 World*, Basingstoke: Palgrave.

Shaw, T. M. (2002), 'Peace-building Partnerships and Human Security, in V. Desai and R. B. Potter (eds), *The Companion to Development Studies*, London: Arnold, pp. 449–53.

Sheahan, J. (1987), *Patterns of Development in Latin America*, Princeton: Princeton University Press.

Shields, R. (ed.) (1992), *Lifestyle Shopping*, London: Routledge.

Shiva, V. (1989), *Staying Alive: Women, Ecology and Development*, London: Zed Books.

Shiva, V. (1993), 'The Greening of the Global Reach', in W. Sachs (ed.), *Global Ecology*, London: Zed Books.

Shivji, I. G. (2007), *Silences in NGO Discourse: The Role and Future of NGOs in Africa*, Oxford: Fahamu.

Short, J. R. (2004), *Global Metropolitan*, London: Routledge.

Sidaway, J. D. (2002), 'Post-development', in V. Desai and R. B. Potter (eds), *The Companion to Development Studies*, London: Arnold, pp. 16–20.

Siddarth, V. (1995), 'Gendered Participation: NGOs and the World Bank', *IDS Bulletin*, July 1995, Brighton: IDS.

Siddique, H. (2007), 'Brown Launches Global Health Plan to Aid World's Poor', *The Guardian Unlimited*, 5 September, www.guardian.co.uk (accessed 28/5/10).

Sidwell, M. (2008), *Unfair Trade*, London: Adam Smith Institute, www.adamsmith. org. (accessed 7/8/08).

Silberschmidt, M. (2001), 'Disempowerment of Men in Rural and Urban East Africa: Implications for Male Identity and Sexual Behaviour', *World Development* 29(4): 657–71.

Simon, D. (1998), 'Rethinking (Post)modernism, Postcolonialism and Posttraditionalism: South–North perspectives', *Environment and Planning D: Society and Space* 16(2): 219–45.

Simon, D. (2002), 'Neo-liberalism, Structural Adjustment and Poverty Reduction Strategies', in V. Desai and R. B. Potter (eds), *The Companion to Development Studies*, London: Arnold, pp. 86–92.

Simon, D. and Närman, A. (eds) (1999), *Development as Theory and Practice: Current Perspectives on development and Development Co-operation*, Harlow: Longman.

Simon, D., Van Spengen, W., Dixon, C. and Närman, A. (eds) (1995), *Structurally Adjusted Africa: Poverty, Debt and Basic Needs*, London: Pluto.

Simon, J. L. (1981), *The Ultimate Resource*, Princeton: Princeton University Press.

Simon, J. L. (1990), *Population Matters*, New Brunswick, NJ: Transaction.

Singer, P. W. (2008), *Corporate Warriors*, 2nd edn, Ithaca NY: Cornell University Press.

Singh, A. (2004), 'Aid, Conditionality and Development', in J. P. Pronk et al., *Catalysing Development?*, Oxford: Blackwell, pp. 77–87.

Singh, K. (2001), 'Handing Over the Stick: The Global Spread of Participatory Approaches to Development', in M. Edwards and J. Gaventa (eds), *Global Citizen Action*, Boulder, CO: Lynne Rienner, pp. 175–87.

Six, C. (2009), 'The Rise of Postcolonial States as Donors: A Challenge to the Development Paradigm?', *Third World Quarterly* 30(6): 1103–21.

Sklair, L. (ed.) (1994), *Capitalism and Development*, London: Routledge.

Sklair, L. (2002), *Globalization: Capitalism and its Alternatives*, 3rd edn, Oxford: Oxford University Press.

Smart, B. (ed.) (1999), *Resisting McDonaldization*, London: Sage.

Smillie, I. and Minear, L. (2004), *The Charity of Nations*, Bloomfield: Kumarian Press.

Smith, A. (1961[1776]), *The Wealth of Nations*, London: Penguin.

Smith, A. D. (1990), 'Towards a Global Culture?', in M. Featherstone (ed.), *Global Culture*, London: Sage, pp. 171–91.

Smith, D. M. (2000), *Moral Geographies: Ethics in a World of Difference*, Edinburgh: Edinburgh University Press.

Smith, M. P. (2001), *Transnational Urbanism*, Oxford: Blackwell.

Smith, S. C. (2005), *Ending Global Poverty*, Basingstoke: Palgrave.

Soto, A. (1992), 'The Global Environment: A Southern Perspective', *International Journal* XLVII: 679–705.

South Commission (1990), *The Challenge to the South: The Report of the South Commission*, Oxford: Oxford University Press.

Spaargaren, G., Mol, A. P. J. and Buttel, F. H. (eds) (2000), *Environment and Global Modernity*, London: Sage.

Sparr, P. (ed.) (1994a), *Mortgaging Women's Lives: Feminist Critiques of Structural Adjustment*, London: Zed Books.

Sparr, P. (1994b), 'Feminist Critiques of Structural Adjustment', in P. Sparr (ed.), *Mortgaging Women's Lives*, London: Zed Books, pp. 13–39.

Speth, J. G. (2003), 'Two Perspectives on Globalization and the Environment', in J. G. Speth (ed.), *Worlds Apart: Globalization and the Environment*, London: Island Press, pp. 1–18.

Spivak, G. C. (1987), *In Other Worlds: Essays in Cultural Politics*, London: Methuen.

Spybey, T. (1996), *Globalisation and World Society*, Cambridge: Polity.

Standage, T. (1998), *The Victorian Internet*, London: Weidenfeld and Nicolson.

Standing, G. (1989), 'Global Feminization through Flexible Labour', *World Development*, 17(7): 1077–95.

Staudt, K. (1998), *Policy, Politics and Gender: Women Gaining Ground*, West Hartford, CT: Kumarian Press.

Staudt, K. (2008), 'Women and Gender', in P. Burnell and V. Randall (eds), *Politics in the Developing World*, 2nd edn, Oxford: Oxford University Press, pp. 148–65.

Stein, H. (2003), 'Rethinking African Development', in H.-J. Chang (ed.), *Rethinking Development Economics*, London: Anthem Press, pp. 153–78.

Stern Review (2006), 'The Economics of Climate Change', www.hm-treasury.gov.uk/sternreview (accessed 12/3/07).

Stewart, F. and Fitzgerald, V. (2001), *War and Underdevelopment*, Oxford: Oxford University Press.

Stewart, H. (2006a), 'No Respite in Struggle to Write off Debt', *The Observer: Global Poverty*, 2 July, p. 3.

Stewart, H. (2006b), 'Is Aid a US$2.3 Trillion Failure?', *The Observer: Business & Media*, 24 September, p. 6.

Stewart, H. (2008), 'US Refuses to Relax its Grip on the World Bank', *The Observer*, 10 August, www.guardian.co.uk (accessed 15/8/08).

Stiglitz, J. A. (1998), 'More Instruments and Broader Goals: Moving Toward the Post-Washington Consensus', WIDER Annual Lectures 2, Helsinki.

Stiglitz, J. E. (2002), *Globalisation and its Discontents*, London: Penguin.

Stiglitz, J. E. (2003), 'Globalization and Development', in D. Held and M. Koenig-Archibugi (eds), *Taming Globalization*, Cambridge: Polity, pp. 47–67.

Stiglitz, J. E. and Charlton, A. (2007), *Fair Trade for All: How Trade Can Promote Development*, Oxford: Oxford University Press.

Stillwaggon, E. (2002) 'HIV/AIDS in Africa: Fertile Terrain', *Journal of Development Studies* 38(6): 1–22.

Stöhr, W. B. and Taylor, D. R. F. (1981), *Development from Above or Below? The Dialectics of Regional Planning in Developing Countries*, Chichester: John Wiley.

Storm, S. (2005), 'Development, Trade or Aid? UN Views on Trade, Growth and Poverty', *Development and Change* 36(6): 1239–61.

Streeten, P. (1995), *Thinking About Development*, Cambridge: Cambridge University Press.

Sutcliffe, B. (2000), 'Development after Ecology', in J. Timmons Roberts and A. Hite (eds), *From Modernization to Globalization*, Oxford: Blackwell, pp. 328–39.

Swain, A., Amer, R. and Oiendal, J. (2007), *Globalisation and Challenges to Building Peace*, London: Anthem Press.

Sweetman, C. (ed.) (2001), *Gender, Development and Humanitarian Work*, Oxford: Oxfam.

Sylvester, C. (1999), 'Development Studies and Postcolonial Studies: Disparate Tales of the "Third World"', *Third World Quarterly* 20(4): 703–21.

Tarp, F. (1993), *Stabilization and Structural Adjustment*, London: Routledge.

Tarp, F. (ed.) (2000), *Foreign Aid and Development*, London: Routledge.

Taylor, D. R. and Mackenzie, F. (eds) (1992), *Development from Within: Survival in Rural Africa*, London: Routledge.

Taylor, P. J. (2001), 'Isations of the World: Americanisation, Modernisation and Globalisation', in C. Hay and D. Marsh (eds), *Demystifying Globalisation*, Basingstoke: Palgrave, pp. 49–70.

Taylor, P. J. (2003), *World City Network*, London: Routledge.

Tehranian, M. and Tehranian, K. K. (1997), 'Taming Modernity: Toward a New Paradigm', in A. Mohammadi (ed.), *International Communication and Globalization*, London: Sage.

Telfer, D. J. and Sharpley, R. (2007), *Tourism and Development in the Developing World*, London: Routledge.

Tews, K. and Busch, P.-O. (2002), 'Governance by Diffusion? Potentials and Restrictions of Environmental Policy Diffusion', in F. Biermann, R. Brohm and K. Dingwerth (eds), *Global Environmental Change and the Nation State*, Potsdam: Potsdam Institute for Climate Impact Research, pp. 168–82.

Thomas, A. (2000), 'Development as Practice in a Liberal Capitalist World', *Journal of International Development* 12(6): 773–87.

Thomas, A. and Allen, T. (2000), 'Agencies of Development', in T. Allen and A. Thomas (eds), *Poverty and Development into the 21st Century*, Oxford: Oxford University Press, pp. 189–216.

Thomas, C. Y. (1989), *The Poor and the Powerless: Economic Policy and Change in the Caribbean*, London: Latin American Bureau.

Thomas, C. (2000), *Global Governance, Development and Human Security*, London: Pluto.

Thomas, C. (2002), 'Global Governance and Human Security', in R. Wilkinson and S. Hughes (eds), *Global Governance: Critical Perspectives*, London: Routledge, pp. 113–31.

Thomas, C. (2007), 'Globalisation and Human Security', in A. McGrew and N. K. Poku (eds), *Globalization, Development and Human Security*, Cambridge: Polity, pp. 107–31.

Thompson, G. F. (2007), 'Global Inequality, the "Great Divergence" and Supranational Regionalization', in D. Held and A. Kaya (eds), *Global Inequality*, Cambridge: Polity, pp. 176–203.

Throup, D. (1995), 'The Colonial Legacy', in O. Furley (ed.), *Conflict in Africa*, London: I. B. Tauris, pp. 237–74.

Thurston, J. (2003), 'Keeping the Poorest on Board', in P. Griffith (ed.), *Rethinking Fair Trade*, London: Foreign Policy Centre, pp. 49–54.

Tickner, J. A. (2001), *Gendering World Politics*, New York: Colombia University Press.

Tickner, J. A. (2008), 'Gender in World Politics', in J. Baylis et al. (eds), *The Globalization of World Politics*, Oxford: Oxford University Press, pp. 262–77.

Timberlake, L. (1985), *Africa in Crisis: The Causes, the Cures of Environmental Bankruptcy*, London: Earthscan.

Timmons Roberts, J. and Hite, A. (eds) (2000), *From Modernization to Globalization*, Oxford: Blackwell.

Tinker, I. (ed.) (1990), *Persistent Inequalities: Women and World Development*, Oxford: Oxford University Press.

Tobin, J. (1974), *The New Economics One Decade Older*, Princeton: Princeton University Press.

Todaro, M. P. and Smith, S. C. (2003), *Economic Development*, 8th edn, Harlow: Pearson Education.

Todd, H. (1996), *Women at the Centre*, Boulder, CO: Westview Press.

Toffler, A. (1970), *Future Shock*, London: Bodley Head.

Tomlinson, J. (1991), *Cultural Imperialism*, London: Pinter.

Tomlinson, J. (1999), *Globalisation and Culture*, Cambridge: Polity.

Townsend, J. G., Mawdsley, E. and Porter, G. (2002), 'Challenges for NGOs', in V. Desai and R. B. Potter (eds), *The Companion to Development Studies*, London: Arnold, pp. 534–8.

Townsend, P. (1979), *Poverty in the United Kingdom: A Survey of Household Resources and Standards of Living*, Harmondsworth: Penguin.

Toye, J. (1987), *Dilemmas of Development: Reflections on the Counter-Revolution in Development Theory and Practice*, Oxford: Blackwell.

Toye, J. (1993), *Dilemmas of Development: Reflections on the Counter-Revolution in Development Theory and Practice*, 2nd edn, Oxford: Blackwell.

Toye, J. (2003), 'Changing Perspectives in Development Economics', in H.-J. Chang (ed.), *Rethinking Development Economics*, London: Anthem Press, pp. 21–40.

Tran, M. (2007), 'World Bank Must Lead on Climate Change, Says Benn', *Guardian Unlimited Environment*, www.guardian.co.uk, 12 April (accessed 9/5/07).

Tran, M. (2008), 'Developed Countries Fall Behind in Meeting Foreign Aid Pledges', *Guardian Unlimited*, www.guardian.co.uk, 3 June (accessed 4/6/08).

Trittin, J. (2004), 'The Role of the Nation State in International Environmental Policy', *Global Environmental Politics* 4(1): 23–8.

Truman, H. S. (1967), 'Inaugural Address', *Documents on American Foreign Relations*, CT: Princeton University Press, 20 January 1949.

Tucker, V. (1996), 'Introduction: A Cultural Perspective on Development', *European Journal of Development Research* 8(2): 1–21.

Tucker, V. (ed.) (1997), *Cultural Perspectives on Development*, London: Frank Cass.

Twist, J. (2004), 'China Leads Way on Broadband', *BBC News Online*, 5 October, www. bbcnews.co.uk (accessed 12/11/08).

Ukeje, C. (2008), 'Globalization and Conflict Management: Reflections on the Security Challenges Facing West Africa', *Globalizations* 5(1): 35–48.

UNAIDS (2009a), *UNAIDS Action Framework: Addressing Women, Girls, Gender Equality and HIV*, www.unaids.org (accessed 11/6/10).

UNAIDS (2009b), *AIDS Epidemic Update*, December 2009, www.unaids.org (accessed 12/6/10).

UNAIDS (2009c), *A Strategic Approach: HIV & AIDS and Education*, May 2009, www. unesco.org/aids/iatt (accessed 13/6/10).

UNCTAD (2001), *World Investment Report 2001*, Geneva: UN.

UNCTAD (2004a), *Economic Development in Africa – Debt Sustainability: Oasis or Mirage?*, Geneva: UN.

UNCTAD (2004b) *The Least Developed Countries Report 2004: Linking International Trade with Poverty Reduction*, Geneva: UN.

UNCTAD (2006a), *Economic Development in Africa: Doubling Aid – Making the "Big Push" Work*, Geneva: UN.

UNCTAD (2006b) *The Least Developed Countries Report 2006: Developing Productive Capacities*, Geneva: UN.

UNDESA (2002), *World Population Ageing: 1950–2050*, UNDESA Population Division, www. un.org/esa/population/publications/worldageing19502050/ (accessed 4/10/09).

UNDP (1994), *Human Development Report, 1994*, Oxford: Oxford University Press.

UNDP (1995), *Human Development Report, 1995*, Oxford: Oxford University Press.

UNDP (1998), *Human Development Report, 1998*, Oxford: Oxford University Press.

UNDP (1999), *Human Development Report, 1999*, Oxford: Oxford University Press.

UNDP (2001), *Human Development Report, 2001: Promoting Linkages*, Oxford: Oxford University Press.

UNDP (2002), *Human Development Report, 2002: Deepening Democracy in a Fragmented World*, Oxford: Oxford University Press.

UNDP (2003a), *Human Development Report, 2003*, Oxford: Oxford University Press.

UNDP (2003b), *Making Global Trade Work for People*, London: Earthscan.

UNDP (2003c), *Forging a Global South: United Nations Day for South–South Cooperation*, United Nations Development Programme, 19 December 2004.

UNDP (2005), *Human Development Report, 2005: International Cooperation at a Crossroads*, New York: UN Publications.

UNDP (2006), *Human Development Report, 2006: Beyond Scarcity: Power, Poverty and the Global Water Crisis*, New York: UN Publications.

UNDP (2007), *Human Development Report, 2007/2008: Fighting Climate Change: Human Solidarity in a Divided World*, New York: UN Publications.

UNDP (2010), *Human Development Report, 2010*, New York: UN Publications.

UNDPKO (2008), *United Nations Peacekeeping Factsheet* (DPI/2429/Rev.2 – February 2008), pp. 1–4, www.un.org/Depts/dpko/factsheet (accessed 8/9/08).

UNECA (2004a), 'Ministerial Statement', Conference of African Ministers of Finance, Planning and Economic Development, Kampala, Uganda, 21–22 May, www.uneca.org/cfm/2004/index.htm (accessed 29/6/08).

UNECA (2004b), 'Trade Liberalization and Development: Lessons for Africa', *African Trade Policy Centre*, No. 6, www.uneca.org/ATPC/Work (accessed 27/6/08).

UNEP (2007), *Global Environment Outlook 4: Environment for Development*, www.unep. org/GEO/geo4 (accessed 28/11/08).

UNESCO (1995), *World Education Report 1995*, New York: Oxford University Press.

UNESCO (2009), *2009 EFA Global Monitoring Report: Overcoming Inequality – Why Governance Matters (Summary)*, Paris: UNESCO.

UNESCO (2010), *2010 EFA Global Monitoring Report: Reaching the Marginalized (Summary)*, Paris: UNESCO.

UNESCO (forthcoming), *2011 EFA Global Monitoring Report: Education and Violent Conflict*, Paris: UNESCO.

UNFPA (2007), 'State of the World Population Report 2007', *United Nations Population Fund*, www.unpfa.org (accessed 4/4/08).

UNFPA (2008), 'UNFPA Statement: Population and Climate Change', *United Nations Population Fund*, 11 February, www.unpfa.org (accessed 3/5/10).

UNFPA (2011), 'Reproductive Health', *United Nations Population Fund*, www.unpfa. org (accessed 23/4/11).

UN–Habitat (2003), *The Challenge of Slums: Global Report On Human Settlements 2003*, London: Earthscan.

UN–Habitat (2007), *State of the World's Cities Report 2006/7*, New York: UN Publications.

UNICEF (1999), *The State of the World's Children: Education*, New York: UNICEF.

UNICEF (2005), *The State of the World's Children: Childhood under Threat*, New York: UNICEF.

United Nations (1995), 'Beijing Declaration and Platform for Action', 15 September, Fourth World Conference on Women, www.un.org/womenwatch/daw/beijing/platform/declar (accessed 3/5/08).

United Nations (1999), *1999 World Survey on the Role of Women in Development: Globalization, Gender and Work*, A/54/227, New York: United Nations.

United Nations (2004), *Basic Facts about the United Nations*, New York: United Nations.

United Nations (2005a), *Draft Reform Document*, 13 September, www.un.org (accessed 22/6/08).

United Nations (2005b), *Report on the World Social Situation 2005: The Inequality Predicament*, New York: United Nations.

UNMDG (2005), *UN Millennium Development Goals*, New York: UN, www.un.org/millenniumgoals/ (accessed 29/11/07).

UNMDG (2007), *The Millennium Development Goals Report 2007*, New York: UN, www.un.org/millenniumgoals/ (accessed 29/1/08).

UNMDG (2008), *The Millennium Development Goals Report 2008*, New York: UN, www.un.org/millenniumgoals/ (accessed 23/1/09).

UNMDG (2009), *The Millennium Development Goals Report 2009*, New York: UN, www.un.org/millenniumgoals/ (accessed 21/6/10).

UNODC (2008), 'Drugs Finance Taliban War Machine, says UN Drug Tsar', 27 November, www.unodc.org/unodc/en/press/releases/2008-11-27 (accessed 15/4/11).

UNPD (2009a), *World Fertility Patterns 2009*, UN Department of Economic and Social Affairs, www.unpopulation.org (accessed 23/4/11).

UNPD (2009b), *World Mortality 2009*, UN Department of Economic and Social Affairs, www.unpopulation.org (accessed 23/4/11).

UNPD (2011), *World Population Prospects: The 2010 Revision*, UN Department of Economic and Social Affairs, 5 May, www.unpopulation.org (accessed 7/5/11).

Vajja, A. and White, H. (2008), 'Can the World Bank Build Social Capital? The Experience of Social Funds in Malawi and Zambia', *Development and Change* 44(8): 1145–68.

Vakil, A. (1997), 'Confronting the Classification Problem: Toward a Taxonomy of NGOs', *World Development* 25(12): 2057–70.

Van Beers, C. and Van den Bergh, J. C. J. M. (1997), 'An Empirical Multi-Country Analysis of the Impact of Environmental Regulations on Trade Flows', *Kyklos* 50(1): 29–46.

Van Rooy, A. (2002), 'Strengthening Civil Society in Developing Countries', in V. Desai and R. B. Potter (eds), *The Companion to Development Studies*, London: Arnold, pp. 489–95.

Varley, A. (2002), 'Gender, Families and Households', in V. Desai and R. B. Potter (eds), *The Companion to Development Studies*, London: Arnold, pp. 329–34.

Vasagar, J. (2006), 'A Failure of Purpose', *Guardian Online*, 3 January, www.guardian. co.uk (accessed 11/12/06).

Vaux, T. (2007), 'Humanitarian Trends and Dilemmas', in D. Eade and T. Vaux (eds), *Development and Humanitarianism*, Bloomfield, CT: Kumarian Press, pp. 1–23.

Verstegen, S. W. and Hanekamp, J. C. (2005), 'The Sustainability Debate: Idealism versus Conformism – the Controversy over Economic Growth', *Globalizations* 2(3): 349–62.

Vidal, J. (2007a), 'China Could Overtake US as Biggest Emissions Culprit by November', *The Guardian*, 25 April, p. 13.

Vidal, J. (2007b), 'Dust, Waste and Dirty Water: The Deadly Price of China's Miracle', *Guardian Unlimited*, 18 July, www.guardian.co.uk (accessed 14/9/07).

Visvanathan, N., Duggan, L., Nisonoff, L. and Wiegersma, N. (eds) (1997), *The Women, Gender and Development Reader*, London: Zed Books.

Wade, R. H. (2000), 'The Asian Debt-and-Development Crisis of 1997–?: Causes and Consequences', *World Development* 26(8): 1535–53.

Wade, R. H. (2003), 'The Disturbing Rise in Poverty and Inequality: Is It all a "Big Lie"?', in D. Held and M. Koenig-Archibugi (eds), *Taming Globalization*, Cambridge: Polity, pp. 18–46.

Wade, R. H. (2004a), *Governing the Market: Economic Theory and the Role of Government in East Asian Industrialization*, 2nd edn, Princeton: Princeton University Press.

Wade, R. H. (2004b), 'Is Globalization Reducing Poverty and Inequality?', *World Development* 32(4): 567–89.

Wade, R. H. (2007), 'Should We Worry about Income Inequality?', in D. Held and A. Kaya (eds), *Global Inequality*, Cambridge: Polity, pp. 104–31.

Wade, R. H. and Veneroso, F. (1998), 'The Asian Crisis: The High Debt Model versus the Wall Street–Treasury–IMF Complex', *New Left Review* 228: 3–24.

Wade, R. H. and Wolf, M. (2003), 'Are Global Poverty and Inequality Getting Worse?', in D. Held and A. McGrew (eds), *The Global Transformations Reader*, 2nd edn, Cambridge: Polity, pp. 440–6.

Walker, A. (2005), 'Lenders Edge Closer to Debt Relief Deal', *BBC News Online*, 22 September, www.bbcnews.co.uk (accessed 25/10/06).

Wallace, T. (1991), 'The Impact of Global Crises on Women: Introduction', in

T. Wallace and C. March (eds), *Changing Perceptions: Writings on Gender and Development*, Oxford: Oxfam.

Wallace, T., Bornstein, L. and Chapman, J. (1999), *The Aid Chain: Coercion and Commitment in Development NGOs*, Rugby: ITDG Publishing.

Walle, N. van de (2005), *Overcoming Stagnation in Aid-Dependent Countries*, Washington, DC: Centre for Global Development.

Wallerstein, I. (1974), *The Modern World System I*, New York: Academic Press.

Wallerstein, I. (1979), *The Capitalist World Economy*, Cambridge: Cambridge University Press.

Wallerstein, I. (1980), *The Modern World System II*, New York: Academic Press.

Wallerstein, I. (2003), *The Decline of American Power*, New York: The New Press.

Ward, H. and Brack, D. (eds) (2000), *Trade, Investment and the Environment*, London: Earthscan for RIIA.

Warren, B. (1980), *Imperialism: Pioneer of Capitalism*, London: Verso.

Watchel, H. M. (2000), 'The Mosaic of Global Taxes', in J. Nederveen Pieterse (ed.), *Global Futures*, New York: Zed Books, pp. 83–97.

Watkins, K. (1995), *The Oxfam Poverty Report*, Oxford: Oxfam.

Watson, J. L. (1997), *Golden Arches East: McDonald's in East Asia*, Stanford: Stanford University Press.

Watson, M. (2001), 'International Capital Mobility in an Era of Globalization', *Politics*, 21(2): 81–92.

Watts, J. (2007), 'Villagers Riot as China Enforces Birth Limit', *The Guardian*, 22 May, p. 22.

Watts, J. and Vidal, J. (2007), 'As Glaciers Melt and Rivers Dry Up, Coal-fired Power Stations Multiply', *The Guardian*, 20 June, p. 23.

WBIEG (2006), *Debt Relief for the Poorest: An Evaluation Update of the HIPC Initiative*, Washington, DC: World Bank.

WCED (1987), *Our Common Future*, Oxford: Oxford University Press.

WDI (2008), *World Development Indicators 2008*, Washington, DC: World Bank.

Weber, H. (2002), 'Global Governance and Poverty Reduction: The Case of Microcredit', in R. Wilkinson and S. Hughes (eds), *Global Governance: Critical Perspectives*, London: Routledge, pp. 132–51.

Weber, M. (1958[1904/5]), *The Protestant Ethic and the Spirit of Capitalism*, New York: Charles Scribner.

Weiner, M (ed.) (1966), *Modernization: The Dynamics of Growth*, New York: Basic Books.

Weiss, T. G. (2004), 'The Sunset of Humanitarian Intervention? The Responsibility to Protect in a Unipolar Era', *Security Dialogue* 35(2): 135–53.

Weiss, T. G. (2007), *Humanitarian Intervention*, Cambridge: Polity.

Weiss, T. G. and Collins, C. (2000), *Humanitarian Challenges and Intervention*, 2nd edn, Boulder, CO: Westview.

Welsh, J. M. (ed.) (2004), *Humanitarian Intervention and International Relations*, Oxford: Oxford University Press.

Whaites, A. (2000), 'Let's Get Civil Society Straight: NGOs, the State, and Political Theory', in D. Eade and J. Pearce (eds), *Development, NGOs and Civil Society*, Oxford: Oxfam, pp. 124–41.

Wheeler, D. (2002), 'Beyond Pollution Havens', *Global Environmental Politics* 2(2): 1–10.

White, H. (1999), 'Politicizing Development? The Role of Participation in the Activities of Aid Agencies', in K. Gupta (ed.), *Foreign Aid*, London: Kluwer Academic.

White, H. (2002), 'The Measurement of Poverty', in V. Desai and R. B. Potter (eds), *The Companion to Development Studies*, London: Arnold, pp. 32–7.

White, H. (2006), 'Millennium Development Goals', in D. A. Clark (ed.), *The Elgar Companion to Development Studies*, Cheltenham: Edward Elgar.

White, S. C. (2000), 'Depoliticizing Development: The Uses and Abuses of Participation', in D. Eade and J. Pearce (eds), *Development, NGOs and Civil Society*, Oxford: Oxfam, pp. 142–55.

WHO (1948), *WHO Definition of Health*, www.who.int/about/defintion/en/ (accessed 5/5/10).

WHO (2002), *The World Health Report 2002*, Geneva: World Health Organization.

WHO (2006), *The World Health Report 2006 – Working Together for Health*, Geneva: World Health Organization.

WHO (2008), *Effective Aid: Better Health*, Report prepared for the Accra High Level Forum on Aid Effectiveness, 2–4 September 2008, Geneva: World Health Organization.

WHO (2009), *World Health Statistics 2009*, Geneva: World Health Organization.

Widner, J. with Mundt, A. (1998), 'Research in Social Capital in Africa', *Africa* 68(1):1–24.

Wieringa, S. (1994), 'Women's Interests and Empowerment: Gender Planning Reconsidered', *Development and Change* 25: 849–78.

Wiesmann, D. (2006), '2006 Global Hunger Index: A Basis for Cross-Country Comparisons', *International Food Policy Research Institute*, www.ifpri.org (accessed 2/9/08).

Wilkinson, R. G. (2005), *The Impact of Inequality*, New York: New Press.

Wilkinson, R. and Hughes, S. (eds) (2002), *Global Governance: Critical Perspectives*, London: Routledge.

Williams, G. (2004), 'Reforming Africa: Continuities and Changes', *Africa South of the Sahara 2004*, 33rd edn, London: Europa Publications, pp. 3–11.

Williams, M. (2001), 'Trade and Environment in the World Trading System: A Decade of Stalemate?', *Global Environmental Politics* 1(1): 1–9.

Willis, K. (2005), *Theories and Practices of Development*, London: Routledge.

Wilson, E. (2010), 'Billions Pour in for India's Insulated Superclass', *The Observer*, 9 May, www.guardian.co.uk (accessed 12/9/10).

Winters, A. L. and Yusuf, S. (eds) (2007), *Dancing with Giants: China, India and the Global Economy*, Washington, DC: World Bank.

Wisner, B. (1988), *Power and Need in Africa: Basic Human Needs and Development Policies*, London: Earthscan.

Wolf, M. (2000), 'The Big Lie of Global Inequality', *Financial Times*, 8 February.

Wolf, M. (2004), *Why Globalisation Works*, New Haven: Yale University Press.

Woods, N. (2000), 'The Challenge of Good Governance for the IMF and the World Bank Themselves', *World Development* 28(5): 823–41.

Woods, N. (2005), 'Making the IMF and the World Bank More Accountable', in A. Buira (ed.), *Reforming the Governance of the IMF and the World Bank*, London: Anthem Press, pp. 149–70.

Woodward, D. (1992), *Debt, Adjustment and Poverty in Developing Countries*, 2 vols, London: Pinter.

Woolcock, M. (1998), 'Social Capital and Economic Development: Toward a Theoretical Synthesis and Policy Framework', *Theory and Society* 27(2): 151–208.

Woost, M. D. (1997), 'Alternative Vocabularies of Development? "Community" and "Participation" in Development Discourse in Sri Lanka', in R. D. Grillo and R. L. Stirrat (eds), *Discourses of Development*, Oxford: Berg, pp. 229–53.

World Bank (1975), *The Assault on World Poverty*, Baltimore: Johns Hopkins University Press.

World Bank (1983), *World Development Report*, Washington, DC: World Bank.

World Bank (1988), *Accelerated Development in Sub-Saharan Africa: An Agenda for Action*, Washington, DC: World Bank.

World Bank (1993), *The East Asian Miracle*, Oxford: Oxford University Press.

World Bank (1996a), *NGOs and the World Bank*, Washington, DC: Poverty and Social Policy Department.

World Bank (1996b), *World Development Report, 1996*, New York: Oxford University Press.

World Bank (1997), *World Development Report 1997: The State in a Changing World*, Washington, DC: World Bank.

World Bank (1998a), *Assessing Aid: What Works, What Doesn't, and Why*, Washington, DC: World Bank.

World Bank (1998b), *Partnerships for Development: A New World Bank Approach*, Washington, DC: World Bank.

World Bank (2000a), *Can Africa Claim the 21st Century?*, Washington, DC: World Bank.

World Bank (2000b), *Higher Education in Developing Societies: Peril and Promise*, Washington, DC: World Bank.

World Bank (2001a), *Poverty in the Age of Globalization*, Washington, DC: World Bank.

World Bank (2001b), *World Development Report 2000/01: Attacking Poverty*, New York: Oxford University Press.

World Bank (2002), *Empowerment and Poverty Reduction: A Sourcebook*, Washington, DC: World Bank.

World Bank (2003), *World Development Report 2003: Sustainable Development in a Dynamic World: Transforming Institutions, Growth and Quality of Life*, Oxford: Oxford University Press.

World Bank (2005a), *The World Bank's Global HIV/AIDS Program of Action*, Washington, DC: World Bank.

World Bank (2005b), *World Development Report 2006: Equity and Development*, Washington, DC: World Bank.

World Bank (2011), *World Development Report 2011: Conflict, Security and Development Overview*, Washington, DC: World Bank.

World Bank NGO Unit Social Development (1998), *The Bank's Relations with NGOs: Issues and Directions*, Paper No. 28, Washington, DC: World Bank.

World Education Forum (2000), *The Dakar Framework for Action – Education for All: Meeting our Collective Commitments*, Paris: UNESCO.

Worsley, P. (1964), *The Third World*, London: Weidenfeld and Nicolson.

Worsley, P. (1984), *The Three Worlds: Culture and World Development*, London: Weidenfeld and Nicolson.

Wriston, W. (1992), *The Twilight of Sovereignty*, New York: Charles Scribner.

Wurm, S. A. (ed.) (1996), *Atlas of the World's Languages in Danger of Disappearing*, Paris: UNESCO.

Wuyts, M. (1996), 'Foreign Aid, Structural Adjustment, and Public Management: The Mozambican Experience', *Development and Change* 7(4): 717–49.

Xavier Inda, J. and Rosaldo, R. (eds) (2002), 'Introduction: A World in Motion', *The Anthropology of Globalization: A Reader*, Oxford: Blackwell, pp.1–34.

Yanikkaya, H. (2003), 'Trade Openness and Economic Growth: A Cross-Country Empirical Investigation', *Journal of Development Economics* 72: 57–89.

Young, K. (1989), *Serving Two Masters*, New Delhi: Allied Publishers.

Young, K. (1993), *Planning Development with Women*, New York: St Martin's Press.

Young, K. (1997), 'Gender and Development', in N. Visvanathan et al. (eds), *The Women, Gender and Development Reader*, London: Zed Books, pp. 51–4.

Young, K. (2002), 'WID, GAD and WAD', in V. Desai and R. B. Potter (eds), *The Companion to Development Studies*, London: Arnold, pp. 321–5.

Young, K., Wokowitz, C. and McCullagh, R. (eds) (1984), *Of Marriage and the Market: Women's Subordination in International Perspective*, London: RKP.

Zack-Williams, A. B. (1995), 'Crisis and Structural Adjustment in Sierra Leone: Implications for Women', in G. T. Emeagwali (ed.), *Women Pay the Price: Structural Adjustment in Africa and the Caribbean*, Trenton, NJ: Africa World Press, pp. 53–62.

Index

LLYFRGELL COLEG MENAI LIBRARY
SAFLE FFRIDDOEDD SITE
BANGOR GWYNEDD LL57 2TP

ST NO	9780745638959
ACC	108441
	890 338·9
	17:09:12
STAFF	SJW 18·99